AF560741

UNITED PROVINCES' POLITICS, 1938: CONGRESS IN MID-TERM

Governors' Fortnightly Reports and other Key Documents

United Provinces' Politics, 1938: Congress in Mid-Term

Governors' Fortnightly Reports and other Key Documents

compiled and edited by

LIONEL CARTER

Former Librarian, Centre of South Asian Studies, University of Cambridge

MANOHAR

2009

First published 2009

ISBN 978-81-7304-810-4

Published by
Ajay Kumar Jain *for*
Manohar Publishers & Distributors
4753/23 Ansari Road, Daryaganj
New Delhi 110 002

Printed at
Salasar Imaging Systems
Delhi 110 035

Contents

Editor's Introduction

This is the second volume in a series which aims to reproduce in full the text of the U.P. Governors' Fortnightly Reports to the Viceroys together with other important documents from the Governors or their Secretaries to the Viceroys or their Private Secretaries.[1] Space considerations do not allow the publication of the Viceroys' replies although these are footnoted where necessary. Enclosures to Governors' letters are only included when they are important. The introduction to the previous volume provides an account of the origins of the Fortnightly Reports.

The first six months of Congress government in the United Provinces, between July and December 1937, were far from smooth and the resignation of the Ministry had seemed possible on more than one occasion. The year 1938, however, opened on a calmer note. The crisis of December 1937 over speeches made by Pandit Parmanand and others had been resolved by a firm statement issued by the U.P. Government on 27 December. The Governor, Sir Harry Haig, was conscious that many difficulties remained. He told the Viceroy, Lord Linlithgow, on 10 January that he certainly did not hold any optimistic anticipations for the future. However he felt 'the present position is in many respects better than might have been anticipated. I myself, for instance, a year ago, thought that a Congress Government could not function in this Province without leading to a very rapid break-down.' (No. 4.)

This period of relative calm did not last long. In the early weeks of January Pandit Govind Ballabh Pant, the U.P. Premier, 'returned to the charge' about releasing all the remaining political prisoners in the Province. (No. 6.) There were some fifteen of these as well as six prisoners who remained in custody for their part in the Chauri Chaura incident of 1922. (Full details of the crimes of, and sentences imposed on, the fifteen political prisoners are given in Enclosure to No. 24.) Pant continued to press the subject and at a Cabinet meeting on 14 February the Ministers demanded that they had the power to order the general release of the fifteen prisoners without further reference to the Governor. (They made it clear that they would not necessarily decide to release all the prisoners.) (No. 14.) In taking this line the Ministry were apparently influenced by anxiety to avoid hunger-strikes by prisoners in the U.P. They also wished to secure the release of prisoners before the 51st Session of the Indian National Congress which was to take place at Haripura between 19 and 21 February 1938. The whole subject raised again the thorny issue of a Governor's special powers to over-rule a Ministry which had caused so many problems in 1937.

Although he had taken a rather stronger line in January, Haig was now clear that it was not worth starting a major constitutional crisis over the prisoner release question. (No. 14.) However the Viceroy did not share this view as he was anxious about the effect which releases in the U.P. and Bihar would have on the political and security situation in Bengal and the Punjab. He therefore issued an Order, under Section 126 of the Government of India Act 1935, requiring Haig to resist his Ministers' demands. In response to this Pant submitted the Ministry's resignation. (See Enclosure to No. 15 for Pant's resignation letter of 15 February 1938.) The Ministry in Bihar submitted its resignation under similar circumstances.

The immediate response of the U.P. Governor to Pant's resignation was to enter into discussions with two opposition leaders – the Nawab of Chhatari and Chaudhuri Khaliquzzaman (of the Muslim League) – on the possibility of forming a minority Ministry. (Nos. 17, 18 and 22.) It soon became clear that this course of action would not be possible and Haig concluded that it was very important to reach a settlement with Congress. (No. 22.) Calls for moderation came from other quarters as well. The Viceroy's Private Secretary, Gilbert Laithwaite, reportedly told B. Shiva Rao that there was 'the necessity of saving of face on either side'.[2] Right-wing Congress leaders in the provinces were reported to have been begged to proceed to Haripura to support the moderate cause.[3] The result was that the All-India Congress Committee passed a very conciliatory resolution on the dispute (drafted by Mahatma Gandhi). (Appendix 4.) For his part the Viceroy issued a statement which stressed that Ministers in the U.P. and Bihar could still pursue a policy of release of prisoners in consultation with Governors. (Appendix 5.) This last statement drew from Gandhi a press statement arguing that Provincial Ministers ought not to be subject to control by Governors over the releases and he indicated ways by which the crisis might be ended. (Appendix 6.)

In the event Haig was able, with Pant, to play a significant part in bringing about a speedy solution. Discussions between them first took place on 24 February and it seems that both parties agreed to a compromise on the basis that release of prisoners should take place after an individual examination of each case. (See No. 30 and Appendix 9.) The Premier however remained worried about the terms of Gandhi's press statement which he felt needed to be taken account of in any settlement. (Appendix 7.) A major contribution was then made by Mr G.D. Birla in Delhi who (in consultation with Pant and Laithwaite) drafted a joint statement which Haig and Pant might issue. (See No. 30, note 73.) This incorporated Gandhi's thinking but avoided the demand that the Governor's special powers should never be used. On the afternoon of 25 February, Haig secured Pant's agreement to some verbal changes to the Delhi draft which the Governor considered essential and their joint statement was swiftly issued. (Appendix 8.) In so doing, Haig managed to forestall both the Congress Working Committee and the Viceroy. For the Working Committee had apparently wished to vet the agreement between Haig and Pant before the Ministers' resignations were withdrawn (No. 30, paragraph 4) while the Viceroy was unhappy that his required amendments to the statement had not been secured. (Appendix 10.) Had Haig not acted so swiftly it seems likely that the settlement would have been a very protracted affair. As a postscript we may note that the Justice Minister, Dr K.N. Katju, evidently tried to follow Gandhi's lead and he issued immediate orders for the release of a large number of the prisoners without an individual examination of their cases. (Appendix 9.) Haig prevented this but, perhaps wisely, did not report the incident to the Viceroy. Documents on the February 1938 constitutional crisis form the subject matter of Chapter 1 of the *Summaries of Documents* with supporting material reproduced in Appendices 2 to 10.

* * *

The ending of the constitutional crisis allowed the U.P. Ministry to concentrate on its programme of legislative and administrative reform. A Tenancy Bill, already the subject of much deliberation within government, was introduced in the Legislative Assembly during April 1938. (See No. 38.) A serving administrator was appointed to head the rural development programme in place of a Congress politician who had previously run the operation in a controversial way. (No. 45, paragraph 8; see also Nos. 63 and 72.) Examination was begun (in a somewhat half-hearted way) of the idea of separating the administrative and judicial functions of district officers. (See Enclosure 1 to No 43 for Katju's note; also Nos. 52, paragraph 3 and 64, paragraph 15.) This was an item of policy which went back to the earliest days of the Indian National Congress in the late nineteenth century.[4] Later in 1938 the question of abolishing Commissioners of Divisions was to come up (No. 76) as well as the idea that district officers should be helped in their work by advice from district advisory committees. (See No. 80 for Pant's impressively researched note on the subject.) Throughout the year there was anxiety that, because of an increasing budget deficit, government might be forced to cut the pay and allowances of the provincial services. (See Nos. 2 and 77.)

The Tenancy Bill was unquestionably the most important of these various measures. It was not that the proposals were particularly revolutionary.[5] A legal commentator wrote that the tenant gained very little by the Bill. Nonetheless it combined the legislation of Agra and Oudh for the first time and created a distinction between the larger and the smaller landlords which was to be important for future Congress strategy. (The boundary between the two groups of landlords was set at 250 rupees a year in land revenue payments.) Tenants were provided with various forms of protection and hereditary tenancy provisions were introduced. Occupancy and hereditary rents could normally only be raised once every ten years. The larger landlords were to lose any *sir* (personal land) which they had gained through legislation in the 1920s. Tenants of landlords with more than 50 acres of *sir* would acquire the new hereditary rights. All in all the Bill was in conformity with the noble aspirations of the Congress creed.

It may have seemed, therefore, that by the time Haig left for his four months' leave on 17 May 1938 the U.P. Ministry was on an even keel. However this would be to ignore a number of changes which were taking place in the political and communal situation. At the Haripura Congress Session in February, the left-wing leader, Subhas Chandra Bose, had assumed the Presidency of Congress. Bose immediately made a call for unity between all factions of the party but it was clear that the left were now in a significant position of power in the high command. Then in April discussions were begun between Gandhi, the Congress and M.A. Jinnah, the Muslim League leader, on the communal question. These continued in a desultory way through the summer but ultimately broke down. Most importantly, from our point of view, on 2 March 1938 Sri Sampurnanand replaced Piyare Lal Sharma in the key U.P. education portfolio. Sampurnanand was a highly intelligent and committed activist. His writings have been described as showing a 'curious dialogue between Marxism and Hindu revivalism' and he came to the Ministry with a determination to propagate the use of Hindi and develop the Congress model of nationalist education.[6] By the end of 1938 some 1,300 primary schools in the U.P. had been converted to the Congress scheme. Sampurnanand's own account of life as a Congress minister is printed as Enclosure to No. 66. His appointment clearly moved the U.P. Ministry in a leftward direction and had major implications for the communal position in the province. Documents on the period from 9 March 1947 until Haig's departure on leave form the basis of Chapter 2 of the *Summaries of Documents*.

* * *

The person chosen to act for Haig during his home leave was Sir Maurice Hallett, at the time Governor of Bihar. There were only two years difference in age between the two men[7] and they had had not dissimilar administrative experience. Between 1932 and 1934 Hallett had been Haig's no. 2 when Haig was Home Secretary in the Governor-General's Council and Hallett had been Secretary to the Home Department, Government of India. It is possible that Hallett knew of Linlithgow's dissatisfaction with Haig. (See Introduction to the previous volume.) In any case it is reasonable to assume that Hallett had his eye on the U.P. Governorship when Haig's term of office ended in December 1939. The documents suggest that the acting-Governor was anxious to use his time in the U.P. to impress and to minimise difficulties. He engaged in a sizeable touring programme; despatched a considerable volume of correspondence; and developed good relations with the Ministry. On this latter front a notable success was the settlement of a damaging general strike in the Cawnpore mills. Hallett wrote that Pant deserved all credit for this.[8] (No. 57.)

In his last Report to the acting-Viceroy, Hallett explained his 'reasoned optimism' about the future. He felt that 'responsibility is begetting reasonableness' on the part of the two Ministries with which he had been involved. (No. 65.) Yet by this time (mid-September 1938) the clouds were darkening in the U.P. Hallett himself had noted a considerable increase in crime in certain divisions of the Province and he had sent Pant a lengthy letter on the subject. (Enclosure to No. 62.) In addition there now appeared to be elements within both Congress and the Muslim League which were behind the formation of 'volunteer' organisations of a semi-military character. (Nos. 62 and 64.) The agrarian and communal situation was also beginning to cause anxiety. (No. 62.) Notwithstanding this, Hallett was able to leave Lucknow with some feeling of satisfaction. On his last day Pant and Katju both called 'to say goodbye and were very friendly'. (Appendix 11.) Documents on Hallett's acting-Governorship form the subject matter of Chapter 3 of the *Summaries of Documents*.

* * *

On his return from leave, Haig soon recognised that the U.P. situation had worsened and it is clear that for the remainder of 1938 he was not on particularly close terms with Pant – a matter which Linlithgow held against the Governor. (See No. 78, note 32.) One of the first problems that Haig faced was the crisis which had developed between Britain and Germany and the implications this had for India. He was asked by the acting-Viceroy on 28 September to ascertain the attitude of the U.P. Ministry towards measures which would be necessary in the event of war. After a discussion with Pant, the Governor felt that the Premier would not be likely to raise objection to the necessary immediate measures but that much would depend on the attitude of the Congress Working Committee. Haig stressed Pant's point that on the outbreak of war 'he [Pant] personally might be satisfied if you were to send for one or more representatives of the Congress, take them into confidence and ask them whether Congress would support the war.' (No. 68; see also No. 84.) It was a pity that Linlithgow did not heed this advice in September 1939.

Foremost in Haig's mind on his return was, however, the relations between the landlords and tenants of the U.P. (See his Report to the acting Viceroy of 26 September 1938 (No. 67).) Not a great deal of progress had been made with the Tenancy Bill during his absence and it had become clear that the landlords were grasping at straws in their hope that the legislation might be prevented. At the end of September 1938 the Working Committee of Congress took up a proposal that it might arbitrate between the U.P. Ministry and the landlords on condition that the landlords accepted its ruling as binding. Haig felt that acceptance of this proposal by all the parties would be a decided triumph for the Congress right-wing. (No. 73.) However although the Agra zamindars were agreeable to arbitration, the Oudh taluqdars rejected it. This development consequently strengthened the position of the left-wing of Congress in the U.P.

Anxiety over the strength of the left-wing and concern that Pant appeared to be losing control of affairs was to be the major theme of Haig's correspondence in the last months of 1938. In a interview on 22 November, Mrs Vijayalakshmi Pandit, the Health Minister, told Haig that 'the position of the Ministry was, in her judgment, definitely weaker than it had been' and that Pant was being continually attacked for his moderation. She felt they would have a very troublesome cold weather. (No. 79.) In a letter to Hallett on 29 November Haig expressed similar concerns. 'It is true that Pant is so friendly, so reasonable, and puts his case with such skill that after talking to him I cannot help feeling reassured; but I fear the facts are against him.' When Haig had tackled the Premier on the semi-military Congress volunteer force, Pant expressed 'ideas so unconvincing that I felt he knew he was not in a position to do anything about it and was simply fencing with me.' (Appendix 13.)

Haig, then, ended 1938 in a state of considerable apprehension for the future. He felt it prudent on 19 December to send both the Viceroy and the Secretary of State for India a lengthy memorandum on the current position in the U.P. with a recommendation on the policy they should follow if things got even worse. He concluded that they must retain intact the framework of the administration and also retain the confidence of the services. On the other hand, they must, 'if the Government comes under the domination of left-wing influences, put up with policies which are dangerous to the peace of the Province, until the point of breaking clearly arises.' It was a policy which Linlithgow endorsed. Indeed the Viceroy felt it was unavoidable given that the decision had been taken to try out representative government in the Indian provinces. (Enclosure to No. 82 and its note 49.) Documents on the period 26 September to 31 December 1938 form the subject-matter of Chapter 4 of the *Summaries of Documents*.

* * *

The documents in this volume are British Crown Copyright and are all taken from the following classes of material in the India Office Records:

L/P&J	India Office – Public & Judicial Department files.
MSS.EUR.F 115	Haig papers.
MSS.EUR.F.125	Linlithgow papers.
R/3/1	Prints of Viceroy's correspondence with the Governors.

I would like once again to express my thanks for help and advice received from Anthony Farrington, formerly head of the India Office Records at the British Library. I am also most grateful to Graham Shaw, Director of Asia, Pacific and Africa Collections at the British Library, for his interest. I owe a special debt to Ram Advani and to Ramesh Dogra, M.B.E. and Urmila Dogra for advice on a wide range of issues. My publisher, Ramesh Jain, has, as ever, extended many kindnesses to me. None of the foregoing bears any responsibility for errors and omissions in the book. The responsibility for these rests solely with me.

Harrow, May 2008 LIONEL CARTER

NOTES

1. The previous volume was published by Manohar in 2008 with the title: *United Provinces' Politics, 1936–1937: Formation of the Ministries and Start of Congress Government.*
2. See Basudev Chatterji (ed.), *Towards Freedom: Documents on the Movement for Independence in India 1938*, Part II (New Delhi: Oxford University Press, 1999), p. 1187.
3. Linlithgow to Zetland, 18 February 1938. Ibid., p. 1184.
4. See Gordon Johnson, *Provincial Politics and Indian Nationalism: Bombay and the Indian National Congress 1880 to 1915* (Cambridge: Cambridge University Press, 1973), p. 29.
5. The material in this paragraph is taken from Peter Reeves, *Landlords and Governments in Uttar Pradesh: A Study of Their Relations until Zamindari Abolition* (Bombay: Oxford University Press, 1991), pp. 231-3.
6. The material in the remainder of this paragraph is taken from William Gould, *Hindu Nationalism and the Language of Politics in Late Colonial India* (Cambridge: Cambridge University Press, 2004), pp. 166-80. This section in Gould's book is an important assessment of the career and thinking of Sampurnanand at this time.
7. Haig was born in 1881 and Hallett in 1883.
8. It is noteworthy that Hallett was markedly more critical of the Cawnpore employers than Haig. This may have been general liberalism on Hallett's part; it may equally have represented the Indian Civil Servant's traditional disdain for the European commercial and industrial class in India.
9. Mrs Pandit was away from her post from 18 August until 15 November 1938. During this time Mr Kidwai was responsible for Local Self-Government and Municipal Departments and Hafiz Muhammad Ibrahim was responsible for the Medical and Public Health Departments.

Abbreviations

A.I.C.C.	All-India Congress Committee.
A.P.	Associated Press.
B.&N.W.	Bengal and North-Western.
C.-in-C.	Commander-in-Chief.
C.I.D.	Criminal Investigation Department.
C.I.O.	Central Intelligence Officer.
C.O.	Commanding Officer.
C.P.	Central Provinces.
Cr.P.C.	Criminal Procedure Code.
D.C.	Deputy Commissioner.
D.I.B.	Director of the Intelligence Bureau.
D.I.G.	Deputy Inspector General.
D.M.	District Magistrate.
D.O.	Demi-Official.
G. of I.	Government of India.
H.E.	His Excellency.
H.M.	Honourable Minister.
H.M.G.	His Majesty's Government.
H.M.J.	Honourable Minister for Justice, Development, Agriculture and Veterinary.
H.M.R.	Honourable Minister for Revenue and Jails.
H.S.R.A.	Hindustan Socialist Republican Army.
I.C.S.	Indian Civil Service.
I.F.S.	Indian Forest Service.
I.G.P.	Inspector General of Police.
I.M.S.	Indian Medical Service.
I.P.	Indian Police.
I.P.C.	Indian Penal Code.
M.L.A.	Member of the Legislative Assembly.
M.L.C.	Member of the Legislative Council.
N.C.O.	Non-Commissioned Officer.
P.M.	Prime Minister *or* Premier.

P.S.	Postscript *or* Parliamentary Secretary.
P.S.V.	Private Secretary to the Viceroy.
P.W.D.	Public Works Department.
Re.	Rupee.
R.I.	Rigorous Imprisonment.
S.D.O.	Sub-Divisional Officer.
S. of S. *or* S./S.	Secretary of State.
S.P.	Superintendent of Police.
S.S.O.	Senior Station Officer.
U.P.	United Provinces.
U.P.P., 1936-7	Lionel Carter (ed.), *United Provinces' Politics, 1936–1937: Formation of the Ministries and Start of Congress Government* (New Delhi: Manohar, 2008.)
U/s	Under Section.

Glossary

Anna	One-sixteenth of a rupee.
Babu	A term of respect; often accorded to Indians who were fluent in English.
Bakhshish	'Gift', tip or bribe.
Bania	Trader, moneylender.
Bhajan	A Hindu devotional song.
Chaprasi	An office messenger; an orderly in government service.
Chehlum	A Shia (q.v.) Religious holiday which occurs forty days after the Day of Ashurah – the tenth day of Muharram and anniversary of the day when Husain (grandson of the Prophet) was slain at Karbala. Forty days is the usual period of mourning in many Islamic cultures.
Chhaoni	Cantonment.
Chowkidar	Watchman in town or village.
Crore	One hundred lakhs or ten million.
Dacoity	Robbery with violence committed by a gang.
Dalali	Brokerage, commission.
Dhoti	Garment for the lower body.
Dussehra	Hindu festival celebrated in September-October in honour of Durga and Rama.
Fasli	Belonging to the harvest; the harvest year. A method of computing time which was prevalent throughout India and was one of the forms used in public orders and regulations. The era was started by the Emperor Akbar and the year began with the month of Asarh (June/July). It is necessary to add 592 to the *fasli* year to compute the Common Era year (593 if the date is more than halfway through the *fasli* year).
Goonda	Hooligan, hired rascal.

Holi	Hindu spring festival celebrated on the full-moon day of Phalguna (February-March). Participants throw coloured waters and powders on one another.
Id	A Muslim holy festival. *Bakr-Id* commemorates Abraham's sacrifice.
Inqilab	Revolution.
Izzat	Honour, credit, reputation.
Kanta	Fork, thorn.
Karinda	Agent.
Khadi	*Strictly:* cloth woven by hand from yarn village-spun also by hand.
Kharif	Grain crops sown in summer and reaped by early winter.
Khudai Kidmatgars	(Red Shirts.) Congress volunteer movement of the North-West Frontier Province started by Khan Abdul Ghaffar Khan.
Kisan	Peasant, cultivator, tenant.
Kist	Instalment, portion.
Kotwal	A chief officer of town or city police; an Indian town magistrate.
Kumbh Mela	A Hindu pilgrimage festival and fair which is held four times every twelve years rotating between Hardwar, Ujjain, Nasik and Allahabad.
Lakh	One hundred thousand.
Lathi	Thick stick, usually bamboo, sometimes bound with iron rings.
Mahant	Priest, monk.
Malkhana	Storehouse, warehouse.
Mandal	Party, team, association.
Maulvi	Muslim religious teacher.
Mazdur Sabha	Trade union.
Milad-i-sharif	Festival celebrating the birth of the Prophet Muhammad.
Mistry	Artificer, mechanic.
Muharram	First month of the year in the Islamic calendar; a Muslim festival held during Muharram. The festival commemorates the martyrdom of Ali, son-in-law of the Prophet Muhammad, and of Ali's two sons, Husain and Hassan.

Mulakatis	People who normally meet each other.
Munsif	An Indian judge of a summary civil court of the first instance.
Panchayat	Court of arbitration (properly of five persons) for determination of petty disputes; village council.
Patwari	Village accountant.
Peon	Messenger of an official.
Rabi	Principal grain harvest sown after the rains and reaped in the spring season.
Ram Lila	A dramatic epitome of the life and adventures of Rama. The public performances often extend over many days.
Sabha	Association, conclave, assembly.
Sanad	A grant, a charter.
Satyagraha	*Lit.:* holding on to truth. Total self-giving; integral to Mahatma Gandhi's concept of victory achieved through non-violent resistance.
Shia	One of the two main branches of Islam (cf. Sunni); followers of Ali, the son-in-law of Muhammad.
Sir	Land held by a zamindar under title of personal cultivation.
Sircar	District, Government.
Sunni	The majority in Indian Islam, who regard Caliphs Abu Bakr, Omar and Osman as spiritual descendants of Muhammad.
Swaraj	Self-rule, independence.
Tahsil	Revenue sub-division of a District. Tahsildar: collector of the revenue within a tahsil.
Taluqdar	Large landholder in Oudh; holder of a revenue subdivision.
Thana	Police station. Thanedar: officer-in-charge of a Thana.
Vakil	Lawyer; authorised pleader in a court of justice.
Zamindar	Landed proprietor paying land revenue to Government, revenue farmer.
Zindabad	Long live!
Zulm	Tyranny, oppression, extortion.

Principal Holders of Office, 1938

UNITED KINGDOM

Secretary of State for India	The Marquess of Zetland

INDIA

Viceroy, Governor-General and Crown Representative	The Marquess of Linlithgow (Lord Brabourne acted 25 June – 24 October 1938)
Private Secretary to the Viceroy	Mr Gilbert Laithwaite (Mr. F.H. Puckle acted late June – late October 1938)
Commander-in-Chief, India	General Sir Robert Cassels

UNITED PROVINCES

Governor	Sir Harry Haig (Sir Maurice Hallett acted 17 May – 16 September 1938)
Secretary to Governor	Mr J.C. Donaldson
Chief Secretary to Government	Mr C.W. Gwynne (Mr Panna Lal acted 2 March – 31 August 1938)

MEMBERS OF THE COUNCIL OF MINISTERS

Premier and Minister of Home Affairs and Finance	Pandit Govind Ballabh Pant
Minister of Revenue and Jails	Mr Rafi Ahmad Kidwai
Minister of Justice, Development, Agriculture and Veterinary	Dr Kailash Nath Katju

Minister of Local Self-Government and Health	Mrs Vijayalakshmi Pandit[1]
Minister of Education	Pandit Pyare Lal Sharma Sri Sampurnanand (from 2 March 1938)
Minister of Communications and Irrigation	Hafiz Muhammad Ibrahim

(The Ministry submitted its resignation on 15 February 1938 but resumed office on 25 February 1938.)

U.P. LEGISLATIVE ASSEMBLY

Speaker	Shri Purushottamdas Tandon
Deputy Speaker	Mr Abdul Hakeem

NOTE

1. Mrs Pandit was away from her post from 18 August until 15 November 1938. During this time Mr Kidwai was responsible for Local Self-Government and Municipal Departments and Hafiz Muhammad Ibrahim was responsible for the Medical and Public Health Departments.

Summaries of Documents

CHAPTER 1 : DOCUMENTS FOR 1 JANUARY – 5 MARCH 1938

Name and Number	Date Jan.	Main subject or subjects
1 Haig to Linlithgow Tel. 103-G	1	Is opposed to release of Sadashiv by Bombay Govt.
2 Haig to Linlithgow Tel. 104-G	4	Ministry are considering pay cuts and reduction or abolition of special pay and compensatory allowances for those members of Provincial and subordinate services recruited after March 1937
3 Donaldson to Laithwaite Letter 916-G.S.P	5	Sends minute by Pant which requests that no titles be conferred in the U.P. whether on officials or non-officials
4 Haig to Linlithgow Report U.P.-47	10	Haig's joint statement with Pant on Parmanand case very well received by Press; assessment of Pant and Ministry; feels power and popularity of Congress in U.P. are near their peak; anxiety over Pant's personal condition; Sharma likely to resign from Ministry; ban is withdrawn on Congress independence day pledge; rural development scheme; tahsildars expected to realise revenue vigorously; Sahajanand's tour of U.P.; speculates on possibility of Congress-League agreement

5	Haig to Linlithgow Tel. 109-G	19	Is seriously disturbed at proposal to declare a holiday in C.P. on 26 January (independence day)
6	Haig to Linlithgow Report U.P.-49	22	Pant presses for release of remaining revolutionary prisoners and Katju passes an order for release of Chauri Chaura prisoners; growth in strength of Congress left; fears Pant could be turned out of office by Nehru; Sahajanand's tour; Pant over-optimistic about the collection of rents; unsatisfactory position on budget; Congress will need to give some material benefits to villagers if it is not to lose ground; Pant wishing to replace Sharma with Sampurnanand; prospects of Congress-League accommodation have not improved; parliamentary secretaries; suggested independence day holiday; Assembly resolutions; Enclosures: (1) Note by Haig on revolutionary prisoners: (2) Extract from note by Haig on Chauri Chaura prisoners
7	Haig to Linlithgow Tel. 114-G	24	Refers to No. 1: suggested guarantee from Sadashiv would no doubt help in U.P. for six months; but important point is that in any conflict with his Ministers, Haig's position would be weakened by release of a U.P. man whose revolutionary activities were more conspicuous than those U.P. prisoners whom Haig was not agreeing to release
8	Haig to Linlithgow Letter U.P.-50	30	Summarises history of prisoner release question; reports on his

No.	From/To	Date	Summary
			meetings with Pant and Katju on 26 and 29 Jan.; proposes to tell Ministers that he will review situation on revolutionary prisoners when hunger-strikes in other provinces come to an end
		Feb.	
9	Haig to Linlithgow Letter U.P.-52	6	Explains why he has had to ask Viceroy to cancel his shoot near Kaladhungi
10	Haig to Linlithgow Letter U.P.-53	9	Pant asks for discussion of prisoner release question at next Cabinet meeting; threatened *kisan* demonstration did not materialise; change in composition of Ministry has not proceeded further; Paliwal tenders his resignation as Rural Development Officer; Haig expects tussle with Ministry over activities of rural development staff; disturbance at Cawnpore involving Ibrahim; nervousness increasing with approach of *Bakr Id*; Madhe Sahaba controversy; state of budget discussions; hot weather move of Govt. to Naini Tal again abandoned; Civil Service Week a great success; talk with Pant on social contacts of Ministers; suggestions for abolition of Secretary of State's Services and Commissioners
11	Haig to Linlithgow Tel. 118-G	10	Pant has indicated that Congress Working Committee consider that prisoner release question must be settled before A.I.C.C. session
12	Haig to Linlithgow Express Letter U.P.-54	10	Reports his discussions with Pant and in Cabinet on prisoner release question; clear there is new note

			of urgency but cannot judge whether Congress intend to push matter to a break; would be no adequate reason in U.P. for facing a break
13	Haig to Linlithgow Letter U.P.-55	12	Refers to circular issued in Nov. 1937 on district officers' relations with Congress; answers Linlithgow's criticisms of it; believes it has led to strengthening of district officers and that they should now leave matter alone; D.I.G. will talk to S.P., Meerut about his circular letter (see No. A1); Enclosure: Answers by Pant in Assembly to questions on Nov. 1937 circular
14	Haig to Linlithgow Tel. 119-G	14	Pant and Cabinet have demanded that they have power to release the prisoners without further reference to Governor; Haig does not consider there are grounds in U.P. for a break with Ministers on this point; seeks instructions from Viceroy; does not anticipate that Ministry would resign immediately
15	Donaldson to Laithwaite Letter 1051-G.S.P.	16	Sends Pant's letter of 15 Feb. to Haig submitting Ministry's resignation; indicates line Haig took at Cabinet meetings
16	Haig to Linlithgow Letter U.P.-56	16	Considers he would need three Advisers under Section 93; suggests who these should be
17	Haig to Linlithgow Tel. 121-G	17	Reports discussion with Chhatari on formation of Ministry; Chhatari not at all hopeful but is exploring situation with League
18	Haig to Linlithgow Tel. 122-G	17	Reports discussion with Khaliquzzaman who seemed clear that

			formation of minority Ministry would be useless and inexpedient; he also felt that Congress would not start civil disobedience; Haig considers he would need to go into Section 93 about 19 Feb.
19	Haig to Linlithgow Tel. 123-G	17	Summarises local press reactions to resignations of U.P. and Bihar Ministries
20	Haig to Linlithgow Tel. 124-G	18	Believes Ministers would agree to their resignations not being accepted until their return from Haripura; important not to force pace
21	Haig to Linlithgow Letter U.P.-57	19	Refers to No. 16; sends alternative proposal on Advisers
22	Haig to Linlithgow Tel. 127-G	20	Reports further conversation with Chattari who would refuse an offer to form Ministry; Haig feels that if Pant Ministry's resignation is confirmed, he should go at once into Section 93; Governor considers it very important to try to reach settlement with Congress
23	Donaldson to Laithwaite Tel. G.S.-128	21	Sends details of tax measures contemplated in forthcoming budget and their estimated yield
24	Donaldson to Laithwaite Letter 1061-G.S.P.	21	Sends note on the fifteen prisoners whose release was under discussion with Cabinet
25	Haig to Linlithgow Report U.P.-58	22	Reactions in U.P. to Ministerial resignations; rent and revenue have been coming in better; budget discussions are reasonable; Ministry accepts Paliwal's resignation; enquiry into attack on Ibrahim's procession in Cawnpore; *Bakr Id* passes off quietly but League feeling against

		Congress is very bitter; Ministry declines to issue orders in Madhe Sahaba dispute; pressure of work affecting health of departmental secretaries
26 Haig to Linlithgow Tel. 129-G	24	Has had long talk with Pant who, he feels, would agree to gradual release of prisoners with examination of individual cases; discusses problems raised by Gandhi's statement (No. A6); is meeting Pant following day and they are considering issuing statement
27 Haig to Hallett Tel. 130-G	27	Not correct that he has agreed to release all U.P. revolutionary prisoners in fourteen days
28 Haig to Linlithgow Tel. 131-G	28	Has agreed to release six prisoners immediately including Chandra Man Singh; proposes to agree to release of Yashpal after two or three days
	Mar.	
29 Haig to Emerson Tel. 135-G	3	Yashpal released previous day; Pant will advise him strongly not to go to Punjab without permission but is unwilling to impose any condition
30 Haig to Linlithgow Letter U.P.-59	5	Refers to No. A10; gives account of background to his settlement with Pant
31 Haig to Linlithgow Letter U.P.-60	5	Reports conversation with Pant who reiterated his objections to award of honours and hinted at possibility of awkward developments

CHAPTER 2 – DOCUMENTS FOR 9 MARCH – 17 MAY 1938

		Mar.	
32	Haig to Linlithgow Report U.P.-61	9	Constitutional crisis may be regarded as finished but landlords are not showing much political sense; possible timetable of tenancy legislation; budget is being criticised as too ambitious; demonstration of cultivators in Lucknow; Sampurnanand appointed in place of Sharma; Ministry has taken a very moderate line on rural development; changing attitude of Ministry towards flying of flags on local government buildings; Haig's fear of communal friction in coming weeks
33	Haig to Linlithgow Report U.P.-63	23	Communal problems in Allahabad and Benares; Ministry behaves sensibly over disturbances and League's criticisms are unfair; believes real causes of ill-feeling are: (1) fact that practically whole of Muslim community in Legislature is in opposition to Govt., (2) Hindu elation at what is in effect a Hindu Govt.; further postponement of report on Madhe Sahaba dispute; twelve political prisoners now released; Cawnpore labour situation; land revenue realisation is satisfactory and great many of Cabinet's tenancy and revenue policies are very reasonable; Rural Development Officer; Pant's attitude to Garhwali mutineers and to Arms Act;

No.	Document	Date	Summary
			Enclosures: editorial comment from *Leader* on communal disturbances
		April	
34	Haig to Linlithgow Report U.P.-64	8	Pant resolute in tackling communal violence; some re-emergence of Mahasabha influence; move to transfer Chhatari's Muslim supporters in Assembly to League Parliamentary Party is dropped; Madhe Sahaba report is received quietly but further trouble possible; attitude of landlords towards Govt.'s tenancy and revenue proposals; more agitation likely from depressed classes; Cawnpore labour inquiry report published but Haig doubts whether there will be agreement on it; Cabinet considers scheme for separation of executive and judicial powers of magistrates; effects of present political conditions on crime; activities of Congress panchayats; burden on Pant very heavy; lapse by Panna Lal; Pant more difficult over I.C.S. appointments; Enclosure: leading article from *Pioneer* critical of leaking of Cawnpore inquiry report
35	Haig to Linlithgow Letter U.P.-66	12	Sends his comments on proposal for a Bill to amend Govt. of India Act; in general is not sympathetic and advises waiting for a time
36	Donaldson to Laithwaite Letter 1220-G.S.P.	14	Contrary to a press report, police in Lucknow are not wearing khadi
37	Haig to Linlithgow Tel. 141-G	21	Feels increasingly strongly about importance of maintaining

			position of Public Service Commission as against Govt.; is opposed to reduction of salaries of members
38	Haig to Linlithgow Letter U.P.-70	22	Seeks legal advice on a question relating to U.P. Tenancy Bill; Enclosures: (1) Opinion of Asthana; (2) Note by Haig; (3) Report from *Pioneer* of discussion in U.P. Assembly on 20 April 1938 including communication from Haig giving his previous sanction to introduction of Bill
39	Haig to Linlithgow Letter U.P.-71	23	Adequacy of senior staff to deal with existing conditions of work and conditions that might arise
40	Haig to Linlithgow Report U.P.-72	23	Pant taking firm line on communal violence; Pipridih train dacoity may lead Pant to re-examine his policy towards political criminals; Hardwar Kumbh Mela, which had been very successful, ends with disastrous fire and fight with police; Mela shows vitality of Hinduism in U.P.; hopes Govt. will make certain concessions to landlords on Tenancy Bill; kisan demonstration a failure after Congress opposed it; position of Govt. on Cawnpore labour inquiry report and problems over its acceptance; difficulties over appointment of Rural Development Officer; Cabinet allowing recessing officers to go up to Naini Tal; appointment of President of Court of Wards; rioting between Sunnis and Shias

		in Lucknow; Enclosures: (1) Circular from Panna Lal on reporting of speeches by communal leaders or those under auspices of communal organisations; (2) extract from *Pioneer* giving text of Congress circular on kisan demonstration; (3) extract from *Pioneer* giving Nehru's statement on kisan demonstration
41 Haig to Linlithgow Tel. 142-G	30	Has been nothing to suggest that Ministers were taking an interest in Orissa developments; Gandhi's attitude, however, creates new situation and Haig will mention subject to Pant
	May	
42 Haig to Linlithgow Tel. 143-G	2	Does not favour cancelling the appointment of Dain as Acting Governor of Orissa as they cannot afford to make open climb-down to Congress; feels they should state that they would not make similar appointment again; Pant does not seem to think that Orissa events will affect U.P.
43 Haig to Linlithgow Letter U.P.-75	7	Sends: (1) Note by Katju on his scheme for separation of judicial and executive functions of district officers; (2) Haig's own comments on this; asks Viceroy to ascertain whether Zetland would require scheme to be referred to him; Pant considers it is impossible politically not to make some move
44 Haig to Linlithgow Letter U.P.-76	9	Reports discussions with Cabinet and Pant on functions of parliamentary secretaries; proposes

		to allow them to note on files subject to definite restrictions; seeks Linlithgow's comments; Enclosures: (1) Note by Pant; (2) Note by Haig suggesting amended working rules of practice that might be tried experimentally
45 Haig to Linlithgow Report U.P.-78	13	No further Hindu-Muslim trouble but feels they must be prepared for more communal outbreaks; Sunnis in Lucknow seem to have started some form of civil disobedience; Pant's letter of appreciation on police work; Haig's visit to Cawnpore; Ministers decide to follow up report on attack on Ibrahim at Cawnpore; Haig's talk with Pant on Cawnpore labour inquiry report; Pipridih train dacoity; letter from an ex-Kakori prisoner seeking assistance; interview with Jehangirabad on Tenancy Bill; likely timetable for Govt.'s legislation; appointment of Rural Development Officer; controversy over role of Public Service Commission; proposal for a committee in each district to advise district officers on corruption questions; conviction of Congress workers for contempt of court; work and climate pressures on Ministers
46 Haig to Linlithgow Letter U.P.-80	14	Reports serious agrarian outrage in Maharajganj tehsil of Gorakhpur; has told Pant he considers situation needs immediate and vigorous action

47 Haig to Linlithgow Letter U.P.-81	17	Reactions in UP. to settlement of Orissa crisis; politicians generally are likely to have impression that Govt. will not stand up to Congress

CHAPTER 3 – DOCUMENTS FOR 27 MAY – 16 SEPTEMBER 1938

	May	
48 Hallett to Linlithgow Report U.P.-85	27	First meetings with Ministers; hopes to discuss important matters with Pant in Naini Tal; report of Anti-Corruption Committee disappointing and inadequate – fears object in some quarters may be to destroy morale of services and bring them under political control; hopes Ministers will adopt harmless approach to separation of judicial and executive functions; jury system unlikely to be extended very widely; parliamentary secretaries; amendments made by Council to legislation; Cawnpore situation; talk with Pant on Gorakhpur developments; is reassured district officers are holding their own; Enclosure: telegram from Employers' Association to Donaldson
	June	
49 Hallett to Linlithgow Tel. 149-G	2	Reports on Cawnpore strike situation following discussions with employers' representative, Pant and Katju; employers' attitude accentuating difficulties; Ministry not proposing any immediate action

50	Hallett to Linlithgow Letter U.P.-86	6	Provincial attitudes to Federation; complete unanimity in Legislature that present scheme is unacceptable; situation might improve if introduction of scheme is delayed; position of services would be very difficult if Federation is attempted in near future
51	Hallett to Linlithgow Letter U.P.-89	17	Reports speech by a parliamentary secretary at a meeting in the Lansdowne military cantonment in which he praised Garhwali soldiers in 1930 Peshawar incident; military authorities have expelled organiser of meeting (Rup Chand Varma) from cantonment; reports discussion with Pant; seeks reactions of Viceroy and Defence Dept.
52	Hallett to Linlithgow Report U.P.-90	17	Govt. Resolution on Cawnpore Labour Inquiry Report; separation of judicial and executive functions; working rules for parliamentary secretaries; extension of jury system; selection of new honorary magistrates; value of police abstracts; question of action against Parmanand for recent speeches; anticipates serious difficulties over Govt.'s land revenue proposals; land revenue situation not unsatisfactory but fears trouble in eastern districts; situation in Lucknow seems to have improved; proposals for additional police; legislative sessions

53	Hallett to Linlithgow Letter (unnumbered)	20	Sends best wishes for his leave; Ministers in the U.P. are more interesting than those in Bihar
54	Hallett to Brabourne Tel. 155-G	25	Reports that Govt. and Cawnpore employers have reached agreement on some important points; indicates Pant's thinking; position still uncertain
55	Hallett to Brabourne Letter U.P.-96	28	Refers to No. 51; explains why he does not feel able to make personal appeal to Pant on Lansdowne question; will seek Premier's co-operation in preventing future speeches of this kind
		July	
56	Donaldson to Puckle Letter 1403-G.S.P.	4	Sends: (1) copy of letter (dated 3 July) from Hallett to Pant giving Governor's views on present state of negotiations between Cawnpore employers and workers; (2) telegram (dated 4 July) from Donaldson to Puckle reporting that settlement of Cawnpore strike had been reached through personal intervention of Pant
57	Hallett to Brabourne Letter U.P.-102	6	Says Pant deserves all credit for settlement of Cawnpore strike; believes settlement is on sound lines
58	Hallett to Brabourne Report U.P.-103	7	Inadequacies of Chief Secretary's reports; general appreciation on Cawnpore strike; believes strike was not solely due to communist agitation and that, in the result, right-wing of Congress has strengthened its position; tenancy legislation and agrarian anxieties; difficult to assess communal

			situation; release of remaining Chauri Chaura prisoners; Parmanand's speeches; is examining whether there has been an increase in crime; honorary magistrates; Enclosure: cutting from *Pioneer* giving U.P. Govt. communiqué on payment of rents
59	Hallett to Brabourne Letter U.P.-113	15	Sends copy of his correspondence with Pant on whether Premier might wish to express his views on recommendations for King's Police Medal and Indian Police Medal; Pant asks to discuss matter with Hallett and expresses certain reservations
60	Hallett to Brabourne Report U.P.-124	22	Visit to Jhansi and Agra – (1) feels increase in crime not yet serious and could have been worse under new Constitution, (2) left-wing members of Congress causing trouble in a few districts, (3) complaints in two districts of interference by Congress in criminal investigations; Mudie feels revenue collections are not satisfactory but Hallett notes problem is confined to certain districts; talk with Pant on circular to district officers; progress of two committees of Legislature; Hancox (D.M.) satisfied with Cawnpore situation; early release of Gulaothi riot case prisoners; communal situation; Pant's suggestion for relieving congestion in petty criminal cases; little apparently being done on rural development; Enclosures: (1) Draft circular to district officers

			on tension between zamindars and tenants; (2 and 3) notes by Hallett and Pant on Gulaothi riot case prisoners
		Aug.	
61	Hallett to Brabourne Report U.P.-142	7	Concern at reports that Muslims and zamindars were collecting volunteers, also that Hindustani Seva Dal has held a training camp; Palestine; communal situation in Allahabad; revenue collections on whole progressing satisfactorily; complaints from local Congress officials of mistreatment of tenants and from landlords of non-payment of rents; private members' resolutions before Legislature; Mudie's debt legislation proposals; Tenancy Bill making slow progress in committee; Mrs Pandit's leave; talk with Sapru; Gandhi's criticisms of Wylie and Khare; Pant's action on 'Tilak Day' meeting at Lansdowne
62	Hallett to Brabourne Report U.P.-157	23	Floods serious in places – everyone turns to district officers in emergencies; Hallett's visits to Allahabad, Benares and Fyzabad; previous fortnight quiet but agrarian and communal situation worrying; Muslim League Council meeting in Cawnpore; Palestine; has received reports that League intends to enrol large bodies of volunteers; Cawnpore situation; taluqdars are reported as not agreeing to any compromise on Tenancy Bill; concern over increase in crime and

			position of subordinate police in some districts; Lansdowne affair; Mrs Pandit's leave; Pant showing tendency to cut down European recruits to I.C.S. and I.P.; Enclosure: Letter from Hallett to Pant, dated 22 Aug., in which Hallett draws attention to the crime situation as recorded in Commissioners' reports
63	Hallett to Brabourne Letter U.P.-158	27	Explains Ministry's proposals for rural development and feels some change in position of district officer was inevitable; recommends continuance of Govt. of India grant with conditions
		Sept.	
64	Hallett to Brabourne Report U.P.-167	6	Ministry's actions over floods; revenue collections and crime; feeling against police may be due to too free use of Sections 109 and 110 C.Pr.C.; agrarian situation – points from Commissioners' reports; uncertain position on Tenancy Bill; riots in Allahabad and Fyzabad – Ministry taking a sound line; Muslim League's claims of anti-Muslim bias; intelligence report on enlistment of Congress volunteers; document giving details of instruction course for 'Congress Volunteer Corps'; Sampurnanand's suggestion U.P. should create an air defence organisation; agitation against Anti-recruitment Propaganda Bill; Palestine agitation; Dible's note on separation of judicial and executive functions; Ministry appears not to be

			appointing honorary magistrates on political grounds; difficult to assess effect of communist activity in Cawnpore; Enclosure: Note by Ibrahim (extract) on floods in U.P.
65	Hallett to Brabourne Report U.P.-173	15	Hallett's reasoned optimism on the ministerial situation in U.P.; gross inaccuracy of some Press reports; U.P. Govt.'s proposals for military training; action in event of European crisis; his final Cabinet meeting
66	Donaldson to Puckle Letter 1615-G.S.P.	16	Sends article by Sampurnanand in *Congress Socialist* on 'Problems of a Congress Minister'

CHAPTER 4 – DOCUMENTS FOR
26 SEPTEMBER – 31 DECEMBER 1938

		Sept.	
67	Haig to Brabourne Report U.P.-175	26	Most crucial problem in U.P. is relations between landlords and tenants – his discussions with Pant, Katju, Chhatari and Jehangirabad; Pant and Katju more conciliatory on Tenancy Bill than expected but U.P. Congress Committee and Kidwai seem opposed to concessions; villagers somewhat restive over lack of progress; fast by some police officers in Cawnpore; Pant's relations with police; effects of Ministry's anti-corruption organisation on police and its possible bearing on increase in crime; communist victory in Cawnpore Mazdur Sabha elections; position of Ministry has

			probably weakened; communal feeling appears particularly bitter; Ministers' attitudes on possible European war; Sampurnanand has suggested U.P. should develop its own air force and take air raid precautions; Congress only likely to co-operate in a war if they feel they are actively involved
68	Haig to Brabourne Tel. 178-G	29	Reports discussion with Pant on his attitude to a European war; believes that in practice Premier would support measures which were immediately necessary; Pant has stressed Congress ought to be consulted and support a war by voluntary act; Sampurnanand has expressed similar views and is concerned at declining recruitment to Army from U.P.
		Oct.	
69	Haig to Brabourne Report U.P.-176	10	Munich Agreement probably appeared to advanced Indian opinion as surrender of principle; talk with Pant on tenancy legislation; Working Committee's rebuke to U.P. Congress Committee; no diminution in ill feeling between Hindus and Muslims; Palestine; League success in Budaun bye-election; Madhe Sahaba dispute; Haig's interviews with a number of Heads of Department; work of certain committees; Enclosure: Resolution of Congress Working Committee passed on 30 Sept. 1938
70	Haig to Brabourne Letter U.P.-177	10	Reports his discussions with Pant and Horton on conditions in

		police; was favourably impressed with Premier's attitude; outlines action Governor will be taking
71 Haig to Brabourne Letter U.P.-180	18	Explains difficulties connected with suggestion that Pant might make a public pronouncement on police
72 Haig to Brabourne Letter U.P.-181	19	Refers to No. 63 and agrees with Hallett's conclusions; explains that Ministry is now seeking to foster rural development on sound and non-political lines; believes they should encourage this and continue Govt. of India grant; indicates how grant should be spent
73 Haig to Linlithgow Report U.P.-185	23	Haig's visit to Bareilly and Dehra Dun – he feels conditions on whole satisfactory; concern over recommendations of Maharaj Singh's Anti-Corruption Committee; growth of communalism in U.P.; Pant's indignation at Muslim League agitation; enquiry into killing of Muslims in Fyzabad district; strain caused by Madhe Sahaba dispute in Lucknow; Agra zamindars agree to arbitration of Congress Working Committee on Tenancy Bill but decision of Oudh taluqdars awaited; Haig's talks with landlords; he believes arbitration would be decided triumph for Congress right-wing; prospects of Oudh taluqdars agreeing to arbitration; Ministry may again consider pay cuts for services; talks with Ministers; Enclosure: Speech by Pant

			reported in *National Herald* of 14 Oct. 1938
74	Haig to Linlithgow Letter U.P.-189	30	Draws attention to the case of an official, Ram Babu Saksena, who was not *persona grata* with the Ministry
		Nov.	
75	Haig to Linlithgow Report U.P.-191	8	Haig's visits to Agra, Jhansi and Etawah; Agra Division suffering from a good deal of gloom; particular problems in Aligarh, Agra district, Muttra and Lalitpur; view in Agra Division that left-wing influence in Congress growing and there was uneasiness in police; Haig's study of rural development during visits; communal relations in these areas much less strained than in Rohilkhand; Oudh taluqdars reject arbitration on Tenancy Bill – Haig's interview with Jehangirabad; Haig discusses situation with Pant; Governor's note on situation; Ministry's discussions with landlords; deputation from Oudh Bar Association; elopement case in Cawnpore – application to transfer hearing; interview with Dholpur; Pant will not immediately visit Delhi; Enclosure 1: Cutting from *Hindustan Times* of 29 Oct. 1938 giving text of resolution passed by taluqdars of Oudh; Enclosure 2: Note by Haig dated 2 Nov. 1938 on possible settlement between landlords and Ministry

76 Haig to Linlithgow Letter U.P.-192	9	Has heard that Ministry intend to take up question of abolishing posts of Commissioners; asks to be brought up to date with discussions on subject
77 Haig to Linlithgow Letter U.P.-196	16	Asks for Linlithgow's advice on points arising from possibility that Ministry may cut pay and allowances of provincial services
78 Haig to Linlithgow Report U.P.-198	22	Inadequacies in Chief Secretary's reports; Pant's apparently uncompromising and threatening speech in Assembly on Tenancy Bill; Haig's discussions with Yusuf, Jehangirabad and Chhatari; further move to try to involve Congress Parliamentary Sub-Committee with Tenancy Bill; Haig feels this opportunity has passed and they may be in for seriously disturbed conditions; situation in Agra and Lalitpur; Pant's discussion on Lalitpur with Ross (Commissioner); Pant subject to constant and serious embarrassment from left-wing; matters Haig has taken up with Pant; nomination to Legislative Council; Patel's contact with Pant over Income-Tax Bill in Central Assembly; Pant's real attitude to European members of services; visit of Muirhead and Keeling: Enclosure 1: Cutting from *Pioneer* giving Pant's speech on Tenancy Bill in U.P. Legislative Assembly on 16 Nov. 1938; Enclosure 2: Circular letter from Gwynne to District Magistrates about the reporting of speeches at

			communal and agrarian meetings; Enclosure 3: Note by Haig, dated 18 Nov. 1938, expressing concern at growth of communal organisations
79	Haig to Linlithgow Letter U.P.-199	23	Reports conversation with Mrs Pandit who said that: (1) position of Ministry was definitely weaker; (2) Pant was being continually attacked for his moderation; (3) she thought they would have a very troublesome cold weather
		Dec.	
80	Haig to Linlithgow Letter U.P.-205	4	Sends note by Pant (circulated to Ministers) on District Advisory Committees; has growing feeling that attack on broad front is being made on whole machinery of present administration
81	Haig to Linlithgow Report U.P.-206	6	U.P. at present quiet but necessary to consider possible developments; Congress Parliamentary Sub-Committee makes it clear it will not intervene on Tenancy Bill; has felt greatly relieved about Bill after discussions with Kidwai and Pant; consideration of Bill starts on restrained note in Assembly; Ministry reported to be examining proposals for reduction of rent roll in U.P.; unsatisfactory talk with Pant on volunteer organisations; Haig's visit to Cawnpore; his concern that communists were very active, that violent speeches were being made and that provocative meetings were being held at mill gates; talk with Pant on Cawnpore situation is not very satisfactory;

			circular to D.M.s on use of Sections 107 and 108 Cr.P.C.; police abstracts; Pant decides not to attend annual police parade; Haig's concern at Pant's present attitude; strength of left-wing in U.P. not a calculated policy of Congress; first joint session of two houses of Legislature; Enclosure 1: cutting from *Pioneer* giving text of statement elaborating some remarks of Pant on Tenancy Bill; Enclosure 2: cutting from *National Hearld* giving Krishna Sharma's statement on Haig's visit to Cawnpore and proposed Bekar Sabha demonstration
82	Haig to Linlithgow Letter U.P.-208	19	Sends lengthy memorandum on existing position in U.P.; this concludes with recommendations as to their policy
83	Haig to Linlithgow Report U.P.-210	23	Haig has long talk with each Minister before he leaves Lucknow; signs right-wing are holding their own on Tenancy Bill; anticipations that Bill might be passed by April 1939; impression from Pant and Kidwai that they do not intend large, general reduction in rents; talk with Tiloi following his election as President of British India Association; Mrs Pandit says Ministry will concentrate on formation of village panchayats; Owen's anxieties for future at Cawnpore; Bal Krishna Sharma real problem at Cawnpore; police situation seems more

		hopeful; Ministers request that consideration of Anti-Corruption Report should be resumed; embarrassing incidents at Lucknow University Convocation; Haig's short tour examining newer tube-well areas; scheme for improving communications; Assembly discussion of Ministry's release of convicted murderer; Sampurnanand's warning of an attack on Benares State; special measures in Shahjahanpur; military training in schools
84 Haig to Linlithgow Tel. 187-G	28	Considers that legislation to give Centre necessary powers in war-time should not be undertaken immediately but left until the outbreak of war

APPENDICES

	Feb.	
A1 Linlithgow to Haig Letter	1	Refers to *U.P.P., 1936-37*, Nos. A9 and A16; expresses concern at a circular issued by S.P., Meerut to police subordinates in district; is also concerned that circular has been published in press
A2 Communiqué by Donaldson	15	Account of release of prisoners since Congress took office; background to the Ministers submitting their resignations
A3 Statement by Pant	18	Comments on No. A2 which he considers to be somewhat incomplete if not inaccurate
A4 Resolution of All-India Congress Committee	21	Congress view of the U.P. and Bihar crises

A5	Statement by Linlithgow	22	Explains reasons for the action he has taken; action leaves open to Ministers, in consultation with Governors, to pursue a policy of release of prisoners; hopes concerned Ministers, in discussion with Governors, may feel able to resume their interrupted labours
A6	Press Statement by Gandhi	24	Comments on No. A5; believes crisis can be avoided and indicates how this might be done
A7	Pant to Haig Letter	24	Refers to No. A6; considers it will be necessary to bear in mind Gandhi's principles for release of prisoners in arriving at solution to constitutional crisis
A8	Statement by Haig and Pant	25	Circumstances in which Ministers are resuming their normal duties
A9	Haig to Pant Letter	26	Is concerned that Katju has directed the release of large number of the political prisoners without detailed examination; this is out of accord with their agreement; very serious situation might be created if Katju issues immediate statement
A10	Linlithgow to Haig Letter	27	Refers to No. A8 and explains his considerable unease that it had not been possible to secure the drafting changes for which he had asked
		Sept.	
A11	Hallett to Brabourne Letter (Extract)	24	His last Cabinet meeting in U.P. discussed report of Anti-Corruption Committee and Public Service Commission; position on Tenancy Bill; Pant and Katju called to say goodbye and were very friendly

		Nov.	
A12	Press Communiqué issued by U.P. Govt.	10	Madhe Sahaba dispute; not at present proper for Govt. to announce its own decision
A13	Haig to Hallett Letter U.P.-203	29	Is more hopeful that Tenancy Bill will go through without provoking serious conflict; remains uneasy about general situation and swing to left; assumes Congress would probably swallow Federation under protest; unsatisfactory talk with Pant on volunteer movement; unhappy atmosphere in Cawnpore; work of Bihar Retrenchment Committee; grave mistake to upset services by agreeing to a cut in their pay

Map of the United Provinces

CHAPTER 1

Documents for 1 January–5 March 1938

1

HAIG TO LINLITHGOW
Telegram
MSS.EUR.F 115/22B

No. 103-G *January 1st, 1938*

Your telegram No. 537-G.C. dated December 30th.[1] My C.I.D. are definitely opposed to release of Sadashiv and I am in full agreement with them. This man was an active member of the most dangerous group of terrorists that have operated in Northern India. He was closely connected with Chandra Shekhar Azad and also with Bhagat Singh. He is, like Parmanand, a resident of Jhansi, and I think there is every likelihood that if he were released he would join up at once with the group of ex-Kakori prisoners.[2] I am afraid I should attach no importance to any assurances he might give. Moreover his release would be a definite embarrassment to me in that his record is much worse than that of several other U.P. prisoners whom I am refusing to release. I trust in view of these facts Bombay Government may abandon proposal to release him.

2

HAIG TO LINLITHGOW
Telegram
R/3/1/73

No. 104-G *January 4th, 1938*

Your telegram No. 496-G.C. dated 24th December.[3] I am in full agreement with conclusions reached by Your Excellency and Secretary of State. I understand in fact my Ministry will not put forward proposals for reducing pay scales of persons appointed before 1st April 1937, though they are likely to propose reduced scales on lines described in paragraph 2 of your telegram for persons recruited subsequently.

2. They have however taken up question of reduction or abolition of special pay and compensatory allowances. The saving would not at most be likely to exceed one lakh annually. The main object on the part of the Ministry would be to show that they were making such economies as are possible. Also on principle they dislike these various additions to pay.

3. The position as I understand it is as follows:

(*a*) In regard to special pay there is a class of officers protected under Section 241(3)(*a*). In the case of these officers the principles accepted in India Office letter No. S.&G.-4663-33, dated 15th November 1933,[4] would apply. In case of officers not so protected it might be desirable to apply the same principles.

(*b*) In the case of compensatory allowances position for all officers is same as in the case of travelling allowance, which was summed up in your telegram No. 1102-G., dated 24th September 1937.[5] It is not of course as easy in dealing with compensatory allowances given on somewhat general grounds, such as expensiveness of a station or compensation for absence of medical practice, to decide regarding continuance or scale of allowance as it is in the case of travelling allowance. I should anticipate that we shall have to consider not only whether there is any definite change in the circumstances in relation to which the allowance was originally sanctioned, but also might have to reconsider if necessary, the principle which has been held in the past to justify grant of any allowance.

4. My view is that I could not take any general objection to proposals for reduction or abolition of special pay or compensatory allowances but would have to consider the various proposals on their merits as indicated in paragraph 3. The matter will come up in connection with budget meeting of Cabinet on 15th January and I should be glad to know whether Your Excellency agrees with line I should propose to take.[6]

3

DONALDSON TO LAITHWAITE
R/3/1/73

Confidential
No. 916-G.S.P.

Camp,
January 5th, 1938

Sir,

Honours and Titles

I am directed to say that at a meeting of the Council of Ministers of the United Provinces held at Government House, Allahabad, on Monday, 20th December 1937, a minute which had been prepared by the Hon'ble Premier on the subject of honours and titles was considered. The request made in the minute is that no titles be conferred whether on officials or non-officials in this Province.

2. His Excellency the Governor pointed out that the grant of honours was not a function of the executive authority of the Province and that in any action he might take he did not act on the advice of his Ministers. He further pointed out that honours were conferred only by authority of His Majesty; and that His Majesty had assigned certain powers in respect of honours in India to His Excellency the Viceroy, but to him only. His Excellency stated that he would forward the minute of the Hon'ble Premier to His Excellency the Viceroy. No order was recorded by the Council of Ministers.

3. I am therefore directed to forward a copy of the minute of the Hon'ble Premier for the information of His Excellency the Viceroy.

I have the honour to be, Sir,

Your most obedient servant,
J.C. DONALDSON

ENCLOSURE TO NO. 3

MINUTE BY PANT

December 19th, 1937

H.E.

I have referred to the question of titles already on several occasions. It is, however, necessary to have a clear decision of the Cabinet on the subject. The Indian National Congress has felt for many years past that honours and titles play a demoralising part in public life. In our country titles have not unoften been conferred for resisting and combating the national movement. Political opinion in the country has been consistently opposed to the institution of honours and titles. The Indian National Congress reiterated its definite opinion again at the A.I.C.C. meeting held in Calcutta last month that no titles should be conferred – at least in the Provinces which are under the administration of the Congress Ministries.

Even in England where His Majesty the King is personally the head of the society and plays an important part in all functions "it is usual, where titles are conferred as a reward for parliamentary or other public services, for the Crown to be guided largely by the advice of the Prime Minister", and all honours are bestowed on the recommendation of the Prime Minister except that "His Majesty reserves to himself an absolute discretion in conferring the Order of Merit and the Royal Victorian Order." (Halsbury – *Laws of England.*) Any other course would be undesirable as it would carry with it the possibility of a conflict between the King and his Ministers.

On a similar principle in several Dominions His Majesty the King, the Governor-General and the Governors refrain, in accordance with the wishes of the Governments of those Dominions, from conferring honours. It is the desire of the Ministry that no titles be conferred whether on officials or non-officials in this Province and that His Excellency the Governor may be pleased to take necessary steps to give effect to this request.

G.B. PANT

4

HAIG TO LINLITHGOW
R/3/1/73

Secret
No. U.P.-47

January 10th, 1938

My dear Lord Linlithgow,

When I wrote my last fortnightly report of December 24th, the Parmanand situation was still unsettled, but I was able to settle the matter finally that night before I went off to my Christmas camp. I drafted out the statement[7] on the lines I had already discussed with Pant. He accepted it, subject to a few suggestions for amendment, some of which I agreed to and others I did not. But he made very little difficulty about the statement, and before we separated that night, I had had a fair copy of it made and he signed it.

2. The statement was very well received by the press, and I enclose cuttings[8] which show both the general impression created by head-lines and the editorial comments. I think it is quite clear that it was regarded by public opinion not as an act of weakness, but on the contrary as a new stage in the development of Congress policy. Like Your Excellency, I am very glad to see that the Working Committee at Bombay has passed a satisfactory resolution on the subject. But they have really done no more than endorse the policy contained in our statement, and I think the impression on the public (who of course are in ignorance of the inner history of the matter) is that the United Provinces Government have taken a firm line. I think this is a very satisfactory outcome of a situation which at one time looked exceedingly difficult.

3. At the same time I am fully in agreement with Your Excellency's general feeling, as explained in your letter of January 6th, which was of great interest and value, that Pant is very far from being a strong and resolute man, and that it will require constant pressure to keep him up to his own declared policy. In their attitude towards law and order I fear my Ministers want watching the whole time. Your Excellency's views in paragraph 3 of your letter about the general right wing attitude are very interesting, but I am afraid my Ministers lag a good way behind that position. On the other hand, Pant's characteristics make him reluctant to push the landlords too far, and generally incline him in policy to a middle course.

4. With regard to my general estimate of the present position and future developments, referred to in paragraph 4 of Your Excellency's letter of 6th January, what I had meant to convey in paragraph 2 of my letter of December 24th was that I thought Nehru was quite right in holding that the existence of the Congress Government had greatly strengthened the hold of the Congress on the Province, and that for some little time to come that tendency will continue. But my own feeling is that the power and popularity of the Congress are now getting somewhere near the peak, that before long opposite tendencies may begin to make themselves felt, and that after a year not only the Congress Government, but the Congress organisation will not command the same degree of popular support which it does at present. I certainly do not wish to suggest any optimistic anticipations of the future. There are plenty of difficulties all round. But the present position is in many respects better than might have been anticipated. I myself, for instance, a year ago, thought that a Congress Government could not function in this Province without leading to a very rapid break-down.

5. I am not very happy about Pant's own condition. During the last week both the Chief Secretary[9] and the Inspector-General of Police,[10] who had been in close touch with him, told me separately and uninvited that Pant seemed to them very tired and beginning to feel that the situation was getting on top of him. With me he keeps up appearances better, but I am frankly uneasy at these signs of over-strain just when he is about to be faced with two and a half months of exceedingly difficult and strenuous work. Rumours have been finding their way into the press that some Cabinet changes are likely in the near future. In particular it is said that Pandit Piyare Lal Sharma, Minister for Education, is likely to resign. I spoke to Pant about this, and he said that, as I knew already, Sharma is not happy in his present post and would be quite pleased to quit it. He is an oldish man and has never really settled down as an effective Minister. He feels the work is too much for him and that he is not the person to make a success of it. Pant has hitherto been pressing him to continue, for he is a man of moderate views and gives no trouble in the Cabinet. But it is quite possible that before long he may have to be replaced.

6. The Home Department wrote to us recently, informing us that the ban on the Independence Day pledge[11] had been withdrawn by the Delhi administration, and that its withdrawal was contemplated by various Provinces. Pant on seeing reports of withdrawal in the newspapers said he wished it withdrawn in this Province. I told him that under present conditions I quite appreciated the difficulty of maintaining the ban and that I would not oppose its withdrawal. At the same time I said that certain passages were clearly objectionable, and that I hoped that at any rate the Ministers would refrain from associating themselves publicly with any such declaration. He said, as he has said before, that "Independence" is the accepted creed of the Congress, and that he felt that Ministers would have to conform to whatever instructions they received from the Congress organisation. He said that at present none had been received, and he did not know what action was proposed for Independence Day. We discussed, not for the first time, the general difficulties arising from the fact that Ministers who had taken the oath of allegiance to the Crown were at the same time members of a party which was pledged to promote the policy of complete independence. One naturally does not wish to bring to the surface unnecessarily this underlying contradiction, but it seems to me possible there may be certain embarrassments in connection with Independence Day celebrations.

7. Another matter which I am watching closely is the working of the Rural Development Scheme, and particularly the behaviour of the members

of the staff. I have already drawn the attention of the Minister to the necessity for checking any tendency in the staff to regard themselves as Congress workers instead of as Government servants, and this is a point which will have to be emphasised very clearly.

8. There is little more that I can say at present about the rent situation. The Tenancy Committee has not yet reached conclusions. Letters have been or are being issued to Commissioners that Tahsildars are expected to realise revenue vigorously and to give any assistance in collecting rent that may be required, and also to report the names of persons suspected to be engaging in no-rent propaganda. I think that so far as the Government machinery is concerned everything possible is being done. The Premier is inclined, as always, to minimise the importance of Kisan Sabha activities. But he was certainly alarmed about the visit to the United Provinces of Sahajanand the Bihar agitator. He spoke at one time of stopping him from touring in the United Provinces, but he evidently felt after reflection that he could not do this, and I think as usual he is relying on bringing influences to bear to prevent the tour having seriously embarrassing consequences. The tour is starting just now.

9. The possibility of some agreement between the Congress and the Muslim League is very much to the fore at present, but I have no detailed inside information as to what is actually happening. The whole political situation seems to me at the moment extraordinarily fluid, and it is impossible to say what may come out of it.

Yours sincerely,
HARRY HAIG

5

HAIG TO LINLITHGOW
Telegram
R/3/1/73

Immediate
No. 109-G

January 19th, 1938

Your telegram No. 124-G.C. of 19th January.[12] I am seriously disturbed at action proposed to be taken in the Central Provinces which is obviously going to make it very difficult for other Provinces to resist similar proposals. I had assumed from your telegram No. 86-G.C. of 12th January that we were going to be quite firm about this point and I myself regard it as of the most serious importance to stand firm.

2. Suggested compromise seems to me from our point of view of no value. It can deceive no one. Public opinion cannot fail to regard this holiday on Independence Day as a holiday to celebrate the policy of independence which is in any case being announced by a patently seditious declaration. Government servants will feel independence is officially recognised and that by grant of a holiday they are in effect being encouraged to celebrate it. I think they would feel resentment and bewilderment. So far as public are concerned it will have a profoundly discouraging effect on all those who believe in British connection.

3. I understood from conversation with Pant a few days ago that he had no intention of raising this issue here and I feel so strongly on the subject that I should have greatest difficulty in bringing myself to agree if he now proposes action similar to that of the Central Provinces. But position will be seriously complicated by the Central Provinces action. The crucial point is that this holiday is to be given on Independence Day.

6

HAIG TO LINLITHGOW
R/3/1/73

Secret
No. U.P.-49

January 22nd, 1938

My dear Lord Linlithgow,

Many thanks for Your Excellency's letter of the 14th January. I am glad that your visit to Madras has been so successful. I have been settled in Lucknow, occupied with a number of problems, and free for the time from public functions.

2. There have been during the last fortnight some plain indications that pressure is being put on the Ministry by the left wing, and those indications have been reinforced by certain definite facts to which I shall refer later. The first matter in which it is clear that the left wing have recently been active is the old problem of release of political prisoners, which I had hoped would be allowed to rest for a time. Early in the month, the Premier returned to the charge once more about releasing the remaining revolutionary prisoners. He wrote a note on the subject, expressed rather decided views, and said that he would like the matter discussed in Cabinet. I think the most convenient course is for me to enclose a copy of the note which I wrote in reply on the 11th January. There has been no further

development, except that on a recent threat of hunger-strike by the revolutionary prisoners in the Allahabad jail the Premier, just as he was starting for Delhi, sent a hasty note saying that, if necessary, a Cabinet meeting on the release of revolutionary prisoners should be held even before he returned. I have no intention of doing anything of the kind. But it looks to me as if he will press this matter before long in a Cabinet meeting. I am not sure, however, that he has as yet thought out what the position will be if I find myself unable to agree to the proposals.

3. Another proposal for release of prisoners came up about the same time. Dr. Katju, the Minister for Justice, passed an order that the six Chauri Chaura prisoners[13] who are serving life sentences and are still in jail should be released. When the matter came to me I wrote a note on the 11th January an extract from which I enclose. I have heard nothing more about this, and I am not sure whether they wish to press it further. Since then there has also been a proposal that Yashpal, who is the most dangerous of our terrorist prisoners, should be released on the ground, certified by the I.M.S. Superintendent of the Jail, that he is suffering from the early stages of tuberculosis. This I have also opposed. I do not believe that all this pressure for the release of prisoners represents any strong convictions on the part of the Ministry; but it is to my mind clear evidence of the difficulties they are having with the left wing.

4. From what I hear the left wing seems to be more active and vigorous than ever, and it is even said that they are becoming so dissatisfied with Pant's comparatively moderate policy that they are seriously contemplating trying to get rid of him. The position appears to be that in the legislature the right wing predominates. But the recent elections of office bearers for the Provincial Congress Committee, which is the party organisation, are significant. The agreed names seem to have been settled after a great deal of private controversy in accordance with the wishes or decision of Jawaharlal Nehru. A right wing man has been elected president;[14] the secretary is Mr. Pandit, who of course is entirely under the influence of Nehru, and the executive committee contains apparently a majority of left wing men. This is an exceedingly weak position for the Premier to find himself in, and I do not think it is going too far to say that he could be turned out of office any day by Nehru.[15] Indeed, I doubt whether he would attempt to put up a fight, if Nehru went against him. He would not take the responsibility of splitting the party. At the present moment Nehru is clearly anxious to maintain Pant in office and is giving him useful support. But at the same time I have no doubt he is pressing on him many points of policy which Pant would not accept if he were a free agent. This situation seems

to me likely to be accentuated after the next Congress session when Nehru will cease to be President of the Congress. He will probably then devote himself more actively and decisively to provincial politics.

5. On the whole the tour of the Province by Sahajanand, the Bihar agitator, seems to have passed off without doing as much damage as might have been feared. But he seems to have stimulated Kisan Sabha feeling to a considerable extent in the Rae Bareli district, adjoining Lucknow, which has for many years been a centre of peasant unrest. A big demonstration of kisans from the neighbouring districts in Lucknow is being organised for the 29th January. The intention is to demonstrate in front of the Council House, and there is some talk of their demanding to see the Governor if they do not get satisfaction from the Premier. It will be necessary to consider with some care what action is to be taken to keep this demonstration under control and to prevent them approaching Government House.[16] The estimates of probable numbers are very speculative and range from 10,000 to 100,000. Meantime the rent situation is much as before. Rents are coming in, but very slowly. The passage in the fortnightly d.-o. which I attach,[17] dealing with the collection of rent, was drafted by the Premier himself and to my mind represents a view decidedly too optimistic. I have told him so, but of course his views have to go forward to the Government of India. In particular the statement that "it is generally admitted that good zamindars are not finding any difficulty in the matter" does not seem to me at all justified by the reports we are receiving. The Ministry have still not made up their minds on the very difficult questions of tenancy and revenue policy which have been under consideration of the tenancy committee. They are anxious to reach conclusions before the end of the month, but they have so much else on their hands that I am not sure whether this will be possible.

6. We have had a preliminary discussion on the budget, but decisions on the most important questions were deferred until the Premier returns from his visit to Delhi. This seems to me to be a clear case in which Nehru must have insisted on his views. A few days before the Cabinet discussion and after the Ministers had been holding their preliminary discussions among themselves the Premier gave me an outline of his views on the budget. At the Cabinet Meeting he had gone back on some of these views, seemed very undecided, and produced two entirely new ideas, which it was fairly clear had only recently been adopted by him and I feel pretty certain must have originated with Nehru. The first was that the deficit must be covered by a cut in pay of all the services; the second that constructive work on a large scale in the villages must be financed by a big loan. The budget position is decidedly unsatisfactory. The budget for

next year shows a deficit of 50 lakhs, less whatever sum may be available from our share in the Central Income Tax. The Premier is putting forward no suggestions at this stage for covering this deficit other than a vague proposal for a cut in pay, which I have indicated to him involves great difficulties, and which of course in accordance with the decision already taken will have to be negatived. If the Congress are to maintain their popularity in the villages it seems to me they will certainly require to spend money somewhat freely. They have already provided in the budget 25 lakhs for rural development, a scheme about which opinions differ widely, many holding that it is going to be used principally for purpose of Congress propaganda. There might be something to be said for raising a moderate loan for agricultural development on a wide scale. Unless the Ministry are able to give some material benefits to the villagers they may well lose ground, owing to the disappointment which is already making itself felt at their exhortations to the villagers to pay their rents, which are in such marked contrast with the election promises of the Congress. Hereditary rights and other provisions of this kind will of course be welcome, but I doubt if they will compensate for rents not being reduced, and any general reduction of rents would give rise to difficulties which I do not think the Ministry would be prepared to face.

7. The Premier spoke to me recently about possible changes in the Cabinet. He said he thought that Pandit Piyare Lal Sharma would have to go shortly and that he would like to replace him by Mr. Sampurnanand. The latter is a prominent left wing man, but for some time has been in favour of accepting office and in this respect at any rate does not seem to see eye to eye with the majority of the left wing. I asked Pant whether he hoped from this proposal to mitigate the opposition of the left wing, and on the other hand, whether he expected that it would lead to some change in the general policy of the Cabinet. He said that he anticipated neither of these results, but that Sampurnanand's ability would strengthen the Government, and that he had some influence over him and did not expect any difficulty in regard to the Government policy. I doubt if this represents the whole truth. I imagine he hopes to disarm left wing criticism to some extent by including Sampurnanand and that his inclusion will not be without its effect on policy. Sampurnanand must in fact be fairly representative of left wing views, for he was the left wing candidate for the Presidentship of the Provincial Congress Committee. Pant finally asked me whether he might have my authority to approach Sampurnanand, and I told him he might. We had some discussion at the same time about the desirability of increasing the number of the Cabinet to nine. But this clearly depends on

agreement with the Muslim League which at the moment seems unlikely. As far as I can judge the prospects of accommodation between the Congress and the Muslim League have not increased lately. The Muslim League seems to be going ahead very vigorously with its organisation, and I do not think it is in a mood to come to any agreement except very much on its own terms, which the Congress are hardly likely to accept.

8. I have taken the opportunity recently of interviewing a number of the Parliamentary Secretaries, and I think they have appreciated being brought into contact with me. They obviously feel that they could do a good deal more to help the over-worked Ministers if they were allowed to deal with files, and if files did not go up to a Minister when the Permanent Secretary and the Parliamentary Secretary were in agreement. In the meantime the question of the functions of the Parliamentary Secretaries is temporarily in abeyance pending receipt of a further communication from Your Excellency.

9. I have been in separate communication with Your Excellency on the question of a holiday on "Independence Day", and I hope that in view of your telegram of the 20th January[18] which I was very glad to get we shall not have any difficulty here. I do not think Pant has any desire to raise the issue unless it is forced on him by action elsewhere. The Assembly has passed resolutions reprehending titles and expressing its strong opposition to federation. In the latter the Muslim League and Congress joined hands, but could not resist the temptation to criticise each other's motives.[19]

Yours sincerely,
HARRY HAIG

ENCLOSURE 1 TO NO. 6

NOTE BY HAIG

January 11th, 1938

I have discussed this matter many times with the Hon'ble Premier, and I think he is fully acquainted with my views. The release of the Kakori prisoners was advocated on precisely the same grounds as are now put forward for the release of the remaining revolutionary prisoners. It can hardly be denied that the anticipations formed at that time have been conspicuously falsified by events. Ideas of revolutionary violence were at that time quiescent; the release of the Kakori prisoners has helped to bring them into marked and continuous prominence. H.M.J. considers that the non-release of these prisoners has been poisoning public life. It is possible to take the opposite view, that if the Government had taken a different line in regard to prisoners convicted of violence and had from the beginning refused to treat them with leniency, we should have been saved from many of our recent embarrassments which have been brought upon us by the activities of the released Kakori prisoners.

2. I quite recognise, and regret, the political embarrassment to which this question gives rise, but I regard it as really only an incident in a much wider issue, and that is whether the Ministry firmly intend to resist the ideas and policy of mass violence and revolution. The recent statement issued on the Parmanand case created the impression that that was their intention, and I cannot help feeling that this was welcomed by a large section of Congress opinion. To release revolutionary prisoners would, I fear, quite apart from its practical results on a situation which must be kept under control, be likely to counteract the salutary impression created by the statement.

3. I notice that though the cases of these various persons have been examined by H.M.J. with reference to such circumstances as the age of the prisoners, the length of sentence and features of the trials, we do not seem to have on record any detailed statement by the C.I.D. of the revolutionary histories and connections of these prisoners, and the nature of their crimes as viewed against that background. These seem to me essential points to be considered in addition to the general aspects of policy which I have indicated above, and if the Hon'ble Premier wishes this case to be discussed in Cabinet, I would suggest that, in the first place, the C.I.D. should be directed to prepare notes of this kind on each prisoner.

ENCLOSURE 2 TO NO. 6

NOTE BY HAIG (EXTRACT)[20]

January 11th, 1938

There seems to me to be in the notes some misunderstanding of the administrative facts. It is assumed that a life sentence is equivalent to 14 years' imprisonment, and that the 14 year rule substitutes this period for a life sentence. This of course is not the case. A life sentence is a life sentence and can only be commuted by a special order of Government. When a life convict has served 14 years with remissions, his case is examined, the opinion of the District Magistrate is obtained and also, I understand, that of the Revising Board. With these recommendations before it, the Government passes orders. But it is by no means the invariable rule to release after 14 years. On the contrary dacoits are normally kept much longer and also other prisoners in whose cases release seems for any reason undesirable.

In the case of the six Chauri Chaura prisoners who are still in jail, I understand that their cases have all been carefully examined by the Government after considering the recommendations of the District Magistrate and the Revising Board, and that definite orders have been passed in the case of each of these men as to the full sentence that they are to serve. Five of them have been ordered to serve 25 years and one 20 years. The proposal on this file therefore is not to remedy an oversight, but to reverse an order of Government issued after careful consideration of the facts.

As H.M.J. (Hon'ble Minister for Justice) remarks, this was no doubt a terrible case. On that account it is in my judgment necessary to be exceedingly careful in extending clemency to those convicted. Sir William Marris[21] when unveiling the memorial to the policemen murdered at Chauri Chaura said that "this very peaceful looking place suddenly became invested throughout India, indeed beyond India, with a hideous notoriety" and this is a fact which must be borne in mind. The name of Chauri Chaura is still universally known throughout India and is sufficiently familiar in England. As Sir William Marris remarked "Chauri Chaura showed us all, as in a flash of lightning, what may happen if once the foundations of law and order are sufficiently loosened," and again "it is a very easy thing to trouble the minds of the masses; but the reckless man who does so is playing with a mighty fire." It is impossible in my judgment to hold that these reflections do not still apply to conditions in the United Provinces, and there have been clear signs in recent months of the re-birth of a spirit of violence, from which for some years we had fortunately been free. This therefore is no time to take action which can be interpreted as indicating a lenient view towards such a striking manifestation of mob violence, arising, be it remembered, from conditions of which there is in many quarters some apprehension of repetition. In the Gorakhpur district recently there have been many references to Chauri Chaura, and last September the Commissioner[22] wrote that "conditions in the opinion of responsible persons are becoming similar to those obtaining before the Chauri Chaura outrage." In the very last fortnightly report we have from Gorakhpur, dated December 21st, the Commissioner[23] writes: "I regret that the latter (i.e. bad speeches) include a speech delivered in the Hata Tahsil by a convict of the Chauri Chaura case who had been released from the jail in the ordinary course." The Kakori prisoners have been making a number of references to the Chauri Chaura case. Ram Krishna Katri said that the Chauri Chaura prisoners who had burnt a thana on police provocation were still rotting in jail. Vidya Dhar Bajpai said that the Chauri Chaura prisoners had killed police officers whose oppression they could not bear. Sachindra Nath Bakshi said that the Chauri Chaura prisoners who had merely set fire to a police station on police instigation were still in jail, and on another occasion he referred to the "unarmed peaceful kisans who on police provocation burnt Chauri Chaura police station." I think these references are sufficient to show the kind of interpretation that may be placed on the release of these prisoners at the present time. There were also threats in some of the scandalous speeches made at Cawnpore at the Anti-Police Day demonstrations that Chauri Chaura would be repeated.

This leads me to another aspect of the matter. Sir William Marris, in the speech to which I have already referred, said: "The news of this tragedy spread not only consternation but very keen and very natural resentment throughout the ranks of the police in India." That feeling I know exists, and I greatly fear that action, which would be interpreted as indicating the sympathy of the Government with the Chauri Chaura prisoners, would create a feeling of considerable uneasiness in the police of this Province in regard to the attitude towards them of the Government which they at once serve and protect.

For the reasons stated above I would strongly urge that the proposal to release the remaining Chauri Chaura prisoners should not be pursued.

7

HAIG TO LINLITHGOW
Telegram
MSS.EUR.F 115/22B

No. 114-G *January 24th, 1938*

Your telegram No. 162-G.C. dated 23rd January. I am grateful for action taken.[24]

2. A firm guarantee that Sadashiv would not leave Bombay Presidency for six months would no doubt for that period lessen direct effect on my local situation. He might still however prove very embarrassing to us after six months.

3. The most important point however at the moment is effect on my general position, which is to refuse release of further revolutionary prisoners. My letter No. 49 dated 22nd January with enclosures shows

attack which is being developed on that position by my Ministers, and is likely to come to a head shortly. If, as seems possible, the matter comes to a direct conflict between me and my Ministers, my position would be appreciably weakened by the release of a U.P. man, whose revolutionary activities in the U.P. have been most dangerous, just at the time when I am declining to accept the advice of my Ministers in regard to others whose revolutionary activities were less conspicuous.

8

HAIG TO LINLITHGOW
R/3/1/73

Secret *January 30th, 1938*
No. U.P.-50

My dear Lord Linlithgow,

I have had two important interviews with my Ministers regarding the release of political prisoners: the first, on January 26th, when the Premier and Dr. Katju came to see me on the subject; the second, on January 29th, when the position was further discussed with the Premier alone, Dr. Katju being temporarily away.[25] As a result of these discussions, which make certain aspects of the problem perhaps clearer than they were before, I feel it is desirable to review the whole situation and try to reach, if possible, some general conclusion about policy.

2. I might briefly recall the earlier history. My Ministers at a very early stage raised, like Congress Ministers in other Provinces, the question of release of political prisoners convicted in connection with offences of violence. Those for whose release they pressed in particular were the Kakori prisoners who were very much in the public eye. After long consideration and full discussion with Your Excellency, I agreed to the release of these prisoners about the 20th August. The releases were followed by some striking and scandalous demonstrations which made a great impression on the public mind. As a result of that situation, I decided that for the time being it was out of the question to proceed with any further releases, and for a time this position was accepted by my Ministers, though I had a great deal of difficulty with them over the question of Dublis, one of the Kakori prisoners who was returning from the Andamans and was not due for release for a month or so after his return. Eventually I declined to let him out on his return, and he was released in the ordinary course about the beginning

of November. Meantime, the Kakori demonstrations having died down and there being something of a reaction of feeling against them, my Ministers again raised the question of release of the remaining prisoners, numbering some ten or twelve. Discussions about these men proceeded during October. I agreed to the release of five, three of whom were believed not really to have been engaged in any revolutionary conspiracy, while two were mere boys who had embarked on a very amateurish exploit. I declined, however, to agree to the release of six other prisoners who were reported to have definite revolutionary connections and one of whom, Yashpal, had been a person of considerable importance in the terrorist movement. The line I have always taken with the Premier was that the question of release depended partly on the record and character of the individual prisoner and partly on the general conditions of the Province; and in October, when I definitely refused to accept his proposal for the release of the six remaining prisoners, I said I would be quite prepared to review my conclusions six months later when the situation would have become clearer and it would be more easy to see whether his anticipations or mine had proved correct. I based my view then largely on the menace of the development of the terrorist communist movement, and said I felt that it was important not to give it further encouragement or accretion of strength. It seemed clear that the Kakori prisoners had joined this group and it was a fair inference that any other men of this type who were released would do the same.

3. In October and November the Kakori prisoners made themselves once more notorious by touring the Province under the leadership of Parmanand, making speeches of a violent tendency, and the situation became such that it was necessary to take action. The statement issued at the end of December in connection with the Parmanand case, together with the firm action which had been taken at the end of November in Cawnpore, produced a salutary effect on general conditions in the Province and, combined with the sentences inflicted on several of the Kakori prisoners at Delhi, have produced an atmosphere which appears to me in respect of these extremist movements to be for the time being reasonably tranquil.

4. As I have already informed Your Excellency, at the beginning of January my Ministers once more took up strongly the question of the release of the remaining prisoners. I maintained the position which I had adopted last October and in which I had persisted ever since. This is the background of our recent conversations.

5. I may mention that whereas, when the Premier raised the question

again at the beginning of January, he had said that he wished it to be discussed in Cabinet, after he received my note of January 11th, a copy of which I have already sent to Your Excellency, he seems to have given up this idea and on the 26th January he merely asked that Dr. Katju should come with him to discuss the problem. The impression I derived from this interview was that the Premier felt that if I continued to refuse to accept his advice he would perforce have to acquiesce, because he was not prepared either to resign on such an issue or to disclose publicly a difference of opinion between us. On the 29th, however, he looked a little further ahead and gave me to understand that in the event of public opinion becoming seriously agitated, as it might be for instance by a hunger-strike, he might find it impossible to continue in office if he was unable to carry out the policy of his party on this matter. That is a possibility that has always been present, and whether it would materialise would depend not I think on the Premier's own attitude so much as on the development of public opinion, which is somewhat more difficult to predict. There was no suggestion that he would wish to resign on such an issue, and I am convinced that he would not; but circumstances might force his hands.[26]

6. While the Ministers put forward a number of old arguments which I need not repeat, the point which they stressed in particular and to which they gave an importance that had not emerged in our previous discussions, was that rightly or wrongly the release of these prisoners had been part of the Congress programme with which they had gone to the country, that expectations had been roused, and that it was hardly possible for them to justify their position in postponing these expectations indefinitely. In this connection they asserted that the demand for release of political prisoners was by no means confined to the left wing, but was supported by all classes of Congress opinion, and I am inclined to think that they are right to this extent at any rate, that in resisting the release of these prisoners they would not have the support of any Congressman. They further emphasized that their proposals were being put forward in the firm belief that they did not involve any danger to the peace of the Province, that conditions in the Province were on the whole remarkably peaceful at present, that so far as could be judged the prisoners were not the kind of men who would be capable of influencing opinion to any great extent or seriously promoting any dangerous revolutionary movement, and that it was believed that they would in fact abstain from any activities in encouragement of violence and that satisfactory assurances could be obtained from them on these lines. Further, they argued that there were very few prisoners involved,

and that the effect of their release on the Province so far from constituting any grave menace would in fact be negligible.

7. I think the real reason for the renewed and urgent insistence of the Ministers on some action being taken now is that they are afraid of being faced with a political development which would shake their position seriously. What they are particularly afraid of is the starting of a hunger-strike. This I should guess they feel would be made the occasion for the working up of feeling against them by the left wing, and they expressed the definite belief that a hunger-strike would be likely to lead to demonstrations which the Government might find it difficult to deal with. They realise very clearly the embarrassments of a hunger-strike. They appreciate the fact that if a hunger-strike developed it would be quite impossible for me to agree to any concessions. At the same time they are afraid that popular feeling might be roused to such an extent as to make it impossible for them to remain in office. In other words, the occurrence of a hunger-strike might produce an insoluble dilemma which might destroy the present prospects of reasonable political developments in the Province.

8. I had recently asked the police to re-examine the individual cases of the six prisoners with whom we are concerned, and also to give me a general picture of conditions in the Province from the point of view of the terrorist and revolutionary situation. Out of the six prisoners the police now hold that one is not primarily a political prisoner, although some of his associates were political criminals, and that one young man might safely be released conditionally. The other four they consider on their records and connections should not be released. With regard to the general estimate of the position it seems to be agreed that there are no indications of any revival of terrorist plans, and it cannot therefore be anticipated that these men if released would re-embark on terrorism. The case for not releasing them really rests on the estimate of the importance of the revolutionary-communist movement and the impetus that they might give to this. The general picture of the immediate danger of this movement to the Province contained in a tentative draft from the C.I.D. which I have seen, is not very impressive and indeed seems to me a little thin. I discussed the situation yesterday with the Inspector-General of Police who has just returned from tour. His position is that on ordinary police standards the opposition to the release of these four men is fully justified. At the same time he is obviously somewhat doubtful whether they would in fact be required or be utilised as organisers of importance in the promotion of any revolutionary movement at present in sight, and his view is that there

are a number of individuals out of jail who are potentially every bit as dangerous as these men. He also appears to consider that the atmosphere of the Province is at present peaceful and this agrees with my own observation. The position therefore is that as against the possibility of very serious consequences from insisting on not releasing these men, one has to put a case which is not altogether convincing about the grave menace that their release would involve.

9. So much for the provincial situation as I see it. But of course I am fully alive to the effect of the all-India aspect and provincial interactions, and in particular to the fact that political prisoners are at present on hunger-strike in Bengal, Bihar and the Punjab. So far as Bengal and the Punjab are concerned, my Ministers urged that the problem is different to ours. They have Ministries which is not releasing prisoners of this type are pursuing a policy in which they believe and in which they are supported by the majority of the legislature. In the Congress Provinces exactly the reverse is the case. The Ministers not only do not believe in the policy of keeping these prisoners in jail, but by so keeping them are going against their own election manifesto and opposing their own followers. On the question of general policy, while I think it is important that the Congress Provinces should keep in line with each other, I think perhaps there is less necessity for them to keep in line with the non-Congress Provinces. With regard to hunger-strikes, I think it would be very undesirable for us in this Province to take any action while the hunger-strikes in the other Provinces are continuing, for this would be likely to encourage the hunger-strikers. What my Ministers are clearly most anxious to do is to ward off a hunger-strike here by giving some hope to the prisoners that their cases will be considered shortly. I think therefore the position of my Ministers would be greatly eased if, without agreeing to any immediate action, I gave them to understand that I would be prepared to review with an open mind the whole question of releasing these prisoners as soon as the hunger-strikes in other Provinces have come to an end. If on further discussion with the police I came to the conclusion that these releases could be carried out without involving any grave menace to the Province, I should propose that they should be carried out gradually, say, over a period of a month, that we should get definite assurances about no demonstrations and satisfactory assurances from the prisoners themselves about their future attitude. With regard to Yashpal, whose case would normally be the most difficult to agree to, both on his record and the fact that he has only served about half his full sentence of 14 years, there is the fact that he is undoubtedly suffering from the early stages of tuberculosis, and there may

be a case on medical grounds for releasing him. All the prisoners under consideration have served a considerable proportion of their sentences. None has been in for less than four years, and some have served nearly six.

10. I should be glad to know whether Your Excellency would agree to my handling the situation on these lines. I am of course aware that one thing leads to another. For instance, if I agreed to the release of the four prisoners whose record is bad there could be no ground for resisting the release of Sadashiv,[27] and there may be one or two other United Provinces men in other Provinces who would come out similarly. Nevertheless it is clear that the release of these prisoners will be pressed continuously and it seems to me that it is only a question of time before these men will all have to be out; on the other hand the present moment is rather crucial, and by anticipating a decision which perhaps would have to be taken in any case in three months' time we might be able to avert a very serious political development. At the same time I should propose to make it clear to the Ministers that I would expect them not to proceed with their proposals for the release of the six Chauri Chaura prisoners. They gave me to understand that these proposals would not in fact be pressed and that the Chauri Chaura prisoners were not looked upon as politicals in the same way as those whose cases I have been discussing above.

11. I have told the Premier that I hope to be able to discuss the matter with him again towards the end of this week. I should therefore be grateful if I could have Your Excellency's views on this letter as early as possible. I am also sending a copy of this letter to Hallett who is of course closely concerned in the policy suggested. I should perhaps explain that I think there may be considerable justification for my Ministers' apprehensions in connection with a hunger-strike. In view of the strength of the left wing influence in this Province and the comparatively weak position of the Ministry in relation to it, a hunger-strike here might have more formidable political reactions than are perhaps likely in Bihar, where it seems to be attracting no undue attention.[28] I should perhaps add that Dr. Katju was more emphatic on this point than the Premier and declared that there was no sufficient justification for our creating administrative conditions which would give rise to such formidable difficulties.

Yours sincerely,
HARRY HAIG

9

HAIG TO LINLITHGOW
R/3/1/73

No. U.P.-52

Camp,
February 6th, 1938

My dear Lord Linlithgow,

I am very sorry that this difficulty about Your Excellency's shoot near Kaladhungi on the 11th and 12th of this month has developed. As soon as the police heard of Your Excellency's plan they were seriously disturbed, and after looking into details, the Inspector-General of Police yesterday wrote in to say that he could not advise that it would be safe in the circumstances to undertake to provide the necessary protective arrangements for Your Excellency's visit. I could not feel that his apprehensions were unjustified. The state of feeling between the Hindus and Muslims throughout the Province has been for some months decidedly strained, and this tension is particularly likely to break out into violence at the time of the Bakr Id which takes place precisely on the 11th and 12th, which were the dates for Your Excellency's proposed visit. Apart from general apprehensions, it is clear that in a number of districts district officers are decidedly anxious about particular danger spots. In these circumstances to withdraw some 1,200 constables from the force available for maintaining order throughout the Province during the Bakr Id would be taking risks which seem to me unwise, and which we might find difficult to justify if in fact any serious trouble arose.

2. I know what a delightful holiday a day or two in the Kaladhungi jungles gives, and I know how much in need of an occasional holiday Your Excellency must be. It was therefore with the greatest reluctance that I had to suggest that your plan should be reconsidered, and I should not have done so had I not felt that a serious practical risk in the maintenance of the peace of the Province was involved. I hope greatly that it will be possible for Your Excellency to carry out the shoot later on some more convenient date.[29]

Yours sincerely,
HARRY HAIG

10

HAIG TO LINLITHGOW
R/3/1/73

Secret *February 9th, 1938*
No. U.P.-53

My dear Lord Linlithgow,

As I have reported separately, I have had some important conversations with my Ministers on the subject of release of political prisoners. I have put my views on the general problem in some detail before Your Excellency. The hunger-strikes in other Provinces appear to be coming to an end, and in this Province the Ministers have by their own methods been able to avert a hunger-strike developing. But they have clearly been very nervous about it, and they will not be able indefinitely to avoid this complication unless some real hope is held out to the prisoners. I told the Premier, when I saw him two or three days ago, that for the present I could not carry the matter any farther than the point reached in our discussions at the end of last month, as reported in my letter No. U.P.-50, dated January 30th, 1938. Yesterday, however, at a Cabinet meeting, he said that he wished to discuss this matter at our next Cabinet meeting which will take place tomorrow. So it appears that after all he wishes to have the views of the Ministers formally on record.

2. The threatened *kisan* demonstration to which I referred in paragraph 5 of my letter of January 22nd did not after all materialise. The Premier was anxious to stop it. He would not have been prepared to take any official action to prohibit it, but he set the Congress organisation to work. It was given out that the demonstration was to be postponed until after the Government had made up their minds about their tenancy policy, and this move was successful. In addition to this, in the Rae Bareli district where the movement was strongest and from which it was supposed that 20,000 men were coming, the Congress committee expelled from the Congress the principal organiser who had been, I understand, in their bad books for some time. This seems to have produced considerable effect. The agrarian position generally seems to me decidedly easier.[30] The continuous exhortations to the tenants from the Congress side to pay their rents are having effect, and rents and revenue are coming in much better. On the whole it looks to me as if the Government will get through this difficult time without any very serious consequences.

3. The position as to a change in the Ministry has not advanced any further. I asked the Premier recently what was happening. I understand from him that Mr. Sharma, feeling that the opportunity was being taken to push him out, has turned a little stubborn and says he does not intend to resign, and the Premier is not prepared to ask him to resign. At the same time the Premier seems to have committed himself rather definitely to Sampurnanand, and there have been numerous paragraphs in the press saying that Sampurnanand is about to be appointed. Administratively, there would be no objection to Sampurnanand being appointed without Sharma resigning, and this is a course to which at the moment the Premier inclines; but I have drawn his attention to the consideration that if another Hindu Minister is appointed, the Muslims, even though they may not have a very strong case for complaint, will undoubtedly seek to raise an agitation, and that it may be unwise for him at the present time to give them a handle of this kind. He is still undecided as to what line to take.

4. Another resignation which is hanging fire in a manner that is bewildering to the public is that of Paliwal, the Rural Development Officer. It was announced in the papers about a fortnight ago that he had resigned, and various very scathing articles have been written in the *Leader* and the *Pioneer* about his giving up his post before he had really been able to do anything effective. The Premier told me that Paliwal has in fact tendered his resignation, but that the Ministers have not made up their minds whether to accept it, though I gather it is likely that they will. My inside information is that Paliwal sent in his resignation on seeing a note which I had recorded. It was reported that he had been elected Chairman of the Agra District Board. I enquired whether this was correct, pointing out that the District Board Act did not permit an official to be Chairman, and that it was clearly understood when Mr. Paliwal was appointed that he would be treated in all respects as a Government servant and would be fully subject to all the restrictions that govern the conduct of Government servants. It has been pretty obvious from the beginning that Paliwal would before long come in conflict with Government regulations about conduct, and that he had no intention of running this department on anything but political lines.

5. This question of the organisation and activities of the Rural Development department is likely to engage my attention seriously during the next few months. There is an almost universal belief that the Government intend to use this movement very largely for purposes of political propaganda. There has already been a great deal of public criticism of the appointment of the lower paid staff, and many rumours are current as to the instructions that have been given to them at their training camps.

I have already taken these matters up with my Ministers and expect to have a somewhat prolonged tussle with them. The two strong points in my position are, firstly, that the staff are Government servants and must be made to behave as such and not as party propagandists; and, in the second place, that I can as an ultimate resort insist on recruitment of the whole staff being made by the Public Service Commission, including those who have already been appointed on a temporary basis. I think the Premier is genuinely anxious that the staff should do real development work in the villages, but I strongly suspect that Dr. Katju, who is the Minister in charge, is primarily aiming at political results. In any case by holding my hand at the beginning, I am now in a position in which, if I have any difficulty with my Ministers over this matter, I should have a considerable volume of public opinion behind me. The Ministers themselves have been a good deal disturbed by the nature of the criticisms that have been directed against them on this subject in the Assembly.

6. A rather ugly, though short-lived, disturbance broke out at Cawnpore last Sunday, when Hafiz Muhammad Ibrahim, one of the Ministers, went over to fulfil certain engagements. Though it was known that the Muslim League were going to demonstrate against him, the local Congressmen insisted on organising a public procession. This was heavily attacked by the Muslim Leaguers with brickbats, and a number of people were injured, the Minister himself being in considerable danger of injury. The Premier is very indignant with the police, and declares that they were negligent and had ample warning of what was going to happen, and talks of taking very serious notice of their failure to prevent this riot.[31] The facts have not yet been fully ascertained; but this is a curiously novel attitude for the Premier to take when one remembers how a few months ago he shrank from their carrying out even the most elementary precautions to deal with disorder provoked by the strikers. He feels, however, that this was an insult to the Ministers (the Education Minister also being there) and he suspects that the police were deliberately negligent, which seems to me very improbable.

7. With the approach of the Bakr Id nervousness in the Province is increasing, and there is a general feeling that we shall be lucky if we get through without any serious disturbance anywhere. The Ministry are finally facing the Madhe Sahaba problem. They had postponed for months reaching a conclusion and had exhausted all the possibilities of discussion and compromise. It is now agreed on all hands that the report of the committee which sat about nine months ago must be published before the Muharram. The Government are accepting the conclusions of the

committee, which are sound and well thought out, but the Sunnis are likely to be dissatisfied and to give trouble. It has been decided that the report and the conclusions of the Government will be published as soon as possible after the Bakr Id.

8. Final discussions on the budget are still being postponed, but the latest edition of the proposals is very much more satisfactory than earlier anticipations, and I hope it may be possible to put forward the budget for next year with a revenue deficit of not more than 12 lakhs. The Premier, however, still seems to be toying with the idea of launching a most ambitious scheme of expenditure on the improvement of rural and agricultural conditions to be financed by a loan. At one time he seemed to have dropped this idea after we had discussed it in Cabinet, but I am told that he has taken it up once again. Our final budget discussions are due to take place tomorrow.

9. I fear the hill move has been abandoned. Pant and the majority of the Ministers would have liked to go to Naini Tal, but when this intention became apparent the party revolted, and they cannot face the criticism that they are becoming demoralised by the sweets of office and losing their pristine and hardy Congress principles. So things are likely to work out much as they did last year, with Ministers, I hope, coming up to Naini Tal for a month or so at the most trying time of the hot weather, and Secretaries also being allowed to get away from time to time.

10. The Civil Service Week which has just concluded was a great success. A large number of officers came in from all parts of the Province and a cheerful atmosphere prevailed. We had over 70 at the Civil Service dinner which is well up to the average. I spoke to them about present day conditions, the difficulties, the interest, the prospects of success, the importance of their individual work and the confidence I had in them. I also assured them that their legitimate interests would be supported. I understand that my speech was very well received.

11. I took up recently with Pant the question of social contacts. The question had arisen whether members of the I.C.S. should invite the Ministers to their "At Home" at the races. While feeling was in favour of doing so, it was also apparent that not a few members of the Services resented the attitude of the Ministers in not calling at Government House and severing themselves from any social contacts with the Governor, and it was felt that if these conditions continued, it would not be altogether easy for members of the Services to establish satisfactory social relations with the Ministers. I felt the force of these considerations and took the opportunity of discussing the whole subject somewhat frankly with Pant.

I told him I realised that the practice they had adopted was due not to any personal reasons but was dictated by political considerations, but that in my opinion those political considerations were fundamentally illegitimate, in that they were in essence directed against the influence of the Representative of His Majesty. I also mentioned the difficulty that was bound to be felt by members of the Services and stressed the point that my desire was that we should all, Governor, Ministers and the Services, work together in the closest co-operation. He had nothing very effective to say in answer to my arguments, but indicated that he was bound by general policy. I did not take the matter any further, but I am not without hope that what I said may fructify later. Not infrequently I find that suggestions made by me which do not seem at the moment to be taken up are acted upon afterwards.

12. By a coincidence the Assembly was discussing during the Civil Services Week the abolition of the Secretary of State's Services proposed by Sir Maharaj Singh, and the usual criticisms were made about them. The Premier's own speech, as reported in the press, was far from happy, but I do not think the Services were unduly disturbed. The Ministers propose shortly to express their desire for the abolition of Commissioners, but they know that nothing will come of this. They profess to be convinced of the uselessness of these posts.

Yours sincerely,
H.G. HAIG

11

HAIG TO LINLITHGOW
Telegram
MSS.EUR.F 115/8

Clear the Line *February 10th, 1938*
No. 118-G

Yesterday the Premier spoke about release of political prisoners, having just sent me a note saying that "the question has assumed very great importance and if the release is delayed grave consequences may follow". He said he and his colleagues felt they must have a decision before the Congress session. I was disposed to think this new development had a local origin and was not due to instructions from Working Committee. The matter was discussed formally in Cabinet today and I elicited from Premier statement that view of the Working Committee was that this matter must be settled before Congress session. I am sending full report by special messenger tonight, but information about attitude of Working Committee is so important that I am telegraphing this in advance. If this information is correct, presumably same line is being taken in Bihar.

Repeated to Governor of Bihar.

12

HAIG TO LINLITHGOW
Express Letter
R/3/1/73

Secret *February 10th, 1938*
No. U.P.-54

Reference your telegram No. 123-G., dated February 3rd.[32] At a Cabinet meeting on 8th February the Ministers expressed a desire to discuss the release of political prisoners at the next Cabinet meeting on February 10th and the Premier said he wished to talk the matter over with me as a preliminary on the 9th. Accordingly on the 9th he saw me, having already sent me a note saying that "the question has assumed very great importance and if the release is delayed grave consequences may follow".[33]

2. The Premier explained that he had been discussing the matter with his colleagues and that they felt very strongly the necessity for an early decision. He gave me two reasons for this urgency: (*a*) In spite of the termination of the Bihar hunger-strike they are very nervous that a hunger-strike may start in the United Provinces. I gathered they must have given some hope to the political prisoners that an early decision was likely. (*b*) Their action will come under critical scrutiny at the Congress session and they consider it necessary to show that they have not been backward in taking action.

3. I pointed out that it seemed improbable that our prisoners would now start a hunger-strike just when the other hunger-strikes were terminating and the Working Committee had pronounced against them. I further explained that the proposals of the Ministry raised difficult problems which required to be thought out carefully, and that I could see no possibility of reaching a decision before the Congress session.

4. As the Premier used language which suggested the possibility of the Ministry taking a very grave view of failure to accept their proposals I thought it as well to ask him precisely what he meant, and said that I had understood from our last interview that the Ministers would not be likely

to contemplate resignation on such an issue unless their hands were forced by public opinion. The Premier said that this was not the impression he had wished to convey and that they felt very strongly on the subject. But when I asked him what the position would be likely to be if I were unable to meet his wishes for an immediate decision, he merely said that the Ministry would have to consider its position seriously.

5. I interpreted this development as having a local and not a central origin. I thought the Premier was being pressed strongly by Katju and Kidwai and that his colleagues considered that he had not taken a firm enough line with me. I was disposed to regard the present threat as bluff, for it seemed to me that they could not proceed to resignation without the prior approval of the Working Committee which it did not look as if they had obtained. At the same time the Premier made it perfectly clear to me that the Working Committee had decided to make this question of release of political prisoners in the Congress Provinces a major issue, and it was clear that the problems discussed in my letter of January 30th would have to be faced at an early date.

6. One point which the Premier makes repeatedly is that when in Bengal, where the terrorist menace is serious, 1,100 detenus have been released and it is said that the release of more is contemplated, it is absurd to hold that the release of half a dozen prisoners in this Province constitutes a risk which cannot be faced. The distinction between detenus and convicts has of course its importance and is a fair debating point which I always use. But if we look at the facts frankly, unless I have a wholly mistaken impression of Bengal conditions, the risks which have already been taken there are immensely in excess of any that I can see here arising from the release of our remaining prisoners.[34]

7. Today the matter was discussed in Cabinet. The Premier spoke strongly, and said that the Ministers felt they could wait no longer. They had given full consideration to all the points I had made, and if on a matter like this they could not be trusted to form a judgment that was not dangerous and could not be allowed to follow their own policy, they were clearly not fit to administer the Province. He made the point that these prisoners had been convicted for crimes connected with individual violence, and that it was not anticipated that they would resume activities of this kind.[35] If there had been any serious anticipations of this, it would have been a different matter, but the mere fact that they might join an undesirable movement was not sufficient justification for holding that their release would be a grave menace. He again stressed the point about the release of the Bengal detenus.

8. I said that they must not suppose that I was trying to defer decision, as I realised that we must reach some conclusions as early as possible. But the issues raised were serious and required consultation, and it seemed to me impossible to reach a decision before the Congress session. I further said that the tone adopted by the Premier did not seem to me consistent with that of the Working Committee resolution. The Working Committee had, it was true, made it clear that they were going to press this as a major point of Congress policy, but there was no suggestion that they must have a decision before the Congress session. The Premier said that tone and substance did not always agree, and that it was in fact the intention of the Working Committee that the prisoners should be released before the Haripura session.[36] I asked him definitely whether this was information or merely inference, and he said that it was information which he had received. If this is correct, then presumably the same line will be taken in the other Congress Provinces, and it will be necessary to decide at once on an all-India policy.

9. Apart from whatever instructions they may have received from the Working Committee, the Ministers are clearly nervous about a hunger-strike. The Premier seems to have promised the prisoners some further communication between the 10th and 12th February. We did not take the matter any further, but the Premier said he was very anxious to see me again before he leaves for Haripura on the evening of the 14th, and we have tentatively agreed to meet and have a final talk on this matter on the 14th. The dominating consideration in the minds of the Ministers at the moment seems to me that they should be in a position to state at Haripura that they are going to release the prisoners.

10. Towards the end of the discussion the question was raised as to how many political prisoners were still in jail. It appears that in addition to the original list, which is what we have always been considering, there are four or five other prisoners in Naini who have been classed as politicals by the jail authorities. I imagine they are of less importance, but they would clearly have to be included in any general scheme of release.[37]

11. There is no doubt to my mind that a completely new note of urgency has come into the discussions on the side of the Ministry in the last two days, and both from the circumstances and from what the Premier said, it must I think be concluded that this is a new policy which the Working Committee have decided upon.[38] I have no means of judging whether this is bluff on the part of the Working Committee or whether they intend, if they cannot get satisfaction, to push the matter to a break. The language used by the Premier was very firm. Doubtless he spoke under instructions.

12. My own general view remains as expressed in my letter No. U.P.-50, dated January 30th. I do not think there is adequate reason so far as conditions in this Province are concerned for facing a break.

13

HAIG TO LINLITHGOW
R/3/1/73

Secret *February 12th, 1938*
No. U.P.-55

My dear Lord Linlithgow,

I have taken some little time to answer Your Excellency's letter, dated the 23rd December 1937,[39] about the circular of 10th November 1937,[40] issued by my Government to district magistrates dealing with their relations with Congress organisations. I have waited deliberately, because I wished to see how the situation was developing in fact, and because the Civil Service Week, which has just taken place and which has brought a large number of district officers into Lucknow, gives an excellent opportunity to find out what district officers are thinking of administrative conditions generally and whether they are in any way embarrassed or have felt that their position has been weakened by the issue of this circular.

2. With regard to the general principles enunciated by Your Excellency I am of course in full agreement. It is of great importance to maintain the position of the Services as an impartial administration, detached from party politics, affiliations or influences, and this is a point which I have in fact been watching carefully from the beginning and taking every opportunity to impress on our officers both publicly and privately. Where I think my outlook in regard to this circular differs from that of Your Excellency is in the estimate of its practical effect. Your Excellency clearly looks upon it as an attempt to bring the administration into undesirable relations with a particular party organisation. I do not deny that this is a possible interpretation to put on the circular, and this is a point which has been taken up by the opposition and especially the Muslim League. I look upon it, as I have from the beginning, as in essence an administrative instruction which is in accordance with our administrative principles in the districts. It is a commonplace of administrative practice in this Province that the district administration is expected to maintain close touch with all the main elements and influences in the district. For special reasons, our

officers have been in the past wholly out of touch with the Congress, but at the present time on ordinary administrative standards there are no elements it is more important for them to be in touch with than the Congress. It would be in my opinion quite an erroneous view that a district officer has to be insulated in order to preserve his independence. Such an idea seems to me wholly foreign to the principles of our service.

3. While bearing in mind carefully the general principles enunciated by Your Excellency, we have at the same time to face facts as they are. I explained in paragraph 7 of my letter No. U.P.-28, dated 28th November 1937,[41] what was the situation which confronted us and led to the issue of the circular, and to this perhaps Your Excellency would refer. To put the matter in a slightly different way, the situation was that the Congress have a very powerful hold on the Province, that an idea prevailed when the Congress Government first took office that the district administration could be cut out, and that everything could be done direct between the Congress organisations, to which the complaints of the public were being made in enormous volume, and Government headquarters. This was not a situation created by the circular, but one to the cure of which the circular addressed itself. Conditions at that time were in my opinion tending definitely to effect the authority of the district administration, as I explained in my letter of November 28th. Now, so far as I can judge, the situation has greatly improved. The Congress organisations, like everyone else, have to approach the district authorities instead of going over their heads. The authority of the district officer so far from being impaired is enhanced and at the same time friction with the Congress organisations has been greatly reduced.

4. You refer to the terms of the Congress circular as reported in the press. Naturally, it is not worded very much to our taste. But it seemed to me that it contains some practical admissions and instructions which have in fact been of very real value. In the first place, it is made clear that redress and relief of wrongs must be secured through Government agencies. This is a point to the admission of which by the Congress I attach the greatest importance, for it is a definite negation of the principle of parallel government, which both Your Excellency and I are very anxious to discourage. The point is emphasised again at the end of the circular when it is said that Congress workers forwarding complaints should leave the investigation to the proper authorities. In the second place, the principle of settling these matters locally instead of going over the head of the local authorities to Government headquarters is emphasised. It is said that Congressmen are requested to endeavour that complaints are in the first

instance dealt with locally, and later it is said that in case Congressmen are not satisfied with the result of an investigation, they may make suitable representations to district officers. These are points to my mind of practical importance, and there is no doubt from what I hear that they have been acted upon and that in consequence the authority of the district officer has been appreciably strengthened.

5. I have talked over general conditions with a number of district officers during the last week. I cannot find that the Government circular has been regarded by them with any apprehension. Frankly they are not worrying about the terms of it. They seem to be satisfied that the conditions which were threatening their authority to some extent have been diminished, and they are in my opinion entirely capable of dealing with their local Congressmen in a suitable manner. As for the general public many district officers have told me that the attitude towards them of the mass of the people is markedly friendly and respectful.

6. In these circumstances I feel that it would be a mistake for me to embark on a controversy with my Ministers about the circular. A question on the subject was asked recently in the Assembly, and I enclose a copy of the Premier's reply to the main question and to certain supplementaries. It seems to me to state a reasonable position, and should serve to dispel the misapprehensions referred to in paragraph 2 above. My own feeling very definitely is that we should now leave the matter alone. I do not think there is any practical misunderstanding on the part of our officers as to their attitude to the Congress and their relations with Congress representatives.

7. In Your Excellency's letter of 1st February 1938,[42] you refer to a circular letter which was said by the *Hindustan Times* to have been issued by the Superintendent of Police, Meerut,[43] to police subordinates in the district. This report attracted my attention at the time and I spoke about it to the Inspector-General of Police[44] who said that he had also observed it and intended to look into the matter and see that the ideas of the Superintendent of Police were corrected. I asked him recently what had been the upshot. I understand that the Superintendent of Police has been asked for his explanation, and that it is the intention of the Deputy Inspector-General when he visits Meerut shortly to take the matter up personally, explain the position clearly to the Superintendent of Police, and ensure that any misapprehensions that may have been caused by the circular in the minds of the Meerut police are removed. There was not of course any kind of necessity for a police officer to issue any instructions on the basis of the circular which is addressed to district magistrates, and this

Superintendent of Police went far beyond the plain meaning of the circular. Your Excellency may be interested to see the attached cutting[45] from the *Leader* of a day or two ago with regard to certain activities of the Superintendent of Police, Allahabad. Mr. Carless' methods are decidedly individual, but his general attitude is, I think, typical of the practical understanding and good sense with which in general our officers are handling their difficulties in the districts. I may add that the publication in the *Hindustan Times* was of course unauthorised.[46]

Yours sincerely,
H.G. HAIG

ENCLOSURE TO NO. 13

QUESTIONS ASKED BY MUHAMMAD ISHAQ KHAN IN U.P. LEGISLATIVE ASSEMBLY ON FEBRUARY 2ND, 1938 AND ANSWERS BY PANT

Question No. 79. – Did the Government issue any circular to the District Officers about their relations with the district Congress leaders and the District Congress Committees? Will the Government be pleased to lay a copy on the table?

Answer. – Yes, a copy is laid on the table.

Question No. 80. – Will the Government state in this connection the names of officials and the Congressmen districtwise who had complained against each other and the nature of the complaint?

Answer. – No useful purpose will be served by supplying this information. It may tend to defeat the very purpose for which the circular was issued.

Question No. 81. – Is it a fact that the District Congress Committees and its workers have been encouraged to watch and report on the activities of the Government officials?

Answer. – No.

Question No. 82. – Is it a fact that the Government has been calling for report[s] from District Congress Committees concerning complaints from the public received by it?

Answer. – No.

Question No. 83. – Will the Government state reasons as to why it did not issue instructions to the District Officers to maintain same cordial relations with other political parties of the district?

Answer. – The Congress has assumed office for the first time. Government officials and Congressmen had for years been arrayed against and were in the discharge of their respective duties called upon to oppose each other. There had been a ceaseless struggle between the two. It was necessary therefore to revise reciprocal attitudes and to remove mutual distrust. There had been besides many complaints and counter-complaints which were embarrassing to Government and which created difficulties. Government therefore considered it desirable to issue the circular. There had not been any such conflict or estrangement between Government servants and other political parties, nor were any such general complaints received by Government from the members of those parties or against them. Government therefore did not consider it necessary to issue any such instructions in the case of those parties nor were Government requested by them to do so.

Question No. 84. – Is it the intention of the Government to run the administration on party lines? If the answer is in the negative, is it the intention of the Government to cancel the previous circular or to issue another circular calling on the District Officers to maintain same cordial relations with other political parties of the district specially the Muslim League?

Answer. – No. The Government expect their officers to maintain cordial relations with the public and with all peace-loving organizations. It is not their intention to cancel the circular nor do they at present appreciate the need for issuing any other circular for the reasons given in the answer to question No. 83.

Question No. 86 [*sic*]. – Will the Government be pleased to make a clear statement of its policy concerning the attitude of the public servants towards the various political parties in the districts respectively?

Answer. – Government servants are the servants of the Government and not of any particular party. They are expected to observe an attitude of neutrality as regards party politics, and under the Government Servants' Conduct Rules may not take part in political movements.

To a supplementary question asking whether the Chief Secretary's circular did not create a privileged position for some Congressmen, the Premier replied (according to the newspaper report): "If anything it means a privileged duty of the Congressman to help the administration so far as he can where he is not even legally bound to do so."

14

HAIG TO LINLITHGOW
Telegram
R/3/1/73

Immediate
No. 119-G

February 14th, 1938

I discussed again with Premier this morning the question of political prisoners as a preliminary to the Cabinet meeting which was held later. I took the line suggested in Your Excellency's telegram No. 194-G., dated February 12th,[47] that appropriate course was that cases should be examined individually. Premier however made it clear that this would not content the Ministers. The difficulties with which they are faced would continue until prisoners as a whole had been released and he said he must press for acceptance of principle of general release. I suggested that first thing was to examine the list which now includes all 15 persons and decide which of them could be eliminated on ground that they are not really politicals but ordinary criminals. Arising out of this he suggested that a committee of Ministers should be empowered to decide on individuals to be released and date of release without any further reference to me. I pointed out that this would hardly be consistent with my constitutional position. He said that he merely put forward this proposal as an alternative which might be less unacceptable to me than immediate release of all the prisoners. He stressed again the difficulty of Ministers carrying on under these unsatisfactory conditions when their carefully considered views on a major matter of policy were not accepted. I made it clear that he must not assume that if this matter merely concerned this Province I would eventually feel that it was necessary for me in exercise of my special responsibility to reject their advice. But I called attention to inter-provincial reactions and said that this was a matter which might concern Your Excellency under Section 126 (5).

3. At Cabinet meeting the discussion followed similar lines. They made it clear that they would be satisfied with having power to release all these prisoners, but that they would not necessarily wish to release all 15 if after examination it were found that some of them had no real political connections. It was also pointed out that out of 15, 4 had less than a year to serve. The core of the matter is the 6 prisoners mentioned in paragraph No. 8 of my letter, dated January 30th, No. 50, to whom one other terrorist

prisoner may be added who appears a person of no great importance serving a three-year sentence.

4. The Ministers made it clear that policy of gradual and individual release would not satisfy them. Premier without actually using the word resignation stated that if the views of Ministers in this case, to which they had given most careful consideration, were rejected they must be regarded as irresponsible people and not fit to continue in their places. I said that I must consider action to be taken in the light of their advice but that case clearly was one of more than provincial significance. I said that on this aspect I must consult Your Excellency. They then pointed out that their position had been for sometime that they desired to be in a position to state their policy before Congress session and they asked for earliest possible answer. They were leaving for Haripura this evening but said they would be prepared to postpone their departure till evening of 15th. I undertook to make an immediate reference to Your Excellency and I said that I hoped to be able to give them an answer tomorrow morning. We have decided tentatively to have another Cabinet meeting in the morning.

5. My own view as Your Excellency is aware is that so far as conditions in the United Provinces are concerned there is not sufficient ground for breaking with my Ministry on this point and I could not hold that a grave menace to Province would be created by the release of these prisoners. I therefore refer the matter to Your Excellency for any instructions you may wish to issue under Section 126 (5). I do not think that there is any advantage in deferring those instructions if Your Excellency has made up your mind in accordance with policy laid down in your telegram No. 178 of February 11th.[48] I should imagine that if I received instructions from Your Excellency tomorrow and communicated them to Ministers they would not immediately resign but would proceed to Haripura knowing precisely how matter stands and that he [?they] would there take counsel as to their action.

6. On Saturday at a Cabinet meeting Ministers were discussing budgeting [in] an atmosphere which suggested they were looking forward to prolongation of period of office. Today Premier at any rate leaves on my mind the impression that he is very seriously contemplating resignation not merely on an all-India policy but because he feels [that] to be overruled in this case would compromise his position and involve political embarrassments which he is no longer prepared to face. This however may be only a passing mood.

Repeated to Governor of Bihar. *Ends.*

15

DONALDSON TO LAITHWAITE
R/3/1/73

Confidential | Camp,
D.O. No. 1051-G.S.P. | *February 16th, 1938*

My dear Laithwaite,

His Excellency wishes me to send you, for the information of His Excellency the Governor-General, the enclosed copy of the letter of resignation which Pant handed to him about 7-30 p.m. last night when he and his colleagues came to Government House to say good-bye. They were very much later than the time which they had originally indicated. The published official communiqué which had been discussed with you was of course prepared without reference to this letter or knowledge of its contents, but it was decided to issue it as it stood.[49]

With regard to the assumptions made about the attitude of His Excellency, he wishes me to say that at yesterday's Cabinet meeting he had merely communicated to the Cabinet the substance of paragraph 1 of His Excellency the Governor-General's telegram No. 209-G. of 15th February.[50] I had spoken to you about this on the telephone and made certain that the contents of this paragraph might be communicated to the Ministers. There was no discussion, at this meeting, of His Excellency's attitude in regard to the Provincial situation. At the previous Cabinet meeting on February 14th His Excellency had been careful, in accordance with paragraph 2 of the Governor[-General]'s telegram of February 12th,[51] to avoid saying to the Ministers that he was rejecting their advice for reasons based on Provincial conditions. He had also avoided saying that he did not consider that his own special responsibility was attracted. This point was left in the air after he had stressed the objections to the course which they were proposing.

Their personal attitude when they said good-bye was extremely friendly and regretful. We hear that after the Cabinet meeting in the morning they telephoned to Haripura and only finally decided on resignation on receiving instructions from there.

Yours sincerely,
J.C. DONALDSON

ENCLOSURE TO NO. 15

PANT TO HAIG

Lucknow,
February 15th, 1938

Dear Sir Harry Haig,

As Your Excellency has now intimated to me and my colleagues that in compliance with the orders issued to you by the Governor-General under Section 126(5) of the Government of India Act you are bound to reject the advice which we thought it our duty to tender to you in regard to the release of political prisoners, we think that the only course open to us is to tender our resignation which we hereby do. The issue now raised is of the widest importance both from the constitutional and administrative point of view.

The release of political prisoners has formed a prominent part of the Congress programme throughout. It was distinctly mentioned in the Congress election manifesto, and the electorate in overwhelming numbers has supported the demand of the Congress. It was again urged in the resolutions passed by the Convention in Delhi in March last year.[52] The British Government must therefore have been fully aware of the Congress policy and its implications in regard to this matter. It is unthinkable that the Governor-General should not have realised that the Congress whenever it accepted office would take the earliest opportunity to implement the Congress programme and to honour its pledges. The Congress was invited to accept office with a full knowledge of all these facts. An assurance was also definitely held out that the Congress in office would be free to carry out its programme. It is exceedingly strange that when after prolonged and patient consideration and discussion we proceed to give effect to the Congress policy the Governor-General issues his orders under Section 126 to thwart the Congress Ministry in this Province in this matter. The reasons which have weighed with the Governor-General in taking this decision are not known to us and in spite of our request to Your Excellency you expressed your inability to disclose them to us. The responsibility for maintaining law and order in the Province is that of the Ministers. No Council of Ministers can discharge its functions satisfactorily if its considered opinion is disregarded arbitrarily in respect of momentous questions strictly falling within their purview by outside authority and when even the courtesy of mentioning the grounds on which such interference is sought is not shown to it. It is inconceivable that the release of no more than 15 political prisoners some of whom were mere boys when they were convicted and several of whom have undergone long terms of imprisonment and are due to be released within a few months in the usual course can be a grave menace to the peace and tranquillity of any Province in India. We have every reason to believe and are definitely assured that they have abjured the path of violence. The jail authorities have formed a similar impression after a close observation of individual prisoners in their charge. We have discussed this question on numerous occasions with Your Excellency and we are inclined to believe that you have come at least to appreciate our point of view. The decision of the Governor-General is attributed to extra-provincial affairs, and it is significant that action has been taken under Section 126 and not under Section 54 which suggests that the Governor of the Province does not consider that there is any menace to the peace and tranquillity inside the Province itself. There is an insistent demand in the country for the release of these prisoners and it has been forcefully voiced in our own Assembly by all sections from time to time. Their non-release is apt to disturb the peaceful atmosphere, to engender tension and to hamper the growth of the non-violent spirit. The Burma Government has recently released all the rebellion prisoners. A general release of all political prisoners followed in 1921 immediately after the introduction of Dyarchy in the Provinces. We have had occasion to discuss this question in all its aspects with you during the last seven months. While there have been hunger-strikes in every other Province, the prisoners here have refrained from doing so and have reposed their trust in us. We had far-reaching and comprehensive programmes of agrarian reforms, rural development, jail reform, overhaul of local self-governing bodies, education, prohibition and excise reform and several other large issues which called for a tranquil atmosphere for their solution. This interference on the part of the Governor-General in the ordinary administration of the Province raises a constitutional issue of the gravest import, and instead of promoting peace and tranquillity is likely to imperil it not only in this Province but elsewhere in India also. In our considered judgment their release is essential in the public interest and the Governor-General has by his order disabled us from performing our elementary duty in this respect. We look upon this interference as an utter abuse even of the provisions of Section 126(5) and it brings vividly home to us the unsubstantial character of the autonomy which the Provinces are supposed to enjoy, when the advice of the Council of Ministers[53] can be trampled upon by one entirely outside the Province and having no direct contacts with it and no live part in its affairs. In the circumstances there is no alternative to the course which we have taken, and we would request you to accept this resignation.

Yours sincerely,
G.B. PANT

16

HAIG TO LINLITHGOW
R/3/1/73

Secret *February 16th, 1938*
No. U.P.-56

My dear Lord Linlithgow,

With reference to Your Excellency's telegram No. 215-G., dated 15th February 1938,[54] no more points have occurred to me in connection with the Proclamation under Section 93 which require further discussion.

2. With regard to Advisers I have been thinking the matter over carefully in the light of the existing situation. As a result of the Congress Ministry's term of office the work of the Provincial Government has increased immensely, and though a good deal of this work could be reduced again if I took over charge under Section 93, there will remain a number of major problems which have been raised by the Congress Ministry and cannot possibly be dropped. Indeed, my feeling is very strong that in the matter of general policy I should endeavour to maintain a large degree of continuity and to avoid abrupt reactions. This will mean, for instance, that I must pursue the search for a satisfactory tenancy policy, that I must carry out with such amendments as may be necessary the main outlines of the rural development plans, very possibly that I should continue with a great deal of the temperance policy, though dropping the actual prohibition proposals. These are only illustrations of the large questions that will have to be handled. I am quite clear, after reflecting on the situation, that it would be impossible for me to do justice to these problems in addition to the difficult questions of law and order that are bound to arise with only two Advisers, and that it is essential to have three. I should propose to appoint Bomford and Gwynne as already reported to Your Excellency. Both of them were going on leave this summer; but I shall have to ask them to forego their leave and I do not think there will be any difficulty in the matter. For the third Adviser it seems to me essential to have an Indian, both from the

point of view of public opinion and from the advantage that I should derive from an Indian who is closely in touch with Indian opinion. The Indian whom I should propose to appoint would be Panna Lal, I.C.S., Commissioner of Allahabad. He seems to me to be the only Indian member of the I.C.S. who would be suitable. He has wide administrative experience and worked for sometime in the Secretariat. V.N. Mehta, his senior, who is just returning to us after having been a year at Bikaner, would be in my opinion unequal to the work.

3. I still propose to pay the Advisers Rs. 4,000 a month.

Yours sincerely,
H.G. HAIG

17

HAIG TO LINLITHGOW
Telegram
R/3/1/73

No. 121-G *February 17th, 1938*

Yesterday evening I saw Nawab of Chhatari whose party in the Assembly claims to outnumber Muslim League party by two or three and discussed with him possibility of forming a Ministry. He said it was clearly impossible even to consider it unless his party and Muslim League combined and it would be necessary to try and get support of other minority parties. Even so they were bound at first to be a very decided minority and difficulty about the budget would at once arise. He was not at all hopeful about the possibility of doing anything but agreed to explore the situation with Muslim League leaders and for that purpose goes to Delhi today to see Jinnah. Meantime I shall try to see Muslim League leader here today. I thought it best not to treat my conversation as a formal invitation to Chhatari to form Ministry, as with two chief minority parties so evenly balanced it is not possible at this stage to be sure what form a combination between them if feasible would take. I propose therefore to leave the matter as it stands until Chhatari returns from Delhi on Friday night. In the light of what he then reports I will make a formal move and invite one or if necessary more than one in succession of minority leaders to form a Ministry.

Repeated to Governor of Bihar.

18

HAIG TO LINLITHGOW
Telegram
R/3/1/73

Important
No. 122-G

February 17th, 1938

In continuation of my telegram No. 121 of February 17th, I have now seen Khaliquzzaman leader of Muslim League party and discussed with him informally as with Chhatari. He seems clear in his own mind that formation of minority Ministry would be useless and inexpedient. He says even if Chhatari's party and Muslim League were to combine there would be no possibility of this, which would be predominantly Muslim, attracting to itself any Hindu support. Indeed he goes so far as to say that he thinks Chhatari's own comparatively few Hindu followers would possibly leave him. He sees no advantage in minority Ministry taking office with no prospect of ever securing majority.

2. I made it clear to Khaliquzzaman that my conversation with him was at present informal but that it was likely that after a day or two I might wish to approach him formally in order to receive from him a formal reply. He leaves for Bombay today and will not be back till February 23rd. I have therefore arranged to telegraph to him and get reply by telegraph. He does not think any further conversation would be of value. Nor do I.

3. As to probability of Congress starting civil disobedience if Governor assumes full powers, he expressed an interesting view. He said he thought they would not do so because if they did they would be vigorously opposed by Muslims and there would be serious riots. I give this view for what it is worth. I have had no means yet of checking its validity.

4. I think everything points to Chhatari giving a definite refusal when he returns from Delhi, and it looks as if about the 19th I shall have to ask Your Excellency to agree to issue a Proclamation under Section 93. Unless there is any possibility of a settlement with Congress it seems undesirable for present situation to continue too long. If however there were any possibility of a settlement I would of course gladly hold my hand for a few days.

Repeated to Governor of Bihar.

19

HAIG TO LINLITHGOW
Telegram
R/3/1/73

No. 123-G

Lucknow,
February 17th, 1938

Your telegram No. 226-G. of February 16th.[55] Press reactions so far available only from *Pioneer* and *Leader*. *Pioneer's* leader of 17th describes local public attitude as one of bewilderment. On Congress side left wing have successfully forced the issue. On the Government side Government of India have chosen to fight on an issue which is of quite secondary importance in the United Provinces. If Bengal is the trouble, why not have waited until the question arose there? Are the very authors of the Constitution snatching for some reasons at opportunity to undo their own work? *Pioneer* cannot credit it but says it is being freely said. *Pioneer's* leading article of February 16th will have already reached Delhi. Theme was that disagreement was not over a vital question of principle but had been engendered for political ends by extremists and that it was a pity Governors of the United Provinces and Bihar should have been forced to make a stand upon an issue.

2. *Leader*, dated February 17th, as received, had no comments. In issue of February 18th leading article is headed 'Why?'. It regards crisis as grave public misfortune pregnant with wide-ranging and probably disastrous consequences. Problem of prisoners was not new. Political prisoners strictly so-called had already been set free. The hands of Ministry were forced by their masters in Congress Working Committee. There was no provincial autonomy on their side. Similarly the Governors acted under instructions of outside authority. There was no provincial autonomy here either and decision was influenced by extraneous considerations irrelevant to the immediate issue. Neither party is to be congratulated. The resignations are a public misfortune.

20

HAIG TO LINLITHGOW
Telegram
R/3/1/73

Immediate *February 18th, 1938*
No. 124-G

Your telegram No. 242-G. of February 17th.[56] I had just drafted telegram to Your Excellency saying that there was some reason to believe that it would be agreeable to Ministers on personal grounds if their resignation was not accepted until after their return from Haripura about February 23rd, that I saw no real objection to postponing action and that if there was any possibility of a settlement it was naturally most important not to force the pace by accepting resignation of Ministers earlier than was absolutely necessary. I am therefore fully in agreement with conclusions in paragraph 2 and paragraph 3 of Your Excellency's telegram.[57]

2. I have also just received telegram No. 263-G.B. of 17th February from Governor of Bihar.[58] My views expressed above will fit in with his situation.

Repeated to Governor of Bihar.

21

HAIG TO LINLITHGOW
R/3/1/73

Secret *February 19th, 1938*
No. U.P.-57

My dear Lord Linlithgow,

With reference to my letter No. 56, dated February 16th, 1938, regarding Advisers under a Section 93 situation, I am beginning to be afraid that Gwynne may not be available. He has been very heavily over-worked recently, and was going on four months' leave. He would have been prepared to postpone his leave, but it has now been found that he is suffering from high blood pressure, and I think it is more than likely that under medical advice he will have to proceed on leave almost at once.[59] In that event I should propose to take Sloan in his place as an Adviser, as having the requisite secretariat and administrative experience. He was of course in the Home Department of the Government of India for many years. At the same time he would, I fear, be much less closely in touch with Indian opinion than Gwynne, and this would make it all the more essential that I should have an Indian also among my Advisers.

2. With regard to pay, I have been considering the matter further, and I think there is a good deal to be said for a suggestion that the Advisers instead of having a fixed pay should draw their present pay *plus* a special pay of Rs. 500. This would mean that Bomford would get Rs. 4,000 and the other two approximately Rs. 3,700. The advantages of this would be:

(*a*) That the proposal would sound less extravagant in that it would appear as a proposal for merely giving Rs. 500 special pay to three officers instead of the creation of three new posts on Rs. 4,000 a month. In view of the great stress laid by the Congress Ministry on moderation in salaries, this would I think be an advantage.

(*b*) It might also to some extent diminish possible feelings of discontent among other senior officers who had not been selected.

If Your Excellency has no objection to this alternative proposal, I should like to be left free to adopt whichever plan seems to me on further consideration and discussion the most suitable.

Yours sincerely,
HARRY HAIG

22

HAIG TO LINLITHGOW
Telegram
R/3/1/73

Important — Lucknow,
No. 127-G — *February 20th, 1938*

I had further talk with Chhatari this morning on his return from Delhi where he had consulted Jinnah and other Moslems. His views represent general trend of opinion. He says that if the present crisis indicated a definite change in policy of British Government and was likely to be real and decisive struggle with Congress then Moslems and conservative forces would be solidly with British. It would be worth while taking office and there would be some prospect of securing a considerable and perhaps growing degree of popular support. But if this is to be what Chhatari calls a friendly quarrel, with periodical waiting on events and hopes of reconciliation before long, then he considers it would be useless and definitely damaging to position of Minority to fill this gap so as really to oblige other parties to dispute. His position thus is not unlike that described by Hallett in paragraph 2 (*b*) of his telegram No. 505 of 18th February.[60] But Chhatari would put the minimum period for which Ministry would require to be maintained in office at two years.

2. From point of view of Minorities this position seems to me not unreasonable. From our point of view I can see no advantage in stop-gap Minority Ministry. It would be weakness at a time when we may want to be strong. It will not lessen hostility of Congress, while expedients that would be required to keep it in office would in my opinion invalidate any claim that we were still substantially working the Constitution. It seems not only that it is impossible in this Province to secure an alternative Ministry but that this is a course which on the whole even if it were possible would not be wise. What I contemplate is that if resignation of Ministry is confirmed I should take over at once under Section 93. In the course of next three or at most six months the situation would clarify itself and we should either have Congress coming back to office or we should be faced with prolonged struggle with Congress. If latter contingency arose we could then consider whether it was desirable by some amendment of the Act or other expedients to try and form a Moslem plus moderate Ministry or in some other way to associate the opponents of Congress with administration.

3. My conversation with Chhatari continued to be on a strictly informal basis. I told him that for the present I did not intend to extend to him any formal invitation but that if and when the resignation of Ministers became effective I should then propose to approach him formally. He made it clear that in that case for reasons explained above his answer would have to be a refusal.

4. Chhatari made it clear, as Khaliq-uz-Zaman had, that in case of civil disobedience the Moslems are likely not merely to be indifferent but actively hostile to such movement. The landlords also to a large extent might come out strongly against it; but this would depend in part on their anticipations of what would happen after civil disobedience.

5. The consequences of complete rupture with Congress are so [?serious] for whole future of present constitutional plan that it seems to me very important to endeavour to reach some settlement with Congress on present issue which from point of view of this Province should not be matter of great difficulty. If there is no settlement either now or after a few months and situation drifts into civil disobedience the resumption of normal working of existing Constitution will present grave difficulties.

Repeated to Governor of Bihar. *Ends.*

23

DONALDSON TO LAITHWAITE
Telegram
R/3/1/73

No. G.S.-128 *February 21st, 1938*

Your telegram No. 268-G. of February 18th.[61] Only new taxation measures contemplated by next year's budget are increases in Court Fees and Stamp Fees. Estimated yield ten lakhs next year. Bills to this effect have gone before Select Committees of Legislative Assembly. Detailed budget and budget papers are not ready.

24

DONALDSON TO LAITHWAITE
R/3/1/73

D.O. No. 1061-G.S.P. Camp,
February 21st, 1938

My dear Laithwaite,

I enclose two copies of an amplified note on the fifteen terrorist prisoners whose release was under discussion with the Cabinet. This contains some additional information to that given in the note sent to you with my letter of February 16th and may be substituted for it.

Yours sincerely,
J.C. DONALDSON

ENCLOSURE TO NO. 24

LIST OF PERSONS AT PRESENT CLASSIFIED AS "B" CLASS REVOLUTIONARY OR TERRORIST PRISONERS WHO WERE CONVICTED BY COURTS IN THE U. P. AND ARE CONFINED IN JAILS IN THE U. P.

February 21st, 1938

1. *Yashpal.* – A prominent Hindustan Socialist Republican Army organiser and leader; aged about 33; educated at the Gurukul Kangri and the National

College, Lahore; an associate of Bhagat Singh, Sukhdeo Raj, Chandra Shekhar Azad and other well known revolutionaries; was wanted in the second Lahore Conspiracy case and the Delhi Conspiracy case. A reward of Rs. 3,000 was offered for his arrest. While in concealment was appointed Commander-in-Chief of the H.S.R.A. Was arrested at Allahabad on 23 January 1932 after exchange of shots with the police in the house of Mrs. Jafar Ali *alias* Savitri Devi (an Irish woman). Sentenced to 7 years' rigorous imprisonment under the Arms Act, and to 7 years' rigorous imprisonment for attempted murder, the sentences to run consecutively. In view of this conviction it was decided not to proceed against him in respect of other offences. Unexpired portion of sentence: 6 years and 6 months.

Was recently reported to be suffering from tuberculosis of the lungs. Has been ordered to be examined by a Medical Board.

2. *Haldar Bajpai.* – Aged about 27; resident at Cawnpore. An important member of the H.S.R.A. with Bihar connections. His house was searched on 12th August 1932 in connection with the Dehra Dun-Cawnpore Conspiracy. He opened fire on the police and was arrested and sentenced to 6 years' rigorous imprisonment for attempted murder. Unexpired portion of sentence: 2 years and 10 months.

3. *Rajendra Dutt Nigam.* – Aged about 29; resides in Hamirpur and Cawnpore. A prominent H.S.R.A. organiser. Son of a Patwari. Associate of Chandra Shekhar Azad, Yashpal and other prominent members of the H.S.R.A. In 1931 was appointed provincial organiser of the H.S.R.A. Was arrested at Cawnpore on 13th August 1932 with two revolvers and ammunition and was overpowered before he could open fire. He was sentenced to 2 years' rigorous imprisonment under the Arms Act and to 7 years' rigorous imprisonment for attempted murder of a police head constable and constable during the previous year. The policemen had followed Nigam and three others and attempted to make their arrest. Nigam's party fired at the police and wounded two of them and made their escape. Unexpired portion of sentence: 2 years, 10 months and 27 days.

4. *Chandra Man Singh.* – Aged about 28; resident of Bihar. Son of a dismissed head constable. Associate of the Bihar terrorist Jogendra Shukul. Was arrested in Cawnpore in 1933. Fired at the police party, but was overpowered. Was sentenced to 5 years' rigorous imprisonment for attempted murder and 2 years' rigorous imprisonment under the Arms Act. Was also placed on trial in the Bettiah approver murder case with Vaikunt Shukul. The latter was convicted and hanged, but Chandra Man

Singh was acquitted. Unexpired portion of sentence: 1 year, 5 months and 16 days.

5. *Ramesh Chandra Gupta.* – Aged about 25; resident of Cawnpore. Belongs to a well-to-do family of Cawnpore. Became an associate of terrorists; on 24th November 1931 at Jalaun attempted to shoot Bir Bhadra Tiwari, a fellow terrorist, but the revolver misfired. Was arrested on the spot with a loaded revolver and convicted and sentenced to 10 years' rigorous imprisonment for attempted murder and under the Arms Act. Unexpired portion of sentence: 3 years and 8 months.

6. *Desraj Singh.* – Aged about 30; resident of Banda. An active member of a Bundelkhand terrorist party; was arrested on 11th January 1935 between Benares and Allahabad on information received with 45 revolver cartridges of various bores in his possession, which he was apparently taking to Allahabad for the use of terrorists. Absconded when on bail, but was convicted under the Arms Act and sentenced to 3 years' rigorous imprisonment. Unexpired portion of sentence: 1 year and 3 months.

7. *Kamta Prasad.* – Aged about 38; resident of Agra. Comes of a well-to-do family. Organised a gang of desperate youths and dacoits in Agra; on 5th August 1932, his house was searched and four revolvers, two pistols, some acid and daggers were recovered. He was put on trial for dacoity with murder and was convicted and sentenced to death by the lower court, but acquitted on appeal. He was, however, convicted for being in possession of a stolen revolver. He was sentenced to 7 years' rigorous imprisonment under the Arms Act, 5 years' rigorous imprisonment under the Explosive Substances Act and 3 years' rigorous imprisonment under Section 411, I.P.C., these sentences to run concurrently. The crimes of which he was accused and acquitted had a revolutionary colouring. Unexpired portion of sentence not stated, but several years.

8. *Balack Ram.* – Aged about 24; resident of Sitapur. Convicted under Section 394 in 1934 in the Lucknow Postal Robbery case and again in 1937 for attempted murder and sentenced to 7 years' rigorous imprisonment. In the Postal Robbery case this man got 2 years' rigorous imprisonment and a fine for robbing a postal cash overseer of Rs. 2,000 and odd in broad daylight. Having served his sentence for that crime he was convicted for attempted murder. An attempt was made to give a political colouring to the first crime, but the second was committed out of pure self-interest. Unexpired portion of sentence: 6 years, 9 months, 23 days. The crime for which he is at present undergoing imprisonment was the attempted murder of an old zamindar's agent, by shooting with a .450 revolver. He was apparently hired to do this by the victim's son as

the result of a bitter family quarrel. Balack Ram followed the victim along a lonely road from the railway station to his village and fired five shots at him, two of which took effect.

N.B. – Balack Ram is classified as a "C" Class prisoner.

9. *Jageshwar.* – Aged about 26; born in Rae Bareli; resident of Cawnpore. Son of a mill employee. On 22nd July 1932 his house was searched by the Excise Staff and ten country-made bombs and explosives were recovered. He was convicted and sentenced to transportation for 14 years. Unexpired portion of sentence: 8 years and 16 days. Nothing is known about this man's early history and political antecedents. He appears to be an ordinary criminal.

10. *Putlu Singh.* – Aged about 32; resident of Farrukhabad. He had two previous convictions in 1922 under the Criminal Law Amendment Act. In 1935 an armed dacoity was committed in his neighbourhood. Two bombs, some moulds and other articles for counterfeiting coin and a seditious pamphlet were recovered from his house. He was convicted and sentenced to 3 years' rigorous imprisonment for being in possession of coining implements, and 3 years' rigorous imprisonment for being in possession of explosives, the sentences to run consecutively. Unexpired portion of his sentence: 3 years, 1 month and 21 days.

11. *Roshan Singh.* – Aged 23; resident of Jhansi. Convicted under Section 394 and sentenced to 1 year and 6 months' rigorous imprisonment in the Jhansi Mail Robbery case. A mail peon was attacked and robbed of his mail bag which contained about Rs. 95 in cash. This man was once employed in Tikamgarh State as a school teacher but either resigned or was discharged and became a Congress volunteer. There is nothing on record to show that he was involved in the Mail Robbery for any other motive than personal gain. Unexpired portion of sentence: 5 months and 24 days.

12. *Ram Sahai.* – Aged 23; resident of Jhansi. Was convicted in the same case and given the same sentence. He had previously taken some interest in *kisan* affairs in Jhansi. Otherwise there is nothing to show that his crime was for anything but personal gain. Unexpired portion of sentence, 3 months and 4 days.

13. *Gurcharan Singh.* – Is a Punjabi of the Hoshiarpur District and apparently the son of a retired sub-engineer. He was employed as a temporary mistry on railway construction on the Great Indian Peninsula Railway at Jhansi. On discharge from there he started travelling on a forged railway pass. In Lucknow he represented himself to be a Railway Land

Acquisition Officer and he committed various other offences of cheating there, and at Jullundur he represented himself to be a Railway Overseer on special duty and cheated various people. After his conviction in the United Provinces on certain cheating charges he was sent to Jullundur for trial on other charges and while there he conspired with another prisoner to manufacture a bomb, apparently because he was not given full privileges of a "B" Class convict. Presumably it was on this account that he was classified as a revolutionary prisoner, since there is nothing else on record to show that he had anything to do with politics. He got the following sentences on various dates:

(1)	25-2-29	u/s 170, 420 and 468 I.P.C.	2 years' R.I.; City Magistrate, Lucknow.
(2)	21-12-29	420 I.P.C.	2 years' R.I. *plus* a fine.
	21-12-29	420 I.P.C.	2 years' R.I. *plus* a fine, from the Special Magistrate of Lucknow; sentences to run consecutively.
(3)	21-12-29	420 I.P.C.	2 years' R.I. *plus* a fine.
	21-12-29	420 I.P.C.	2 years'R.I. *plus* a fine, sentences to run concurrently, from the same court.
(4)	14-4-30	468 I.P.C.	1 years' R.I.
	14-4-30	471/465 I.P.C.	1 years' R.I. from a Magistrate, Jhansi; sentences to run consecutively.
(5)	19-5-31	419 I.P.C.	9 months' R.I. from a first class Magistrate at Jullundur.
(6)	9-10-31	4 and 6 Explosive Substances Act	3 years' R.I. from a Sessions Judge of Jullundur.

The total sentences amounted to 13 years, 9 months' rigorous imprisonment, or with imprisonment in default of payment of fine, 15 years and 3 months' rigorous imprisonment.

Out of a total fine of Rs. 1,000 he is reported to have paid all but Rs. 70-15-6. In January 1938 he had served all his sentences except a sentence of 3 months' rigorous imprisonment awarded to him by the Magistrate in Jullundur and 1 month and 21 days in lieu of payment of his fine.

14. *Ganga Prasad* alias *Jagdish* alias *Master.* –Aged about 23; resident of Unao and Cawnpore. First came to notice in 1932 when two boxes

containing materials for bomb-making and H.S.R.A. literature were recovered from his possession. He stated that he was keeping them (the boxes) for another man. He was later suspected in the Cawnpore Bomb case in 1934 and for dacoity. In 1936 he was convicted under Section 397 in the Sachendi dacoity of district Cawnpore and sentenced to 4 years' rigorous imprisonment. This was a case of a road dacoity of a bullock cart, which was apparently committed without premeditation by a band of dacoits who had assembled to commit some other crime. As far as appeared, there was no revolutionary object for this crime. Ganga Prasad appears to be an ordinary criminal who was made use of by a revolutionary group in Cawnpore. Unexpired portion of sentence: 2 years, 4 months, 28 days.

15. *Asutosh Ganguli.* – Aged 27; resident of Calcutta. Was employed in the Railway Workshops, Lucknow; but had for some time been under observation as a communist agent. He took delivery of a large parcel of communist literature consigned to the Lucknow Railway station for which he signed under a false name. Was sentenced on 10th August 1937 to 1 year and 3 months' rigorous imprisonment under Section 17 (1) of the Criminal Law Amendment Act (for having taken part in the operations of an unlawful association, the Communist Party of India) and under Section 18 (1) of the Press Emergency Powers Act, 1931 (for being in possession of a parcel containing a large amount of Communist literature, unauthorised news-sheets and leaflets emanating from the Communist Party). Unexpired portion of sentence: 9 months and 8 days.

J.C. DONALDSON

25

HAIG TO LINLITHGOW
R/3/1/73

Secret *February 22nd, 1938*
No. U.P.-58

My dear Lord Linlithgow,

Recently everything has been overshadowed by the resignation of the Ministry on the 15th February and its effects. While a number of the more old-fashioned landlords are inclined to look upon this as an interposition of providence in their favour, public opinion generally has shown itself regretful of these developments and apprehensive about the future. There has been no trace so far of any ugly feeling. I think the state of public opinion affords a rather striking confirmation of the view that, in spite of many difficulties, the Constitution has been working in this Province better than might have been expected, and that people in general were looking forward to orderly developments on constitutional lines. Everyone shrinks from the prospect of plunging the Province into a state of turmoil with a civil disobedience movement, and though the movement could no doubt be put down, there is a widespread feeling that this would provide no permanent solution of problems which seemed on the way to solving themselves by constitutional processes. My Ministers and I parted on the 15th with genuine regret and expressions of good will, and a feeling that, if the parting were final, a great deal of arduous work and effort on both sides would have been wasted.

2. Apart from this crisis over the release of political prisoners, the situation in the Province seemed to be improving steadily. Rents and revenue were coming in much better, and the situation which at one time had seemed definitely disturbing looked like settling itself as a result of the persistent pressure exercised by the Congress organisation in favour of payment of rent. The budget too, while conceived on lines that would make a considerable popular appeal, was restrained within the bounds of reasonable financial prudence. The revenue deficit was estimated at only 12 lakhs, and though it was contemplated that a loan of something like a crore of rupees might have to be raised, some 50 lakhs of this represented capital expenditure commitments, for the most part of a productive character, and another 30 lakhs would represent advances for seed, fertilisers and agricultural implements which would be recoverable. By various expedients a sum of nearly 40 lakhs recurring was to be made available for rural development, and the Ministers seemed anxious that this money should be spent in really practical ways and on well thought-out schemes. Considerable provision was also being made for improvement of roads. At the end of the budget discussion the Premier indicated that there were other matters which he wished to raise later, though they could not be included in his budget proposals. These were:

(*a*) The question of reduction or abolition of special pay, about which I have had correspondence with Your Excellency; and

(*b*) proposals for a cut in the pay of existing members of the services.

With regard to the latter the Ministers indicated no definite plan, but said they proposed to raise the matter when they returned from Haripura. I indicated to them that I thought any such proposals would give rise to great difficulties, but we did not carry the matter further.

3. The resignation of Mr. Paliwal, the Rural Development Officer, was

accepted by the Ministry just before they resigned, and this I regard as a very definite advantage. Among other things, Mr. Paliwal is involved in a charge of assaulting the police at Agra.

4. The Congress indignation at the attack on the Minister's procession in Cawnpore has subsided in face of the more serious issues that have been occupying public attention. The Commissioner[62] has held an enquiry, and though he has not yet submitted his report, it seems pretty clear from what I hear that the police were not to blame and that when the disturbance broke out they dealt with it most effectively and promptly.

5. In spite of general apprehensions the Bakr Id passed off peacefully practically throughout the Province. A very difficult situation developed at Gorakhpur, but was handled with skill and firmness by the District Magistrate,[63] and though a number of Muslims, including some M.L.As., were arrested for breach of an order under Section 144, I think the situation is likely to settle down now. Muslim League feeling however against the Congress is very bitter, and if nothing is done to allay this, it will become increasingly difficult to prevent communal clashes.

6. The last act of my Ministry at the time they tendered their resignation was to say that under the circumstances they could not assume the responsibility for issuing the contemplated orders about the Madhe Sahaba dispute in Lucknow and they advised me to postpone action until after the Muharram. It had been decided that the orders would be issued last Saturday, which was considered to be about the latest date on which they could safely be published, if publication were to be made before the Muharram. After discussing the matter with the local officers, I came to the conclusion that the only sound course in the circumstances was to postpone publication till after the Muharram, and so far there seems to have been no criticism of this decision, though it must have been well known in Lucknow that orders were to have been passed last Saturday.

7. The excessive pressure at which the Secretaries have been working since the Congress Ministry took office is beginning to have its inevitable results. I am very sorry to say that Gwynne, the Chief Secretary, whose work during all these difficult months has been invaluable, has broken down seriously in health.[64] He is suffering from high blood pressure and has been ordered Home at once. He goes on leave at the beginning of March and will be away for at least five or six months. Waugh, the Revenue Secretary, is going on long leave in the middle of April, and though I know that the Premier is anxious for him to return to his post, he has told me that he feels he could not undertake it. Turner, the Finance Secretary, is also proceeding on leave from the beginning of April, and will probably

have to undergo an operation at Home. The Secretariat will in this way be much weakened during the summer, for these three officers are all first class and it will be extremely difficult to replace them.

Yours sincerely,
H.G. HAIG

26

HAIG TO LINLITHGOW
Telegram
R/3/1/73

Immediate *February 24th, 1938*
No. 129-G

I had a long talk this morning with Pant. His attitude was entirely friendly and we discussed matters quite on terms that prevailed before rupture. He is clearly most anxious that there should not be a break-down and I do not think there will be any serious difficulty about practical measures to deal with release of prisoners. I discussed these with him in some detail and I think he would be satisfied if we had these prisoners out gradually over a period of a month with special examination of individual cases.

2. The difficulty however we both feel lies in Gandhi's statement[65] which we had both read only a few minutes before we met. He understands difficulties that this presents. I made it clear to him that I could not compromise my constitutional position. He made certain tentative suggestions to me on the lines that after my examination of cases I would be satisfied to leave the question of release to Ministers. I pointed out that this would compromise the whole of our position and he appreciated the difficulty. I am quite prepared in practice to leave the Ministers to satisfy themselves in each individual case that assurances of future behaviour that they will obtain from prisoners are satisfactory, but I cannot surrender in advance my right of judgment about releases.

3. We decided to meet again tomorrow morning and in the meantime we will both consider the possibility of some statement that would not be likely to compromise the position of either. Unless the statement is to be of a somewhat colourless kind, which from his point of view might present embarrassment, it seems to me it is going to be difficult to reach agreement.

Repeated to Governor of Bihar.

27

HAIG TO HALLETT
Telegram
R/3/1/73

Immediate *February 27th, 1938*
No. 130-G

Your telegram No. 634-G.S. of 26 February.[66] It is not correct that I have agreed to release of all prisoners in 14 days. My understanding with Premier is that releases will be spread over one month. I agreed to take up immediately case of three terrorist prisoners and subsequently I found that three non-terrorist prisoners of no importance are due for release almost at once and I shall raise no objection to their early release. My intention was to take up the remaining three or four terrorist prisoners, one of whom is Chandra Man Singh, after about ten days. Statement in this morning's *Pioneer* that seven prisoners are being released at once is incorrect and will be contradicted.

Addressed Governor of Bihar. [Repeated to Viceroy.]

28

HAIG TO LINLITHGOW
Telegram
MSS.EUR.F 115/22B

Immediate *February 28th, 1938*
No. 131-G

Reference my telegram G-130 dated February 27th. Premier explained yesterday that as orders for release of ten prisoners in Bihar had already been passed, he would be placed in difficulties if orders were not now issued for the six prisoners whose cases I had agreed to. This was accordingly done. At his request I substituted Chandra Man Singh whom he was particularly anxious to release for one other terrorist prisoner.

2. We have had the Medical Board's report on Yaspal. He is suffering from the early stages of tuberculosis. Premier has seen him personally and is pressing strongly for his release. I presume Punjab have nothing of importance to say but am verifying this. I propose to agree to this release after two or three days.

29

HAIG TO EMERSON
Telegram
R/3/1/73

No. 135-G *March 3rd, 1938*

Your telegram No. 16-G. of 28 February.[67] Yashpal was released yesterday. Premier who has had more than one talk with him is convinced that his outlook is genuinely changed and that he will not attempt to renew his old activities. He is proceeding immediately to Bhowali sanatorium for treatment but talks of going later to the seaside or if he can get a passport to Switzerland. I explained to Premier the embarrassment that would be caused to the Punjab if Yashpal attempted to return there. He will explain the position to Yashpal and advise him strongly not to attempt to return without permission of the Punjab Government. He was not however prepared to impose any definite condition.

Addressed to Governor of the Punjab. [Repeated to Viceroy.]

30

HAIG TO LINLITHGOW
R/3/1/73

Private and Personal *March 5th, 1938*
No. U.P.-59

Dear Lord Linlithgow,

With reference to Your Excellency's private and personal letter, dated 27th February 1938,[68] about the terms of the settlement with my Ministry,[69] I think there was clearly some material misunderstanding in connection with the telephone conversation about the weight which was meant to be laid on the points raised by Your Excellency. There were a number of these conversations, and the general impression I had derived from what was reported to me was that while Your Excellency did not like three particular points[70] in the draft which had been communicated to me from Delhi, you did not attach special importance except to the point about "conventions". On the afternoon of the 25th a further telephone message came through. My Secretary then understood that you considered it would be better, even if it led to delay, not to accept the draft unless the sentence about conventions was omitted, and that you also attached substantial importance to the other two points. At this time I was holding my final conversation with the Premier, and before my Secretary could send in the note which he was writing immediately on the conclusion of the telephone conversation, the settlement had been reached and it was too late.

2. With regard to the three points raised, I felt in connection with the sentence about conventions that the substitution of the word "maintaining" for "establishing" took, as Your Excellency says, the sting out of the sentence. I appreciated that there were some objections to talking of conventions at all, as to some extent convention is a term of art in constitutional parlance. At the same time in practice my working arrangements with the Ministers and the procedure for dealing with them are in the nature of conventions, and I think would generally be regarded as such in the popular mind.

3. With regard to the other two points, I was not altogether clear about Your Excellency's wishes. I understood that you did not like the word "appropriate". On the other hand, it seemed to me that if the statement was to take the general form suggested, a vague word like "appropriate" was as suitable as anything we could secure. The form of the statement was in any case bound to give an opportunity to those who wished to claim a victory to do so. But it seemed to me that the words finally adopted did not in fact compromise the constitutional position of the Governor, a point on which I have been extremely emphatic with the Premier. As to the phrase about usurpation of functions of Ministers, I did not understand that Your Excellency attached very special importance to it. Actually as the statement was worded, I think the natural reading would be that certain apprehensions had been expressed, but that there was no foundation for them. It is I think of some interest to see that the *Hindustan Standard* of February 26th, the extremist paper of Calcutta, has from its point of view taken objection to the use of the word "appropriate" and has strongly criticised the words "legitimate functions" which are the really crucial words in the "usurpation" sentence, and had not been used by Gandhi.

4. The background of the settlement was as follows. When the Premier came to see me on the 24th, he was exceedingly reasonable about all the practical questions, but he was clearly a good deal upset by Gandhi's statement,[71] with its open criticism of the Congress Ministers for being weak and not understanding and exercising their powers. He said at the time, and later on the 24th wrote to me,[72] that account must be taken of Gandhi's statement. On the morning of the 25th I found he was still harping very much on the constitutional position. I told him plainly that I could

not for a moment accept Gandhi's constitutional views, that I could not possibly agree to compromising my own constitutional position, and that if this was his demand I was afraid there could be no settlement. He went away apparently depressed and uncertain as to what to do. In the afternoon when he came back he brought the Delhi formula[73] and was ready to settle at once on that. I thought myself it was desirable to reach at once a settlement that would be satisfactory myself, not having understood at that time that Your Excellency had any really strong feeling against the points which I was accepting, with the exception of the one about "conventions" which I thought I had largely overcome by the change in phrasing. My main reasons for wishing to conclude a settlement immediately were that the Premier was in a very wavering mood, that he had not as far as I was aware referred to the Working Committee, that if we broke off for further consideration it seemed to me likely that he would refer to the Working Committee and that he might receive from them (in the light of Gandhi's attitude) instructions which might make a settlement a great deal more difficult than the one we were considering. I was interested to see subsequently that evening in the Associated Press telegrams a telegram from Bombay, sent off before the settlement with Pant was known, to the effect that the intention was that the Premiers should after discussion with the Governors refer to the Working Committee and only withdraw their resignations if permitted by them. I do not think this telegram was published next day in the newspapers, having presumably been suppressed as soon as news came through that the settlement had been concluded. But it lends some corroboration to my view that by delay we might have got back to the position which I understood it was considered desirable to avoid, namely, that the negotiations should in effect be conducted between the Working Committee and Your Excellency. If the Working Committee had come in, it would in any case have involved a good deal of delay, and at a time like that every day's delay was likely to make the position more difficult and emphasize the fact that serious difficulties were being experienced in reaching a settlement. That was my general approach to the situation, and this coupled with the misunderstanding about Your Excellency's precise intentions led me to conclude a settlement.

5. As I mentioned above, I have always made it perfectly clear to the Premier that I did not consider our settlement as in any way compromising my constitutional position. When he was about to make his statement in the Assembly on March 1st (a copy of which I enclose) he brought it to me in the morning and said he felt he ought to let me see it. It was in the main a reasonable and colourless statement from his point of view, but in the

last sentence he had said that the clarification of the constitutional position had been of great value and that it had strengthened the position of the Ministers. I told him at once that it was impossible for me to agree to any such sentence, and that if he felt it necessary to put any gloss on our agreed statement, I should almost certainly find it necessary to put out a statement of my own making the constitutional position perfectly plain. After some discussion he agreed to omit this sentence, and the statement as made by him in the Assembly was quite harmless. Another complication was subsequently threatened. A member of the opposition said he wished to discuss the Premier's statement and a motion was put in by him the next day censuring the Ministry for the action they had taken in withdrawing their resignations. I spoke again to the Premier about this and said that while I recognised that he could not control the actions of the opposition, a debate on such a motion was likely to give rise to very serious embarrassment both to myself and to him, and I told him again that if anything was said in the debate which seemed to me to create a false impression of my constitutional position, I might find it necessary to put out a statement making my position clear. Meantime, a Congress member had tabled another motion approving the action the Ministers had taken, and I believe that some of the left-wing Congressmen were anxious to have a debate in order to try and claim a victory, whether practical or constitutional. But the Premier realised after his conversations with me the great dangers of this and co-operated in getting both motions withdrawn. I hope now we shall hear no more of the matter.[74]

Yours sincerely,
HARRY HAIG

ENCLOSURE TO NO. 30

COPY OF STATEMENT BY PANT IN U.P. LEGISLATIVE ASSEMBLY ON MARCH 1ST, 1938

I think that I owe to the House that I should make a short statement on the events of the last two weeks which have attracted widespread attention both in India and in England. Ever since the assumption of office by the present Government, the question of release of political prisoners had been under our consideration. Some were released in August and in October and the release of the remaining prisoners had been a subject of frequent discussion between the Governor and the Ministers.

As these discussions had proceeded for a long time and the public excitement was growing, we came to the conclusion that a final decision was necessary and we expressed this view before His Excellency in January and also in February. Ultimately in response to our request His Excellency informed us on February 15th that he had, in accordance with instructions issued to him by the Governor-General under powers reserved to him under Section 126 (5) of the Government of India Act, been unable to accept the advice tendered to him by the Ministers about the release of these prisoners.

In view of this action we thought that we could not discharge the responsibilities of our office in a satisfactory manner. We had therefore no option but to tender our resignation.

We mentioned the reasons for our doing so in a letter[75] which I addressed to His Excellency. This letter, I think, Hon'ble Members have already seen. It has led to the issuing of statements by the Governor[76] and another by myself.[77]

The Congress naturally took cognisance of this important matter, and it adopted a detailed resolution upon it at Haripura.[78] Later the Governor-General stated in a communiqué[79] the reasons for the action taken by him and on his statement Mahatma Gandhi expressed his own views.[80]

I and my colleagues returned to Lucknow by February 23rd, and the Governor asked me to discuss the whole situation with him. We had lengthy discussions and as a result, I am glad to say, that the differences were composed and a joint statement[81] was issued by His Excellency and myself.

As the controversy has now been settled and as I am laying all the relevant papers on the table, I do not think that the House will desire me to discuss its merits any more.

31

HAIG TO LINLITHGOW
R/3/1/73

Secret
No. U.P.-60

March 5th, 1938

My dear Lord Linlithgow,

In connection with the submission of my recommendations for the Birthday Honours, I saw the Premier yesterday and explained to him that I had been asked to submit recommendations, that I was anxious that he should not be embarrassed by any recommendations I might make, and that I should be very glad to inform him of the recommendations I was making if it would be agreeable to him.

2. He reaffirmed at considerable length his constitutional arguments. Briefly, they were that while he recognised that the grant of honours was a matter lying constitutionally outside the sphere of the Provincial Government, it was a matter which was bound to be of concern to the Provincial Government, and might even affect its working, in particular its relations with Government servants; that in the Dominions when Ministers had expressed their desire that honours should not be given His Majesty had respected their wishes, and that it seemed to him not unreasonable that the wishes similarly expressed by Ministers in this Province should be respected. He also referred to the fact that while no reply had been given to his representation, the conferment of honours was being continued, and he said he had hoped that His Excellency the Viceroy would have done Ministers the courtesy of explaining why he was unable to fall in with their wishes. I said that I had no doubt that Your Excellency had transmitted their representation to the Secretary of State, but we did not pursue this point any further.

3. He also hinted at the possibility of certain awkward developments if the wishes of the Ministry were ignored; for instance, they might instruct Government servants not to make any recommendations for honours, or they might issue instructions that titles were not to be used or recognised in official correspondence. I am not sure how far he would really be prepared to go in practice. But the Ministry have committed themselves very publicly to the discontinuance of honours, and he might feel that their credit was involved in pushing the matter somewhat far by way of demonstration and protest against the system.

4. Meantime, he will have nothing to do with honours and does not want even to be informed about them. I do not think that the anticipations in paragraph 10 (*b*) of Your Excellency's secret letter of February 7th, 1938,[82] are likely to be realised in this Province.

Yours sincerely,
HARRY HAIG

NOTES

1. In telegram 537-G.C. of 30 December 1937 Lord Linlithgow repeated a telegram from Sir Roger Lumley (Governor of Bombay) who was proposing to agree to the release of Mr. Sadashiv Raghunath Malkapurka. Sadashiv had been sentenced to 15 years' rigorous imprisonment for his part in the Bhusoval bomb case of 1930. He was said now to have abjured violence and had served about two-thirds of his sentence. MSS.EUR.F 115/22B.

2. The so-called 'Kakori case' came out of action taken by a group called the 'Hindusthan Republican Association' which had for its object the establishment of a Federal Republic of the United States of India by organised and armed revolution. Four dacoities were committed by the group in 1924 and 1925 in three of which it murdered people. The last dacoity took place on a railway train at Kakori on the main Lucknow-Dehra Dun line. Twenty-two persons stood trial for the dacoities and twenty were convicted. Four received death sentences, five were sentenced to transportation for life and the remainder received terms of rigorous imprisonment. L/P&J/7/1261: f. 251.
3. In his telegram 496-G.C. of 24 December 1937 to Provincial Governors, Lord Linlithgow reported on the outcome of his discussions with Lord Zetland on the attitude they should take towards any proposals for cuts in the pay of the provincial or subordinate services. In paragraph 2 Linlithgow said that Ministries would be within their rights to reduce the pay scales of persons recruited after 31 March 1937 and Governors should not oppose this unless it was clearly against the public interest. Similar considerations would apply to people promoted after 31 March. However Governors should refuse to agree to cuts in pay for those recruited before 31 March. MSS.EUR.F 125/127.
4. The India Office file containing this letter has been destroyed.
5. MSS.EUR.F 125/127. See also *U.P.P., 1936-7*, Nos. 70 and 90, paragraph 7.
6. Lord Linlithgow replied in telegram 87-G.C. of 13 January 1938. He agreed that no general objection should be taken to proposals for reduction or abolition of special pays or compensatory allowances. He proceeded to outline the principles they should adopt in particular cases. R/3/1/73.
7. See *U.P.P., 1936-7*, Appendix 17 for the text of the statement as issued.
8. Not included in R/3/1/73.
9. Mr. C.W. Gwynne.
10. Mr R.A. Horton.
11. In January 1930 the Congress Working Committee passed a resolution calling on the country to celebrate 26 January each year as 'Purna Swaraj Day'. In January 1935 the Working Committee further asked members to hold public meetings on 'Purna Swaraj Day' (or household meetings where public meetings were prohibited). At these meetings a lengthy resolution (worded in Hindustani or the local languages) was to be passed. This resolution began: 'We remind ourselves on this, the solemn national day, that Complete Independence is our birthright and we shall not rest till we have achieved it....' The independence resolution had been banned in the U.P. in 1937. See *U.P.P., 1936-7*, No. 5.
12. In telegram 124-G.C. of 19 January 1938, Lord Linlithgow reported that the Premier of the Central Provinces (Pandit Khare) had told the Governor (Sir Hyde Gowan) that he wished to declare 26 January a holiday 'to celebrate

partial assumption of power by people of the Province'. Lord Linlithgow had suggested the holiday should be 'to celebrate Provincial Autonomy'. Eventually Gowan asked Khare not to press the proposal and the Governor had little doubt that that was the end of the matter. R/3/1/73.

13. Early in 1922, during Mahatma Gandhi's civil disobedience campaign, a mob set fire to a police station at Chauri Chaura, a village in the Gorakhpur district of the U.P. Twenty-two police constables were killed. It was this incident that led Gandhi to call off the civil disobedience campaign.
14. Mr Mohan Lal Saksena had been elected President of the U.P. Provincial Congress Committee in January 1938.
15. Lord Linlithgow minuted: 'Quite! Then why pet Pant at the expense of sound practice and sound principle when in fact you are up against no one but Nehru.'
16. Lord Linlithgow minuted: 'More important to consider whether it should be allowed to assemble *at all*.'
17. The relevant portion of the U.P. Chief Secretary's Report for 19 January 1938 read: 'It is reported that the rents are generally coming in except in certain parts of the Gorakhpur and Benares Divisions, the collections in the estates under the management of the Court of Wards having actually exceeded the usual percentage. There are still complaints on the part of some zamindars here and there, but it is generally admitted that good zamindars are not finding any real difficulty in the matter. In some cases it is suggested that zamindars themselves are really responsible as they are not making any real effort to collect rent or still insisting on the payment of more than their lawful dues. In several cases, as the zamindars refused to accept the recorded rents, tenants made payments by money-order or in tahsils. Commissioners report that on the ordinary processes of law being enforced payment speedily follows. A certain amount of difficulty was also due to the poverty of crops or deterioration in sugarcane due to pyrella in certain areas. Congressmen generally have been helpful in inducing tenants to pay their rents.' L/P&J/5/265: ff. 265-6.
18. See note 12 above.
19. Lord Linlithgow minuted: 'P.S.V. – This letter disturbs me.'
20. Only this extract was enclosed with Sir Harry Haig's letter.
21. Sir William Marris was Governor of the U.P. 1922-8.
22. Mr C.W. Grant was Commissioner, Gorakhpur in September 1937.
23. Mr C.F. Wood was Commissioner, Gorakhpur in December 1937.
24. See No. 1. Although Sir Roger Lumley (Governor of Bombay) saw no very strong reason to resist the release from prison of Mr Sadashiv, Lord Linlithgow had a number of objections. The prisoner's record was much worse than that of several U.P. prisoners whom Sir Harry Haig had refused to release. Sadashiv had also not served two-thirds of his original sentence which was the standard required for release. Linlithgow hoped that Lumley could persuade Mr K.M.

Munshi (the Bombay Home Minister) to drop the proposed release. Lord Zetland wondered if they could make use of Munshi's offer to be responsible for Sadashiv's good behaviour if released and if Sadashiv could be bound not to leave Bombay for six months. L/P&J/7/1261: f. 6.

25. Haig's note of his discussions with Pandit Pant and Dr Katju is printed in Basudev Chatterji (ed.), *Towards Freedom: Documents on the Movement for Independence in India 1938*, Part II (New Delhi: Oxford University Press, 1999), pp. 1147-8.
26. Lord Linlithgow minuted: 'And even, perhaps, more upon Nehru's views and instructions.'
27. Mr Sadashiv was in fact released in early March 1938.
28. In a telegram of 31 January 1938, Lord Linlithgow instructed the Governor of Bihar (Sir Maurice Hallett) to stand firm and not to agree to his Premier's proposal to the early release of political prisoners during the hunger-strike. MSS.EUR.F 115/22B.
29. Lord Linlithgow minuted: 'P.S.V. – I, of course, have only to be told of such difficulties to be willing at once to change my plans.'
30. Lord Linlithgow minuted: 'I wish he could tell me how far short Revenue is.'
31. Lord Linlithgow minuted: 'This is the action of a weak man and I begin to suspect that that is what Pant in fact is.'
32. Lord Linlithgow's telegram 123-G, actually sent on 2 February 1938, was an interim reply to No.8. Linlithgow said that very important issues of policy were raised for which there was no hope of an early answer. The Viceroy asked Sir Harry Haig to play for time if pressed by his Ministers. R/3/1/73.
33. Lord Linlithgow minuted: 'Any suggestion of a threat to the King's representative to deprive him of his Ministers' services ought to be most firmly discouraged. It will *never* do.'
34. Lord Linlithgow minuted: 'P.S.V. – This makes me glad that I showed my hand at length.'
35. Lord Linlithgow minuted: 'All undertakings should include abjuration of mass violence.'
36. Lord Linlithgow minuted: 'Government by Working Committee is most important.'
37. Lord Linlithgow minuted: 'Or perhaps released in place of worse.'
38. Lord Linlithgow minuted: 'I think it quite essential that no Governor should in Cabinet admit even to knowledge of the existence of the Working Committee, much more to any view of that body bearing upon the issues before the Ministry.'
39. See *U.P.P., 1936-7*, Appendix 16.
40. See *U.P.P., 1936-7*, Appendix 9.
41. See *U.P.P., 1936-7*, No. 112.
42. Appendix 1.

43. Mr G.G. Field.
44. Mr R.A. Horton.
45. Not included in R/3/1/73. The *Leader* of 10 February 1938 contained a lengthy report of a speech which the Superintendent of Police, Allahabad, Mr H.A. Carless, had made in Hindustani the previous week to villagers in Karchchana. Carless admitted frankly that he had been dissatisfied with both the method and amount of patrol that was done. He had instituted a new method and several constables and sub-inspectors had been punished for failure to carry out such patrols properly. Carless had also stressed the need for *thana* staff to record honestly and intelligently reports of crime.
46. Lord Linlithgow thanked Sir Harry Haig for this letter in a letter of 10 March 1938. Linlithgow wrote: 'I cannot, I must say, pretend that my anxieties are entirely removed; but as matters stand I think there is nothing for it but to see how the situation develops and for us to continue to keep a close watch on this question of official morale.' MSS.EUR.F 115/12.
47. R/3/1/73.
48. Ibid.
49. See Appendix 2.
50. Paragraph 1 of Lord Linlithgow's telegram 209-G of 15 February 1938 to Sir Harry Haig read: 'I have carefully considered position in relation to my own responsibilities but with a full sense of the gravity of the issues involved I have no choice but to instruct you under the provisions of Section 126(5) that despite the advice in the contrary sense of your Ministers you should decline to agree to the proposed general release of your "political" prisoners.' In paragraph 2 Linlithgow said that Zetland (with his own agreement) suggested that Haig should not, if possible, disclose to his Ministers that he (Haig) believed that his own responsibility was not attracted. There was everything to be said for a united front. R/3/1/73.
51. Lord Linlithgow's telegram 194-G of 12 February 1938. Ibid.
52. I.e. the All-India Convention of Congress Legislators held at Delhi in March 1937.
53. Pandit Pant's letter had the words here 'even though acceptable to the Governor' but these words were omitted in the text sent to Mr Laithwaite. MSS.EUR.F 115/22B.
54. In telegram 215-G of 15 February 1938, Lord Linlithgow asked Sir Harry Haig to confirm that there were no other points in connection with a Section 93 situation on which he needed further advice or information. Linlithgow also asked Haig to confirm that he would use the same Advisers as those proposed in 1937. R/3/1/73.
55. In telegram 226-G of 16 February 1938 Lord Linlithgow asked for a brief summary of general press reactions to the situation created by the resignation of the U.P. and Bihar Ministries. Linlithgow said that Lord Zetland would probably make a statement in Parliament that day or the following day.

Linlithgow himself might subsequently make a statement but he would await developments before deciding whether to do so.

56. Telegram 242-G of 17 February 1938 repeated to Sir Harry Haig the text of a telegram which the Viceroy had sent Sir Maurice Hallett (Governor of Bihar). Hallett was concerned about the problems of getting a budget passed by 31 March with a minority Ministry. Linlithgow said that they must all hope that Congress could be got back into office without an unduly long interval. His advice to both Hallett and Haig would be 'to play for time, to go as slowly as possible; to confine your discussions with possible Leaders of alternative Ministries to very preliminary soundings; and in any event to avoid any commitment until we have been able to discuss matter further together (and if necessary with Secretary of State) after Haripura....' R/3/1/73.
57. In telegram 277-G of 20 February 1938, Lord Linlithgow asked Sir Harry Haig to see Pandit Pant on his return from Haripura and 'that you put it to him in whatever manner you think best that so long as there is prospect of amicable settlement you think it best not to take further action in connection with acceptance of his resignation, and suggest that he and his colleagues should (without prejudice to fact that they had tendered their resignation and that this is in your hands) continue their ordinary work. I have no objection to your saying that you make this suggestion after consultation with me.' Ibid.
58. This telegram was evidently a repetition of telegram 262-G.B. of 17 February 1938 from Sir Maurice Hallett to Lord Linlithgow. In it Hallett said that if the U.P. went into Section 93 as early as 19 February it would stop any possibility of a minority Ministry being formed in Bihar. R/3/1/17.
59. Lord Linlithgow minuted: 'This is disappointing. I can but concur.'
60. In telegram 505-G.S. of 18 February 1938, Sir Maurice Hallett reported to Lord Linlithgow the results of a conversation he had had with the leader of the Bihar opposition. The opposition leader felt a minority Ministry would be possible but in paragraph 2 (*b*) he was reported as saying that such a Ministry must have a term of at least 18 months to carry out a programme for the betterment of the people. R/3/1/17.
61. In telegram 268-G of 18 February 1938 to Mr Donaldson, Mr Laithwaite asked (in connection with a possible Section 93 situation) for details of the broad features of any taxation measures contemplated by the Ministry for the following year's budget. Laithwaite also asked for the approximate yields of the measures and, if there were no objection, copies of the detailed budget and all budget papers. R/3/1/73.
62. Cawnpore District was a part of the Allahabad Division. The Commissioner in February 1938 was Mr Panna Lal.
63. Mr J.E. Pedley was District Magistrate of Gorakhpur in February 1938.
64. Lord Linlithgow minuted: 'P.S.V. – This is a very serious statement.'

65. Appendix 6.
66. Sir Maurice Hallett's telegram has not been traced.
67. MSS.EUR.F 15/22B. The position of the Punjab Government was that they would not have released Mr Yashpal if he had been in a Punjab prison. They did not, however, wish to oppose his release if this meant they would make the constitutional crisis worse. Nonetheless they hoped a condition of the release would be that Yashpal would be kept out of the Punjab. Emerson to Linlithgow, 24 February 1938. R/3/1/59.
68. Appendix 10.
69. See Appendix 8 for the Statement issued by Sir Harry Haig and Pandit Pant on 25 February 1938.
70. See Appendix 10, note 8.
71. Appendix 6.
72. Appendix 7.
73. It is evident that the first draft of the Statement made by Sir Harry Haig and Pandit Pant (Appendix 8) was drawn up by Mr G.D. Birla in consultation with Pant and Mr Laithwaite (P.S.V.). See Birla to Gandhi, 25 February 1938, printed in Basudev Chatterji (ed.), *Towards Freedom: Documents on the Movement for Independence in India 1938*, Part II (New Delhi, Oxford University Press, 1999), pp. 1168-9. This first draft is presumably the 'Delhi formula' referred to by Haig. According to Birla, Pant wished to receive an assurance from the Governor that he would never use his special powers again. Birla advised against pressing this point as it would mean that the blame for the crisis would then fall on Congress. Birla argued that 'if Pantji issued a statement on the lines of the draft I had suggested with the full consent of the Governor and if that statement was followed by release it will very much strengthen the position of Congress.' Birla reported that Pant was also concerned about the attitude of Mahatma Gandhi to the proposed settlement. However Pant rejected a suggestion that he should refer the settlement to an associate of Gandhi as 'this would prolong the matter and he [Pant] was already getting tired of it.'
74. Lord Linlithgow acknowledged this letter on 10 March 1937. The Viceroy did not wish to pursue the matter further but made two points: (1) the use of the word 'appropriate' in the Statement (Appendix 8) was open to misunderstanding of a damaging character; (2) the agreed Statement (being the first issued in the affected Provinces) had implications for Bengal and Bihar as their Governors would have difficulty in refusing to follow the wording. Linlithgow hoped that the 'somewhat exhausting period through which we have had to pass will result in Congress being more careful next time.' R/3/1/73.
75. Enclosure to No. 15.
76. Appendix 2.
77. Appendix 3.

78. Appendix 4.
79. Appendix 5.
80. Appendix 6.
81. Appendix 8.
82. Paragraph 10 (*b*) of Lord Linlithgow's letter of 7 February 1938 to Sir Harry Haig dealt with the possibility that critics of honours might challenge individual awards when they were made. R/3/1/73.

CHAPTER 2

Documents for 9 March – 17 May 1938

32

HAIG TO LINLITHGOW
R/3/1/73

Secret
No. U.P.-61

March 9th, 1938

My dear Lord Linlithgow,

There was a general sense of relief when the Ministers returned to office as a result of the settlement reached on the 25th February. I have communicated in some detail to Your Excellency subsequent developments. I think the whole affair may now be regarded as finished, except for the release of the prisoners which is still proceeding gradually. As I indicated in my last letter, the feeling of relief was not shared by a considerable number of the more old-fashioned landlords, who hoped for some respite from conditions which are naturally causing them apprehension. I fear the landlords do not show much development in the quality of political sense. I am told that some of them have reached the conclusion, as a result of the Congress returning to office, that their best course is to join the Congress. But unless they are to pay considerable sums as blackmail I do not quite see the outlines of a bargain.

2. The Ministers will I believe within the next week make up their minds about the tenancy policy. We shall probably be having a Cabinet meeting on the subject shortly. Many of the measures under discussion are reasonable and indeed desirable, though there are certain points of importance in which they may wish to go too far. But when it comes to a decision I am a little afraid that the Ministers may find themselves pushed by the opinion of their followers beyond the point at which they might themselves have preferred to stand. At the same time it is clear that there is a certain amount of political influence even on the Congress side which

does not desire to go too far in the direction of antagonising the landlords or upsetting the zamindari system. If developments work out as at present seems probable, a Bill could be ready for introduction in the Assembly about the middle of April, and after it has gone to a select committee it might come back for final consideration at a session in July or August. This would in my opinion be a wise programme. But it is possible that if the Ministers contemplate something of this kind, they would feel at the same time that they must take some earlier steps in the way of dealing with particular points by short Bills which might be passed before the Assembly rises in April.

3. The budget was introduced on the 3rd March. The revenue deficit has now gone up from 12 lakhs to 15 lakhs, and the expenditure on rural development has been dressed up so as to make the greatest show possible. The Premier's rather light-hearted reference to the deficit has not been well received by more sober opinion, and the budget is receiving a good deal of criticism on the ground that it is too ambitious and that the rural development schemes on which such large sums of money are to be spent have not actually been worked out and are still in the air. Criticism of this kind will I hope have a salutary effect.

4. Revenue payments have improved greatly, and I think it may safely be assumed that rents have been coming in pretty well. There was a remarkable demonstration of cultivators in Lucknow on the 1st March. It seems to have been the product of two separate factors. A *kisan* demonstration had been advertised for the end of January to bring pressure on the Ministers to carry out their election promises. The Ministers succeeded in stopping this by putting about the story that it had been postponed and would come off later. To some extent therefore this was the postponed demonstration of January, though instead of large numbers of cultivators coming from all the surrounding districts it was in the main confined to cultivators from the Unao district. The other contributing factor was that when the Ministers had resigned the Congress organisation had called for a great demonstration of *kisans* for the 1st of March in Lucknow as a protest against the action of the Governor. Though there was no occasion for such a protest and the Ministry had tried to stop this demonstration taking place, it was too late to stop it altogether. According to the best estimates I have had the number of cultivators who came into Lucknow was approximately 20,000. They were well organised and remarkably orderly, and entered into conversation in the most friendly way with various Europeans who happened to talk to them. Their leaders however uttered the usual revolutionary slogans with fervour and venom.

The cultivators repeated the slogans, but without apparently much personal conviction. Kisan Sabha influence was prominent and there were a number of red flags on which Jawaharlal Nehru who addressed the crowd commented unfavourably. The crowd dispersed in the evening still perfectly orderly and rather tired, and I am told that a good many of them expressed disappointment. Indeed the Ministers could give them nothing except some comforting words and exhortations to patience. Several people have commented to me on the contrast between these orderly and almost dull proceedings and the excitable demonstrations, when the Congress Ministry entered upon office, on the first day of the meeting of the Assembly.

5. One of the first communications made to me by the Premier after his return was that Mr. Pyare Lal Sharma, Minister of Education, had finally confirmed his resignation and that he wished it to be accepted and Mr. Sampurnanand to be appointed in his place. I had discussed this some time ago with the Premier and agreed to his proposals. When I was wishing good-bye to Mr. Sharma he made it clear that one thing he had resented very much was the criticism he had incurred from the Congress party when he proposed to stay at Allahabad with Sir Tej Bahadur Sapru. He is a man of considerable independence of character, and he found this interference with his personal affairs and friendships very galling. He also hinted that he did not approve of the Congress ban on social relations with the Governor. Sampurnanand is a man of a very different type, more able and extreme. It is too early yet to say whether his inclusion in the Cabinet will have any marked effect on policy.

6. On the whole I have found the Ministers since their return very reasonable. In particular their attitude towards the rural development movement is far more satisfactory than it was. I hope they have now realised that a big movement of this kind cannot be run for the benefit of their party. They have agreed to the issue of instructions emphasizing the point that the rural development staff must conform strictly to the Government Servants' Conduct Rules and not take any part in politics. Moreover, while at the beginning they insisted that the district officer should as far as possible be kept out and said that this was the main difference between their conception of rural development and the scheme which I had initiated, Dr. Katju has now told me that he is convinced that the movement cannot succeed without the full co-operation of district officers and that he intends to seek it. They have also said that they desire the co-operation of landlords. I only hope that these new resolutions will be maintained. It is a very great advantage to have got rid of Paliwal, the Rural Development Officer. As long as he remained the movement was bound to be primarily political. I

hope they will agree now to appoint an official in his place.

7. Another matter in which events appear to be changing the views of the Ministers is the flying of flags on buildings of local bodies. When the Congress Ministry first came in, they initiated a regular campaign for Congress flags being flown in this way, and the Ministers themselves were constantly taking part in ceremonial hoisting of flags on municipal and district board buildings. Since however the Muslim League have been claiming to fly their flag in the same way, and also the communists, there has been a great cooling off on the Congress side in regard to this principle of flag flying, and it is not impossible that they may eventually, in order to avoid the considerable embarrassment that is now being experienced, adopt the principle of refusing to allow local bodies to display party emblems.

8. I fear there may be a good deal of communal friction during the next few weeks owing to the near conjunction of Muharram and Holi. I have just heard that the Muharram has started rather inauspiciously in Allahabad with an attack by Muslims on a Hindu marriage procession.

Yours sincerely,
HARRY HAIG

33

HAIG TO LINLITHGOW
R/3/1/73

Secret *March 23rd, 1938*
No. U.P.-63

My dear Lord Linlithgow,

The matter which has almost monopolised interest during the last fortnight his been the communal situation. As I mentioned in my letter No. U.P.-61, dated March 9th, the Muharram started inauspiciously in Allahabad with an attack by Muslims on a Hindu marriage procession. Feeling was very strained in Allahabad during the whole Muharram period, but strong and impartial handling of the situation by the local authorities was successful in avoiding any serious outbreak of trouble, though on more than one occasion trouble was very narrowly averted. Throughout the Province there was a great deal of tension during the Muharram period, and in more than one place there were short-lived disturbances. We were just beginning to congratulate ourselves on having got through this very difficult time when the Holi celebrations coming immediately on top of the Muharram led to unfortunate outbreaks, first at Benares and almost immediately afterwards at Allahabad. In both places the situation was very well handled by the local officers and most valuable and cordial assistance was rendered by the military. In the case of Benares, the normal garrison of which is not adequate to deal with any serious trouble, two extra companies of British troops were sent over promptly as a reinforcement. In Allahabad the troops were employed freely in the city throughout the period of tension and subsequent disturbances, and their presence had a very steadying effect. In Benares the situation returned to normal fairly quickly, but in Allahabad the long period of tension during the Muharram had created conditions in which certain members of the two communities were ready to be at each other's throats and considerable panic also prevailed. The result was that the trouble continued longer than might have been expected. In neither place, however, was there anything in the nature of a serious riot, though the police opened fire on one occasion in Allahabad, and the deaths were to a large extent due to isolated assaults and stabbings. I think in both towns now it is safe to conclude that the trouble is over.

2. The Ministry behaved in a most sensible way over these disturbances. Indeed, the situation was handled in effect just as it would have been under the old conditions. In both cities we had capable and reliable officers. The Ministry did not attempt to dictate to them how they were to handle the situation. They kept closely in touch with what was going on and gave every assistance that was required in the way of providing extra temporary staff. But they did not fuss the officers on the spot with unnecessary suggestions, and made it clear that they would support them in whatever action the situation called for. Two Ministers were present in Allahabad during part of the time, but they behaved with the most commendable restraint, and made no attempt to interfere with the handling of the situation by the District Magistrate. In these circumstances the political attack made upon the Ministry yesterday in the Assembly by the Muslim League was very unfair. The Muslim League in the course of a motion of adjournment suggested that the Ministry had not taken all reasonable steps to maintain order and that local officers were afraid to act impartially for fear of offending the Congress Government. This was deliberate falsity to a degree which even the manoeuvres of politics can hardly excuse. I enclose two interesting and reasonable editorial comments by the *Leader* about the communal troubles and their handling.

3. At the same time it is interesting to consider what are the real causes of the very bad feeling which prevails at present throughout the Province

between the Hindus and Muslims, and which manifested itself almost inevitably in these outbreaks. To my mind they are to be found in the present political grouping. As I have mentioned more than once, a position in which practically the whole of the important minority community of Muslims is ranged in the legislature in opposition to the Government is bound to lead to serious communal friction. The minority cannot get their own way in the legislature, and as a permanent communal minority have no prospect of ever getting it, and they are tempted inevitably to redress the weakness of their parliamentary position by rousing religious feelings and emphasizing the importance of the community outside the legislature, even at the risk of communal outbreaks. This is the Muslim contribution to the trouble. But the Muslims are not solely responsible for the ill feeling. There is also a reverse side to the picture. The Hindus have been undoubtedly elated by the establishment of what is in effect a Hindu Government. There is a good deal of popular feeling that this is Hindu raj, and several officers have told me that they think the Hindu attitude towards communal questions has been aggressive lately. The Holi is particularly a time when provocation is likely to be given to other communities. The Ministry undoubtedly find these conditions an embarrassment, and it remains to be seen whether anything will be done to revive the ideas of a coalition between the Congress and Muslim League, without which I should anticipate that this state of communal tension will continue and will come to a head again whenever there is a provoking cause, which is bound to arise not infrequently.

4. I have frequently referred to the Madhe Sahaba dispute in Lucknow between Sunnis and Shias. It had been decided to publish the report of the committee and the conclusions of Government on it on the 19th March, but the Government decided, wisely I think, not to run the risk of further disturbances at a time when the demands on the police were very considerable. They therefore postponed publication again, and it is now intended to publish on the 26th.[1]

5. Twelve out of the fifteen political prisoners who were the cause of the Ministerial crisis have now been released. Little public attention has been paid to them and they themselves have behaved with restraint. Of the remaining three I have received notes from the Ministers about two, and I think they are likely to be released within the next few days. The third is hardly a political case at all, but I think the Ministers will feel bound in view of what has gone before to release him.

6. There have been reports recently from Cawnpore that the extreme labour leaders are getting active again in anticipation of the publication of

the report of the Inquiry Committee. The Employers' Association sent in a representation complaining that dangerous incitements were being made and that intimidation was once more beginning to manifest itself. Cawnpore, however, has remained perfectly quiet during the Muharram-Holi period. The Enquiry Committee's report has now, I understand, been signed and the Government will be faced with important problems of policy. The prospects for something like an amicable settlement seem decidedly brighter than they were some months ago, but there are of course many influences working against peace, and the extremists will certainly try to provoke a strike.

7. Land revenue realisations continue to be satisfactory, and I think we may now assume that the danger which at one time threatened, that there would be refusal on a considerable scale to pay rent, has now passed. We have had two important Cabinet meetings to consider the general tenancy and revenue policy of the Government. A great many of the proposals are very reasonable. In certain respects what they propose will be decidedly unwelcome to the landlords, but I think it possible that on certain points the Ministry may compromise if faced with strong and convincing opposition. With regard to further taxation of the landlords, the decision is not to impose any agricultural income-tax on the landlords of temporarily settled areas but to raise the maximum pitch of land revenue from 40 per cent of assets to 55 per cent, and to allow for a good deal of graduation among those revenue payers whose land revenue at 55 per cent would come to Rs. 2,000 or less. For the small cultivating proprietor class the rate would go down to 25 per cent. Another issue of great importance is the final decision about the arrears of rent, recovery of which has been stayed. The present conclusion of the Ministry is that all these arrears should be written off, but that the writing off should be connected up with future payments of rent, a certain portion being written off for every complete payment of the half-yearly rental demand, the process extending over two or three years. I think this is a reasonable solution which will certainly act as a strong inducement to tenants to pay rents in the future. The Ministers are most anxious to establish a rent-paying mentality among the tenants. The programme contemplated for legislation is that a Bill should be introduced about the middle of April and then referred to a select committee. The committee would be given at least two months, and possibly more, to report, and public opinion will have plenty of time to declare itself. The Bill will then be taken up in July, or possibly as late as August. The Ministers realise fully the importance of the matters they are dealing with and the necessity of considering and weighing carefully the

arguments of the opposition. If they continue in this spirit, I hope that it may be possible to pass a Bill which will prove more or less acceptable to the landlords, and at any rate that it will not be rejected in the Upper House.

8. The Ministry are still considering the appointment of a new rural development officer. They realise the advantages of appointing an official, and I think are coming round to the view that this offers them the best chance of getting practical results from the money they propose to spend. There is difficulty, however, about finding a suitable official. We are undoubtedly short of good officers at present. If an official is appointed at the head of the rural development movement, I hope that it may progress on really sound lines. At present the whole scheme is very much in the air and no practical work is being done.

9. I have had to take up recently with the Premier two matters in which his attitude tends not to be satisfactory. One is the question of praise of the Garhwali mutineers[2] which has been referred to me by the Eastern Command. This is a matter in which I have always found the Premier decidedly difficult to deal with and extremely lacking in appreciation of obvious military considerations. I think the fact is that he himself some years ago took rather a prominent part in these activities, but I hope I shall be able to get him to see reason. The other question is that of the administration of the Arms Act. A circular to all district officers of a somewhat ambiguous character enjoining the freer grant of licences to agriculturists for crop protection was issued last month, and through inadvertence[3] was not shown to me before issue. I am taking up with the Premier the question of what his precise intentions are, and whether it is necessary to refer to the Government of India, which would clearly be the case if any substantial departure from existing policy was intended. When I first raised the matter with him, he was inclined to take the line that if he could not administer the Arms Act on principles that seemed suitable to him he would not take any responsibility for it at all and would leave the Government of India to appoint their own officers. I do not think he had appreciated that the Government of India could, as I think they could under Section 124 (2) of the Government of India Act, appoint District Magistrates to carry out their policy. But of course this would be a very unfortunate development. I hope I may be able to get him to take a reasonable attitude, but I think it is well to warn you that he may prove difficult on this matter.

Yours sincerely,
H.G. HAIG

ENCLOSURE 1 TO NO. 33

LEADING ARTICLE FROM THE *LEADER* NEWSPAPER OF ALLAHABAD, DATED MARCH 24TH, 1938

Our Shame

No patriotic, no self-respecting Hindu or Muslim can contemplate the orgies of the five or six days of communal riots at Allahabad and Benares except with a sense of deep humiliation and great shame. Once again have Hindu and Muslim mobs demonstrated with violence their utter unworthiness to be regarded as members of a civilized community. What for, after all, did they go at each other with a frenzy akin to that of wild beasts more than of humankind? If a Hindu marriage procession accompanied by music, passed through a thoroughfare, how on earth was the Islamic religion insulted? And where in the whole of Hindu religion is it prescribed that crowds should march on the streets to drench innocent and unwilling passers-by in dirty coloured water? We shall never forgive ourselves if we wrote in the language of levity of the doctrines or the faith of a single religious system in the world. Toleration, defined by a great man as reverence for every possible form of truth, is to our mind the very essence of a devout religious faith. But it is not religion, it is a disgraceful travesty of it for adherents of one creed to treat with contumely and afterwards to butcher their fellow-men of another faith. The whole thing is so silly and ridiculous and, if it were not so tragic, would be so eminently fit a subject for ribald laughter – this mob madness to fly at one another's throats on the slightest pretext or on none at all. All talk of our culture and our civilization and our lofty mission in the world is sheer moonshine by the side of such savage happenings as have disgraced the two sacred cities of Kashi and Prayag last week. On some former occasions of communal riots there was at least a plausible reason for dissatisfaction by one community or the other at the orders of authority as being partizan and as showing insufficient regard for the civic rights of the aggrieved community. But last week the most inventive of human minds could not think of any such excuse. To be candid, it was sheer criminal lunacy on the part of both Hindus and Muslims and no one who had any hand in initiating or prolonging the riots deserves any quarter whatsoever from any person of whatever religious faith.

The only redeeming feature of the disgraceful happenings was the effort of authority to control the grave disturbances of public peace. We are aware of the criticism privately uttered by not a few that the police and the executive were more lenient than they should have been. But we are not unaware of the criticism to which both were subjected not unoften in the past for what appeared to be excess of severity. We do not mind confessing after what happened last week, that perhaps the latter would be more of an error on the right side than laxity. It is not difficult for people sitting comfortably in their arm-chairs in their cosy homes and offices to blame this officer or that for a supposed mistake on one or another occasion. Nor do we say that the function of criticism should be abdicated. Certainly not. But it should be exercised in a responsible spirit and the benefit of every doubt ought to be given to the harassed officers, who on such occasions have to work not only during the live-long day but far into the night regardless of food or sleep and in circumstances of the utmost difficulty, anxiety and not unoften, of delicacy. Looking back on the past week we can honestly offer to the officers, executive and police, who were involved, full credit for efficient and dutiful action, all in the interest of the general public.

One word of caution we feel called upon to utter. It was the unfortunate practice on occasions of previous communal riots for Governments to withdraw the cases that were instituted against persons caught in the act of rioting. This the authorities did at the instance of so-called communal leaders who pleaded that for the restoration of communal harmony, the unhappy memories of the riot should be wiped out by the withdrawal of prosecutions. We never favoured this course. It was carried to such excess that it almost began to be felt by the criminally-disposed that to participate in a communal riot was not wholly unsafe as, after the event, they would not be sent to jail or kept there for any long time. A former Inspector-General of Police, Sir Robert Dodd, adversely criticized this policy as putting a premium upon communal rioting. We earnestly hope that this time the Government will not listen to any such appeal if it should be made to them, and that those who are proved to be guilty will receive the punishment which is their just due and which they have richly earned.

ENCLOSURE 2 TO NO. 33

EDITORIAL COMMENT IN THE *LEADER* NEWSPAPER OF ALLAHABAD, DATED MARCH 24TH, 1938

There is not a word that can be said in support of the Muslim League's resolution against the Government of the United Provinces in connection with the riots at Allahabad and Benares. There is not a scintilla of evidence that the Government imposed their will on the district officers in respect of the steps taken by the latter to control the riots. And there is absolutely none that those officers showed any communal preference or betrayed any communal bias in the performance of their police and executive duties to put down the disturbances. Nor has the Muslim League taken pains to make out a *prima facie* case for its reckless condemnation of authority in the service of both the Hindu and Muslim communities against their own hooligans and *goondas*. The resolution recorded by Muslim League at Lucknow is not only deplorable but discreditable; and it is a great public disservice not less to the Muslims than to the Province as a whole.

34

HAIG TO LINLITHGOW
R/3/1/73

Secret *April 8th, 1938*
No. U.P.-64

My dear Lord Linlithgow,

As I mentioned in my last fortnightly report, dated March 23rd, the communal trouble has now subsided. Nevertheless, acute feeling still persists in Allahabad and considerable nervousness, and one cannot be sure that there may not be another flare up. In Benares the situation seems to have returned to normal. So far as I can judge, the Premier has not been affected by the unpractical remarks of Gandhi about how to deal with communal riots,[4] and he is not in the least shaken in his policy of using force vigorously. If there is any further recrudescence of trouble in Allahabad, I should anticipate that he would wish for the strongest possible action to be taken.

2. A new development which might perhaps grow in importance in its effect on communal relations, and even on the general political situation, is some re-emergence of the Hindu Mahasabha influence. This was almost completely submerged at the time of the general election, but Savarkar has been touring in this Province and, I am told, has addressed big meetings both in Cawnpore and in Lucknow. His policy is violently anti-British, but the support he receives is probably mainly based on Hindu communal feeling. He has been attacking the Congress for neglecting the interests of

the Hindus, and has been trying to rouse Hindu feeling in just the same way as the Muslim League has been rousing Muslim feeling. The Congress of course, though consisting predominantly of Hindus, always professes and to a large extent pursues a non-communal policy. But, as I suggested in my letter of March 23rd, the idea of Hindu raj appeals strongly to the Hindus and if the Hindu Mahasabha come out with a strong Hindu communal policy, they may gain some support at the expense of the less communal Congress. At present however the Congress predominance is firmly established.

3. A development in Muslim politics of some interest took place recently. As I think I have told you before, the opposition in the Assembly consists of two parties of approximately equal strength, one being the Muslim League Parliamentary Party, the other being Chhatari's Independent Party, which includes a number of the more conservative Muslims of the landed type and a small number of Hindu landlords and conservatives. A move was made from the Muslim League side to insist on the Muslims in the Independent Party transferring their allegiance to the Muslim League Parliamentary Party, and a meeting of the Muslims was held to decide on their policy. Chhatari appears to have expressed his readiness, and even eagerness, to join the Muslim League Parliamentary Party, and thus to unite all Muslims under one banner for purposes of Parliamentary opposition. This readiness to fall in with their own proposals somewhat alarmed the Muslim Leaguers. They felt that perhaps Chhatari and his followers were anxious to displace them in their leadership of the Muslim League Party. Consideration was given to the obvious fact that if Chhatari's party was broken up, the handful of Hindus would be left in the air, and finally it was agreed unanimously that the two opposition parties should remain as they were and that the idea of Chhatari's Muslims joining the Muslim League Parliamentary Party should be given up. Chhatari is very pleased with this result, and I think considers that he has out-manoeuvred his opponents.

4. After many postponements the Madhe Sahaba report and the Government resolution on it were published on the 28th March, and I enclose copies.[5] Contrary to some of the apprehensions that had been expressed, the publication has been very quietly received. The Ahrars, who initiated this trouble on the Sunni side, seem definitely unwilling at the present stage to embark on any direct action. The Shias express themselves satisfied with the conclusions, which indeed to a large extent reaffirm the existing position. Nevertheless, we cannot expect to have heard the last of this troublesome problem. All that the Government

decision amounts to is that while the Sunnis have a right to recite the Madhe Sahaba under suitable conditions and at suitable times, they must not do so to the annoyance or danger of the public, or in a manner provocative to the Shias. The question whether in practice they can be allowed to make any public recital of the Madhe Sahaba in Lucknow remains a matter for executive decision, and may prove a difficult problem. It is not, however, impossible that the two sects may reach some agreement on the lines of a conspicuous public assertion of the right of the Sunnis on a single occasion, with a clear understanding that it will not be repeated. In any case, at the moment feeling in favour of peaceful settlement is much stronger than it has been ever since this troublesome question was revived in 1935.

5. The proposals of the Government for the reform of the tenancy and land revenue law (a copy[6] of which I enclose) have now been communicated to the landlords and will be embodied in a bill which will be introduced just after Easter. The landlords are of course very critical of these proposals and show signs of getting together to oppose them. There is even some talk of Congress landlord M.L.As. throwing in their influence to secure modifications. At the same time if they can secure compromises on certain points the future may not be too black. They maintain, and probably with justice, that the 55 per cent rate of land revenue is excessive, and a strong effort will be made to get this reduced. Some of them are exploring the idea of keeping the land revenue at its present percentage of 40 and agreeing to an agricultural income-tax in addition. They seem to think that the total effect would be less severe. Also they feel that they would then know the worst, for the agricultural income-tax could hardly be put above the ordinary income-tax rates, and there is thus an assured upper limit for this tax, while if the existing rate of land revenue were reaffirmed it would be very difficult for any Government in the future to raise it. On the other hand, they feel that if the rate of percentage of land revenue is now put up as proposed by the Government, even on the understanding that an agricultural income-tax will not be imposed, it is possible that another Government in a few years' time might impose an agricultural income-tax on top of this, and taxation on such a scale would completely ruin them. The Taluqdars are still playing with the idea of countering these political proposals by legal opinions. I am afraid they are wasting their money and their energies. The Taluqdars have a pathetic faith in their *sanads*, and eminent lawyers will always give encouraging opinions at high fees. What they really need to do is to concentrate on practical opposition and establish a sound case before the public.

6. The *kisan* leaders are said to be dissatisfied with the Government proposals as not going far enough, and there is talk of another big *kisan* demonstration to be held in front of the Council House when these proposals come up for discussion after Easter. The Ministry will no doubt do all they can to discourage such a demonstration, and it will be interesting to see what happens if it materialises. The political lesson of demonstrations is being learnt very rapidly. The latest demonstration was one organised by the depressed classes on the 4th April, when a procession of several thousands marched through the streets of Lucknow and assembled at the Council House. This was organised by the non-Congress depressed class leaders who, for the most part, were defeated at the elections owing to the system of joint electorate, but who claim very vigorously to represent the real interests of the depressed classes. At any rate, it is not without significance that they have been able to organise a demonstration on this scale, which consisted, I understand, largely of delegates from a number of districts. The Premier made a long speech to them, but does not appear to have carried conviction. I think we are likely to hear more of this development, for the depressed classes are beginning to be really stirred. The Ministry have done little for them, and I do not think are likely to secure the confidence of the mass of the depressed classes.

7. The Cawnpore labour inquiry report has not made a promising start. The Premier was anxious to prepare the way both with the employers and labour before the report was published and appears to have shown an advance copy in confidence to both sides. The result has been leakage and the creation of a good deal of suspicion and prejudice, concentrated particularly in a leading article in the *Pioneer*, a copy of which I enclose. The Premier is greatly hurt at these attacks, and perturbed. The position, so far as I can judge, is this. The forecasts of the report which have appeared are substantially accurate. I do not suppose the Government attempted actually to interfere with the recommendations in the report, but they were certainly hoping for proposals on these lines and the constitution of the committee made it pretty certain that they would get them. Labour will regard these proposals as the minimum; the employers, even making allowance for the tactical necessity of denouncing what they may be prepared eventually to accept, are not, I think, likely to agree to these proposals, which seem to them to go very far. In these circumstances the prospects of agreement are not hopeful. There will be considerable temptation to the employers to challenge a strike, for economically it would seem impossible for it to be maintained more than a month or so. A strike would almost certainly be the occasion for serious disorder in Cawnpore,

and it might well turn into communal rioting. It is not impossible that the Muslim workers might take a different line to the Hindu workers and refuse to support the strike. This would almost certainly lead to communal trouble. However, it is not much use at the moment speculating as to developments that cannot be foreseen with certainty, but it may be said with confidence that Cawnpore is going to provide some difficult problems in the next few months.

8. At a recent Cabinet meeting we discussed at very short notice a rather vague scheme for the separation of executive and judicial functions of Magistrates which had been prepared by Dr. Katju, the Minister for Justice. This question of course has had a very long history, and in this Province not only was the principle accepted as long ago as the time of Sir Harcourt Butler, but a detailed scheme was then drawn out and forwarded to the Government of India for sanction. It was not accepted, and the matter has been in abeyance ever since. When the Congress Ministry took office, they were pressed to proceed with this time-honoured part of the traditional Congress programme. Dr. Katju was evidently not particularly anxious to take it up, and during the rains session indicated some very mild changes which he proposed to introduce for the purpose of satisfying the popular demand. But the Ministry were strongly denounced by the opposition, and particularly by the *Leader*, Mr. Chintamani, the editor, having been Minister in the time of Sir Harcourt Butler and one of the principal authors of the scheme then prepared. These criticisms made a considerable impression on the Ministers, and they felt it was necessary during this session to go much further. This was the origin of Dr. Katju's scheme which he intended to disclose in answer to criticisms in the budget discussion. In considering the proposals in Cabinet I made three general points:

(1) that it was by no means clear that Dr. Katju's proposals could be carried out, as he hoped, without legislation;

(2) that there was no assurance that the scheme would not involve appreciable expenditure, and that the financial implications had not been examined; and

(3) that it might turn out on examination that the Secretary of State might be concerned if the functions of the District Magistrate were to be seriously modified.

As a result of Cabinet discussion it was decided that Dr. Katju should put forward his ideas with a good deal of caution; and this he did. It was decided to appoint a committee to examine the problem. I do not think the Ministers are really very keen about pursuing this question; but the opposition as a whole, and not merely the convinced Liberals, are I am afraid, driving them into action, not because they really want this change carried out, but because they feel that they are putting the Government to some embarrassment. This is, I fear, rather typical of the opposition tactics. They took a somewhat similar line in connection with canal rates and pressed the Government strongly to reduce them, though there is no real justification for such action, and though it is to my mind quite clear that if canal rates were reduced there would be no source for making good the revenue surrendered save by increasing the land revenue, that is, taking the money out of the pockets of the landlords who have raised this question. Nevertheless, the opposition cannot resist the temptation of snatching at a temporary tactical advantage. Another matter connected with judicial procedure was discussed at the same Cabinet meeting, and that was a proposal to abolish assessors in sessions trials and extend the jury system. Here again I got the Ministry not to commit themselves, but the matter will be examined further.

9. I have recently had an interesting talk with the Deputy Inspector-General, Criminal Investigation Department,[7] who has just returned from a fairly extensive tour in the west of the Province. His observation and judgment about the working of the police administration in the districts he visited was on the whole reassuring. On the other hand, the Inspector-General of Police[8] recently complained to me that the police were feeling the lack of public acknowledgment of their services on the part of the Congress Ministry. I have taken up with the Premier, on the basis of a formidable though in all probability temporary rise in dacoity figures, the whole question of the effect of present political conditions on crime, and I have sent him a note dealing with what appear to me to be various important aspects. It is desirable to keep these things pretty constantly before the minds of the Ministers. I have been receiving during recent weeks a good many reports of the activities of Congress panchayats. To a large extent these activities appear to be beyond the reach of the law, and in so far as they attempt to settle small disputes and complaints, which would never be taken up by the police, they do not [*sic*] meet a real want in the district administration. But the right course undoubtedly is to multiply our official panchayats and not to allow these unofficial panchayats to establish themselves on a large scale. I am expecting before long to receive more detailed reports from the police about the activities of these panchayats. This is a matter also which I have taken up with the Premier who, I think, is likely to prove reasonable on the subject.

10. I mentioned in my last letter that I had taken up with the Premier the question of the circular about the administration of the Arms Act and also the praise of the Garhwali mutineers. He has not given me a written answer yet on either point, but in conversation with him two days ago I formed the opinion that he will take a more reasonable line on both points than I had at first anticipated. There is no doubt that the burden on him during this session is very heavy and he finds great difficulty in getting through his essential work.

11. You inquired whether the inadvertence, as a result of which the Arms Act circular was issued without my seeing it, was on the part of the Ministers or on the part of the departmental Secretary. No circular of this kind can issue except under the signature of the departmental Secretary, and no instance has come to my notice of any attempt to ignore this well established rule of procedure. The inadvertence was on the part of the Chief Secretary, who issued the circular without showing it to me, as he ought to have done. It is very seldom that anything of this sort happens, and our Secretariat procedure is, after some initial difficulties, working, in my judgment, very satisfactorily now.

12. During the last fortnight I have had to devote a good deal of time to questions of important appointments, particularly those of the I.C.S. officers, for the hot weather. I have found the Premier decidedly more difficult than he was previously. For this there are, in my opinion, several reasons. In the first place, some of the appointments were of great importance and practical difficulty, particularly the replacing of the two Secretaries in the Finance and Revenue departments, and this would have entailed in any case considerable discussion between us. Secondly, the Premier is finding his feet and has a closer knowledge of district administration than he had six months ago, when we were considering the cold weather postings. Consequently, he has ideas and, I fear, some prejudices, about particular officers which I have to contest. Thirdly, there is the political pressure to which Ministers are undoubtedly subjected in regard to postings and against which I have to be constantly on my guard. Though it has taken up a lot of my time as well as that of the Premier, we have finally reached conclusions which satisfy me. But it is beginning to be difficult to find good men for all our important posts, particularly in the hot weather. In order to get the two new Secretaries whom I have mentioned above, it was necessary to withdraw the District Magistrates from the very important posts of Allahabad and Agra. I have been concentrating particularly on ensuring that our more important district

posts are well and securely held. I attach the greatest importance to this, and the value of this policy has been very clearly demonstrated in the communal and other troubles that we have had in the last few months. Ineffective handling of some of these situations in the districts would have given rise to most serious embarrassments with my present Ministry. At the same time I have to see that there is at any rate a minimum of capable Europeans in the Secretariat.

Yours sincerely,
H.G. HAIG

ENCLOSURE TO NO. 34

COPY OF A LEADING ARTICLE IN THE *PIONEER*, DATED APRIL 5TH, 1938

Whose Report?

Government have behaved in a very extraordinary and, to our mind, reprehensible fashion in the matter of the Cawnpore Labour Inquiry report. Having, for reasons best known to themselves, refused to accept the suggestion of the employers that the inquiry should be a judicial one, they ought to have been particularly careful not to give the slightest cause for suspicion that they were attempting to influence the findings of the non-judicial committee which they had themselves appointed. They had no right to see the report until it was delivered to them in its final form, duly signed by the members. Our information is, however, that the first draft was read and considered by the Premier before it had received the signature even of the Chairman. Whether he suggested any emendations and, if so, whether they were adopted, we do not know. But clearly this was a highly improper procedure which must make the whole report suspect. For the obvious inference is that Government, with one eye on Labour and their own left wing, were anxious to make sure in advance that the Committee had taken a sufficiently "popular" line. A fact-finding inquiry conducted in such circumstances is a farce and Government, if only to clear themselves of suspicion, ought to lay on the table of the House the report as originally drafted by Professor Rudra.

This is not all, however. We print in our news columns today a summary of the report which we have every reason to believe is substantially accurate. We have "lifted" it, quite frankly, from a Cawnpore Labour paper controlled by a Cawnpore Labour leader who is also a Congress M.L.A. In this country some leakage of news is inevitable and, in view of the preferential treatment given by the local Congress Government to an outside newspaper not hitherto suspected of Congress sympathies, we have, we confess, ourselves been obliged on occasion to anticipate the official release of official documents. But in a case as delicate as that of Cawnpore, Government should have been at pains to see that the Inquiry Committee's report was made available to the public as soon as possible and not circulated in advance amongst its own sympathisers. Finally, we would ask whether it is a fact that the Premier has gone over the heads of Sir Tracy Gavin Jones and the Employers' Association and discussed the terms of the report with individual millowners in an endeavour to secure a favourable reception of it from at least a section of the employers. If so, he has, in our opinion, acted most improperly. We shall discuss the recommendations of the Committee tomorrow. But if it transpires that they are, in effect, the recommendations of the Congress Government, influenced by its Cawnpore Labour M.L.As., then they are not the result of an objective and impartial study of the problem and are hardly worth discussion.

35

HAIG TO LINLITHGOW
R/3/1/73

Most Secret
No. U.P.-66

April 12th, 1938

My dear Lord Linlithgow,

I am writing in answer to Your Excellency's most secret letter, dated March 24th, 1938,[9] regarding proposals for a Bill to amend the Government of India Act. I am grateful to have been placed in possession of the facts and to have been given the opportunity of offering comments. I should explain, however, as a preliminary point that I have not felt it advisable to consult any of my officers, other of course than my Secretary. The reasons for this are partly constitutional and partly practical. On the constitutional side, there is the fact that those whom Your Excellency describes as my official advisers are primarily working under the responsible Ministry. To consult them in detail on matters which are in many cases of considerable technical complexity and directly concern the interests or policy of the Provincial Government, while at the same time enjoining on them the strict necessity of concealing from the Ministers that any such consultation had taken place, or that any such proposals were under consideration, would, to my mind, be placing these officers in a somewhat unfair position, and would be a course which from my own point of view also I should constitutionally be somewhat reluctant to take. Apart from these constitutional scruples, it so happens that at the moment there are none of the Secretaries whom I could usefully consult. Gwynne, the Chief Secretary, could have given me a valuable general estimate of the probable political effect of an Amending Bill of this nature, but the officiating Chief Secretary cannot quite take his place. The Finance Secretary, Turner, might also have been in a position from his general knowledge to give a useful opinion on a number of the financial proposals, but he has just proceeded on leave, and I could certainly not usefully consult the officer who has temporarily assumed charge for a month. In the circumstances Your Excellency will doubtless excuse the fact that my comments are of a very general character.

2. The main question at this stage, however, I take to be the general policy of such a Bill, and on that I can give my own judgment so far as it goes. It must of course be based on conjecture as to the attitude of the Congress. My own feeling is that a Bill which was confined to one or two points, which it was plainly imperative to deal with, might go through with comparatively little comment or agitation. On the other hand, anything that bore the aspect of a general Amending Bill might, I think, give occasion to widespread opposition. The fact that Parliament was prepared to consider an Amending Bill of the scale indicated in the enclosures to your letter would be felt to weaken the argument, so frequently used in regard to Federation, that Parliament could not be expected to devote more time to the Government of India Act so soon after it was passed. The fact that very numerous amendments were being made, hardly any of which could be regarded as desirable from the popular point of view, might stimulate opposition. Indeed, the opposition might be considerably influenced by the size of the Bill and the time it would take to get through Parliament; in other words, the nature of the target on which opposition would be able to concentrate. My general feeling may be summed up as follows:

(*a*) Any Bill will give occasion for working up some feeling.

(*b*) A Bill which appears to be of a comprehensive character would give occasion for working up feeling on a larger scale.

(*c*) If the Bill can be confined to obviously essential and as far as possible non-controversial amendments, such as that arising out of the Niemeyer proposals,[10] then I do not think the opposition would be likely to be appreciable.

(*d*) On the other hand, anything in the nature of a controversial political amendment, such for instance as the one dealing with the establishment for reserved posts, (clause 26) is bound to give opportunity for agitation.[11]

(*e*) My own view is that the temptation to put right numbers of minor difficulties or ambiguities in the Act should be resisted. We submitted to these for many years under the old Government of India Act, and they do not in my judgment justify running appreciable political risks.

3. There is another consideration on which I have not hitherto touched, and that is whether there is any likelihood that the introduction of Federation will cause any amendment in the Act. If so, it might be better to postpone the amendments now proposed until the Federation situation is clearer. Indeed, the question whether any formidable agitation will be roused on the basis of an Amending Bill next autumn depends to my mind very largely on the Federation position. If the Congress have made up their minds to fight vigorously on the Federation issue, then they will welcome this Bill as giving them additional opportunities for criticism. If, on the other hand, there is any possibility of Federation coming in without a formidable struggle, then certain amendments to the Act might be got through without serious trouble. In general I should be disposed to advise waiting. We do not want during the next six months to introduce any new controversial points into the Provincial situation, or to accentuate the issues of independence which are never far below the surface, but are nevertheless better left where they are.

4. I would add that if it is eventually decided to proceed with a Bill on these lines, I should regard it as most desirable constitutionally that the Provincial Governments should be consulted formally on all points which have any bearing on Provincial interests or policy. I think the Ministers might very justifiably resent any proposals to introduce amendments in such matters without giving them an opportunity of even expressing their views.

5. I add some comments[12] of a general nature on certain of the provisions of the Draft Bill.

Yours sincerely,
HARRY HAIG

36

DONALDSON TO LAITHWAITE
R/3/1/73

Confidential
D.O. No. 1220-G.S.P.

Camp,
April 14th, 1938

My dear Laithwaite,

You may have noted on page 3 of the *Hindustan Times* of April 13th, second column, a statement that Police dressed in white khadi uniform can now be seen controlling the traffic at Hazratganj in Lucknow city and that this is connected with the resolution passed by the United Provinces Assembly in its first session. That resolution is dealt with in His Excellency's secret D.O. to His Excellency the Governor-General, No. U.P.-8 of October 7th, 1937,[13] and connected correspondence. I am desired to let you know that this statement is quite untrue. The Superintendent of Police, Lucknow put the Traffic Police at the busy crossing at the foot of Hazratganj into white coats so that they should be more easily visible to motorists at night. These coats are made of mill-made white drill. His Excellency does not propose to raise the question of correcting this misstatement with his Ministers, as he thinks it better to let the khadi resolution lie peacefully dormant.

Yours sincerely,
J.C. DONALDSON

37

HAIG TO LINLITHGOW
Telegram
R/3/1/73

Important
No. 141-G

April 21st, 1938

Your telegram No. 570-G. of April 17th.[14] I am feeling more and more strongly the importance of maintaining position of Public Service Commission as against Government. There is no doubt that my Ministers dislike the necessity of having to refer appointments to Commission and there is a marked tendency to try and encroach on the authority of the

Commission. The object of Ministers I fear is to have much greater control over appointments in order that they may exercise political patronage, the very danger to provide against which the Commissions were appointed. I would therefore regard question of pay of two of the Members of the Commission not merely from point of view stated in paragraph No. 2 of your telegram (i.e., to secure persons who would be free from sinister private influence) but equally from point of view of obtaining persons who can be trusted to maintain an independent attitude as against Government. Taking this view I am naturally very much opposed to reducing pay of Members of Commissions at the suggestion of Ministers.

2. In any case I see no necessity for taking up this matter at present moment. It is not, for reasons I have indicated above, a suitable item to include in a Ministerial programme of retrenchments. The practical question whether the pay should be changed will arise when new appointments have to be made. I see no reason for taking anticipatory decisions now which might be unsuitable when vacancies actually arise.

3. The pay of Chairmen here is Rs. 2,500, and of Members Rs. 2,000. At present I see no reason why these salaries should be reduced. The pay of Secretary and Assistant Secretary is also reasonable. To sum up I am on merits opposed to any change now in rates of pay fixed and I am particularly opposed to any changes on recommendations of Ministers.

38

HAIG TO LINLITHGOW
R/3/1/73

Confidential
No. U.P.-70

April 22nd, 1938

My dear Lord Linlithgow,

I wish to report for Your Excellency's information, and also with a view to obtaining your advice on a point of law, a question which has arisen in regard to the applicability of Section 299 (3) of the Government of India Act to the United Provinces Tenancy Bill. This Bill was down for introduction in the Legislative Assembly on the 20th April, and the programme for the remainder of the session was directly dependent on this date being observed. The question whether Section 299 (3) applied to the provisions of this Bill and consequently whether my previous sanction was required had not been raised during the departmental discussions, and the point had not attracted my attention. At a Cabinet meeting however on the 19th April when the draft Bill was for the first time available, the Premier stated that this question was likely to be raised. He argued at some length that Section 299 (3) did not in fact apply, and stated that if such a wide interpretation were given to the terms of that Section as to bring this Bill within it, it would mean that no Bill making any change in tenancy rights could be introduced without the sanction of the Governor and, in view of paragraph XVII of the Instrument of Instructions, without being referred subsequently for the consideration of the Governor-General. He said that he understood from the general trend of the discussions at the Joint Select Committee that there was no intention to restrict to such a degree the discretion of the provincial legislatures in dealing with tenancy problems. He also stated that in the case of certain tenancy legislation recently passed by the Bihar Legislature no previous sanction was given by the Governor, nor was the legislation reserved for the consideration of the Governor-General.

2. I said that while giving due weight to these considerations I had to try and interpret the section of the Government of India Act as it stands, and that on a first perusal it appeared to me that its terms were sufficiently wide to cover the United Provinces Tenancy Bill. I said, however, that I should be glad to have the opinion of the Advocate-General on the point.

3. Accordingly the matter was referred to the Advocate-General who, later in the day, furnished me with the opinion, a copy of which I enclose. His conclusion was that no provision of the Bill falls within the provisions of Section 299 (3) of the Government of India Act. Thereupon I wrote a note, copy of which I enclose, stating that in spite of the opinion of the Advocate-General, I entertained considerable doubt whether Section 299 (3) does or does not apply to the Bill. At that time the matter had only reached the stage of discussion inside the Government, and I therefore said that from the practical point of view it seemed unnecessary for me to go out of my way to give previous sanction in view of the opinion of the Advocate-General. At the same time I made it clear that by refraining in these circumstances from giving previous sanction, I did not in any way pre-judge the question whether in accordance with the provisions of Section XVII of the Instrument of Instructions I should feel it necessary subsequently to reserve the Bill for the consideration of the Governor-General.

4. At that time it was not present to my mind that the question was likely to be raised in the Assembly in such a way that I should be called upon to

give a formal decision. This, however, is what happened. When the Revenue Minister moved for the introduction of the Bill, the Leader of the Opposition raised the question at once whether the previous sanction of the Governor had been obtained. After some discussion the Speaker made a written reference to me under rule 24 (3) of the United Provinces Legislative Assembly Rules, and I sent him a reply according my previous sanction to the introduction of the Bill. Copies of these documents are enclosed. When the point was raised in this formal and public manner I was not prepared to hold that my previous sanction was not required.

5. Your Excellency will observe that I refrained from committing myself to a definite legal view as to whether Section 299 (3) applied or not. I had had no time to consider the matter carefully, the only legal opinion I had received, namely that of the Advocate-General, was opposed to my own view, and my Ministry were extremely anxious that, if possible, an official ruling on the point of law contrary to their view should not be given at this stage. In the circumstances while I felt that it was necessary to proceed on the assumption that sanction was required and that the most practical course in any case was to give my sanction, I left my considered view about the application of Section 299 (3) for further determination. The position now is that it is still open to me, after obtaining further advice, either to hold under paragraph XVII of the Instrument of Instructions that it is necessary, or in the alternative, that it is not necessary, for me to reserve the Bill for the consideration of the Governor-General. In these circumstances I should be most grateful for Your Excellency's view, after consulting your legal advisers, as to whether Section 299 (3) of the Government of India Act does or does not apply to the United Provinces Tenancy Bill. My own view is that such provisions as the modification of the landlord's rights in *sir* land and the grant of hereditary rights to tenants do amount to modifications of rights in land, those rights including the right of a landlord to decide how and by whom the land should cultivated, at what rate of rent and so on. I may mention that I have verified from Bihar the fact that previous sanction was not given to the recent Bihar tenancy legislation. The point does not seem to have definitely arisen.

6. Further action dependent on the interpretation of Section 299 (3) will not have to be taken with reference to the present Bill until it is passed, and this is not likely to be before next August or even perhaps September. At the same time I should be grateful if I could have Your Excellency's advice as early as is convenient. The question of the application of Section 299 (3) will also be coming up in connection with the Land Revenue Bill, not yet drafted, which will provide for raising the present percentage of

assets to be taken as land revenue by the Government from 40 per cent to 55 per cent. This again would appear to me to attract the provisions of Section 299 (3) but I should be grateful if Your Excellency could give me an opinion about this also. Though the Bill has not been drafted, I send a copy[15] of the conclusions of the Government on this point, paragraphs 61 *et seq* of which show the line that the Bill will follow. I enclose also a copy of the United Provinces Tenancy Bill.[16]

Yours sincerely,
HARRY HAIG

ENCLOSURE 1 TO NO. 38

OPINION OF ASTHANA

April 19th, 1938

Chief Secretary,

I have looked into the provisions of the new Tenancy Bill rather hurriedly during the time at my disposal. So far as I have been able to make out there are no provisions in the Bill which affect the rights of the landlords in the land except those relating to *sir*. It might be argued on behalf of the landlords that the provision as to the extinction of *sir* rights and creation of hereditary tenants in *sir* land is a modification of the landlords' rights in land within the meaning of Section 299 (3) of the Government of India Act and consequently the Bill requires the previous sanction of His Excellency the Governor.

Reading Sections 299 and 300 together (the former Section lays down restriction on legislative powers and the latter on executive powers), it is clear that both the Sections relate to the relation between the State and the landowners. There is no question of the transference to public ownership of any land, nor of the extinguishment or modification of rights in the land, including rights or privileges in respect of land revenue in the present Bill. The last clause is rather important because it indicates the nature of the rights which are contemplated by the Act, and the same rights are referred to in Section 300. If there were any legislation modifying, i.e. taking away any portion of the rights acquired by or conferred upon landlords it might have fallen within the provisions of Section 299 (3). But the provisions of the present Bill only govern the relation between the landlord and the tenant, namely, *sir* holder and his sub-tenant, making the latter hereditary tenants; they do not amount to extinguishment or modification of the landlords' rights. Their right to eject the hereditary tenants under certain conditions remains in tact as well as their right to cultivate the *sir* land by themselves is recognised. Moreover, the *sir* rights which are statutory rights of cultivating the land, have been provided for by a succession of Tenancy Acts and can, therefore, be regulated by legislation without affecting the proprietary rights of the landlords.

As there is no question of any expropriation of land by the State, or of modification of owner's rights in land in favour of the State, I do not think any provision of the proposed Bill falls within the provisions of Section 299 (3) of the Government of India Act and, consequently, the previous sanction of His Excellency the Governor is not required for its introduction.

N.P. ASTHANA
Advocate-General, United Provinces

ENCLOSURE 2 TO NO. 38

NOTE BY HAIG

April 19th, 1938

I have read the opinion of the Advocate-General with attention. He holds that no provision of the Bill falls within the provisions of Section 299 (3) of the Government of India Act, and consequently that previous sanction of the Governor is not required for its introduction. It is, as I think the Advocate-General himself feels, a matter of some difficulty to decide on the interpretation of Section 299 (3). For instance, the Advocate-General bases his opinion to some considerable extent on the view that the Section concerns the relation between the State and the landowners and not the relation between landowners and tenants. But I should find great difficulty in holding that Section 299 (3) applied to a case where the State were transferring the rights of landlords to the State, but did not apply to a case in which the State transferred the rights of landlords to tenants or any other third party. I only wish to make it plain at this stage that I do myself entertain considerable doubt whether Section 299 (3) does or does not apply to the Bill.

2. The immediate question, however, for decision is whether my previous sanction to the Bill should or should not be given. The Advocate-General has given his opinion that my previous sanction is not necessary. Even if my previous sanction were necessary, there would be no question of my withholding it in view of the terms of paragraph XVII of the Instrument of

Instructions. Therefore it seems to me unnecessary from the practical point of view for me to go out of my way to give a previous sanction which may not be required, more particularly in view of the fact that if previous sanction in fact is required and has been mistakenly omitted, the omission can be cured by the grant of subsequent assent under the provision of Section 109 (2) of the Government of India Act.

3. I must however make it quite plain that in refraining in these circumstances from taking action to give previous sanction, I do not in any way pre-judge the question whether, in accordance with the provisions of paragraph XVII of the Instrument of Instructions, I shall feel it necessary subsequently to reserve the Bill for the consideration of the Governor-General.

H.G. HAIG

ENCLOSURE 3 TO NO. 38

EXTRACT FROM THE *PIONEER*
DATED APRIL 21ST, 1938

United Provinces Legislative Assembly, April 20th, 1938

The Minister of Revenue sought leave of the House to introduce the United Provinces Tenancy Bill.

An Objection

The Nawab of Chhatari said that the Bill could be introduced in the Legislature only with the sanction of the Governor under Section 299 of the Government of India Act. He asked Government whether they had secured the sanction of the Governor.

The Minister of Revenue asked under what Section of the Rules of Business the Nawab of Chhatari objected to the motion.

The Speaker pointed out that he was doubtful whether the question required a ruling. According to the relevant Section of the Government of India Act it was primarily a matter between the Governor and the Ministers. He did not want to make his rulings cheap by giving them where they were not needed.

Raja Bisheshwar Dayal Seth (Independent) suggested that as an objection had been raised the Speaker should postpone this item and in the meantime refer to the Governor whether he had given his sanction.

Sheikh Muhammad Habibullah asked Government to state whether they had received the Governor's sanction for the introduction of the Bill.

The Premier: Government are doing only what they are entitled to do.

Nawab Sir Muhammad Yusuf: Does that mean admission of the fact that Government have got the sanction?

The Premier: It was not an admission, but assertion of a claim.

Premier's Reply

There was some further discussion when the Premier intervening said that he had hoped that every member of the House wanted to enlarge their rights and privileges. He had hoped that none wanted to cripple their rights and privileges. But yet such an objection had been raised. Government were quite clear in their mind that the Bill could be introduced without the previous sanction of the Governor. He pointed out that Government could if they wanted get the sanction of the Governor within a few minutes, but they did not want to cripple the privileges of the House.

The Nawab of Chhatari said that it was not Premier Pant who made the last speech but the politician Pant and he had tried to put the Opposition in the wrong. The Premier had often referred to the limitations of the Government of India Act when the Opposition urged the reduction of certain posts. But now the Premier objected to the Opposition referring to its limitations. As they were working the Government of India Act it was but proper that they should follow it in letter as well as spirit.

Advocate-General's View

The Advocate-General, when asked to express his opinion, said that the question of sanction concerned the Ministers and the Governor. It did not concern the Speaker. The Speaker should follow the rules of procedure laid down for the House. As regards the necessity of previous sanction of the Governor he pointed that Section 299 referred to by the Nawab of Chhatari could apply only in cases where some rights were being taken away or modified.

The Speaker said that he had decided to refer to the Governor whether it was necessary to obtain his sanction in the matter.

Meanwhile they would proceed with other business on the agenda.

* * * 17

Governor's Sanction

At this stage the Speaker said that he had received the Governor's reply to the question referred to him. The reply was:

"The question whether the previous sanction of the Governor to the introduction of the United Provinces Tenancy Bill is required under the terms of the Government of India Act appears to be one of some doubt. In the circumstances I consider it prudent that I should proceed on the assumption that previous sanction is necessary and I hereby accord sanction to the introduction of the Bill."

The House then granted leave for the introduction of the United Provinces Tenancy Bill and the Minister of Revenue introduced it.

The House then adjourned till Thursday.

[*The following Enclosures are omitted:* Enclosure 4: Copy of Rule 24 (3) of the U.P. Legislative Assembly; Enclosure 5: Copy of letter dated April 20th, 1938 from Secretary to U.P. Legislative Assembly to Secretary to U.P. Governor; Enclosure 6: Copy of letter dated April 20th, 1938 from Secretary to U.P. Governor to Secretary to U.P. Legislative Assembly (giving Haig's sanction as cited above).]

39

HAIG TO LINLITHGOW
R/3/1/73

Confidential
No. U.P.-71

April 23rd, 1938

My dear Lord Linlithgow,

I am writing in answer to Your Excellency's secret and personal letter, dated March 26th, 1938, regarding the adequacy of the superior staff of the administration to deal with existing conditions of work and conditions that might conceivably arise.[18] As a preliminary general point, I would mention that it has been the traditional system of administration in India to work with an absolute minimum superior staff. The reason doubtless is that the superior staff is, as compared with other countries, very well paid, and in order to restrict the consequent financial burden to reasonable proportions, the numbers have been very rigidly limited. This is a point which cannot fail to strike anyone who has seen something of the system of administration in England, and I feel sure Your Excellency will agree that our staffs, and more especially in the Provinces, are conspicuously small compared with the standards that prevail in the important Government offices in England.

2. I will take paragraph 3 of Your Excellency's letter, and give my detailed answers under the headings there suggested.

(*a*) and (*b*) – (1) The introduction of Provincial Autonomy, but more especially the existence of the Congress Ministry, has imposed an immensely increased strain on the Headquarter Secretariat. A larger Legislature and a more active public life, which are essential concomitants of the new Constitution, would in any case have meant a very considerable addition to the work of the Secretariat. But the serious strain has come from the existence of the Congress Ministry, and from the date of its taking charge. The reasons are clear enough.

(2) The Ministry came in on a wave of popular enthusiasm and announcing that they were the servants of the people and were there for the purpose of redressing every kind of grievance or injustice. The result was an enormous flood of applications from all over the Province on every conceivable petty and personal matter, and in the earlier stages at any rate the Ministers in their inexperience insisted on treating these applications with great attention. This involved a very large increase in the routine work of the Secretariat. I am told, for instance, that in the Revenue Department, over a period of six months, there has been an increase of 50 per cent. in the number of references. I do not however wish it to be understood that the whole of this increase can be attributed to mere routine and unimportant applications. Every kind of question has been ventilated.

(3) The most important cause of the increased burden on the Secretariat has been the policy of the Ministry in undertaking far-reaching changes in almost all Departments of Government simultaneously, or making enquiries with a view to such changes. In all cases the Ministry has been acting moreover under a sense of extreme urgency. Their followers have been impatient for immediate results, and they have endeavoured to secure such results often with little regard to what is physically possible. They have in consequence been driving the Secretariat machine at an excessive speed. Among the major problems that have been taken up during the past eight months are the examination of fundamental portions of the structure of Government, such as the rent and revenue system, the local self-government system, the excise system, the system of honorary magistrates and assistant

collectors, jail administration, police organisation, the amalgamation of the engineering services, and so on. Besides this, they have been examining the vital and complicated problems connected with rural development, and questions of debt legislation, trade disputes legislation, the whole education system, measures against corruption, and irrigation rates. They have also had to deal with a elaborate system of regulation of sugar factories, and the examination of large numbers of suggestions put forward in order to secure economy. All these matters have required intensive work at high pressure in the Secretariat, and work largely of an original and not of a routine character. Innumerable committees, official, mixed, select committees of the Legislature, have been set up. Nearly all have involved the attendance of a Secretary, Deputy Secretary or Special Officer, and the recommendations and proceedings of all of them must be considered in detail in the Secretariat. While the Legislature is sitting Secretaries have often been attending one and sometimes two committees from 7-30 a.m., and possibly others in the evening and on Sundays.

(4) Since the middle of July, when the present Government assumed office, up to the 31st March, the Legislative Assembly sat on 66 days and the Legislative Council on 33 days. The existence of a Second Chamber, even though of only 60 members, has increased Secretariat work considerably, since a number of questions are asked in the Legislative Council and non-official resolutions are discussed. The new Legislative Assembly of 228 is much larger than the old Legislative Council of 123. The number of questions asked is very large, and most Secretaries complain of the great strain on their time caused by the questions during the session of the Legislative Assembly. The system recently introduced, by which the answers to all questions are translated both into Urdu and Hindi, also means an appreciable increase in work for the Secretariat establishment.

(5) As Secretary to the Cabinet a considerable additional burden has fallen on the Chief Secretary, who is responsible for the circulation of the agenda and notes on matters for discussion, as well as for the minutes of proceedings. Cabinet meetings have often been held at short notice, and in such cases the chief burden of seeing that cases are ready falls on the Chief Secretary. The attitude of the Ministry towards the Services has, partly owing to inexperience, been very much more suspicious than in the past, and it has fallen to the Chief Secretary to explain and defend the actions of officials. Ministers have been receiving numerous complaints against officials, many of them without foundation or in which the facts have been entirely distorted. The Chief Secretary has had a most difficult

task in presenting the case for the administrative machinery and in dissuading Ministers from courses which would impair its efficiency.

(6) The Finance Department has had to prepare three budgets instead of one during the last financial year: a budget for 1937-8 for the Minority Ministry, another budget involving drastic changes for the present Ministry, and the ordinary budget for the year 1938-9.

(7) With this immense increase in the volume and speed of the work, the abolition of the move to the hills has undoubtedly told heavily on the Secretariat and its effect has perhaps been cumulative. The strain of intensive and unremitting office work in the hot weather is probably greater than that of the more active and varied work of the District Officer, which is also normally conducted under conditions of less pressure.

(8) When the present Ministry came into office, we had six Civilian Secretaries and two Irrigation Secretaries (Chief Engineers). The Secretariat work has been taken away from the Chief Engineers and a seventh Civilian Secretary has been added. This new Secretary has been able to take over the work of the Buildings and Roads Branch also, which was previously dealt with by the Revenue Secretary. But on the whole his appointment has given little relief to the ordinary Secretariat organisation. There are at present seven Deputy Secretaries, and a certain number of officers have been temporarily working on special duty. But these appointments have not gone far enough to meet the additional strain on the Secretaries. We probably need one or two extra Secretaries; but apart from the question of expense, it is not going to be easy to find them without weakening other parts of the administrative machine.

(9) I should add in mitigation of this very gloomy picture that I think there is reason to suppose that the volume of work now is likely to diminish rather than increase. Important progress has been made with many of the big questions in which the Ministry have been interesting themselves, and it does not look as if there are many more big questions which they can take up. The flood of miscellaneous applications has undoubtedly diminished. Even so, the burden on the Secretariat has undoubtedly increased permanently, and before long it will be necessary to consider some permanent increase in the staff.

(10) With regard to the work of the District Officers it is not easy to form a definite opinion. When the present Ministry came into office, District Officers suffered, like the Secretariat, from the immense flood of applications arising from the new conditions. They were also greatly plagued by every kind of Congress busybody, and they were faced by

innumerable administrative difficulties, great and small, arising from the new conditions and new policies.

In all these matters I think there has been a great improvement in the last three or four months, and the District Officers are much less worried than they used to be by perplexing and irritating problems. But even now one or two troublesome Congress leaders in a District, particularly if they are M.L.As., can cause a great deal of trouble to the District Officer by sponsoring and instigating unfounded complaints and bringing them to the notice of the Ministry. On the other hand, one of the hopeful features in the situation is that a great number of the more moderate Congressmen show signs of settling down into public-spirited and useful citizens who are not an embarrassment to District Officers, but on the contrary are helpful. During the last few months the communal situation has put an appreciable strain on District Officers throughout the Province, and in some places a very severe strain. Relations between landlords and tenants also in some areas give cause for anxiety and increase the work of District Officers. But on the whole the main strain was, I think, caused by the activities of Congressmen in the first two or three months after the Congress Ministry came in, and that I believe to have diminished now considerably.

(*c*) I am not sure that the burden can be said to have shown itself more markedly in the case of officers of a particular standing. It is a question rather of the posts than of the seniority of the officers. Actually most of our Secretaries have recently been officers of round about 20 years' service. There is no doubt that a great burden has been placed on the better European officers, who have not only been filling some of the most important Secretariat posts, but nearly all the most important District charges.

(*d*) I have paid a great deal of attention to the filling of key positions. Recently we have lost, either permanently or temporarily, no less than five of the six Secretaries who were functioning when the new Constitution came in, and it has been a matter of considerable difficulty to replace them. As I mentioned to you in a recent letter, in order to secure satisfactory Secretaries in the Revenue and Finance Departments, I have had to take away the District Magistrates of Allahabad and Agra. This illustrates the kind of difficulty I am now experiencing. I have barely enough good men to fill the key positions, particularly in the hot weather. I also have a certain amount of difficulty with the Premier over postings, but I have succeeded in getting decisions satisfactory to myself without any major disagreement.

(*e*) From what I have said above, it will be apparent that I have really no reserve at the present moment. Every good man in the Province is being employed in an important post, from which it would be difficult to spare him; and if the situation were to deteriorate further, I might have to ask Your Excellency to let me have back some of the good men whom we have recently placed at the disposal of the Government of India. For instance, the Delhi administration at present has two of our men, Hume and Evans, who would be of great value to us. We have given Rampur State an excellent officer as Finance Minister. I know it is important from the point of view of the State that he should remain, but if circumstances necessitated it, I might have to ask for his return.[19] Among the junior officers I may mention that when as a result of the Allahabad riots we wanted to send a European Joint Magistrate to Allahabad to take the place of one who had been granted leave, it proved absolutely impossible to find one. This will perhaps bring into relief our very serious shortage of European officers in the junior ranks – a point which I have stressed in connection with the recruitment to the Political Department and the taking by them of two of our European officers in the last two years.

(*f*) I would mention the possibilities under three heads:

(1) The normal working of the Constitution under present conditions. As I have already explained, I have no reserve available except by asking the Government of India to return valuable officers who have been lent to them. I hope that we may be able to carry on without any such necessity; but while our posts are adequately filled at the moment, we have no margin of good men. Men of the type required cannot be improvised at short notice from anywhere. If for any reason we were to lose some more of our good men, I see no course except to ask the Government of India to let us have some of our valuable officers back again.

(2) Section 93 situation. This would no doubt result in an increase of work under the head of Law and Order; but many of the causes given above for increase of work, particularly those connected with the Legislature and the complete overhaul of policies would cease to exist. I am disposed to think therefore that the personnel sufficient to man the Province effectively under present conditions would also be sufficient to deal with a Section 93 situation. Moreover, in a temporary emergency of this kind we could, if absolutely necessary, reduce our settlement operations and thereby release a certain number of valuable officers.

(3) An emergency caused by the outbreak of war would certainly make heavy demands on the personnel. The numerous activities connected with a war, combined possibly with very difficult political conditions, might make it essential to have assistance. On the other hand, it might be easier to obtain that assistance, as the less important activities connected with war conditions could be carried out by men of less specialised ability than

those required for our ordinary administration. At the same time one of the great difficulties would be that whereas ordinarily for men of this type one might look to the Army, this source would obviously be closed. We might perhaps in an emergency of this kind be able to secure the return of a certain number of retired officers. Special measures of permanent recruitment would of course take effect slowly, and I would not recommend that anything should be done which would upset the balance of the cadre and give rise to many difficulties in the future. But I do think that steps should be taken at once to recalculate our cadre so as to provide for the large demands which the Government of India make on it. Our cadre provides only for ten superior posts under the Government of India. Actually we have 27 officers serving under the Government of India. This is a very serious depletion of our resources. I also attach the greatest importance to the maintenance of the full proportion of European officers which, under the Secretary of State's orders on the Lee Commission Report,[20] we are entitled to have. I may mention that it was accepted that for the United Provinces the proportion of European officers should be well over 50 per cent. I have not at the moment the exact figure, but my recollection is that the proportion of European to Indian officers, was to be 45 to 35. In this connection I would like to stress once more one expedient by which I consider the Government of India could give us some really valuable and immediate assistance, and that is that the present system of recruitment for the Political Department should be discontinued. It constitutes a continual drain on the very limited number of European officers in the Province, and under present conditions I regard it as definitely dangerous to continue this drain. It comes to this, that we are not retaining the proportion of European officers which it was decided was necessary for the proper administration of the Province. To show how that proportion is being upset by the demands of the Government of India, I would mention that out of 27 officers of this Province serving under the Government of India, which includes those who have gone to the Political Department, 21 are Europeans and only 6 Indians. We have at present 11 men in the Political Department alone, none of whom are Indians.

(*g*) I have already in my remarks on the Secretariat referred to the increased strain imposed on Secretariat officers by the discontinuance of the move to the hills. In addition to the Secretariat, a large number of officers have in the past been entitled to recess in Naini Tal for various periods ranging from one month to three months. This includes Members of the Board of Revenue, all Heads of Departments, Commissioners, Superintending Engineers, Deputy Inspectors-General of Police and so on. If this privilege had been withdrawn, it would have reacted very seriously on the contentment of the Services. I am glad to say that as a result of a Cabinet meeting held a few days ago the Ministry have agreed to allow recessing officers to continue to go to Naini Tal for the periods previously sanctioned. But they have insisted that any clerks or peons they take up must be taken at their own expense and not that of Government. In view of the fact that Government have cancelled the hill move for themselves and the Secretariat on the ground of the expenditure, it would have been impossible for them to agree to incur expense on behalf of Heads of Departments, etc., going to Naini Tal for their own convenience. But I do not think the new rule will be felt as a serious grievance, or will impose any unreasonable financial burden on the officers. On the whole I was considerably reassured by the general tone of my Ministers in discussing this matter. It was clear that they had no desire to pin-prick officers or to deprive them unreasonably of old-established privileges. Nevertheless, in minor matters there are doubtless constant little rubs, and I do not underestimate their cumulative importance. All I can say is that at the moment the main body of superior officers seems to be content to go on with their work, recognising that it is full of interest, though at the same time full of difficulties, and hoping that gradually conditions, at present irksome, will improve. If those anticipations are not fulfilled, I fear that after a year or two we may be faced with a considerable drain from officers retiring earlier than they would have normally or taking proportionate pensions.[21]

Yours sincerely,
HARRY HAIG

40

HAIG TO LINLITHGOW
R/3/1/73

Secret — *April 23rd, 1938*
No. U.P.-72

My dear Lord Linlithgow,

I mentioned in my last fortnightly report, dated April 8th, that though the communal trouble had subsided, acute feeling still persisted in Allahabad and considerable nervousness, and one could not be sure that there might not be another flare up. Not long after I wrote this, there was a further outbreak in Allahabad due to the discovery of a pig's head in a mosque. The trouble was strongly and effectively handled, and after a day or two things settled down again. My anticipation about the attitude of the Premier towards this communal trouble has been fulfilled. He was anxious that the firmest action should be taken in Allahabad, and he has, without any prompting from me, issued a letter dealing with the reporting of communal speeches, a copy of which I enclose. When I remember his attitude eight months ago towards any restrictions on public speaking, I am encouraged to feel that the logic of events is having its natural effects, and that some of the Premier's theories are beginning to yield before the stubbornness of facts. Another interesting development was that the Premier, again without any suggestion from me, ordered the prosecution of a Hindu under Section 153 (A) for making a dangerous communal speech. It does not of course follow that because he is prepared to take action of this kind in the case of communal trouble, which from every point of view he is most anxious to stop, he would be equally ready to act against other kinds of trouble. Still it is something that in communal cases when he is once convinced that speeches are having a plainly deleterious effect, he is prepared to stop them; but he wants to be convinced by facts observed by himself and is not inclined to act on mere apprehensions, particularly those of others.

2. In this connection his attitude towards the Pipridih train dacoity is interesting. I have reported separately to Your Excellency about this, explaining the reasons for the Police reticence on the subject.[22] But the Premier was evidently uneasy at the possibility that this was the work of political revolutionaries, and I think this is precisely the kind of incident which would lead him to re-examine the policy he has hitherto been pursuing towards political criminals. He has always hitherto persuaded himself that there was no real risk of any recrudescence of violence owing to the policy he was pursuing.

3. While I was at Dehra Dun for the Easter holidays, I went over to Hardwar to see the Kumbh Mela. The Mela had attracted an enormous crowd, and though estimates of numbers must be highly speculative, it seemed to be agreed on all hands that the pilgrims present on the great day, April 13th, must have numbered over a million, and that this was the largest gathering that had ever taken place. The relations between the crowds and the Government officials, particularly the Police, had been one of the most cordial and satisfactory character. The great day passed off without accident, but just as the authorities were beginning to

congratulate themselves on the successful results, the whole situation was changed by a disastrous fire which took place on the 15th and burnt out the whole of a large temporary bazar. The question as to what precautions are possible against fire under these conditions will no doubt be examined in the course of the enquiry which is now being made; but once the fire started with a strong wind blowing, the thatched huts were ablaze instantly and it seemed unlikely that any precautionary measures could have stopped the fire.[23] There was little or no loss of life, but very serious losses of shopkeepers' goods of all kinds, particularly cloth and silk. A most unfortunate feature was that in the excitement of the moment a dangerous fight broke out between the Police and the public. A rumour, quite groundless, was put about that the Police were looting property and the crowd attacked them. For a time the situation looked very threatening, but eventually the fight was stopped without any loss of life. I was in Hardwar the next day, but the officers in charge considered that the temper of the people was still very uncertain and they made a point of my not visiting the scene of the fire. Actually feelings have quietened down and there have been no more incidents, but it was an unfortunate end to a gathering which up to that time had been conducted with marked success and goodwill. One point struck me which has some bearing on what I said in paragraph 2 of my letter of April 8th. The gathering appears to have been the largest ever known. It is said that times are comparatively prosperous, particularly in the Punjab from which a large number of the pilgrims came, and that the Pandits had spread it about that this was a quite exceptionally auspicious conjunction of the stars. But when allowance is made for this, I think it is fair to conclude that this enormous gathering of pilgrims shows that the Hindu religion is at the moment exceedingly vigorous and displaying a very marked vitality. That is my general judgment, as I have indicated in some previous letters, and I think the Kumbh Mela at Hardwar offers confirmation of this view. When an attempt was made at the time of the general election to use Hindu religious feeling for political purposes in opposition to the Congress, it was a complete failure. But it would be a great mistake to conclude from that that Hindu religious feeling in its own sphere is not an exceedingly important and vigorous factor in the life of this Province.

4. The Tenancy Bill was introduced in the Assembly on the 20th April, and I have reported separately to Your Excellency the developments which resulted in my giving previous sanction to its introduction. There will be an important debate on the motion for Select Committee, and after that the session will end. The landlords are making vigorous protests and are

trying to organise their opposition. I am inclined to hope that in the end this measure will go through as the result of certain concessions made to the landlords without involving a conflict between the two Houses. The two main points on which the landlords will concentrate, and with justice, are the provisions about *sir* and the provisions about ejectment. I hope that the Government may be prepared to make substantial concessions on both these points. The vital question of the pitch of assessment for land revenue is not included in this Bill and will have to be taken up in a separate measure which has not yet been drafted. This is probably the least reasonable of all the Government's proposals. After further examination of the matter I am beginning to feel that 55 per cent of assets is clearly an unreasonable figure, and I think the Government will have to modify their proposals later in this respect. It is even possible that they may tackle the subject on slightly different lines by imposing a graduated cess on the higher land revenue payers. This would certainly be a much simpler solution than the one they have hitherto been considering. In view of the fact that the Tenancy Bill contains over 300 clauses I should not be altogether surprised to find that the measure was still under consideration when I return from leave in the middle of September.

5. I mentioned in my last letter the proposed *kisan* demonstration which was being organised by the left wing to protest against the inadequacy of the Government's tenancy proposals. The official Congress machinery was brought into action vigorously in order to oppose this. The *kisans* were told that they should demonstrate in their own districts on the 17th April, expressing their support of the Government proposals, instead of marching into Lucknow on the 20th to oppose them. Jawaharlal Nehru also made a strong statement opposing this march on the 20th. I attach copies of his statement and of the circular sent out by the Provincial Congress Committee. As a result of these measures, the *kisan* demonstration was a failure. The supporters of it tried their best, but in the end collected only some five or six thousand *kisans*, and feeling their weakness, appear to have toned down their opposition to the Government. In fact the result of this trial of strength was a very definite victory for the official machine as against the left wing. I am told that the majority of the demonstrators came from the neighbouring district of Bara Banki. The last demonstration which took place in March consisted almost entirely of *kisans* from the districts of Unao and Rae Bareli, and at the time it was said that it was going to be very difficult to get them to come again as they were disappointed with the results. The fact that on this occasion the *kisans* had

to be collected from a different district bears out the correctness of that anticipation. Nevertheless, the habit of demonstration goes on, and only two days ago I understand that a thousand *kisans* marched in from an area not far from Lucknow to demonstrate against certain orders passed by the Joint Magistrate[24] in connection with a local agrarian dispute, and they too after having interviewed the Deputy Commissioner[25] proceeded to present themselves like other demonstrators in front of the Council Chamber.

6. At a recent Cabinet meeting a long discussion took place about the procedure in connection with the Cawnpore Labour Enquiry Report. The Premier's original intention had been to withhold publication while he attempted by mediation to secure an agreement between the employers and workers. It had become however increasingly clear from the attitude of the employers that no such agreement could be expected. In the meantime there was growing criticism of the Government's failure to publish the Report. It was accordingly decided to publish the Report on April 23rd with expressions of hope that the two parties would reach an agreement and a statement that if they did not, Government would take the Report into consideration on the 10th May. The present position is that the Government, without having really gone at all into the merits of the case, are very anxious to get the recommendations of the Report accepted because they know that labour will be prepared to accept them. On the other hand, the employers appear to be more and more determined, as they examine the Report, that it is impossible to accept the proposals as they stand. In particular they criticise most strongly the proposal for a general percentage increase in wages, pointing out that the discrepancies in actual wage standards between one mill and another in Cawnpore are very great, and that while increases are required in the lower paid mills probably little if any increase is required in the mills where the highest wage is paid. Nevertheless, on the proposal of the Committee the increase will be the same and indeed slightly larger in those mills where the wages are already the highest. I understand the millowners look upon the Report as an exceedingly amateurish production, which it probably is. I gather the present idea of the millowners is that after exposing the impracticality of many recommendations of the Report they should make their own proposals to labour and try to negotiate a settlement direct. This would no doubt be the most satisfactory course if labour were prepared to agree, but I feel considerable doubt whether they would, for as the Premier has said more than once, they will look upon the proposals in the Report as

the minimum. At the same time there is always a chance that as discussions proceed, and if a strike is not immediately precipitated, they may come to an amicable settlement.

7. The Ministry are still very much in the air about their rural development plans, and have been finding great difficulty in selecting a rural development officer. They had at one time practically made up their minds to appoint a very competent Indian I.C.S. officer[26] who is at present Registrar, Co-operative Societies, and would probably have done the work better than anyone else available. But I am told that a party meeting raised objections to him on personal grounds, and this shook the Ministry. The latest proposal is to take a comparatively young Indian Forest Officer[27] who has shown some initiative and keenness in dealing with rural development in some of the Tarai villages. I do not think he has anything like the administrative experience or standing that would enable him to make a success of a very big organisation of this kind. However, the Ministers must be left to make their own selection and to bear the responsibility for any resulting disappointment in their plans.[28] At any rate it would be a great thing to have an official in charge and one who will be genuinely trying to achieve practical and not political results.

8. The Cabinet decided recently to allow recessing officers to go up to Naini Tal this year as usual, the only change being that instead of taking, as some of them were allowed to formerly, a clerk and one or two *chaprasis* at Government expense, they would have to pay themselves for any staff they might wish to accompany them. This decision is one of very considerable importance, for any attempt to withdraw this concession would have resulted in the most serious discontent.[29] The recessing officers include Members of the Board of Revenue, Commissioners, Heads of Departments and a number of other officers, and they are allowed to go up to Naini Tal for periods varying from one month to three months during the hot weather. I hope that the Secretaries will in practice be allowed also to go up to Naini Tal for reasonable periods.

9. It may interest Your Excellency to hear something of the way in which the appointment of President, Court of Wards, was settled. The Court of Wards is a non-official body constituted by Statute, but it is provided that the President, who does the whole of the important administrative work, should be appointed by the Governor exercising his individual judgment after consultation with the Court of Wards. The late President, who was a very senior officer of the Indian Civil Service, has just taken leave preparatory to retirement. I was anxious to put in another senior Indian Civil Service officer. When, however, the matter went up to

the Court of Wards the whole body was unanimous that a non-official should be appointed. It is difficult to imagine any decision more unwise in the interests of the estates which the members of the Court of Wards are supposed to represent. But this I fear is a typical illustration of the practical incompetence of the landlords. Fortunately, however, the Court was equally divided as to the individual to be appointed. The Agra Zamindars had neglected to elect their representatives in time. Three representatives of the Taluqdars of Oudh voted for a Taluqdar, three representatives of the Congress voted for a somewhat obscure Congressman. I told the Ministers that in my opinion it was most undesirable to have a non-official at all, and they were content that I should reject the Congress nominee if I also rejected the Taluqdar. They were I believe even prepared to agree to the appointment of the senior Indian Civil Service officer whom I had in mind,[30] but his services were urgently required to officiate as Commissioner at Gorakhpur. I finally suggested that the present Secretary of the Court,[31] who is a very competent Provincial Service officer, should be appointed. The appointment may possibly be reconsidered after six months. The Ministers agreed to this proposal, which in the circumstances I regard as a very satisfactory result.

10. The Chehlum yesterday unfortunately led to rioting in Lucknow between Sunnis and Shias. The Sunnis must evidently have been the aggressors.

Yours sincerely,
HARRY HAIG

ENCLOSURE 1 TO NO. 40

PANNA LAL TO HORTON

Confidential
D.O. No. 1855-Police

Lucknow,
April 21st, 1938

My dear Horton,

I am desired to refer to the correspondence resting with Gwynne's demi-official letter No. N.-325-Police, dated December 3rd, 1937, in which District Magistrates were authorised to order at their own discretion the reporting of speeches when they apprehended incitements to violence or attempts to arouse communal feeling. In view of the prevailing communal tension, Government desire that District Authorities should keep a vigilant eye on any activity likely to exacerbate such tension. When any speeches are to be delivered by communal leaders or under the auspices of communal organisations, it may reasonably be presumed that the speeches will be such as will arouse ill-feeling between different communities. Such speeches should therefore as a rule be reported by the Police unless for special reasons the District Magistrate considers reporting to be unnecessary in any particular case. The reports of the speeches should be submitted to Government as early as possible after they are delivered and particulars should at the same time be furnished about the speaker and the size of the meeting.

2. A copy of this letter is being forwarded to the Deputy Inspector-General of Police, Criminal Investigation Department, and all District Magistrates and Superintendents of Police.

Yours sincerely,
PANNA LAL

ENCLOSURE 2 TO NO. 40

EXTRACT FROM THE *PIONEER*
DATED APRIL 15TH, 1938

Kisans' Demonstration Opposed

In an urgent circular issued to the Congress Committees the Congress Secretary states: "It is inadvisable to use the march *en masse* as a political weapon too frequently as its frequency is apt to blunt its edge and make it ineffective."

The following is the full text of the circular letter:

"I have seen in the papers report of a contemplated march of peasants to the Council Chamber at Lucknow on April 20th. I have since seen a notice purporting to have been issued by a member of the Assembly, advising Kisans to march in lakhs from all Districts and arrive in front of the Council Chamber at 11 a.m. on April 20th when, according to the notice, the Government proposals regarding Rent and Revenue are to be introduced in the Assembly.

"I wish to draw the attention of all District Congress Committees to the circular issued from this office that April 17th should be observed as a Kisan Day in support of the Bill which the Congress Ministry propose to introduce some time in the present session of the Assembly. It is inadvisable to use the march *en masse* as a political weapon too frequently, for obviously its frequency is apt to blunt its edge and would thus tend to make it ineffective. The Kisans will suffer in this season great hardships by such a march which, after the demonstration to be held by them on April 17th, will be uncalled for and will be a wholly unnecessary stimulant for their representatives in the Assembly who are themselves equally determined to secure the passage of the Bill. As it happens the Bill is not coming up on April 20th, as wrongly advertised, and the Kisans will have borne the serious strain of the long march to no purpose. Those who have advised the Kisans to march will, I hope, think over this and drop the proposed march.

"The District Congress Committees will please notify without delay accordingly and also advise the Kisans to muster in as large number as possible in their local meetings on the Kisan Day on April 17th in support of the Rent and Revenue Bill."

ENCLOSURE 3 TO NO. 40

EXTRACT FROM THE *PIONEER*
DATED APRIL 15TH, 1938

Grossly Unfair to *Kisans*
Pt. Nehru on Proposed Demonstration

Allahabad,
April 14th, 1938

The following Press statement has been issued by Pandit Jawaharlal Nehru on the proposed *kisan* demonstration before the Lucknow Council Chamber:

"I find from the newspapers that a Kisan demonstration is being organised before the Council Chamber in Lucknow on April 20th. I do not know definitely who has done so. On enquiry I find that the Provincial Congress Office or any local Congress Committee has nothing to do with this.

"It seems to me highly undesirable for repeated demonstrations to be held before the Council Chamber. The very object of such demonstrations is frustrated by such repetition and they are made cheap and ludicrous. We have recently had several demonstrations of this kind organised by odd groups with a grievance. To demonstrate peacefully is a right which we must protect, but to demonstrate so as to interfere frequently with the work of the Assembly seems to me highly improper. Those who encourage this set a bad example which all manner of people will follow to the public detriment.

"To ask Kisans to march long distances and gather before the Council Kisan Day on April 17th and all of us should co-operate in making this a unfair to them [*sic*]. It is far better for them to demonstrate in their local areas and give expression to their wishes there.

"The Provincial Congress Committee has called for the observance of a Kisan Day on April 17th and all of us should co-operate in making this a success. That is the right way. The Congress Committees should make it perfectly clear that the demonstration organised for April 20th has nothing to do with the Congress. This is a matter which will have to be considered by the Council of the Provincial Congress Committee, for the Congress organisation cannot remain a passive spectator when its name and prestige are used for a purpose that is considered undesirable. It is also necessary that no Congressman should do anything that may be inconsistent with the Provincial Congress Committee's policy." – A.P.

41

HAIG TO LINLITHGOW
Telegram
R/3/1/73

Important *April 30th, 1938*
No. 142-G

Your telegram No. 314-G.C. of April 30th. Hitherto there has been nothing to suggest my Ministers taking any interest in Orissa problem[32] or regard it as having any bearing on themselves. Until yesterday when I came to Naini Tal I have been in very close touch with them on a number of Provincial problems of importance and we have spent long periods discussing future policy.

2. Gandhi's attitude creates new situation. Premier arrives Naini Tal today and I can get in touch with him at any time. So far however I have deliberately abstained from raising question with him as I did not want to suggest that I thought serious complications for this Province were likely to ensue. Now however I shall mention matter when I next see him.

42

HAIG TO LINLITHGOW
Telegram
R/3/1/73

No. 143-G *May 2nd, 1938*

Your telegram No. 326-G.C. of May the 1st.[33] Strong point on Congress side is that it appears to be admitted that this appointment is wrong in principle. On the other hand, it seems to me that it would seriously compromise constitutional position if appointment were in whatever guise cancelled as result of open threats that Ministry would not work under new Governor. This might be claimed as establishing a principle which is wholly wrong in itself, and one which Congress would certainly try to develop and exploit for future. It would be the first step in campaign against appointment of Indian Civil Service Governors.

2. While Gandhi has advantage that he is fighting for a principle which would generally be accepted as sound, I think if he attempted to wreck the Constitution on this point by bringing out other Congress Ministries, a large body of public opinion would be against him, both Congress and non-Congress. The Congress would doubtless obey orders, but they would be as dissatisfied as they were when Office was originally refused.

3. My conclusion therefore is that it should be stated authoritatively and at once that principle is accepted that an officer serving in a Province will not in future be appointed Governor either temporarily or permanently. This concedes Gandhi's specific (gr. omitted) [?objection] on merits. But I would not cancel arrangements already announced, even by device of Hubback cancelling his leave. Although his going at a time of crisis would normally be open to strong objection, yet in this case his remaining means surrendering whole position. This would be dangerous for reasons explained in paragraph No. 1, and in my judgment would be serious blow to prestige of British authority and would have very damaging effect on minds of non-Congress elements.

4. If in circumstances described in paragraph No. 3, Orissa Ministry persists in resigning, their position would be intelligible and they would have some support. In that case I should be disposed to suggest that no attempt should be made to exploit situation to their disadvantage by appointing Interim Ministry if this would have that effect.

5. If in circumstances described in paragraph No. 3, Gandhi called out other Congress Ministries, I think he would be on very weak ground. They

would not be directly concerned, but would only wish to establish a principle. But *ex hypothesi* that principle would already have been established by authoritative statement. They would only be fighting therefore for limited and temporary local issue in Orissa. I see my proposal is in effect the same as Rajagopalachari's as reported in Erskine's telegram,[34] but I had reached my conclusion independently.

6. I do not anticipate any special Service reactions to policy suggested by Secretary of State, other than those referred to in paragraph No. 3. But I consider these would be serious and that we cannot really afford to make open climb-down to Congress. My own anticipation is that if action is taken as in paragraph No. 3, Congress would not precipitate all-India crisis, but in any event I would face the risk.

7. Since drafting the above I have seen Pant this afternoon. He seems to have no personal knowledge about the policy of the Working Committee and does not seem to have any serious apprehension that it is likely to affect us. Indeed he showed little interest in problem. He said he imagined that no decision about all-India policy would be taken until Provincial Premiers had met at Bombay on 12th. His mind is entirely occupied with problems of Provincial policy and he clearly does not contemplate their interruption on account of Orissa.[35]

43

HAIG TO LINLITHGOW
R/3/1/73

Secret | Camp,
No. U.P.-75 | *May 7th, 1938*

My dear Lord Linlithgow,

In paragraph 8 of my secret letter No. U.P.-64, dated April 8th, 1938, I referred at some length to the scheme for separation of judicial and executive functions which Dr. Katju had prepared, and gave some account of the Cabinet discussion. The Government were pressed strongly in the Legislature to take action. Dr. Katju outlined both in the Legislature and in a subsequent speech at Cawnpore the scheme which I mentioned in my letter, but was criticised in the *Leader* for departing from some of the essentials of the original scheme prepared by the Stuart Committee.[36] There the matter rested until a Cabinet meeting at the end of April, just before I left Lucknow, when the question was brought up again with a suggestion that Dr. Katju should be authorised to go ahead with working out the details of his scheme. I pointed out that the Cabinet had given very little consideration to the important factors involved, and I said that before they went further, I should like to have an opportunity myself of examining Dr. Katju's scheme with some care and of recording for the consideration of the Ministers any observations that I might have to make upon it.

2. I now enclose for Your Excellency's information a copy of Dr. Katju's note, outlining his scheme, and a copy of the note which I have recorded for the consideration of the Ministers. You will observe that in paragraph 5 (4) of my note, I have definitely called attention to the possibility that it might be necessary to refer the scheme to the Secretary of State. I should be grateful if Your Excellency would ascertain from the Secretary of State whether in the event of the Ministers wishing to pursue this proposal he would desire that a reference should be made to him. I am not at present raising the question what action should be taken on such a reference, but merely the point whether the proposals contained in Dr. Katju's note would amount, in the opinion of the Secretary of State, to such a material change in the duties of the District Magistrate as to necessitate a reference to him. I am disposed to think that they would.

3. I have had in the last few days some talk with the Premier on the general question of separation of judicial and executive functions. I found him a little uncertain about the practical effects, and my impression is that if it were not for political pressure, particularly from the Opposition, he and Dr. Katju might not wish to go forward with these proposals. But he thinks from the political point of view it is impossible not to make some move, and he regards the Government in fact as being committed to taking some action. He realises that if something on the lines of Dr. Katju's scheme is adopted, it will be open to the criticism of officials who contend that it will weaken the administration, and at the same time to the criticism of the Liberals, headed by Chintamani, who will say that the scheme does not go nearly far enough and does not establish a satisfactory separation of the two functions. I am disposed to hope that the financial argument may carry weight, but I think it is certain that the Ministers will again be pressed strongly on the subject when the Assembly next meets, say in August. At present I think that the wisest course will be to put an official on special duty to work out the details.[37] This would be decidedly preferable to appointing the usual non-official committee. If a scheme is finally approved,

I have little doubt that the Ministers will themselves be glad to try it out in the first instance experimentally in a few districts.

Yours sincerely,
H.G. HAIG

ENCLOSURE 1 TO NO. 43

NOTE BY KATJU

Separation of Judicial and Executive Functions

The demand for the separation of judicial and executive functions has been of long standing. In the past the dominating motive for the demand was the apprehension that the District Magistrate and Superintendent of Police were in a position to exercise pressure upon the subordinate magistrates and that affected both the efficiency and the impartiality of such magistrates in the conduct of their judicial criminal business. There was the further apprehension that inasmuch as the promotion and future advancement of the subordinate magistrates depended upon the good opinion of the District Magistrate, the subordinate magistrates were in a state of perpetual subjection to the District Magistrate and through him to the Superintendent of Police and dared not go contrary to the wishes of the District Magistrate. Being the head in the district both of the police and the magistracy we had the unfortunate situation of the prosecutor being virtually the trying magistrate. It was, therefore, urged that to insure a fair and impartial trial to accused persons it was absolutely necessary that the trying magistrate should be freed from all possible influences of the police and the District Magistrate, and that could only be achieved by the separation of the magisterial functions from the executive functions and by putting the magistrates under the direct control of the High Court. There was no difficulty in the olden days in such a scheme because the authority of the British Government was supreme and therefore whether the magistrates were under the control of the District Magistrates or that of the Sessions Judges it was ultimately the control of the British authority in both cases.

The situation has now considerably changed because of the introduction of the principle of Provincial Autonomy and the allocation of a sphere of authority separately to Ministers responsible to the Legislature. The question is whether it would be consistent with constitutional propriety as well as national prestige to surrender a part of the hopelessly inadequate powers given under the Act to the High Court. If it is thought that from the constitutional point of view it would be humiliating to do so, then some means should be devised to free the trying magistrate from the apprehended evil influences of the District Magistrate and the police. Before going further I should like to point out that in one sense all criminal jurisdiction is exercised directly by the High Court which is *prima facie* utterly beyond the influence of the District Magistrate and in theory even that of the local Government. The Sessions Judge is not supposed to be under the control of the District Magistrate. He and his assistants try all criminal cases of any importance in the sessions courts. Then in every case tried by a magistrate, first class, there is an appeal to the Sessions Judge, an officer supposed to be free from executive control. Therefore, you have it that either in the first instance or in appeal every accused in a criminal case can go up to a judge presumably impartial and free from executive bias.

I may further add that magisterial business is being largely performed in the United Provinces by honorary magistrates. 66 per cent of magisterial cases in Oudh are decided by honorary magistrates and nearly 50 per cent in Agra. Up till now, the method of recruitment of honorary magistrates was faulty and they were rightly supposed to be entirely under the thumb of the District Magistrate. Their appointment depended on the pleasure and recommendation of the District Magistrate and so did their removal. They dared not go against the wishes of the District Magistrate. Government have now with the concurrence of the Legislature promulgated rules which it is hoped will ensure the recruitment of a body of independent and efficient magistrates. If these expectations are fulfilled, then to the extent that these honorary magistrates function magisterial powers will be exercised by magistrates who should have no fear either of the police or of the District Magistrate and should mete out even-handed and absolutely impartial justice to the accused.

In 1922 the Stuart Committee examined this problem in all its aspects and formulated a scheme for the separation of judicial and executive functions in the United Provinces. They recommended that there should be two separate staffs in each district – an executive staff and a magisterial staff. The executive staff should consist of a Chief Executive Officer and his deputies; and there should be a magisterial staff consisting of as many magistrates as may be necessary to perform the original criminal work of the district. (*Vide* paragraphs 22 and 23 of the Report, pages 8-9.) The recommendations of the Committee, however, proceeded on the fundamental assumption that so far as the Executive Officers were concerned the appointing authority would be the local Government, but so far as the magisterial service was concerned it would be under the absolute control of the judiciary, viz., the High Court and would be appointed by the High Court. (*Vide* paragraph 33 of the Report.) If that principle is to be accepted, then the Stuart Scheme can easily be proceeded with slight modifications; but, as I have already indicated, I am not prepared to recommend that the Provincial Government should be willing to transfer the control of the magistracy to the High Court, and I also very much doubt whether in view of the relevant provisions of the Government of India Act that is even feasible. I may also add that legislation consisting of substantial amendments of the Criminal Procedure Code and many other Imperial and local Acts would also be necessary to give effect to the Committee's scheme. This would involve pretty extensive work of a detailed description.

I think that we can achieve our main object by proceeding on somewhat simpler lines. With a view to obviate the necessity of any amending legislation the head of the district may continue to be called District Magistrate and the staff under him deputy magistrates of varying classes as at present; but in each district there should be an officer known as Additional District Magistrate. (See Section 10 (2), Criminal Procedure Code.) The whole Provincial Executive Service should be divided into two compartments, one for executive work and the other for magisterial judicial work. In every district the District Magistrate, while he has in name the designation and under the Criminal Procedure Code the powers of a District Magistrate, should never perform any magisterial judicial functions. Those functions must be entrusted to two or more magistrates, one of whom should be a senior magistrate and have the rank and designation of Additional District Magistrate, and all other magistrates entrusted with case work should be subordinate to him. (*Vide* Section 17, Criminal Procedure Code.) The Additional District Magistrate should have control not only over the stipendiary magistrates dealing with judicial case work but also over honorary, special and bench magistrates in the district. The Additional District Magistrate and the stipendiary staff under him should have nothing to do with any executive work in the district. They should never go out on tour and should have nothing to do with the police in the district. They should be confined solely and exclusively to the trial of criminal cases in the district. All these magistrates while having concurrent jurisdiction throughout the district should have areas allotted to them (*vide* Section 12, Criminal Procedure Code). The Additional District Magistrate should be the appellate authority for the disposal of criminal appeals from second and third class magistrates. He should ordinarily be, in the case of more important first class districts, a member of the Indian Civil Service while in the other districts he need only be a senior deputy collector. But I should like to emphasise here that it would be open to the District Magistrate in times of real emergency to call upon these magistrates to assist him in the maintenance of law and order and to quell disturbances.

The District Magistrate and his deputies should discharge executive duties in the district. They should initiate prosecutions and one of their functions should be to supervise all police prosecutions so that there may be no harrassment. The Criminal Procedure Code at various places has entrusted both executive and quasi-judicial powers to magistrates. For instance, there are powers to issue search warrants and warrants for arrest under Sections 98 and 100. There is the power to issue an order for the dispersal of unlawful assemblies. There is also the power to issue orders for abatement of public nuisances under Section 133, and prohibitory orders under Sections 144 and 145. These powers should, in my opinion, be in the first instance exercised by officers discharging executive functions. Whenever any proceeding assumes the shape of a judicial proceeding in so far as any order issued *ex parte* by an officer is challenged, then the proceeding should be transmitted to the magistrate whose function is to try cases for disposal. For instance, a notice under Section 133 may be issued by an officer discharging executive functions, but the notice should clearly say that if the person to whom the order is issued desires to contest it he should appear before a magistrate whose duty it is to try cases. The powers under Sections 144 and 145 are mainly of an executive nature and the issue is simple and therefore may well remain with executive officers. Any injustices can easily be cured by appeals or revisions already provided for to the Sessions Judge or the High Court.

The Additional District Magistrate and magistrates under him should in no sense be subordinate to the District Magistrate. Subordinate magistrates should be under the administrative control of the Additional District Magistrate. They should apply to him for leave and such other matters. The Additional District Magistrate should be under the direct administrative control of the Provincial Government.

Inasmuch as the Additional District Magistrate and the magistrates subordinate to him will only exercise judicial functions the Sessions Judge should be called upon to report periodically (every year as the normal procedure) upon their judicial work and such reports would normally be taken into consideration whenever the question of promotion arises.

The Sessions Judge should have the power to inspect the office of the

Additional District Magistrate and other magistrates and also to call for records and papers to see that everything is being done properly.

The staff of all magistrates' courts should be subject to the administrative control of the [?Additional] District Magistrate.

It seems to me that this scheme should prove practicable. The Stuart Committee thought that it was desirable that all appeals from the decisions of all magistrates should be heard by Sessions Judges and in this view they recommended the creation of eight additional posts of District and Sessions Judges. I do not think that this additional expenditure need be incurred. Appeals from the orders of second and third class magistrates can be heard even by magistrates of the first class, and the proposal for appointing an Additional District Magistrate will do away with the necessity of creating any extra posts of District and Sessions Judges.

The Stuart Committee in working out the details of their scheme appended a statement showing the distribution of magisterial and executive officers in each district. There is nothing to indicate in the report whether the Committee ever considered the question that their Chief Executive Officer might require the assistance of the entire district staff including the magistrates for the purpose of meeting emergencies or restoring law and order. I think we must make a clear provision in our scheme, as I have suggested above, that the District Magistrate will be entitled to invoke the aid of the magisterial staff in times of emergency. These are days of communal tension and the District Magistrate must not be left short-handed. I have no doubt that if a part of the present district staff is assigned for the discharge of purely magisterial judicial duties and the District Magistrate is not empowered to seek the aid of these magistrates in times of emergency there will be real danger to the preservation of peace and tranquillity in the district.

I have not yet touched upon another point. The Stuart Committee definitely expressed the opinion that the executive service should be clearly divided into these two compartments and there should be no transfer *inter se*; that even the Indian Civil Service officers should be called upon at an early date in their service to say whether they would go in for magisterial work or for executive work. In my opinion, that is a somewhat thorny problem. The Stuart Committee reported 15 years ago. I think the times have changed and so have the demands of the situation. I think it is worthy of consideration whether we should not give due weight to the fact that the class of officers whom we recruit as members of the executive service is far superior to those recruited 20 years ago. We are getting men of superior calibre and I think of sturdy independence not liable to be browbeaten by the District Magistrate, even if the latter cares to do so. Furthermore, we should make allowances for the growth of vigilant public opinion as expressed in the press and platform and in the legislature. These are wholesome influences and I hope will keep the magistracy straight. It is well worthy of consideration whether we should, to begin with, make the two branches of the executive service water-tight. There should be no transfer from one branch to another branch while the officer is serving in the same district, and it should also be understood that when a particular officer has been posted either as a magistrate or as one in charge of executive duties in a particular district he must remain there, barring exceptional circumstances, for a continuous period of three or four years; but there should be no bar to his transfer from one branch to another branch when he is transferred from one district to another district. I am not wedded to this view, but I put it forward because a splitting up of the executive service into two compartments might give rise to serious administrative difficulties as regards the promotion of existing officers. The listed posts are at present divided into two definite classes – those of Collectors and Magistrates and those of District and Sessions Judges. If you were to assign a particular deputy collector to magisterial functions alone and if he were to remain in charge of such magisterial work for five or ten years, that might subsequently prejudice his chances of promotion to one of the listed posts on the executive side, while it would not be feasible to promote him as District and Sessions Judge because of his want of familiarity with civil law. It is therefore to be considered whether in the beginning it would not be more expedient to refrain from making any definite rules. We might wait and see how the experiment works and it would be enough time after two or three years to come to a definite decision in this matter. For two or three years it will be understood that those officers who are assigned to discharge magisterial functions will remain as magistrates throughout and will not be transferred to the executive side.

This procedure to my mind is the more necessary because we must wait and see what will be the effect of the proposed agrarian legislation on rent and revenue work now performed by deputy collectors. Similarly we must see how the work of civil courts, particularly those of munsifs, will be affected by the aftermath of the Encumbered Estates Act and other debt legislation. It is apprehended that there will be serious diminution in the business both of the civil and revenue courts. After two years the effect will become somewhat crystallised and Government will be in a position to judge (*a*) how the system now recommended has worked; (*b*) how many officers would be necessary for the disposal of rent and revenue litigation; (*c*) how many munsifs would be required for the disposal of ordinary civil business in their courts and whether it would be possible to utilise these munsifs as part-time magistrates; (*d*) how the courts of honorary magistrates recruited under the revised rules are working; and (*e*) how the proposed establishment of panchayats on a larger scale authorised to dispose of petty criminal business will affect the business of the criminal courts.

I must also mention another aspect of this problem. For the last 80-90 years district administration has been carried on on the present lines and rightly or wrongly District Officers have come to think that deprivation of criminal powers will seriously impair their authority in the districts and it will become more difficult for them to maintain law and order in their charge. People have also become accustomed to associate the District Officer with a person who has got magisterial powers. We have just started on a new era. Different forces are coming into place and we are confronted with problems arising out of communal difficulties and such other matters. It would, in my opinion, be lamentable if by any sudden change of system the forces of law and order were to be weakened in the districts and our services who are not entirely under our control were to retort that they were not to blame for a breakdown because their prestige and authority had been diminished by a change of system. We must proceed, therefore, cautiously. Separation on the above lines should be tried in some selected districts and the results watched.

I must say that during the last eight months I have noticed a distinct change for the better in the administration. Complaints about interference by District Magistrates or by the police with subordinate magistrates in the discharge of their magisterial duties are very infrequent. I attach great importance to this fact, because the assumption of office by the Ministry has led to the flooding of the Secretariat by complaints. Hundreds and thousands are received regarding every department, and while public opinion has become so vocal it is noticeable that complaints about miscarriage of justice in criminal courts owing to police interference or interference by District Magistrates are comparatively so few. That bears out the observation which I made in the Assembly in September last that it would not be quite correct to be guided solely by considerations which might have had force 30 years or 40 years back. Now every deputy magistrate knows, and has been made to know, that if he is a party to a miscarriage of justice, then he is liable to be punished and any plea based on superior orders or interference would be no defence at all. Similarly,

District Magistrates and police officers, I believe, also realise that the present Government will not take a very light view of such interference, and over and above all these the pressure of public opinion through the legislature has a great purifying and improving influence.

To summarise, my proposals are:

(1) Ascertain in each district the amount of criminal business which must be performed by stipendiary magistrates working as whole-time officers for five hours a day.

(2) Assign magisterial duties to two or more present deputy magistrates and collectors in each district.

(3) These officers should do purely criminal case work at headquarters and should do no executive work of any sort or description.

(4) The senior-most of these officers should have the rank and status of Additional District Magistrate and the other officers should be administratively subordinate to him.

(5) This Additional District Magistrate should hear appeals from all stipendiary and honorary second and third class magistrates.

(6) The Additional District Magistrate should in his turn be subordinate directly to the Provincial Government.

(7) The Sessions Judge alone should be required to report periodically upon the work done by the Additional District Magistrate and his subordinate magistrates.

(8) The Sessions Judge should have along with the Additional District Magistrate the power to inspect magistrates' courts and call for information and necessary papers.

(9) These magistrates should try every case the moment it reaches the stage of judicial proceeding including cases under the preventive jurisdiction, viz., those under Sections 107 and 210, Criminal Procedure Code.

(10) The District Magistrate and his subordinate magistrates and deputy collectors should do all executive work and rent and revenue work and should be in charge of police and prosecutions.

(11) Neither the District Magistrate nor the Police Superintendent should have any concern of any sort or description with the Additional District Magistrate and subordinate magistrates excepting that in cases of real emergency when the District Magistrate feels it absolutely necessary for the maintenance of law and order he should have the authority to invoke the aid of the Additional District Magistrate and his subordinate magistrates for the purpose of maintaining order.

(12) The District Magistrate and his subordinates should have authority to issue orders under Sections 144 and 145 and preliminary orders under Sections 107 and 133, Criminal Procedure Code.

(13) The scheme should be tried not throughout the province but, to begin with, in some division.

ENCLOSURE 2 TO NO. 43

NOTE BY HAIG

May 6th, 1938

I have now had an opportunity of studying with care the minute recorded by H.M.J. which embodies his suggestions for a scheme of separation of judicial and executive functions. I have also read the report of the Stuart Committee, which prepared a scheme in 1921, and the very interesting discussions which took place within the Government at that time. The Stuart Committee's report was generally accepted by the Provincial Government and forwarded to the Government of India in February 1923. The Government of India decided in 1928 that they were not prepared at the time to proceed further with schemes of this kind, and the matter was consequently dropped.

2. I appreciate the fact that H.M.J.'s proposals differ in many respects from those of the Stuart Committee. Nevertheless, I think it would be convenient for me to examine, in the first place, broadly the main objections that have been urged to the proposals of the Stuart Committee, and then to see to what extent these objections have been mitigated in H.M.J.'s proposals. I feel that it is desirable that I should bring to the notice of Hon'ble Ministers the difficulties that have been felt in the past in accepting proposals of this kind, and ask them to give full weight to these considerations.

3. The main objections to the proposals of the Stuart Committee I would state as follows:

(1) The most important general objection is the view, which is held I think by nearly all those who have had practical experience of the conditions, that the change would weaken the authority of the District Magistrate and make it more difficult to maintain order. Admittedly, this is only a general opinion, it rests largely on psychological factors, it is not susceptible of proof except by experience. Nevertheless, if true, it is a point of crucial importance. The position is stated very clearly in the

admirable note of Sir Selwyn Fremantle, dated July 3rd, 1922, the whole of which will repay perusal. On this point he wrote as follows: "It is generally maintained by the advocates of this change that it is resisted by the official because he loses in prestige. There is a great deal of truth in this. But why does the District Magistrate wish to maintain his prestige? Surely it is because he is responsible for the peace of the district and his prestige assists him greatly in maintaining order. He requires magisterial powers to establish his influence and authority in the eyes of the people." I think myself this is broadly speaking true. I need not emphasise the importance at this time of maintaining the authority of the District Magistrate, and being careful to do nothing which is likely to impair it. H.M.J. has himself referred to these considerations, which are very present to his mind. Indeed, what he says is very similar to the point made by Sir Selwyn Fremantle. H.M.J. writes: "For the last 80 to 90 years district administration has been carried on, on the present lines, and rightly or wrongly district officers have come to think that deprivation of criminal powers will seriously impair their authority in the districts and it will become more difficult for them to maintain law and order in their charge. People have also become accustomed to associate the district officer with a person who has got magisterial powers."

(2) There is a danger that a service of magistrates completely divorced from all concern with the practical problems of maintaining order and having no direct responsibility for the peace of the district may tend to take unduly technical or lenient views and to acquit unreasonably. That certainly would be the line of least resistance. There is always the fear of critical remarks being made by the appellate court if a person is convicted. On the other hand it is very seldom that any Magistrate would find himself called to account for wrongful acquittal. Moreover, if a Magistrate sits in court day after day hearing, as he is bound to hear, constant attacks upon the honesty and conduct of the police (that being the normal line of defence taken in criminal cases) and is entirely out of touch with all practical knowledge of police work and police conditions, it would not be surprising if he developed an unreasonable prejudice against the police, which might result in an undue proportion of acquittals. One of the great merits to my mind of the present system is that Magistrates are brought in touch with the working of the police. Further the District Magistrate is in a position of some authority both with the police and with the Magistrates. He is able to prevent an antagonism developing between them which would be dangerous to the administration. He is able to take a reasonable middle view, and to foster a general attitude, both in the police and in the

magistrates, which is likely to make for sound and just criminal administration and an absence of unnecessary friction.

(3) The combination of functions in the subordinate magistrates is administratively useful. In any kind of emergency the district officer is able to utilise the whole of his staff. This would not be the case when the existing staff has been broken up into two entirely separate organizations. For instance, in time of famine the district officer at present can call upon the whole of the district staff. Under the Stuart Committee's proposals he would have at his disposal only about half the number of officers. Similar considerations apply to an emergency when the peace of the district is threatened. No doubt in particular cases (for instance, the occurrence of riots in a large city) it might be possible to call upon the judicial authorities for temporary assistance. But quite apart from the fact that by their training and experience they would not be as valuable as ordinary magistrates are now, this expedient is of little help when conditions generally throughout a district may be dangerous, and it may be of great importance to have a sufficient staff of magistrates available for precautionary purposes in a number of centres.

(4) Moreover, in the normal working of a district the division of functions will certainly lead to loss of efficiency on the executive side. Unless the cost is to be prohibitive, the executive officers will have to be responsible for much larger areas than at present. This means that they will know their areas less intimately.

(5) Even with this handicap, the cost will be appreciably greater. It was reckoned when the Provincial Government were considering the proposals of the Stuart Committee that to give effect to them it would be necessary to create no less than 94 new posts, of which 8 would be posts of District and Sessions Judges. This would mean a very considerable burden on the provincial finances. It was estimated that the recurring cost would be approximately five lakhs in the first instance, rising ultimately to about nine lakhs. It was also reckoned that appreciable expenditure would be required on new buildings, the estimate being put at about three lakhs.

(6) There is a considerable body of opinion that Section 107 cases at any rate, and possibly also Section 110 should be tried by the executive officers. But this is an obvious breach in the principle. If however it is not accepted there is appreciable risk of danger to peace or growth of crime.

4. Now I recognise that H.M.J. has taken certain of these difficulties into account, and that some of them are present in a less acute form in his proposals than they were in the scheme of the Stuart Committee. I proceed to examine them in turn:

(1) The Stuart Committee proposed that the executive officers should cease to be termed magistrates, though they would be given certain executive powers which are magisterial in nature. Their proposals underlined the fact that the district officer responsible for maintaining the peace of the district was being deprived of magisterial powers. The effect on public opinion would be pronounced. H.M.J. proposes that the District Magistrate should still remain the District Magistrate, at any rate in name, and indeed that he should still possess all his existing legal powers, though he would, I understand, by executive order be directed to leave the exercise of certain of these powers to the Additional District Magistrate. I think under this scheme the authority of the District Magistrate in public opinion would stand higher than it would have under the Stuart Committee Scheme.

(2) The dangers of undue divorce and friction between judicial and executive authority under the Stuart Scheme, which to my mind are very great, would also be mitigated by H.M.J.'s proposals, if I understand them correctly. The Stuart Scheme put the Magistrates definitely under the administrative control of District and Sessions Judges. As Sir Selwyn Fremantle pointed out, the District Officer under that system would be subject to animadversions and criticisms of the magisterial staff which had hitherto been under his control. H.M.J. proposes that the Magistrates in a district should be under the general control of the Additional District Magistrate and that the Additional District Magistrate should be considered administratively to be under the Provincial Government and not under the Sessions Judge and the High Court. I take it that H.M.J.'s view is that the Additional District Magistrate should be administratively under the control of the Commissioner, or at any rate that the Commissioner should have a definite responsibility for reporting on the efficiency of the criminal administration of a district. The District Magistrate also, however much he may be directed to abstain from concern with the details of the criminal administration, cannot possibly be indifferent to the criminal administration of the district as a whole, and must, I should suppose, be entitled to draw the attention of the Commissioner, and through him of the Government, to any features which appear to him to be unsatisfactory. It seems to me that it is most important to have the Commissioner as a co-ordinating authority between the District Magistrate and the Additional District Magistrate, and that he might be able to a considerable extent to prevent friction arising between them. Moreover, though the subordinate Magistrates would be working directly under the supervision and control of the Additional District Magistrate, it is not possible to ignore the legal position that under Section 17 of the Code of Criminal Procedure all Magistrates are subordinate to

the District Magistrate, even though he may not directly be exercising his powers over them.

(3) The legal position which I have just mentioned, namely, that all Magistrates in a district are subordinate to the District Magistrate, would greatly facilitate the use of judicial Magistrates for executive work in cases of emergency as contemplated by H.M.J. At the same time the objection remains that these Magistrates would not be available to help in any emergency of a general character, such as a famine.

(4) The objection under this head remains.

(5) I fear the financial cost under H.M.J.'s scheme would be about the same as under the Stuart Scheme, except that eight new posts of District and Sessions Judges would not be required.

(6) H.M.J. proposes to run the risks involved in having Sections 107 and 110 cases tried by judicial magistrates. I myself consider that in Section 107 cases at any rate this would be taking too grave risks with the maintenance of order.

5. There are certain other features of H.M.J.'s proposals which seem to me to involve difficulties:

(1) H.M.J. proposes that the District Magistrate and his staff should be responsible for initiating prosecutions, and the District Magistrate should supervise all police prosecutions. This would, I think, involve great difficulties with the police administration and would seriously affect the position of the Superintendent of Police. My own view is that the present system under which to all intents and purposes the initiation of prosecutions rests with the police is sound. I do not think the District Magistrate would have the time or be in sufficiently close touch with the details of police work to be in a position to supervise the initiation of prosecutions nearly as well as the Superintendent of Police does. Indeed, I have always felt that one of the main attacks upon the present system is misconceived so far at any rate as concerns present-day conditions in the United Provinces. The attack on the system in the old days, I think, originated in Bengal where I understand, the District Magistrate has always taken a much more definite part in the initiation of prosecutions than he has in the United Provinces. The main aim of the Stuart Committee in their own words is: "That no officer who is responsible for the prosecution in criminal matters should be in any way connected with the trial of the case." It is only in special cases to my mind that the District Magistrate can be regarded as responsible for the initiation of prosecutions, and even where he is responsible for the initiation of a prosecution, he does not as a rule concern himself with the actual course of the trial. I feel myself that it would be

quite wrong to make the District Magistrate in effect the public prosecutor, and that this would be a completely new departure so far as this Province is concerned.

(2) I take it that members of the Indian Civil Service filling the post of Additional District Magistrate would be officers only on the junior scale of pay. They would presumably be officers who had elected for the judicial branch and would look forward to promotion on the judicial side. It is, of course, a feature of the proposals which I regard as very desirable, that the Additional District Magistrate both in designation and status would normally not be the equal of the District Magistrate. This I think would tend to diminish occasions of friction.

(3) I am not very clear about the legal position. As I understand it, it is that the District Magistrate retains all the powers concurred on him by the Code of Criminal Procedure, but is directed in practice not to exercise certain of them. But in general it seems to me impossible to say that the judicial Magistrates shall not be in any way subordinate to the District Magistrate when Section 17 of the Criminal Procedure Code plainly and definitely says that they shall be. As I have said, I should not regard it as a disadvantage that judicial Magistrates, though not working directly under the orders of the District Magistrate, should still feel that he was in a general way their superior officer.

(4) The post of District Magistrate is one of the posts which are shown in the cadre of the Indian Civil Service in the Superior Civil Service Rules (1934), which rules continue in force at present by virtue of Section 276 of the Government of India Act, 1935, until rules have been made by the Secretary of State under Section 246. No rules under Section 246 have yet been made, but draft rules were sent out some time ago by the Secretary of State and are still under his consideration. Rule 24 (*a*) of the C.C.A. rules (which are similarly still in force) provides briefly that the Governor of a Governor's Province may only make changes in the duties of a post borne on the cadre of an all-India Service if the changes which it is proposed to make are not material changes. If the changes which it is proposed to make are material changes, they cannot be made without the previous sanction of the Secretary of State in Council. A similar provision to this rule was shown in the draft rules to be made under Section 246, and it may be assumed that some such provision will be made in those rules. It will, therefore, be necessary for me to consider whether the proposals of H.M.J. amount to a material change in the duties of the post of District Magistrate. At present it seems to me that the changes are very material and that therefore it will be necessary to refer the scheme to the Secretary of State.

6. If proposals on these lines are finally approved, I certainly think it would be most desirable, as suggested by H.M.J., that they should be tried out experimentally first in certain districts or in one division. The changes are too important, the effects too doubtful, for it to be safe to introduce the new system at once all over the Province. On the whole I think it would be preferable to try it in selected districts in several divisions rather than in all the districts of one division. In this way we should get the judgment of a number of Commissioners, and we should also be able to estimate the effects in different parts of the Province, which might well vary.

H.G.H.

44

HAIG TO LINLITHGOW
R/3/1/73

Secret
No. U.P.-76

Camp,
May 9th, 1938

My dear Lord Linlithgow,

I had a long discussion with my Cabinet on April 20th and again on April 27th regarding the functions of Parliamentary Secretaries. This is a matter which has been down for discussion for some months past, but owing to various reasons it has not been possible to take it up earlier. The Ministers are particularly anxious to get the present rather indefinite position regularised and defined. When Parliamentary Secretaries were appointed, it was decided that they would assist Ministers in administrative and legislative matters, but that they would not be regarded as in charge of a department or part of a department (meaning the Secretariat department of which the official Secretary is head) and would not be interposed between the Secretary and the Minister. They would have no power to dispose of files, but should be able to call for files for information from the Secretaries. They would assist Ministers in any way directed by the Ministers in dealing with departmental cases.

2. These instructions have not in fact been observed with any strictness, and there has been a growing tendency for Ministers to use Parliamentary Secretaries to advise them on files, and in some cases Parliamentary Secretaries have even attempted to pass orders on files, though when this has happened it has always been checked.

3. The pressure for giving more definite functions to Parliamentary Secretaries comes from two directions. In the first place, the Ministers consider that they could safely get rid of a considerable amount of routine work if they could in some way allow the Parliamentary Secretaries to function for them. In the second place, the Parliamentary Secretaries feel that their position is very unsatisfactory and wish to have some kind of authority and responsibility.

4. A day or two before the first Cabinet discussion took place, the Premier handed me a note, of which I attach a copy, saying that this represented briefly the arrangements that the Ministers would like to introduce. At the beginning of our discussion I referred to this note, and said that while I did not wish to lay too much stress on phraseology, it seemed to me that the note had been drafted without due consideration of the constitutional position, which I proceeded to emphasise. Suggestions that Parliamentary Secretaries could dispose of cases or pass orders were, in my view, inconsistent with the principles of the Constitution as laid down in the Government of India Act. The Premier at once admitted that this criticism was valid. He had no wish in any way to weaken the ultimate responsibility of the Ministers, and he was quite prepared to admit that some of the language used in the note was unsuitable. But he urged that while the ultimate responsibility in all matters must be that of the Ministers, in working practice they had to delegate powers and responsibility to a number of subordinate authorities, and all they wished to do was, in the working of the headquarters machinery to delegate as a matter of working convenience certain powers to Parliamentary Secretaries. In fact the powers they desired to delegate were of little importance, and the object was to relieve themselves of an appreciable amount of routine work. They had no desire that Parliamentary Secretaries should relieve them of work in any matters in which decisions of any importance have to be taken.

5. I then asked the Premier to develop in more detail his ideas as to the manner in which Parliamentary Secretaries could in a practical way relieve the Ministers of some of the very heavy burden which undoubtedly falls upon them. He explained that, in the first place, there were files which might be regarded for various reasons as confidential. His idea was that files of this kind should not be submitted to the Parliamentary Secretary. All other files, however, should go to the Parliamentary Secretary after they had been noted on by the official Secretary. In cases of a routine or unimportant nature, where the Parliamentary Secretary was in agreement with the official Secretary, there would be no need for the Minister to see [them] at all. In such cases the Premier appeared to accept the position

that technically the order would be passed on the authority of the official Secretary, but that the Parliamentary Secretary would in effect be authorised to relieve the official Secretary from the necessity of submitting the case for the orders of the Minister. In more important cases, even if the Parliamentary Secretary was in agreement with the official Secretary, the cases should be submitted to the Minister, and all cases in which the official Secretary and the Parliamentary Secretary differed, however unimportant, should also be submitted to the Minister.

6. I questioned all the Ministers about the practical effects of such a system. They were generally of opinion that they might in this way be relieved from the necessity of seeing some 25 per cent of the files that at present come to them. This would of course, be an appreciable relief, but my own belief is, after discussing with Secretaries, that the number of files that could be handled in this way would be nothing approaching this figure. I put it to the Ministers that if Parliamentary Secretaries were to note on all the files, which at present go from the official Secretary to the Minister, it was likely in fact to increase their work appreciably, because the Parliamentary Secretary might raise a number of new points and would in any case be contributing an additional note to the file. Their view was that this would not in practice increase their work, and indeed would diminish it. The outlook of the Parliamentary Secretary would be in general very much the same as that of the Minister. Criticisms or views he might express would in many cases be similar to those the Minister himself would express. In any case they felt that the Minister would be in a better position for reaching sound conclusions when he had before him not only the departmental point of view, but the political point of view as represented by the Parliamentary Secretary.

7. I pointed out the danger under such a system of interrupting the very essential practice of direct personal contact which at present exists between the official Secretary and the Minister. I also pointed out the necessity of maintaining the position and authority of the official Secretary. Some suggestion was made that where the Parliamentary Secretary differed from the official Secretary, the latter should have an opportunity of discussing with the Minister.

8. At the second Cabinet meeting I expressed the view that while Ministers could arrange for Parliamentary Secretaries to see files and could ask them to note, it was desirable that the notes should not be recorded on the files. We had a long discussion on this and it was clear that an arrangement whereby the Parliamentary Secretaries did not note on the file would not be acceptable to the Ministers. On the other hand, I felt that

such a system might impair the authority of the official Secretary. We reached no conclusion, but it was decided that I should talk the matter over further with the Premier in Naini Tal. I have had a further discussion with him and I put to him quite frankly my apprehensions. He took a very reasonable line and said that what he wanted done amounted to nothing more than the system that was being followed in certain departments at the present time though he desired to have it regularised. He said that Ministers are quite capable of keeping the Parliamentary Secretaries in order, and that they would not surrender their judgment to them, and that if they found that the Parliamentary Secretaries were continually differing from, and criticising, the official Secretaries to the detriment of business, they would have no hesitation in calling Parliamentary Secretaries to account. He explained that there were only half a dozen Parliamentary Secretaries who were capable of noting on the files in any effective manner and he was quite prepared to see that if any complaint were made about the tone or substance of their notes, this should be examined and the matter put right. He assured me that he did not in any way wish to weaken the position of the official Secretaries or to diminish the responsibility of the Ministers.

9. I understand that the constitutional position is that orders of the kind which Ministers desire to be passed could only be made as rules under Section 59 of the Government of India Act, and that consequently it rests with me in my discretion to take action after consultation with my Ministers. Your Excellency in your letter of 6th January 1938 gave certain cautions against using Section 59 in this connection. But I take it that it is only in virtue of Section 59 that I can prevent the Ministers doing what they in fact desire to do. The matter has been discussed hitherto on the basis of trying to reach an agreement between myself and the Ministers. But I think from the general tone of it that their view is that ultimately the decision lies with me. I should be glad to know whether you agree with this view of the constitutional position.

10. Assuming, however, that I have the power to act in my discretion in this matter, I am naturally not anxious to provoke a serious difference of opinion with my Ministers. There is some reason to believe that if I decline to do anything to meet their wishes, several of the Parliamentary Secretaries who are dissatisfied with their present position will resign, and this would create a difficult political situation for the Ministry which I should have precipitated. I feel, therefore, that the wise course is to meet them on the question of Parliamentary Secretaries noting on files, but to impose certain definite restrictions. I have accordingly drafted a note embodying my

conclusions which I propose to record before I go on leave. I lay down certain working rules of practice to be tried experimentally. I am not proposing to make them formally under Section 59. Nevertheless, the procedure will be sufficiently definite. I propose to discuss this note with Hallett on the 16th May before I make over charge. I think it is probable that he will have no objection because in Bihar the Parliamentary Secretaries already note on files. I should be grateful if Your Excellency could send me before 16th May any comments that may occur to you on my note. I feel it is necessary for me to reach some conclusion before I hand over.[38]

Yours sincerely,
H.G. HAIG

ENCLOSURE 1 TO NO. 44

NOTE BY PANT

Administrative matters

1. Files should ordinarily be sent to Parliamentary Secretary.

2. Parliamentary Secretary will dispose of all cases of a routine or unimportant nature, but all cases which raise questions of policy or relate to grants, or in which Parliamentary Secretary differs from the recommendation made by the department, shall be discussed by Parliamentary Secretary verbally with the Minister before passing orders, or shall be referred to the Minister by Parliamentary Secretary with his written note.

3. Decision of the Cabinet relating to particular departments should also be communicated to Parliamentary Secretaries concerned.

ENCLOSURE 2 TO NO. 44

NOTE BY HAIG

The question of the functions which Parliamentary Secretaries can properly and conveniently exercise in connection with Secretariat files has been discussed at length at two Cabinet meetings, and I have since had the opportunity of discussing the matter further with the Hon'ble Premier. The existing rule is that Parliamentary Secretaries will assist Ministers in administrative and legislative matters, but that they will not be regarded as in charge of a department or part of a department and will not be interposed between the Secretary and the Minister. They will have no power to dispose of files, but should be able to call for files for information from the Secretaries. They will assist Ministers in any way directed by the Ministers in dealing with departmental cases.

2. In different departments a different practice has grown up during the last few months in regard to these functions of Parliamentary Secretaries. In some departments when the Parliamentary Secretary records a note for the assistance of the Hon'ble Minister, the note does not form part of the file. This is in accordance with the intention of the original orders. In some departments, however, the practice has grown up of Parliamentary Secretaries recording their notes on the files, and this has, in certain cases, led to some degree of friction and some uncertainty as to the precise powers and constitutional position of Parliamentary Secretaries.

3. The Hon'ble Ministers desire that the functions of the Parliamentary Secretaries should be more precisely defined, and I agree. In defining those functions they desire that the Parliamentary Secretaries should have a more definite status than can, strictly speaking, be enjoyed by them under the existing rules. They also hope that it may be possible to devise some means by which the Ministers themselves may be relieved from the necessity of seeing a certain number of routine and unimportant files which at present come to them.

4. My own attitude in these discussions has been to emphasise certain principles to which I attach the greatest importance:

(*a*) The Governor can be advised only by the Ministers. Parliamentary Secretaries have no existence in the constitutional scheme laid down in the Government of India Act for the executive administration of the Province.

(*b*) It is necessary to maintain the position that it is the duty of the official Secretary to advise the Minister and take his orders.

The observance of these principles clearly limits the functions that can be assigned to Parliamentary Secretaries. In particular, it is essential that nothing should be done which would derogate from the position of the official Secretary as being the official adviser of the Minister, and that there should be no question of the Parliamentary Secretary gradually coming to share that position, or even being regarded as in a position of superiority in relation to the official Secretary.

5. Bearing these principles in mind and, at the same time, endeavouring to give full weight to the wishes of the Hon'ble Ministers, I suggest that we might try experimentally for some months the following working rules of practice:

(1) All files will be marked by the Secretary to the Hon'ble Minister.

(2) It will be for Hon'ble Ministers to decide how far, when files have been marked to them, they wish to have the assistance of the Parliamentary Secretary. The only definite restrictions would be that:

(*a*) the Parliamentary Secretary should not see any confidential files;

(*b*) he should not note on files which raise questions of the special responsibilities of the Governor, or in which action will be taken by the Governor in his discretion or in his individual judgment;

(*c*) he should not note on files dealing with appointments or postings, or with the internal arrangements of the Secretariat.

(3) Hon'ble Ministers can therefore issue orders in regard to any particular class of cases, other than those excepted above, [?and] that, as a matter of office routine, cases, where time permits, should be sent to the Parliamentary Secretary and the Parliamentary Secretary will have the right to record a note on the file before it reaches the Hon'ble Minister.

(4) When the Parliamentary Secretary records a note he will do so under his full signature. The use of initials is, as a matter of Secretariat practice, confined to members of Government, viz., the Hon'ble Ministers and the Governor. If, however, a Parliamentary Secretary does not wish to record a note, he may put his initials on the file merely in token of having seen the file.

(5) It is most important that in recording notes, Parliamentary Secretaries should realise clearly the constitutional position. Their notes are intended to be advice to the Hon'ble Ministers. A Parliamentary Secretary cannot record any order. Moreover, in stating his views, it is assumed that a Parliamentary Secretary will be careful to avoid writing in a controversial style or making any general criticism of the attitude of the Secretary. He will not regard himself as occupying any position of authority over the Secretary merely because he happens to record his note on the file after the Secretary has noted.

(6) It is desirable that the Parliamentary Secretary should normally abstain from noting on personal cases and minor matters of administrative detail. If a practice grows up of the Parliamentary Secretary noting views which differ from the Secretary on numerous matters of detail, the new system will, so far from helping the Hon'ble Ministers in their work, prove an embarrassment and lead to delay and additional work for everyone. The general principle, therefore, should be that Parliamentary Secretaries should confine their noting to matters of some importance in which they think that a point of view different from that of the Secretary, or

supplementary to what the Secretary has said, should be placed before the Hon'ble Minister.

(7) When a Parliamentary Secretary has noted a view in opposition to that of the Secretary, the Secretary should have an opportunity of explaining further his point of view before the Hon'ble Minister finally passes orders. This, I understand, is the practice in England. I am told that it would be unusual for a Minister to accept the view of his Parliamentary Secretary in preference to that of the permanent Secretary without giving the latter an opportunity of stating his reasons for maintaining his own view, if he wishes to maintain it. Normally this result would be achieved by the permanent Secretary seeing again, before submission to the Minister, any file upon which the Parliamentary Secretary had expressed a view differing from his own. Following the English practice, therefore, the Secretary should see the note of the Parliamentary Secretary where it differs from his own before the case goes to the Hon'ble Minister. The Secretary of course might not wish to press his own view, in which case he would indicate this on the file. If he did wish to maintain his view he would probably explain his opinion verbally to the Minister. It may be said that this rule will make the procedure somewhat cumbrous. But it seems to me an essential rule, and it emphasises the fact that if the Parliamentary Secretary is to be continually differing from the official Secretary, the business is bound to be impeded, and the system will not work satisfactorily.

(8) When a case comes to the Parliamentary Secretary and he is in agreement with the official Secretary and considers that the case is not of sufficient importance to be seen by the Minister, he should note on the file his opinion to this effect and the file will then be returned to the Secretary. Unless for any special reason the Secretary considers that the Minister should see the file, in which case he will, notwithstanding the opinion of the Parliamentary Secretary, submit it to the Minister, the Secretary will then dispose of the file without submission to the Minister. It will be understood that the Secretary takes this action on his own responsibility just as he takes action on his own responsibility to dispose of a number of routine and unimportant files. But he will have, in this case, the added assurance that the case has been seen by the Parliamentary Secretary, who would look at it from the point of view of political considerations, and that the Parliamentary Secretary considered it was unnecessary to submit it to the Minister.

(9) As an exception to the general rule that all cases will be marked direct by the Secretary to the Hon'ble Minister, leaving the Hon'ble

Minister to give his own directions as to the class of cases which should be seen by Parliamentary Secretaries, the following cases should be marked by Secretaries "to H.M. through P.S.", viz., files dealing with answers to questions in the Legislature, or resolutions or bills, official and non-official. This emphasises the point that the primary duties of the Parliamentary Secretary are parliamentary and that in all business which concerns the Legislature, the files should, as a matter of settled practice, be seen by the Parliamentary Secretary.

6. I suggest that these rules should be tried experimentally for some months. Whether they prove convenient or the reverse will depend in the main in the spirit in which they are worked. If they are worked in a spirit of good-will and with full acceptance of the necessary limitations, I hope that the new system will be of assistance to the Hon'ble Ministers and prove more satisfactory to the Parliamentary Secretaries, and, at the same time, that the authority and position of the official Secretaries will be in no way impaired.

45

HAIG TO LINLITHGOW
R/3/1/73

Secret
No. U.P.-78

Camp,
May 13th, 1938

My dear Lord Linlithgow,

I am glad to say that there have been, since I last wrote, no further serious manifestations of Hindu-Muslim ill-will. The underlying situation, however, remains unchanged and general opinion does not seem to anticipate any settlement arising from the Gandhi-Jinnah conversations.[39] Failing a settlement I think we must be prepared for communal outbreaks to continue whenever there is any exciting cause, such as the occurrence of festivals, &c.

2. I mentioned at the end of my last letter that the Chehlum had led to rioting in Lucknow between Sunnis and Shias. This caused a good deal of anxiety for some days, but the Police handled the situation very vigorously and peace was restored before long. The rioting, however, must I fear have left a legacy of increased bitterness between the two sects, and the Government have under consideration in consequence a temporary addition

to the Lucknow Police Force, though owing to political apprehensions they are not prepared to make the Muslim inhabitants pay for it. The Sunnis seem now to have started some form of civil disobedience similar to that which was practised for a considerable time in 1936 and led to the appointment of the Allsop Committee.[40] I imagine that apart from the genuine feeling between the two sects, there are certain elements among the Sunnis which are not sorry to have an opportunity of embarrassing the Government by trying to maintain disturbed conditions in Lucknow. On the other hand a real attempt is being made by some of the more responsible leaders to reach a settlement.

3. The Premier was very well impressed by the active measures taken by the Police in Lucknow to bring the disturbances under control, and I think this personal experience has made him more appreciative of the work done by the Police elsewhere. At any rate, after having in spite of suggestions made to him, delayed many weeks to express any appreciation of what the Police did in Allahabad and Benares, he has recently sent to the Inspector-General an admirable letter expressing his satisfaction and appreciation of the Police work in Lucknow, Allahabad and Benares.

4. At a time when this appreciation of Police work seemed to be rather markedly lacking, I made a point of visiting Cawnpore on April 26th to open a very fine Kotwali that has just been built. I enclose a copy of the speech I made.[41] In the case of Cawnpore I was particularly anxious to give the Police some encouragement; for they had done well under most difficult conditions, and the Ministers were inclined to ignore all their good work on account of indignation at the violent attack which had been made on Hafiz Muhammad Ibrahim, the Minister, early in February when he was proceeding in procession through the heart of Cawnpore. Briefly what happened was that the local Hindu Congressmen, who are an exceedingly mischievous and unreliable lot, wished to organise a demonstration in favour of Muhammad Ibrahim. They know perfectly well that this would be greatly resented by the Muslim League, seeing that Muhammad Ibrahim had deserted the League for the Congress. Nevertheless they insisted on organising this provocative demonstration. It was unfortunate that just at this time both the District Magistrate[42] and the Superintendent of Police[43] were away on casual leave for a few days attending the Civil Service Week in Lucknow. The officers on the spot got information about this procession and the probable reactions to it rather late and did not convey any warning to the Minister against coming to Cawnpore. When, however, he arrived in the morning, they told him at the station that there was likely to be trouble, and they advised him not to

proceed with the arrangements. He felt, however, that things had gone too far and that he would be disgraced if he cancelled the arrangements at the last moment. Consequently, the procession took place and though a considerable body of Police were present along the route, at two points Muslims attacked the procession with brickbats, and at the second point, when the procession was broken up, the Minister himself was in some danger. The Police cleared up the situation very rapidly, but the Ministry as a whole felt that they had been insulted by this attack on one of their members and were persuaded that the Muslim Kotwal had shown indifference in the arrangements for the protection of the procession. The matter fell into the background as the constitutional crisis almost immediately supervened and I had hoped that it would not be pressed further, particularly as the Commissioner[44] who held an inquiry sent in a report which on the whole justified and exonerated the local officers. However, the Ministers insisted on discussing the report of the Commissioner at a Cabinet meeting held at the end of April just before I left Lucknow, and after prolonged debate decided to record a general expression of dissatisfaction with the arrangements made in Cawnpore in this connection, and also called upon the Kotwal to give his explanation on a charge of either being unacquainted with the conditions or, if he realised the conditions, taking inadequate steps to deal with them. I think it is probable that the Kotwal will be able to give a reasonable explanation, but it is clear that the Ministry are very anxious to transfer him. I have warned them that the transfer of the Kotwal at the present time is a step that may involve some danger to the peace of Cawnpore, and I hope that the matter may at any rate be postponed for some time until the labour situation has declared itself.

5. With regard to the labour situation, I have little to add to what I said in my last letter. The employers have been engaged, I understand, in drafting an elaborate rejoinder to the Inquiry Committee's report. The Ministry decided to take the report into consideration on the 10th of May, but I have not yet heard whether the employers' representation has been received. I had some talk recently with the Premier about the probable course of events. He had always maintained that labour would regard the recommendations of the report as the minimum, and I put it to him that as it was evident that the employers would reject some of the most important recommendations, a situation of considerable danger was likely to arise, and I asked him what line of action he contemplated taking. He said that if the employers could establish the fact that certain of the recommendations of the Committee were unreasonable, that was certainly a factor that the

Government would have to take into account, and he evidently contemplated the possibility of being able to get labour to accept something less than the recommendations of the report, if a convincing case against them was made out. He thus still hopes that the Government will in effect be able to mediate between the two parties and bring them to an agreed settlement. This is, I think, the only chance of avoiding trouble, and I am glad that the Premier seems to be taking a reasonable attitude in the matter. I feel that one of the dangers is that, economically, labour is in a position of hopeless weakness. If a strike were to take place, I fancy the employers are confident that it could not last more than about two months, and indeed the workmen have no financial resources behind them. This may tempt the employers to take up an unduly stiff attitude. On the other hand, if they did, public opinion would be against them, and I think public opinion will count for a good deal. On the whole, it seems to me not impossible that there may be some settlement, though it will obviously take time.

6. There have been no further developments in the investigation into the Pipridih train dacoity, and I understand that there is nothing at present to suggest that this gang had any extensive connections, or was part of any of the well-known revolutionary organizations. In connection with this question of revolutionaries, you may be interested to know that recently I had a communication from one of the ex-Kakori prisoners forwarding for my favourable consideration a copy of a letter he had addressed to the Premier, in which he explained that he was entirely without financial resources and that therefore he should either be provided with a Government post or be given a substantial loan to enable him to set himself up in business, in return for which he was prepared to abstain from all further undesirable activities while the loan was outstanding. He proceeded to state the proposition that it was necessary for a man to live, particularly if he were a revolutionary. I fancy, in fact, that one of the main difficulties with men of this type is that they have no means of livelihood, and that extremist agitation does offer them some prospect of being able to collect a little money. I imagine this is a problem which must be facing the Bengal Government on a much more extensive scale.

7. Contrary to expectations, the debate in the Assembly on the motion to refer the Tenancy Bill to a Select Committee petered out in less than a day. Though there seems to have been some understanding as a result of which the debate was cut short, the general impression left on the public was that the landlords' opposition had been much weaker than had been anticipated. Just before I left Lucknow, the taluqdars sent me a memorial claiming that the proposals in the Tenancy Bill were in conflict with their

sanads and asking for my protection. I gave the Raja of Jehangirabad an interview in connection with this memorial and asked him, in the first place, what action he wished me to take about it. He explained that he wished me to treat it as a memorial specially addressed to myself personally and did not wish me to make it over to Sir Maurice Hallett for disposal, and that he hoped I would take the memorial to England and show it to the Secretary of State and have some discussion with the India Office about it. I explained to him that I had little belief in the validity of their legal arguments, expounded to him what my constitutional position was in regard to legislation of this kind, and advised the taluqdars to concentrate on political opposition to such of the proposals as they felt were most seriously contrary to their interests and to ensure that their case was put before the public in a convincing way. I found him very reasonable, though naturally somewhat depressed about the future, and I hope in fact the landlords will devote their energies to trying to secure modifications on certain important points, rather than rely on outside authorities to save them. I may mention that the Premier gave me recently in conversation his anticipation of the future course of business in connection with these tenancy and revenue measures. In addition to the Tenancy Bill, there remain still to be drafted a revenue bill and a bill dealing with the arrears of rent that were suspended last autumn. The Select Committee on the Tenancy Bill is not expected to start work until about the middle or end of June. It is expected that its report will be ready for submission to the Legislature about the end of July or the beginning of August. In the meantime, the bills dealing with revenue and the stayed arrears of rent will be available before the end of June. They also will be taken up by the Legislature early in August. On this programme it certainly seems that when I return from leave in the middle of September the legislation will still be under discussion, and this is in fact the anticipation of the Premier.

8. I referred in my last letter to the question of appointment of the Rural Development Officer. Since then the I.F.S. officer whom I mentioned has been appointed, and I hope he will do reasonably well. The question of the scope and organization of the Rural Development Movement is now under active consideration, and I am hopeful that practical schemes of work will be evolved. I hope, too, before long that the question of the recruitment of the staff will be settled on a satisfactory basis and that the principle of utilizing the Public Service Commission for recruiting to the more important posts will have been firmly established. There has been a good deal of controversy recently in connection with the functions and authority of the Public Service Commission. It is a somewhat prolonged tussle, for there are elements within the Government, particularly Dr. Katju,

which are most reluctant to submit to the restriction of the Ministry's powers over appointments. I think however my position is being steadily consolidated and that this struggle will end satisfactorily. The Public Service Commission themselves, under the guidance of Sir Digby Drake-Brockman, their Chairman, are very properly insistent on their position and rights.

9. I am afraid this letter has run to considerable length, and I will only refer briefly to a few other topics. I have addressed Your Excellency separately and in detail on the question of the functions of Parliamentary Secretaries and the proposal for separation of executive and judicial functions in the districts. The report of the Anti-corruption Committee set up by the Government is about to be published. One of the proposals of the Committee on which they lay great stress, and which appears to me to be fundamentally unsound, is that a Committee should be set up in each district which would include all the local members of the Legislature to advise the District Officer in dealing with corruption. When this matter was discussed in the Cabinet, I told the Ministers plainly that in my opinion if they wanted to secure real results, they should make their wishes known unmistakably to the officials and require their full and determined co-operation. I said I was convinced that if this were done, the co-operation required would be forthcoming in full measure. But if officials felt, as they do at present, that the anti-corruption campaign is being used largely for the purpose of satisfying personal or political enmities, then it could not be expected that they would take up the matter with any enthusiasm or conviction. I told them that if non-officials were to play any appreciable part in this campaign I felt that the results were bound to be disappointing, and a great deal of ill-feeling would be created. Somewhat to my surprise I found that several of the Ministers appeared to be impressed by what I said, though the Premier is still inclined to cling to the ideas on which he has been proceeding for several months past.

10. The selections of Honorary Magistrate under the new system are being made now. I have not received any definite information as to the nature of the results. Your Excellency will no doubt have noticed in the papers two strong judgments (copies enclosed)[45] passed by the Allahabad High Court convicting Congress workers of contempt of court in respect of representations they had addressed to certain subordinate courts in the districts. These judgments will have an excellent effect and will, I hope, put a stop to a practice which had probably become not uncommon. One of the persons convicted, Dr. Bishwanath Mukerji, M.L.A., is one of the most troublesome Congressmen in the very troublesome district of Gorakhpur, and this reminder of the limitation the law places on his actions

will be very salutary. My attention was drawn some months ago to a similar case in Oudh when a Congress official made a representation to a Munsif in connection with a case before him. In that case the Ministers seemed inclined to interest themselves on behalf of the Congress worker. The officiating Chief Judge mentioned the matter to me, and I said I hoped that the Court would take a strong line. Eventually, the Congress worker gave a full apology and the Chief Court did not proceed further.

11. I have been in Naini Tal for the last fortnight, and one cannot fail to appreciate the advantages, from the point of view of work, of being in a good climate. The Premier has also been up here most of this time and I have had some useful talks with him. He is feeling better, but I think certainly requires to take care of himself. I have urged him to return here as soon as Sir Maurice Hallett has taken over charge in Lucknow, and I think he will be only too ready to do so. Meantime Kidwai, the Revenue Minister, has been ordered a fortnight's complete rest by the doctors. As his trouble is heart, he is not coming up to Naini Tal, but is disappearing to some unknown destination. It was also reported in the papers that Sampurnanand, the Education Minister, had been suffering from sunstroke. There is no doubt that all the Ministers have been feeling the strain of working at high pressure in a trying climate, and I hope that the experience of this year will convince them of the unsoundness of abandoning the hill exodus and that next year we may go back to something more nearly resembling the old conditions. The Ministers themselves would, I am convinced, be very ready to do this, but the majority of the party is still strongly opposed to it, and it may take a good deal of argument to convince them.

Yours sincerely,
H.G. HAIG

46

HAIG TO LINLITHGOW
R/3/1/73

Secret — Camp,
No. U.P.-80 — *May 14th, 1938*

My dear Lord Linlithgow,

Since the despatch of my fortnightly report No. U.P.-78, dated 13th May 1938, I have received official details of the serious agrarian outrage in the

Maharajganj Tehsil of the Gorakhpur District. Following on a prolonged period of ill-feeling, a body of 200 villagers marched two miles, attacked and broke open the *chhaoni* of a small zemindar, who had at one time been the *karinda* of the zemindar of their own village and deliberately murdered him. This took place on the 8th May and on the 9th May the Police arrived on the spot in adequate force and arrested about 40 persons. So far as the immediate situation is concerned, it appears to be in hand. But I regard this affair as very disturbing in view of the fact that for months past the Maharajganj Tehsil has been the danger spot of the Gorakhpur District and the relations between landlords and tenants throughout the Tehsil are reported to be very strained. The District Magistrate[46] and the Superintendent of Police[47] evidently consider the situation in the Tehsil generally to be serious, and think there are some prospects of its deteriorating. I have sent a telegram to the Premier who is in Bombay, giving him the bare facts and saying that in my judgment immediate and vigorous action is required in order to reassert respect for authority in the Maharajganj Tehsil, and that I hope to discuss the matter with him on the 16th May when he returns and when I shall be in Lucknow. The root of the trouble in this place is Mr. Shibban Lal Saksena, M.L.A., who has secured a very powerful hold on the tenants throughout the area. Doubtless the zemindars have been oppressive, but the local officers attribute the present aggressive spirit among the tenants to the activities of Mr. Shibban Lal Saksena and his followers. I have written a detailed note for the Premier expressing my apprehensions and urging that the situation needs to be dealt with firmly at once. The Commissioner[48] has been asked to give his recommendations as to the action required and I hope these will be available for discussion on the 16th May when it would be possible to go into the whole matter with the Premier and also with Sir Maurice Hallett. I feel that now that violence has actually shown itself in this area, the situation requires to be handled firmly if further trouble is to be avoided. On the other hand, I know that the Premier will be extremely reluctant to take action to interfere with Mr. Shibban Lal Saksena's activities. I have repeatedly pressed him in the past to take some action, but he has never done more than remonstrate with Mr. Saksena, with no apparent effect.[49]

Yours sincerely,
H.G. HAIG

47

HAIG TO LINLITHGOW
R/3/1/73

Secret *May 17th, 1938*
No. U.P.-81

My dear Lord Linlithgow,

I have had to wait until my return to Lucknow to be able to sound opinion in various quarters and to reply to Your Excellency's telegram of 6th May about reactions to the settlement of the Orissa crisis. As I wrote to Your Excellency at the time, my Premier, who was in Naini Tal, did not seem to be taking any interest in Orissa developments or show any signs of apprehension that the ultimate result could affect his Ministry.

2. The first Press reactions indicated feelings of thankfulness that the crisis had been averted, followed by something of a chorus of triumph in the Congress Press and attacks on the system of Civilian Governors. The attitude of the *Pioneer* was rather apologetic; the *Leader*, which is opposed to the Civilian Governors and wishes "Indian public men" to be given opportunities of governing Provinces, was at first rather inclined to be thankful that the crisis had been avoided. On May 7th, however, there appeared a short and extremely malicious leaderette, which seemed to indicate that the Chief Editor (a Liberal) was not at all pleased that the Congress should have been able to claim a success.

3. Lucknow opinion in general appears to be that the mass of the population knew nothing of the crisis at the time, and would not have understood the issues at stake if they had; and that they have not, therefore, been greatly interested or influenced by the settlement. The immediate effect of the settlement in this Province is not, therefore, very noticeable and will die down fairly soon, but the ultimate effect is likely to be an impression both among Congress and non-Congressmen that the Government are not prepared to stand up to the Congress, and it is possible that Congress leaders may regard this as an encouragement for making further claims of a constitutional nature. One political leader, with whom I conversed today, was of the opinion that the settlement was only sound course in regrettable circumstances and that if a break had occurred on this question, Indian public opinion would have been very unsympathetic with the British Government, that is to say, he considered that it would have been bad ground on which to fight. Another thought that the fact that

the withdrawal was made at the last moment was very damaging. If the Government thought they were in the wrong, they should have modified their decision as soon as the point was brought to their notice. Not having done this, they should have seen the matter through. The decision is generally attributed to the European situation, and is therefore taken as an indication that the British Government feel themselves to be in a weak position and therefore attacks on them may be pressed home. Service opinion in general seems to be that the cancellation of his leave by Sir John Hubback was quite a natural and proper solution in the circumstances, and that, while the Congress may consider themselves to be "one up" on the score, the gain is not an important one, nor is it final.

4. Among the vernacular Press, the Congress papers have mostly claimed the result as a victory, while the *Bharat* of Allahabad holds the view that "the move of the Viceroy in this matter shows his far-sighted statesmanship." The *Aj* of Benares, the *Sadaquat* of Cawnpore and the *Oudh Akhbar* take the same line and praise Sir John Hubback's decision.

Yours sincerely,
H.G. HAIG

NOTES

1. The report of the Committee under Mr Justice Allsop appointed to examine the Madhe Sahaba dispute in Lucknow was published in *Government Gazette of the U.P., Extraordinary*, 28 March 1938.
2. In 1930 two platoons of Garhwalis refused duty in Peshawar. They had been facing an excited mob of Pathans hurling bricks and bottles and had not been allowed to retaliate. The N.C.Os. of the platoons were sentenced to various terms of imprisonment and the riflemen were dismissed. The last N.C.O. was released from prison in 1938 or 1939.
3. Lord Linlithgow minuted: 'Whose'.
4. In an article in *Harijan* on 26 March 1938, Mahatma Gandhi advocated a large non-violent army of volunteers which would be equal to every occasion where the police and military were required. He wrote that 'a few hundred, may be a few thousand, ... spotless deaths [of members of such an army] will once and for all put an end to the riots.... To the extent that the Congress Ministers have been obliged to make use of the police and the military, to that extent, in my opinion, we must admit our failure.'
5. See note 1 above.
6. Not printed.
7. Mr B.G.P. Thomas.
8. Mr R.A. Horton.

9. The date of Lord Linlithgow's letter was in fact 29 March 1938. In this letter to provincial governors, the Viceroy said that he and Lord Zetland had been considering a Parliamentary Bill for the purpose of removing defects or ambiguities that had been shown up in the Government of India Act. Linlithgow enclosed three documents (not included in the print) one of which was a revision of the draft Bill. R/3/1/73.
10. The Niemeyer proposals evidently related to financial shortcomings in the Government of India Act.
11. Clause 26 was designed to protect against cut motions in the provincial legislatures in respect of establishments which served reserved posts. R/3/1/73.
12. Sir Harry Haig's comments are not printed.
13. See *U.P.P., 1936-7*, No. 91.
14. In telegram 570-G of 17 April 1938, Lord Linlithgow reported that the Madras Ministry had asked the Governor (Lord Erskine) to reduce the salaries fixed for the Chairman and Members of the Madras Public Service Commission. Linlithgow was disposed to think that it would be difficult for a Governor to refuse to agree to a reasonable reduction in the rates of pay for new entrants to the Commission. He asked for Governors' views on the subject. R/3/1/73.
15. Not included in R/3/1/73.
16. The text of the Bill is not included in R/3/1/73.
    Lord Linlithgow replied to this letter on 8 May 1938. He said: (1) that on the question of the Governor's previous sanction for the introduction of the Tenancy Bill, the Viceroy's advisers entirely supported Sir Harry Haig's line in the preliminary discussions with Pandit Pant and Mr Asthana; (2) that unless further changes were made, the Bill would require reservation as several of its provisions were repugnant to the existing Indian law; (3) that the Ministry's proposals in the forthcoming Land Revenue Bill would certainly attract the provisions of Section 299 (3) of the Government of India Act. This was because the Bill would modify the rights in land. Ibid.
17. Asterisks in R/3/1/73.
18. R/3/1/73. In paragraph 3 of this letter to provincial governors, Lord Linlithgow asked for a frank expression of views by Governors on a range of questions.
19. Lord Linlithgow minuted: 'Haig does not mention the possibility of missing of Provincial Service Officers which I think Hallett referred to.'
20. The Royal Commission on the Superior Civil Services in India, chaired by Lord Lee of Fareham, had reported in 1924. (Cmd. 2128.)
21. Lord Linlithgow minuted: 'Not a healthy picture but a very interesting contribution. I suppose we have now most of these letters from G[overnor]s in.'
22. A train dacoity took place at Pipridih on 10 April 1938. In his letter U.P.-68 of 19 April 1938, Sir Harry Haig said that his C.I.D. believed the dacoity to be the work of an organisation similar to the Hindustan Socialist Republican

Army. The C.I.D. hoped that by saying nothing about their suspicions 'the men who are at present absent from their homes may return, and that then they may be able to pick them all up simultaneously with some hope of securing valuable evidence.' R/3/1/73.

23. Lord Linlithgow minuted: 'The sole effective step is insistence upon "fire lanes" or wide streets breaking up the area in blocks so that the fire can be confined to one block.'
24. Mr D.P. Hardy.
25. Kunwar Jasbir Singh.
26. Mr V. Sahay.
27. Mr Manohar Das Chaturvedi.
28. Lord Linlithgow minuted: 'Having I hope had the benefit of the Governor's advice.'
29. Lord Linlithgow minuted: 'I hope that Pant's own collapse may bring home to him the inexpediency, in the public interest, of pandering to the prejudice of a few people in Lucknow who say, "We have to stew in the plains, so why should not the Ministry do the same!"' [Pandit Pant had gone to Naini Tal to recover from the heat of Lucknow.]
30. Mr G.L. Vivian.
31. Babu H.S.K. Maheshari.
32. The Orissa Ministry had indicated their opposition to the appointment of Mr J.R. Dain, the Revenue Commissioner and 'their subordinate', as acting Governor during the Governor's leave of absence. They had now decided to resign on the day Dain assumed office. Mahatma Gandhi had telegraphed Lord Linlithgow saying that he regarded the point of principle of such importance that the possibility of an all-India crisis 'must be looked for'. He begged that the Viceroy reconsider the appointment. In telegram 314-G.C. of 30 April 1938, Linlithgow asked Governors to keep him informed of ministerial reactions and of developments in their provinces. R/3/1/73.
33. In telegram 326-G.C. of 1 May 1938 Lord Linlithgow said that Lord Zetland felt the best solution to the Orissa crisis was for the Governor (Sir John Hubback) to cancel his leave. Zetland was anxious to know whether this compromise would have unfortunate reactions on service morale. R/3/1/73.
34. Telegram 49-C of 1 May 1938 from Lord Erskine (Governor of Madras). Mr Rajagopalachari was certain that all Congress Ministries would resign if Mr Dain became Acting Governor of Orissa. Rajagopalachari thought it was just possible this would not happen if a statement was issued that the appointment was an isolated case which would not recur. However he was not sure that even such a statement would be acceptable to Congress. R/3/1/38.
35. In the event it was decided that the Governor of Orissa should cancel his leave. See No. 47.
36. The Report of the Stuart Committee, which was submitted in 1921, is on V/26/248/2 in the India Office Records.

37. Lord Linlithgow minuted: 'I agree and to make a pretty voluminous memo. with plenty of references to other authorities &c. – to keep them busy.' Mr W.C. Dible was appointed Commissioner on Special Duty to work out the details of the scheme. On 29 June 1938 Dible sent a lengthy note to all District Magistrates in the U.P. (with the exception of four districts) outlining the principles of the scheme. He asked the District Magistrates to prepare proposals for their districts and submit them by 20 July 1938. After that Dible proposed to visit the divisional headquarters and discuss them with Commissioners and District Magistrates. Dible's note is on R/3/1/73.
38. Lord Linlithgow did not reply to this letter before Sir Harry Haig went on leave as he decided to consult Lord Zetland about the proposals. On 3/4 June 1938 Linlithgow wrote to Sir Maurice Hallett to say that he thought it would be entirely proper to go ahead with the Ministers on the lines of Haig's proposals. R/3/1/73.
39. Mahatma Gandhi and Mr Jinnah had three hours' discussion on the Hindu-Muslim question in Bombay on 28 April 1938. Further contacts between Congress and Jinnah took place over the summer but the dialogue had ended without result by October 1938.
40. See note 1 above.
41. Not printed.
42. Mr L. Owen was District Magistrate, Cawnpore in February 1938.
43. Mr G.A. Pearce.
44. Mr Panna Lal.
45. The copies are not included in R/3/1/73.
46. Mr J.E. Pedley.
47. Mr W.H. Baldock.
48. Mr G.L. Vivian.
49. Lord Linlithgow minuted: 'P.S.V. – S./S. to see. I am not a bit surprised that the chickens are coming home to roost; indeed I only marvel that they have been quiescent so long.'

CHAPTER 3

Documents for 27 May – 16 September 1938

48

HALLETT TO LINLITHGOW
R/3/1/73

Secret
No. U.P.-85

Camp,
May 27th, 1938

My dear Lord Linlithgow,

This, my first Fortnightly Report from the United Provinces, will consist partly of first impressions. First impressions may not be correct, but as you know, I always give the views which I have at the time of writing, even though they may be modified later. I have already met four of my Ministers, all the Secretaries and some heads of departments. While in Lucknow, I saw the Premier, Dr. Katju, Mr. Muhammad Ibrahim and Mr. Sampurnanand. From my interviews with them, I formed the impression that they have far greater intellectual ability than any of the Bihar Ministers and that opinion has been confirmed by what I have seen of their notes on the files. I have not yet seen Mrs. Pandit or Mr. Qidwai.

2. All the four Ministers who were present in Lucknow attended the ceremony at Government House when I assumed Office; three Parliamentary Secretaries also came as well as the President of the Council and the Speaker of the Assembly. This was satisfactory. I saw a report in the Press that the Provincial Congress Committee were going to take the Ministers to task for attending, but either the report was untrue or the Premier succeeded in getting an adverse resolution withdrawn.

3. The Premier has come up to Naini Tal mainly because of the illness of his daughter, and I hope to be able to discuss fully with him the important questions which are pending and which, as at present arranged, we will

discuss at full meetings of the Cabinet about June 9th. In particular it is essential to discuss fully with him the Cawnpore situation. I put forward some provisional views on the question later in this letter and will keep you informed if anything of importance comes out of my discussion with the Premier.

REPORT OF THE ANTI-CORRUPTION COMMITTEE

4. I enclose a copy of this Report.[1] It is disappointing and inadequate. The Committee were of course rushed over the report; they made no real enquiries; they issued a circular letter and a questionnaire giving the persons consulted very little time to submit a considered opinion. They have given in one paragraph a description of the "occasions of corruption" which, as far as I can see, is a list of the main activities of every department of Government. They do not go into details and though in an earlier paragraph they have attempted to define "corruption" and have rightly suggested that extortion and bribery can be distinguished from customary payments (i.e. tips or *bakhshish*), they have made no attempt to show which form of corruption is prevalent in any particular department. Nor have they shown whether those guilty of corruption are the superior or subordinate staff. Having omitted to deal with these important points, the Committee has put forward certain recommendations for the prevention and punishment of corruption which appear to me to be little real help for dealing with the problem. The most difficult is the suggestion that in each District there should be an anti-corruption committee, consisting largely of non-officials. I have not completed my examination of the Report, but I hope to put a considered minute on it before my Ministers and will send Your Excellency a copy. Probably the Committee and my Ministry are honest in this matter, but I have an uneasy feeling at the back of my mind, that even though corruption may be prevalent, this crusade is inspired in some quarters not so much by a desire to secure a pure administration as by a wish to destroy the morale of the services and to bring them more under political control. This you will understand is a purely tentative opinion, but this point must not be lost sight of.

SEPARATION OF JUDICIAL AND EXECUTIVE

5. Sir Harry Haig has kept you informed of these discussions. I do not think the Ministry are really very keen on these proposals; it is liberals such as Chintamani who are pushing this question, though their motive in

doing so is obscure. If they had not taken this attitude, the Ministers here might have dropped the whole question and followed the line adopted by Rajagopalachari in Madras. I discussed the question with Dr. Katju who deals with it, and though he would not admit in reply to a blunt question that he wanted merely eye-wash, I feel myself that he did not want any drastic action. Of course in dealing with this question I am prone to base my views too much on my Bihar experience where the magisterial system differs materially from that in force here. But in dealing with the question my main object is to see that nothing is done to lessen the power of the District Officer to maintain law and order. I feel that the Ministers will support me in this and that their final decision will be, I hope, harmless.

TRIAL BY JURY

6. This is one of the questions marked for discussion by the Council of Ministers. The opinions received are voluminous and interesting; it is generally agreed that assessors are little use, but there are a good many opinions in favour of trial by Judges without a jury or assessors. I doubt whether the Ministry will introduce any radical change of system, the Judicial Minister recognises that many cases cannot suitably be tried by juries, e.g. communal cases, serious dacoity cases or cases which owing to the large number of accused or the intricacy of the case involved long hearings. Thus if the jury system is extended, the extension will not be very wide.

PARLIAMENTARY SECRETARIES

7. I have kept you informed of developments. It has been reported in the Press that the Parliamentary Secretaries here are still restive and this I understand was the reason why only three attended the assumption of office ceremony. I cannot give you more information about this matter till I have discussed with the Premier.

LEGISLATIVE COUNCIL

8. The Council has been discussing the Bills sent up by the Assembly and has made material changes. I have not yet discussed the position with the Premier and as I have not seen the original Bills, it is not very easy for me to appreciate the effect of the amendments that have been carried. Judging mainly by the Press, it looks as if the Assembly would not accept the

amendments made in the two Taxation Bills, the Stamp (Amendment) Bill and the Court Fees (Amendment) Bill, and that therefore we may be faced with a joint session. The Members' Emoluments Bill also led to a difference of opinion about Travelling Allowance; but I gather from the Press that the Council has at last accepted the Bill. I feel doubtful, and Haig was I think also doubtful, whether the Council was wise in differing from the Assembly over these Taxation Bills and thereby facing a joint session.

The Council has also discussed the rules of procedure, but I have not been able to study this question yet or to see whether the rules will give rise to any difficulties. As far as I can see, they give the Council power to delay legislation.

CAWNPORE SITUATION

9. I have just discussed the position with the Chief Secretary and hope to be able to discuss it either today or tomorrow with the Premier. But I am experiencing some difficulty in getting in touch with him, as he is very troubled over the serious illness of his daughter. You have of course seen all that has appeared in the Press; as usual the reports appearing in the Press from whichever side they may emanate are often exaggerated and distorted. The local officers judging by a telephone message from the District Magistrate received by the Chief Secretary this morning have still got good control, while it is also satisfactory that there have not been up to the present any indication of violence on the part of the strikers. But we cannot tell how long this will last. One of the main difficulties is now regarding the clerical staff and other non-worker staff who are prevented access to the mills and this is probably the reason for the telegram which the Employers' Association addressed to me and the Premier yesterday, of which I annex a copy. Hancox, the District Magistrate,[2] says that this contains some misstatements and inaccuracies and he is also doing his best to secure access for the clerical staff, &c. to the mills. The workers are anxious to stop this because they anticipate that this will help the employers to smuggle in workers and so cause a breach in the strikers. A possible solution which I will discuss with the Premier would be to get the employers to declare a definite lock-out.

10. As regards public utility services, the District Magistrate has taken necessary steps, and so far, the strikers seem to be against interference with those services, but of course if they become more desperate you cannot tell what will happen.

11. The real question is what can be done to settle the dispute and I

must admit that I cannot help feeling that the employers are considerably to blame. Further information may lead me to modify this opinion. But the following points strike me:

(*a*) The employers in their reply to the Report start off with a vigorous attack on the Committee, its personnel and the terms of reference. If they felt so strongly on these points, surely they should have put them forward at an earlier stage. On the contrary, at least so my Premier tells me, they did not raise any objection and even helped in drafting the terms of reference.

(*b*) The Premier gave them an opportunity of giving their views before the Report was published, in the hope that there might be an agreed settlement. They did not take advantage of this, but after the Report had been published, waited till the last moment before putting out their very provocative reply.

(*c*) I am told that at one time they contemplated concluding their reply by stating what concessions they were prepared to give, but this idea was given up. All they did say was they would be prepared to adopt any really practicable proposals which would bring about close co-operation between the employers and workers. Attention is being drawn to these more conciliatory statements in recent articles in the *Pioneer*. But the inevitable impression conveyed by the reply was that it was a wholesale rejection of the Committee's proposals and this impression was, I feel, strengthened by the fact that the employers or many of them at once left India.

(*d*) The workers accepted the Report, though I believe it is now contended that they did not indicate their views.

(*e*) The workers put themselves in the wrong by the strike, as even Pandit Jawaharlal Nehru recognises, but their action is hardly surprising.

12. The question seems to me to be whether the employers will reconsider their attitude. There are some signs of this as I hear they have asked for an interview with the Premier for the purpose of "elucidating their position". If they do not become more reasonable, it seems to me they will drive my Government into adopting a more pro-workers attitude than they would have done.

13. When I discussed the position briefly with my Premier, he seemed to take the not unreasonable view that the present low price of cotton and high price of piecegoods justified an increase of wages. He recognised that adjustments would be necessary if cotton rose in price and was, I gathered, in favour of some form of Wage Adjustment Board. To me, very much of an amateur in these matters, this seems quite sound and possibly this may be a possible solution. He showed no desire to break the capitalist

and recognised the incalculable harm that would result from any action tending in this direction.

14. All this is rather vague and indefinite, but I feel we must take action to avoid prolongation of the strike, which means a loss of a lakh of rupees a day. How far the whole agitation is "communist" in origin, I cannot very well say. I feel doubtful whether it is and our intelligence does not give us very much information on this point. I shall be in a better position to let you know how things stand after I have seen the Premier. Meanwhile I should be most grateful for any advice which you can give me, for I feel very much at sea over this difficult problem.

AGRARIAN SITUATION

15. Haig reported to you the case from Gorakhpur, where a zamindar was murdered. I discussed the matter with the Premier, and he at one time said he would go to Gorakhpur. I impressed on him the desirability of reinforcing the Police if the local officers wanted this and pointed out that my experience in such conditions was that even if the extra Police were not used, the moral effect of their presence was good. That was my experience in Bihar. I gather things have quietened down and that the local officers do not want more Police and in view of this, or possibly because of Cawnpore, or his domestic troubles, the Premier has not gone there. He has also I understand promised to get hold of one of the fire-brands, Shibban Lal Saxena (an M.L.A.) and restrain him. I hope he will do so. As far as I can see, Gorakhpur is a District, rather at the back of beyond, where landholders have been oppressive, but I cannot claim any detailed knowledge of the situation which seems to be in hand at present and not to have deteriorated.

GENERAL SITUATION

16. I have studied the Commissioners' Reports and the various Police Reports with care; they are rather depressing; but the reassuring feature is that District Officers, in spite of their difficulties, are holding their own. I refrain from further comment; written Reports may be misleading, and I hope to meet Commissioners when on recess in Naini Tal and also to do some touring in the rains.

Yours sincerely,
M.G. HALLETT

ENCLOSURE TO NO. 48

COPY OF TELEGRAM FROM EMPLOYERS' ASSOCIATION, CAWNPORE TO DONALDSON

May 26th, 1938

Association much concerned over recent developments of picketting. Although factories closed by strike essential certain office supervisory Watch and Ward and Maintenance Staff should attend factories daily. Picketers including women using obstructive intimidatory and abusive methods which may lead to breach of peace as picketting by no means peaceable. Association are of opinion picketers are depriving the right of civil liberty and the right to work of those willing to work. The attention of Government is drawn to the fact that there is a right to work of those who desire to do so and these persons are entitled to the full protection of Government in carrying out their lawful vocations. There is evidence that the right of civil liberty is being restricted and the Mazdoor Sabha have assumed authority to issue permits for the use of the public thoroughfares. Request immediate necessary action.

49

HALLETT TO LINLITHGOW
Telegram
R/3/1/73

Important
No. 149-G

June 2nd, 1938

Cawnpore strike. Reference my letter, dated May 27th, No. 85. Wilkinson representing employers has discussed situation with Premier and also with me and has given us written note which I will send tomorrow. Have discussed situation fully with Premier and Industry Minister today.

2. *Pioneer* regards Report of Committee as falling into 3 portions: (*a*) additional social benefits, (*b*) wages, (*c*) right of dismissal of employers. His association regard (*a*) as all-India question and Ministers accept this or at least agree that these questions can be left over for further consideration.

3. In regard to (*b*) and (*c*), which Ministry rightly regard as of primary importance for settlement of present dispute, Wilkinson makes no

suggestion of any concession by employers or even of any possibility of discussion of these questions with workers. He reiterates view that strike is communist in origin which I personally cannot regard established. Cawnpore situation seems to me very different from Bombay situation in 1934. He urges Government to take more steps to eradicate spirit of revolt and indiscipline, and presses Government to enunciate its position on question of wages.

4. Ministers not unnaturally regard this attitude as entirely unhelpful. They suggest in fact that employers wish to starve workers into submission. They recognise that mere statement of their views on committee's recommendations regarding wages will not solve problem and that only solution is agreement between parties. Ministers consider that more drastic action against strikers will be provocative and having regard to support given to strike I cannot contest this view.

Position is most difficult but I cannot help feeling that "non-possumus" attitude of employers accentuates our difficulties. Ministers are not proposing any immediate action or statement and though fully recognising danger, I feel we must await developments. There is some talk in Cawnpore of possibility of arbitration.

50

HALLETT TO LINLITHGOW
R/3/1/73

Secret — Camp,
No. U.P.-86 — *June 6th, 1938*

My dear Lord Linlithgow,

I find that Haig had not sent a reply to your letter of May 7th, 1938,[3] about "Federation". I think one of his reasons was that Federation is not a live issue in this Province and that he had not been able to collect much information about the views held about it. That too is my difficulty and I think that in the short reply which I sent to your letter from Patna I took the view that in a Congress Province people are more concerned with their domestic problems. These are sufficiently serious and it is hardly surprising that tenancy questions, communal questions or labour questions attract attention to the exclusion of other problems.

2. It is no doubt true that any statements regarding the policy of His Majesty's Government in regard to Federation, such as that made in the Legislative Assembly,[4] or the more recent statement of the Secretary of State,[5] excite comment and criticism in the Press, but the criticisms as far as I have been able to follow them are all of an adverse nature. Politicians also take interest in the intentions of the British Government in this matter, not because they approve of Federation but because they anticipate that Federation will be forced upon India.

3. I have examined carefully the discussions in the Provincial Legislative Assembly on a resolution moved by the Secretary[6] of the Muslim League regarding Federation, on January 20th 1938 (see *Proceedings of the Legislative Assembly of the United Provinces*, Volume III, No. 4). The resolution was as follows:

"This Assembly recommends to the Government to intimate to the Central Government its firm resolve to be no party to the inauguration of the proposed Federation", and "That this Assembly further recommends that no money should be spent out of the Provincial revenues and no arrangements should be made by the Provincial Government in connection with the inauguration of the Federal scheme, whether in the matter of holding elections to the Federal Legislature or in any other matter connected therewith."

4. The second clause is rather significant; whether similar recommendations have been made in other Legislatures, I am not aware, but as far as I recollect the resolution moved by the Prime Minister[7] in the Bihar Assembly did not contain this suggestion of a boycott of the Federal elections. If a Provincial Government did refuse to co-operate over the elections, it would create a difficult, not to say impossible, situation.

5. The main point put forward by the mover of the resolution was that though the Muslim League had made its opposition to the Federal Scheme clear, the attitude of Congress was more indefinite and he was apprehensive that Congress might be prepared "to accept Federation and to combat it by accepting offices under it in the same way as it is professedly doing in the Provinces". Unfortunately many of the subsequent speeches were in the vernacular, but I gather that at one stage the debate degenerated into rather an acrimonious fight between the Congress and the Muslim League party. It is significant however that Kunwar Sir Maharaj Singh speaking on behalf of the Indian Christians supported the resolution, and pointed out that that community had always regarded the Federation proposals as inadequate. Towards the close of the debate the Hon'ble Minister for Justice

(Dr. Katju) fully supported the resolution and asserted that Government would adopt the methods suggested, and if necessary other methods for stopping the system of Federation.

6. I do not think a debate of this kind can be disregarded, especially in view of the fact that similar debates have taken place in other Legislatures. When questions are discussed in Provincial Legislatures, as at present constituted, there is usually some opposition, but in regard to Federation there was complete unanimity that the present scheme is unacceptable.

7. I have recently discussed the position with the Nawab of Chhatari; he referred to the consistent opposition of the League and of Mr. Jinnah to the scheme; he even suggested that the late Sir Fazl-i-Hussain was opposed to it; he also pointed out how the League had increased its strength as a result of the support given to it by the Hon'ble Sir Sikander Hayat Khan and the Hon'ble Mr. Fazl-ul-Haq.[8] The League, he contended, would only be content with some form of Federation of the Muslim Provinces which might later be united with a Federation of Hindu India. Even if this was not possible, they would press for one-third or at least one-fourth of the total number of seats in each of the Houses of the Federal Legislature.

8. On the attitude of Congress, I am not really competent to speak; I have not discussed the question with my Ministers and I do not think discussion would serve any useful purpose; they would merely reiterate in general terms their opposition to the scheme, emphasising in particular their opposition to the proposal regarding Defence, External Affairs, Finance. They would also, no doubt, as did the Hon'ble Minister for Justice in the debate to which I have referred, point out that Federation presupposed equality of citizenship and that such equality did not exist so far as the Indian States were concerned, but that the scheme gave the States a very strong, if not a dominating, position. Congress might of course be prepared to bargain and might try to secure at the same time a modification of Provincial Autonomy. Further it is probable that those members of Congress who are sympathetic with the Hindu Mahasabha would accept Federation even if it was not substantially modified.

9. It may be thought that Congress realising the power which it has, in particular in the Congress Provinces, would be reluctant to surrender that power in order to fight the Federal Scheme. This no doubt would be true if there was any chance in these Provinces of getting an alternative Ministry, but if Congress Ministries went out over Federation, they would have the support of the minority parties and suspension of the Constitution would be even more inevitable than it would be if they went out for any other reason. Suspension of the Constitution on the Federal issue would suit

Congress policy and as far as I can see would be almost certain to lead ultimately to a modification of the Constitution, with all its attendant difficulties.

10. The comments made in the last paragraph are based on the assumption that the attempt to introduce Federation will be made in the near future. If it is made in the near future, it will be at a time when Congress Ministries are still firm in the saddle. If however the introduction of the scheme is postponed, if Provincial Autonomy is allowed to continue as at present for some time longer, Congress may lose credit; the Opposition may grow in strength and we may have a split between the right and left wings of Congress. If the political situation develops on these lines, Federation may then become possible, provided of course that the communal question can be solved. Provincial Autonomy has, it is true, been started without any very serious difficulties, in spite of the opposition to the scheme, but it cannot be inferred from this that Federation can also be thrust upon India. The opposition to Federation seems to me far stronger than the opposition to Provincial Autonomy, mainly because of the attitude of the Muslims, and it will be admitted, I think, even by the opponents of Provincial Autonomy that the present Constitution has enabled the Ministries to implement their election pledge and to rectify many real grievances. Federation will give them no such opportunity.

11. I regret that I have felt bound to give at this stage a view, based possibly on very inadequate information, which is so hostile to the immediate introduction of the Federal Scheme. There is one further point which I would make; it is based on conversations with some of my District Officers. The Services have had a difficult time during these early months of the new Constitution, but every month that elapses seems to me to improve the position, though there are still many threatening clouds on the horizon. If Federation is attempted in the near future, their position will become far more difficult, I would almost say impossible. The Services may make a success of Provincial Autonomy, if we carry on as at present; if we provoke a controversy, I cannot see what the final results will be.[9]

Yours sincerely,
M.G. HALLETT

51

HALLETT TO LINLITHGOW
R/3/1/73

Secret
No. U.P.-89

Camp,
June 17th, 1938

My dear Lord Linlithgow,

The question of speeches at Lansdowne in the Cantonment has again come to the fore and rather a difficult situation has arisen. I have carefully studied the previous correspondence about this question. Briefly the facts are that a Parliamentary Secretary, Ajit Prasad Jain, who deals with Revenue matters, visited Lansdowne with the object of seeing how some Settlement work was being done. He was entertained first by the Bar Association at a party which the Sub-Divisional Officer[10] attended and made there a very reasonable speech saying that he considered that the Settlement work had been well done. He then went on to a meeting in the Bazar organised by the local Congress Association at which 300-400 persons were present, the audience consisting of local Congressmen, shopkeepers, clerks, lawyers and Marwari women. He opened his speech with a reference to the bravery of the Garhwalis in the War and to the Peshawar incident[11] and the following is an extract from the report which I have received of the speech:

"He recalled the Peshawar firing incident and said that Britishers taking advantage of the long-standing enmity between Hindus and Muslims they directed about 100 or 120 Garhwali soldiers to fire at [an] unarmed mob of the Muslims in 1930 believing that Hindus would take a great pleasure in firing at a Muslim mob, but they refused to fire. This was an act of heroism on the part of soldier Chandar Singh. (Note. At this time Rup Chand shouted 'Bir Chandar Singh-ki-jai' followed by others.) This incident, he said, would associate Garhwal with the act of heroism for ever and by fighting in Great War would prove that a black man can easily fight against a white man. He said Chandar Singh could never be forgotten. He regretted the inability of the Congress in not setting him free. He said that it was beyond their power. Chandar Singh, he said, was a prisoner of the Central Government – nevertheless they had been successful in bringing him to Lucknow and classing him as a 'B' class prisoner. In time to come they hope to restore him to Garhwal and already the Premier was in correspondence with the Government of India."

2. The rest of the speech referred only to the Settlement operations and certain local matters and was not open to any objection. He did however refer briefly to the "fight against Federation" and asked the local Garhwalis to organise themselves on the lines of the Khudai Khidmatgars in the North-West Frontier Province.

3. This speech was delivered on June 3rd. On the 9th June the Officer Commanding, Lansdowne,[12] issued a notice against one Rup Chand Varma who is said to be President of the local Congress Committee under Section 239 of the Cantonment Act calling on him to show cause why he should not be expelled from the Cantonment (I enclose a copy).[13] Rup Chand had been previously warned in January last that such action would be taken if flag salutation ceremonies were held at which speeches applauding the mutineers were made. The Officer Commanding also stated that at that time he had clearly explained the position to the local Congress clique. The notice was served on Rup Chand early on the morning of the 9th and the S.D.O. reports as follows:

"The notice to show cause was served on Rup Chand at 9-30 a.m. this morning. He was told to appear at 12-30 p.m. to show cause but he apparently came with a written application to the S.S.O. (not Col. Clarke) at about 11 a.m. to say that he required at least a week in which to take legal advice before he would appear to show cause and when told that he had better appear at 12-30 before the C.O. and then ask for more time he went away saying that he would not appear before the C.O. Consequently when he did not turn up at 12-30, the notice was made absolute and he was ordered to leave the Cantonment in 48 hours."

4. We had a brief telegraphic report on the night of the 8th June that this action was contemplated and after the King's Birthday Parade on the morning of the 9th, I discussed the situation with the Commissioner (Mr. Ibbotson) and the Military authorities. As the telegraphic report was very brief, I told the Commissioner to ascertain full details. He also reported the matter to the Premier who passed very similar orders. But meanwhile, as I have explained above, the order had been issued and had been confirmed. Rup Chand has, I understand, not complied with the order and is being prosecuted.

5. No action could be taken by the Cantonment authorities against the Parliamentary Secretary who had left Lansdowne.

6. I have had a discussion with my Premier and it is desirable that I should explain at some length his views in the matter. The two points which arose were: (*a*) the action taken by the Cantonment authorities against

Rup Chand; (*b*) the fact that a Parliamentary Secretary had made an objectionable speech.

7. I may note that at my discussion with Military authorities I learnt that the Defence Department had issued orders probably in January last that action under Section 239 of the Cantonment Act should be taken in such cases.

8. The Premier asserted that the action of the Garhwal Mutineers in Peshawar had been taken at the request of Congress; that Congress were therefore bound to support them; they had done so before they took office and had secured a reduction of the sentence passed on some of the mutineers; that it was in accordance with this policy that Mr. Gandhi had taken up with the Viceroy the question of the release of the remaining mutineer Chandar Singh. This explanation of Congress position was presumably only given with a view to justifying the speech of the Parliamentary Secretary, a point to which I refer below.

9. The main point which he made was that action against Rup Chand was unjustifiable, even having regard to the fact that he had been previously warned. Even if he had organised or arranged the meeting, it was quite impossible for him to know what form the speech of the Parliamentary Secretary would take and that he could not be held responsible for it. He was not anxious to embarrass the Military authorities, but he felt that in a matter of this kind the Military authorities might have consulted the Local Government before taking action. I would refer in amplification of this point to the last paragraph of Mr. Panna Lal's letter to the Defence Department, No. 1962-C.X. of May 14th, 1938, which was as follows:

"While the Provincial Government are anxious to render all reasonable co-operation in preventing an attack on the discipline or loyalty of the troops, the Government of India must be well aware that their general policy includes as one of its main items the maintenance of freedom of speech and of association. If an attempt is made to carry out in small areas like cantonments a policy which is sharply in conflict with the policy pursued generally throughout the Province, considerable misunderstanding and friction are likely to be engendered and the Provincial Government would find it difficult to justify a breach of the principle for which they stand."

10. Another point, though the Premier did not actually mention it, is that the warning notice referred to flag salutation ceremonies, while this speech by the Parliamentary Secretary was delivered at an ordinary meeting held apparently mainly to enable him to explain to the people about the Settlement operations.

11. As regards the speech itself, the Premier reasserted the point which was made in the letter which I have just quoted that the Local Government had been advised in the days of the Interim Ministry that such a speech did not come within the mischief of the Criminal Law. He also said that though he had at that time warned people in Lansdowne that such speeches were objectionable, he had not given wider circulation to that warning and that the Parliamentary Secretary in the Revenue Department could not have known anything about the matter. His main point was that a speech on those lines would have little effect, as similar speeches had been made in the past. In fact he reiterated the view which he took in January that the Military authorities were making a lot of fuss over nothing.

12. Under the Cantonment Act as amended by Order-in-Council, Rup Chand if dissatisfied with the order of expulsion can appeal to the Defence Department. Whether he will do so is uncertain, but if he does, and if the Defence Department referred to the Provincial Government, the Provincial Government would be almost certain to take the point made by the Premier that even if he organised the meeting, he had no knowledge beforehand that the Parliamentary Secretary would refer to the Garhwal Mutiny and that it was inequitable to punish him for an act committed by another person. I admit there is some force in this argument. Even if Rup Chand does not appeal, it is possible, though the Premier did not say definitely that he would do so, that the Provincial Government will protest against action being taken by the Military authorities without some consultation with them. This point is also not without force. As matters stand at present, we must await the results of the action taken against Rup Chand and of the case said to have been instituted against him. The case can only result in the imposition of a fine or of a recurring fine, but it is possible that my Government might be anxious to remit the fine and I believe, though I have not examined the point closely, they would have power to do so.

13. As regards the Parliamentary Secretary, it is clear, having regard to the previous ruling, that he cannot be prosecuted. It cannot be proved that he knew of the previous discussions between this Government and the Defence Department, unless he had heard of the warnings given to the local Congress people in Lansdowne, but it seems very probable that he had some knowledge of the general position regarding Garhwali Mutineers. The attitude of the Premier is not easy; and the quotation which I have made above from Panna Lal's letter of May 14th shows that though he renders lip service to the necessity of maintaining discipline, he emphasises the right of free speech. These two propositions are hardly consistent. The Premier also did not seem to appreciate the point made by me that the fact

that the speaker held the post of Parliamentary Secretary made the position worse. He did not seem in the least prepared to point out his fault to the Parliamentary Secretary.

14. Such being the position, I am at a loss to know what action to take. The incident has not yet attracted attention in the Press and possibly it may not do so. I have already suggested that in the case of Rup Chand we should wait and see what happens. In the case of the Parliamentary Secretary, I shall probably have a further opportunity of discussing with Pant. But I should be glad to know what the Defence Department and Your Excellency think in this matter. In particular I should like to know whether an isolated speech containing a reference to the Peshawar incident has great effect on the troops or on recruitment; as Your Excellency frequently emphasised when I was in the Home Department, it is necessary to take into account not so much the actual words used as the effect on the audience or the public generally.[14]

Yours sincerely,
M.G. HALLETT

52

HALLETT TO LINLITHGOW
R/3/1/73

Secret *June 17th, 1938*
No. U.P.-90

My dear Lord Linlithgow,

This is my fortnightly report which I am afraid is a little late.

CAWNPORE STRIKE

1. You will have seen in the Press the resolution which my Government have issued on the Report of the Committee.[15] I am, however, sending to your Secretary a copy of it and also printed copies of the Report of the Committee and of the employers' reply to it, so that you may have them on record. The resolution which had been drafted originally by the Premier was discussed by me with all my Ministers at a meeting last Saturday which lasted from 10 a.m. till 4 p.m. The draft resolution was on the lines which my Premier had indicated previously that he would take, viz., that

the textile industry of Cawnpore was flourishing at present owing to the low price of cotton and could afford the increase in wages proposed by the Committee; that there should be in future a Wage Adjustment Board; that there should be also a Labour Commissioner following the Bombay precedent and that the general questions regarding amelioration of the conditions of the workers should be considered later. The resolution seemed to me to be not unreasonable, and to be, on the whole, an effective reply to the employers. I fully admit that it would be advantageous if we could get the parties together round a table and I agree with the suggestion that you put forward in paragraph 2 of your letter of June 3rd.[16] But when Wilkinson, the representative of the employers, interviewed the Premier and myself, he would not agree to any such suggestion and was anxious for Government, first of all, to put forward its own views. It was therefore hardly possible for my Government to refrain from issuing the Resolution and it seemed dangerous to delay the matter further. It is not easy at present to make out exactly what the reactions to the issue of the Resolution have been, but at first sight they seem to be not unfavourable and it is possible now that some sort of discussion or conference may be arranged.

2. When the Resolution was under consideration in Council, the point that gave rise to most discussion was in regard to the last paragraph.[17] The Education Minister wanted Government to state more definitely that they would undertake legislation if the employers did not accept these proposals, so that the present deadlock might be removed. The Premier, however, held that this Resolution was intended only to refer to the Report of the Committee and that it was undesirable to say too much about the strike or the reasons for it. He was, in my opinion rightly, not in favour of definitely stating what action will be taken if the differences between the employers and workers were not solved and hence he had drafted the concluding paragraph in somewhat vague language.

SEPARATION OF JUDICIAL AND EXECUTIVE

3. This matter was also considered during the Council meetings last week. I had myself written a long note for the Council and they agreed that the Executive Officer should have powers under Section 144 and also power to start proceedings under Section 145. They also agreed that he should have power to bind over people under Section 107, Criminal Procedure Code for periods not exceeding three months, but should not have power under Sections 108, 109 or 110, Criminal Procedure Code. I think myself judging by my Bihar experience that these powers will enable a District

Officer to maintain law and order but I know there is a feeling here that the prestige and consequently the authority of the District Officer will be reduced. The Council did not agree with the point that Haig had made and which he had referred to you, that their proposals made such a radical change in the position of the District Magistrate as to render the sanction of the Secretary of State necessary. They held that the powers of the District Magistrate under the Criminal Procedure Code would only be held in abeyance and agreed that they might at any time be restored if Government considered that there was a state of emergency in a district. They also pointed out that in the past changes had been made in the powers of a District Officer, e.g. when he ceased to be the Chairman of the District Board. Nothing, however, will be done at present, for they contemplate now appointing a senior officer, probably Mr. Dible, to work out a scheme for all districts of the Province and to see whether any additional staff will be needed and how the existing staff can be divided up. Mr. Dible is well suited for this work which will take some time. Though they wish the schemes worked out for all districts, I think they will agree ultimately to introducing the scheme tentatively in certain districts of each division. But this matter has not yet been finally decided and clearly some time will elapse before the full scheme has been worked out. I have thus succeeded to some extent in playing for time. I shall probably refer the question of the sanction of the Secretary of State to you formally, while the scheme is being worked out. My present view rather is that the rule under which the sanction of the Secretary of State is required hardly applies to a case of this kind; for, as far as I recollect, it was framed originally to prevent local Governments combining under one officer such posts as Inspector-General, Civil Hospitals, Inspector-General, Prisons and Director of Public Health. I also feel that if the scheme is introduced merely tentatively, it might be undesirable for the Secretary of State to interfere, but I have not yet fully made up my mind.

PARLIAMENTARY SECRETARIES

4. The question of Parliamentary Secretaries was also discussed, and the Premier put in a short draft of the order which he considered should be passed.[18] That was as follows:

(1) Parliamentary Secretaries shall assist the Ministers in their parliamentary work and shall represent them in the Legislature whenever necessary.

(2) The Ministers may entrust to their Parliamentary Secretaries such administrative work as they may deem fit. As a rule, final orders shall be passed by the Ministers.

During the discussion I pointed out that this seemed to be too indefinite and did not make sufficiently clear the position of the Permanent Secretary *vis à vis* the Parliamentary Secretary. The Council appeared to agree that the Permanent Secretary should submit his notes to the Hon'ble Minister and that in the event of a difference of opinion between the Parliamentary Secretary and the Departmental Secretary, the case should be referred to the Hon'ble Minister. If a Parliamentary Secretary dealt with a case without reference to the Minister, he should sign his note, which might appear on the file, as on behalf of the Hon'ble Minister.

5. After the meeting was over, the Chief Secretary tried to embody in definite language the result of the discussion and the points that had been raised. But when these were shown to the Ministers they said they did not want such precise instructions to be recorded or issued. I am not quite certain what their reason for this is. But it may be that they themselves are not quite certain what powers they should give to their Parliamentary Secretaries and possibly some of them do not wish to give any powers at all. On the other hand, it is clear that indefinite orders will only lead to confusion, and I trust I shall be able to get the Premier to agree that instructions dealing with these points of detail should be issued, even though the order in Council takes the somewhat vague form which I have quoted above.

JURY SYSTEM

6. Another question which was discussed in the Council was the question of the extension of the jury system. Though the Council were generally in favour of the extension, it was decided that yet another committee should be appointed to work out details. The Minister for Justice in his notes on the subject pointed out that assessors were in all cases unnecessary, but seemed to be in favour of certain cases being disposed of by judges sitting singly, e.g. cases arising out of communal disputes; cases giving rise to complicated issues; or cases which would involve protracted trials. Their proposals, e.g. regarding assessors, will involve an amendment of the law, but the matter has been shelved for the time at least by the appointment of the committee.

HONORARY MAGISTRATES

7. As Your Excellency is, I believe, aware, Government decided to cancel the appointment of all Honorary Magistrates who, in this Province, do a very large percentage of the criminal work, and to make fresh appointments on the recommendations of local Committees. These Committees consisted of the District Officer, the Sessions Judge, one member elected by the local Bar Association and four non-officials nominated by the local Government, three of whom might be members of the Legislature. There was some apprehension that these Committees would allow political considerations to influence their recommendations. But I have talked to some District Officers and Commissioners and find that at least in some districts, the new method of selection has not worked badly; in some cases former Honorary Magistrates have been re-appointed. I am trying to find out more about the matter and will look further into it when on tour. There have been some protests from Depressed Class Associations regarding these appointments but I do not think these merit much attention.

PARALLEL GOVERNMENT

8. That some of the reports received regarding the institution of "police stations" by Congress workers are exaggerated is shown by a report received in February to the effect that Congress workers were making preparations for setting up 48 centres for registering reports of crime in Hardoi district. Haig naturally enquired about this and we have at last ascertained that only one such centre had been established and that the Secretary in charge thereof referred complainants to the Police if he could not deal with them. This has led the Premier to take up the question of discontinuing the Police Secret Abstract as containing reports that are "highly exaggerated and coloured, if not unfounded". It would of course be impossible to do without the Police Secret Abstract, but I will see whether it cannot be improved. I have noticed that in reporting speeches inadequate information is given and nothing is said about the size or character of the audience or the effect of the speech upon them. At the same time the Premier does not assess intelligence reports of this kind at their correct value. I find that Haig gave you his views on this "Abstract" and I agree with much that he said in a letter to Laithwaite from Donaldson.[19]

SEDITIOUS SPEECHES

9. My Chief Secretary has made a collection of speeches delivered recently by Parmanand and intends taking up with the Premier the question of action against him. It looks as if action under Section 108, Criminal Procedure Code, would be more suitable than a prosecution (possibly the Premier might agree to this). I am reporting to you in a separate letter the recent incident at Lansdowne.

TENANCY LEGISLATION, &C.

10. The Select Committee on the Tenancy Bill will meet about June 26th, and there will no doubt be prolonged discussion. It is not easy to follow the details of this complicated Bill; the main points to which the landholders take exception are those regarding *sir* lands and realisation of rents, but the real difficulty will arise over the proposed increase of Land Revenue, partly because Government wish to combine together two proposals: (*a*) reduction of revenue of the smaller landholders, and (*b*) increase of revenue of the wealthier landholders. Both proposals have some justification, but I anticipate serious practical difficulties in carrying them into effect. I admit however that the question is so complicated that I do not fully understand the alternative proposals. Fortunately Government have very competent official advisers on these problems.

COLLECTION OF REVENUE, &C.

11. The position in regard to this important matter is also not easy to follow, but my Finance Secretary[20] told me recently that the revenue position was at present by no means unsatisfactory. Judging by the Commissioners' Reports for the first half of May it is rather too early to forecast the results of the *rabi* collections. In Gorakhpur which seems the most difficult district, the position is being examined on the spot by the Junior Member of the Board of Revenue.[21] He reports the satisfactory fact that Mr. Pedley the Collector has the situation well in hand. In some of the eastern districts the situation appears to be not unlike that with which I was confronted in Gaya and there is anticipation of trouble at the time of cultivation. The local officers appear alive to the necessity of prompt local enquiries in land disputes and to having adequate police available.

COMMUNAL MATTERS

12. Lucknow and the Shia-Sunni controversy still gives rise to anxiety, and there have been one or two troublesome incidents, which the local officers have dealt with very tactfully and they deserve great credit for this. Temporarily the position appears to have improved, as I see from the Press that the Curfew Order has been withdrawn. Pant took up a very reasonable attitude regarding this order and the protests against it and held that even if people were not encouraging the agitation, they must suffer this inconvenience because they did not discourage it.

13. I hear that the Inspector-General has put up proposals for additional police. I feel rather doubtful myself and have expressed my doubts to Pant whether it is desirable to impose additional police in Lucknow only at the cost of the Muslims; this might enhance the Hindu-Muslim controversy. We appear to need more police not merely because of Lucknow, but because of Allahabad, Benares, Cawnpore and certain districts where there may be agrarian trouble. The Province as a whole should therefore pay for this.

LEGISLATIVE SESSIONS

14. These will probably not begin till the end of July. Dr. Katju is taking up the point of the right of the Council to interfere over a Money Bill, as they did over the Court Fees Bill, but I have not seen his note and so refrain from further comment.

Yours sincerely,
M.G. HALLETT

53

HALLETT TO LINLITHGOW
R/3/1/73

Personal

Camp,
June 20th, 1938

My dear Lord Linlithgow,

This is to wish you a good holiday. I hope you will enjoy your well-deserved rest for the short period of four months and will not be called upon to do too much work. I hope also things will be quiet here during your absence.

I feel I am getting to know something about the Province by degrees, but a Province with such a huge number of districts is not easy. I hope to go on tour in July and August and so get more personal acquaintance with persons and places. I vary between optimism and pessimism, but I have always done so during the last year!

My Ministers are certainly far more interesting than my Bihar quartette. My Lady Minister, Mrs Pandit, is very charming and most interesting to talk to, as she is very outspoken. One yarn she told me will interest and amuse you. She said she had recently had a long letter from Mrs. Gunther, the wife of the author of *Inside Europe*,[22] the theme of which was that it was quite impossible for India to hope for *swaraj* or independence as long as Indians dressed so badly and the men wore *dhotis*. I enquired where [whether] *saris* were also condemned and I think they were.

Another matter which may interest you and which I almost included in my fortnightly is this. We had a six-hour meeting to discuss Cawnpore. It was enlivened in the middle by a lunch party given at the Club by Panna Lal, the Chief Secretary, which all the Ministers attended except Pant and Sampurnanand, the Education Minister. They all seemed to enjoy it!

Again with my best wishes for a good holiday and with best regards to Her Excellency and to Your Excellency from my wife and myself.[23]

Yours sincerely,
MAURICE HALLETT

54

HALLETT TO BRABOURNE
Telegram
R/3/1/73

No. 155-G *June 25th, 1938*

Cawnpore strike. Negotiations between Government and employers have been adjourned till Sunday at Lucknow. They have not been entirely infructuous and agreement has been arrived at on some important points, e.g. wage adjustment, Board and appointment of Labour Commissioner. Main difficulty arises from fact that employers though (group omitted) admitting that they can afford temporary increase of wage proposed, are reluctant to give them without (*a*) a definite assurance from Government that they will in future take action against subversive activities and enforce the law, and (*b*) possibly also a more definite assurance that Government will not impose other charges on the employers for ameliorative conditions. Point (*b*) is not of great importance for Government resolution is fairly clear on this point. Premier with whom I discussed position yesterday feels that it is undesirable to make temporary increase of wages appear as a bargain in return for promise of action against agitators. He is of course somewhat afraid of left wing, but I think that if the present deadlock were removed and strike ended he would be more ready to take action, but he is reluctant to make too definite a statement. He suggested to me, though he had not mentioned point to employers, that he might be prepared to declare lightning strikes illegal. Much depends also on reform of Mazdoor Sabha so as to include reasonable workers, and I suggested to employers that they could help in this matter and that Labour Commissioner would be very helpful in securing this.

2. Trust negotiations will prove successful, but position is still uncertain.

55

HALLETT TO BRABOURNE
R/3/1/73

Secret | Camp,
No. U.P.-96 | *June 28th, 1938*

Dear Brabourne,

May I invite your attention to His Excellency Lord Linlithgow's letter of 21st June 1938,[24] about the unfortunate incident at Lansdowne and to my letter[25] to which it is a reply. I shall be very glad to hear the views of His Excellency the Commander-in-Chief, which no doubt you will communicate to me in due course. Though it is not strictly speaking my concern, I should be glad to be informed beforehand of any action which the Defence Department propose to take, if you or His Excellency the Commander-in-Chief have no objection. My reason for making this request is that any action taken by them may have reactions which I am in a better position to appreciate than they.

2. His Excellency Lord Linlithgow has suggested that I should make a strong *personal* appeal to Pant. I feel that both you and Lord Linlithgow will recognise that most of my conversations with Pant are of the nature of personal appeals and my first conversation with him was of the nature of a personal appeal, or at least an appeal to look at the matter from my or our point of view. He is however rather obstinate in this matter. I doubt

whether this particular speech had any very deleterious effect; it dealt mainly with other subjects. What is important is that I should do my best to get Pant's co-operation in preventing any speeches of this kind in future, rather than attempt to persuade him to take action in this particular case. I am prepared to do what I can to secure this.

Yours sincerely,
M.G. HALLETT

56

DONALDSON TO PUCKLE
R/3/1/73

Confidential — Camp,
D.O. No. 1403-G.S.P. — *July 4th, 1938*

My dear Puckle,

His Excellency has asked me to send you a copy of his letter of yesterday to Pant. He thinks that His Excellency the Viceroy might like to see it, as it gives the position as Sir Maurice understood it to be yesterday.

2. I have just sent you a telegram giving news received from Kharegat, Labour Commissioner, on the telephone about 11 a.m. this morning. We had previously heard through the Police that the situation today was better and that the mill-owners, as a result of the negotiations last night, had agreed not to attempt to open the mills today. The D.I.G., who is in Cawnpore, told the I.G. that he considered the Police arrangements adequate to deal with any emergency.

Yours sincerely,
J.C. DONALDSON

ENCLOSURE 1 TO NO. 56

HALLETT TO PANT

No. U.P.-99 — *July 3rd, 1938*

My dear Premier,

I have purposely refrained from worrying you about Cawnpore affairs while you were busily engaged in negotiations with the parties. There appeared at one time good hopes of a settlement and I regret very much that recent developments show that an even more difficult situation may arise in the near future.

2. As I appreciate the position, the hitch which has occurred is partly due to the precipitate action of the employers in issuing the notice about the increase of wages without reference to you or to Kharegat at a time when certain questions were still outstanding. Government had at that time given the employers, as I understand it, the assurances which they required. I have seen the notice as published in the *Leader* this morning and see that it ends up with a sort of threat that this increase of wages will be withdrawn in the event of workers not returning by the date fixed, or in the event of there being any departure from the understanding with the Association (what exactly the understanding is is not clear) or in the event of an illegal strike. It also emphasises that the proposed scale is conditional and temporary. We could not stop the employers making these points but I feel that if Kharegat or you had seen the notice, you could have got it put in more suitable language and could also have got it issued at more suitable time.

3. However the notice has been issued, and the result has been the meeting of the workers on the night of July 1st. Though, as reported in the leading article of the *Leader* of today (Sunday), labour leaders such as Balkrishna Sharma and Raja Ram Shastri were showing signs of becoming more reasonable, no doubt thanks to your good influences, the meeting was definite in rejecting the offer of the employers, and we are faced with a very difficult position, with threats of picketing on a very increased scale.

4. Mr. Hancox in a telephone message to Chief Secretary (received yesterday evening) said he had been considering forbidding the opening of the mills by an order under Section 144 Cr.P.C. but had decided to wait and see. This action was of course taken in Madras but as far as I know the facts, circumstances were different; in that case the mills proposed to introduce new workers; here the employers have agreed to the main point recommended by the Committee, and accepted by Government, an immediate increase of wages, though as I have pointed out in the previous paragraph, they have done so in a somewhat half-hearted manner; there must be many workers who have suffered severely from the strike who would be only too glad to come back on these terms, and hence an order closing the mills hardly appears justifiable or desirable. If you can persuade the parties to agree to further time for discussion of outstanding points, no doubt you or Kharegat could persuade the employers to extend the date by which labour should rejoin.

5. As I understand the position, the main point outstanding is in regard to recognition of Mazdur Sabha. Hancox in his telephone message to Chief Secretary seems to me to have given a pretty sound opinion; he points out that it is largely a matter of words and that the employers might give a conditional recognition of the Sabha, provided it would reorganise itself within a certain period. This after all is in accordance with the views of the Committee and of Government, but of course neither the Committee nor Government dealt very fully with the point whether the reorganisation should involve insisting on the Sabha consisting of a certain proportion of the workers. I gather however from a Press telegram just received that the workers are prepared to accept the settlement provided it is agreed (*a*) that membership of the Sabha will not be less than 20 per cent of the total labour force; (*b*) that 15 days' noticc of a strike shall be given; (*c*) opinions of workers including *non-members* shall be taken by secret ballot and strike shall be declared only if 60 per cent votes are polled in favour of strike.[26] This does not seem to me unreasonable; it meets the employers' views that there shall be no lightning strikes and also their appreciation that if the Sabha were authorised to declare a strike if there was a majority vote of Sabha members in favour of it, it might happen that the Sabha was not really representative of the workers by only including a very small percentage. If these proposals of the Sabha are correctly reported, it looks to me as though this might form the basis of a *bona fide* Trades Union and I hope the employers will not turn down this proposal, merely because of their "izzat".

6. This latest news makes me somewhat more hopeful and if you and Kharegat have got the workers to agree to this view, I congratulate you. However we may still be faced with intensive picketing and with objectionable action by extremists. Now that there is, as far as I can see, very little substantial differences between the parties and now that Government have succeeded to some extent in bringing them together, I feel that it will be necessary for Government to deal very firmly with extremist agitation, whether their activities take the form of more intensive picketing or in inflammatory speeches. This will of course throw a strain on the Police but they have dealt with the situation so far very tactfully and I hope they will be able to carry on. Hancox I gather from the telephone message to which I have referred, proposes to give necessary help to workers wishing to return and I feel sure you will agree that he is right. The order under Section 144 must be kept in force and Government must, if necessary, issue the order required by sub-section (6) of that Section. I asked the I.G. on Thursday evening to send down the D.I.G. (Mr. Inglis) and he has gone down; he will be able to help the local officers.

7. I hope therefore that all will still go well. If I can be of any help to you, I shall be only too glad and if you would like me to come to Lucknow before I go on tour to Jhansi I shall be glad to do so. But you and your colleagues and the local and Secretariat officers seem to me to be doing all that is possible to get an equitable solution of these difficult problems.

Yours sincerely,
M.G. HALLETT

ENCLOSURE 2 TO NO. 56

DONALDSON TO PUCKLE
Telegram

Confidential *July 4th, 1938*
No. G.S.-157

Cawnpore strike. Telephonic information has come this morning from Labour Commissioner, Cawnpore, that settlement of strike has been reached through personal intervention of the Premier. Latter met representatives of employers and Mazdur Sabha at Cawnpore last evening and after sitting up to 3 a.m. agreement reached, subject to ratification by general meeting of Mazdur Sabha to be held today. Main difficulty was over recognition of Sabha and formula finally reached was that Sabha will be recognised by employers' association as soon as it has been reorganised to satisfaction of Labour Commissioner. It is expected that general meeting will ratify and that mills will reopen tomorrow. Details of negotiations during the past days follow by letter.

57

HALLETT TO BRABOURNE
R/3/1/73

Private and Personal *July 6th, 1938*
No. U.P.-102

My dear Brabourne,

It was extremely good of you to send me last night your telegram of congratulations on the settlement of the Cawnpore strike. I feel that the Premier deserves all the credit; from the beginning of the strike he made up his mind what he would do and stuck to it; overcoming by degrees the opposition of the employers and of the Mazdur Sabha. The settlement is, I think, on sound lines and I hope the Premier will be willing to keep effective control over the extremists.

Another officer who deserves good credit is Mr. Kharegat of the Indian Civil Service, whom we have appointed Labour Commissioner. He is the son-in-law of my old friend Sir Maneckji Dadabhoy and a very hard-working and level-headed officer who will command the confidence of both parties. I ventured to pass on your congratulations to him as well as to the Premier.

The local officers, in particular the District Magistrate (Mr. Hancox) and the Superintendent of Police (Mr. Pearce) have also dealt with the situation throughout tactfully and efficiently and it is very satisfactory to know that one has such efficient and reliable officers in this difficult place.

Haig, just before he left, gave me the wise advice that he thought that Pant could be trusted to effect a good settlement of the difficulties. That advice has proved very correct.

Yours sincerely,
M.G. HALLETT

58

HALLETT TO BRABOURNE
R/3/1/73

Secret *July 7th, 1938*
No. U.P.-103

My dear Brabourne,

I am afraid that I have been rather irregular in submitting my fortnightly reports, but I hope I have kept you pretty well informed of the situation. I now enclose two official fortnightly reports, the first dated June 20th/21st, 1938, the second dated July 5th. These reports are a little on the short side, especially the first one, but it is not easy to dig out the really important matter from the mass of material which confronts a Chief Secretary when he is drafting this report. I also feel that possibly these reports are tainted by "political bias", but that after all is inevitable and we cannot expect the reports of a local Government to be as impartial as they were in pre-reform days. This fact makes it the more incumbent on me to endeavour to give an impartial appreciation of the situation, not an easy task! But I feel on first reading these two official reports are inclined (*a*) to over-emphasize the objectionable activities of the Muslim League; (*b*) to attempt to show that the zamindars are more in the wrong than the Kisans (cf. paragraph 2 of the report for July 5th, which after giving a fairly long list of objectionable activities by zamindars, merely refers incidentally to the fact that "irresponsible persons are reported to be going about holding out false hopes of rent remissions"); (*c*) even in dealing with the Cawnpore situation the reports tend to convey the impression that the prolongation of the strike is due, mainly if not wholly, to the attitude of the employers. This being my *prima facie* view, I have tried to examine the original material with some care.

CAWNPORE STRIKE

2. I deal first with the subject which has been very prominently before me during the past fortnight and indeed ever since I took over charge, the Cawnpore Strike. It now appears to be settled and it is unnecessary for me to go into details of the settlement, which will be known to you from the Press or from the reports which I have submitted from time to time to supplement the Press reports. I propose only in this report to give a more general appreciation of the situation; I admit it is rather rash to do so at this stage, for subsequent developments may show my views to be wrong, but I am always prepared to reconsider my views and therefore take the risk.

3. My first impression when the strike started just about the time I took over charge, was that the employers were asking for trouble by submitting a very intemperate reply to the report of the Labour Committee. Apart from attacking the appointment, constitution, and proceedings of the Committee, to which Government could make quite an effective reply, they had hardly a good word to say for any of their proposals. It looked rather as if they hoped for a prolonged strike, which would break the spirit of the workers and the result of this would have been to force them to agree to the terms of the employers and this view was rather supported by the fact that many of the employers left Cawnpore. Their excuse for adopting this "non-possumus" attitude was that trouble which had occurred last year in August was due to communist agitation and that it was therefore essential for the well-being of the industry to destroy once and for all that evil influence.

4. Their reply to the report was countered by the workers by declaring an immediate strike. The most significant features of the strike were that

all the workers went out practically simultaneously, that the strike was on the whole entirely peaceful, that no attempt was made to interfere with the essential services, such as electric light, water and conservancy, and that there was a very considerable volume of public opinion from all sides in favour of the strikers. These facts seemed to me to show that the strike was not due solely to the activities of communist agitation, but that the workers had some real grievances which should be remedied. Some years ago there was a strike in Bombay – Your Excellency will know far more about it than I ever did – which was undoubtedly due to communists; in order to get the workers out, there was very intense picketing even of workers' homes, and the strike collapsed when the leaders were arrested by the Bombay Government. If my recollection is correct, this marked difference goes to show that this strike was not wholly communist; if it was communist, it shows a very efficient and widespread organisation. I admit that in forming this view I am going rather against the views of my Intelligence officers, one of whom in a report dated July 1st says that he does not believe that "the communist element which has obtained complete control over the workers has any desire for permanent peace". A later appreciation, produced, I presume, by the Director, Intelligence Bureau[27] and written before the strike was settled and hence in a somewhat pessimistic strain, has just come to my notice. This points out that though communist agitation unquestionably played a large part in causing this unrest and directing these strikers, yet there is no direct evidence in support of the suggestion of "Moscow gold" or "foreign assistance" and most of the so-called communist "leaders" are paid professional agitators who have as yet made no great headway in contaminating the masses but are nevertheless exceedingly active in exploiting every industrial strike or disagreement. With much of this appreciation I agree and if this is correct, the policy to be followed is to remedy legitimate grievances as far as practicable and to restrain the professional agitators.

5. The attitude taken by my Government throughout and in particular by the Premier, who is a dominating personality, was, in my view, reasonable. They did not flirt with any extremist ideas such as nationalisation of the industry, though that was suggested in some quarters. They took hold of the most obvious grievances and set about getting the employers to agree to rectify them; it took some time to do so, possibly because the employers felt that hunger would make the workers more amenable. However in the end the employers agreed and possibly it may be said that they gave more than they got. But my Government had made it clear that they were not against capital, that they were anxious to get capital and labour working harmoniously together and to devise some

organisation such as Wages Adjustment Board by which future disputes could be decided. On paper at least they have succeeded and there is hope that the Mazdur Sabha may be reorganised on sound lines.

6. My Government are criticised for not taking sufficiently vigorous steps for dealing with agitators or even with restraining picketing. A pre-reform Government would no doubt have been more vigorous, but if a Congress Government had been too drastic, they would have raised a storm of opposition and would in my view have intensified the strike and increased the support given to the strikers. They should be judged by the results of their policy and I feel that the result has been that the right wing of Congress has scored, has strengthened its position and has not made any undue concessions to the left wing. I have dilated at some length on this topic, but I hope it may be of some interest to Your Excellency.

AGRARIAN SITUATION

7. I do not propose to deal at length with the arguments for and against the proposed Tenancy Legislation. Having been brought up in a Province in which Tenancy Acts have always been more in favour of the tenant than those in force in the United Provinces, I may have rather a prejudiced view, for I feel that many of the proposals regarding "sir" land or regarding recovery of rent are not open to serious objection. The landholders are putting forward their opposition to the Bill as usual at a very late hour and are receiving support from such bodies as the Upper India Chamber of Commerce; it is to be hoped that their opposition will be on constitutional lines and will be successful in securing suitable compromises on various points. Judging by the policy adopted by my Government in regard to Cawnpore, my Government will not be unreasonable and it is satisfactory that the provincial Congress Committee have rejected by a large majority the proposed abolition of "zamindars". I enclose in case it may interest you a copy of the communiqué issued by my Government about payment of rent.

8. I have expressed the view above that possibly the official report is rather one-sided and I have therefore examined the reports received from Commissioners and from the Police with a view to checking this report. In a recent report from Gorakhpur district it was stated that at a recent meeting *kisans* had been asked to boycott zamindars and to fight for the retention of their land. I have drawn the Premier's attention to this. The Commissioner[28] of this division referring to this meeting reports that two M.L.As. were present and makes the pertinent comment: "if inflammatory speeches like this can be made in the presence of (responsible?) legislators,

it is small wonder that the district is in a disturbed condition". He is discussing with the District Magistrate[29] the question of action against the speaker. In this division collections do not appear very satisfactory, owing to the friction between landlords and tenants.

9. In the Ballia district of Benares Division, intemperate speeches are said to have been delivered at a Kisan Conference; they are being examined by the District authorities. In that district also the agrarian situation is said to be not free from anxiety, but such land disputes as have occurred seem to have been settled promptly by the courts or by arbitration.

10. From the Fyzabad sub-division there is a report that a member of the Central Assembly (Sardar Jogendra Singh) advocated the shoe-beating of zamindars, if they misbehave. In the same district the Taluqdars are reported to be collecting volunteers, dressed in khaki and armed with spears, but this has not been verified.

11. I need not trouble you with further petty details; there is nothing as yet very serious in the situation, but there is no doubt that it is six of one and half a dozen of the other and that in many areas the Kisans are as much to blame as the zamindars.

COMMUNAL SITUATION

12. I find it rather difficult to make an appreciation of the communal situation. A recent report which I have seen from Bihar goes to show that the disputes of Congress and the League are leading to an increase in communal friction, so the same may be assumed to be taking place here. My most recent reports do not draw much attention to it. The facts reported in the official report of July 5th appear correct but possibly that report conveys the impression that anti-Hindu agitation by the Muslims, e.g. in regard to the wearing of khaddar, is more widespread than it really is.

13. Two rather troublesome matters have recently come before me. The first is a proposal from the Hon'ble Minister in charge of Jails (Mr. Kidwai) supported by the Hon'ble Minister in charge of Justice (Dr. Katju) that the six remaining Chauri Chaura prisoners should be released. Haig wrote a long minute in January last[30] when the proposal was first made giving the general objections to this proposal, and the Ministers, possibly because of their preoccupation with the cases of other political prisoners, did not press the matter. Recently various Congress bodies had advocated the release of all these six men. I have noted on the case and referred it to the Premier on the ground that it is primarily a "law and order" matter and that we must consider what will be the effect of the release both on the Province generally and in particular on the Gorakhpur district, where the

outrage occurred and which is at present disturbed. I have suggested releasing two of the oldest men, whose records are not particularly bad, in the first instance, so that we can see the effect. I have also pressed the Premier who is, I think, visiting Gorakhpur, to consult the local officers, for the release of the whole lot apart from encouraging the spirit of lawlessness might have a disheartening effect on the Police.

14. The second troublesome case is that of Parmanand; as you probably know, his prosecution was sanctioned by Haig for a violent speech at Dehra Dun but was withdrawn after he had been run in at Delhi. The Government issued at that time quite a good communiqué,[31] saying they would not tolerate such speeches and would in future take action against such speakers without any further warning. The full papers will of course be in your Secretariat. Parmanand's speeches have been gradually deteriorating and the Police had in more than one case recommended prosecution. The Premier after examining some of the earlier and less bad speeches was against action on the ground that he was rather a spent force, that in some speeches he had been content with advocating social reform and that even his occasional lapses were not as venomous as his speeches immediately after his release from jail. He thought that prosecution would bring him too much into the limelight and suggested that he was bringing other influences to counteract him. This note was recorded before he had seen all the speeches; I have gone carefully through the whole lot and find that there is no doubt that he is gradually becoming more venomous; in his most recent speech, he advocated repeal of the Arms Act, and was very directly inciting to violence. Having traced this gradual deterioration in tone, I am asking the Premier to reconsider the question in the light of these further facts. It is rather difficult to estimate the effect of these speeches and I shall try to ascertain that during my forthcoming tour in Jhansi division where many of them were made. This matter as well as the Lansdowne affair have not been mentioned in the official report! In regard to the latter, I have not had a chance of talking to the Premier again.

CRIME

15. I was impressed by the large number of murder and dacoity cases reported by Commissioners in their fortnightly reports. I had of course no means of judging whether the number was in excess of the normal and I am examining this question, with a view to seeing whether crime generally, and not merely the more serious crimes of murder or dacoity, is increasing as a result of the disturbed conditions prevailing in the Province. I have not been able to complete my examination of this problem and I intend to

look further into it during my forthcoming tour. I do not myself think at present there is any cause for anxiety, but crime statistics are the best index of disturbed conditions, whether disturbed conditions are due to agitation (agrarian, communal or industrial). What I feel is that we get numerous reports of inflammatory speeches but that we have very little evidence of their results.

16. Such reports as I have seen show that though many serious dacoity cases have occurred (whether above or below the average, I cannot yet say), yet in many cases the Police or the local inhabitants have acted with courage and efficiency. In a recent case in Fyzabad district, a notorious dacoit was waylaid by the Police under the Superintendent of Police, Mr. Lahiri, and as he showed fight, he was shot dead. This is one of the many examples I have had of good Police work.

HONORARY MAGISTRATES

17. Some progress is being made in appointing new Honorary Magistrates and I am trying to get the matter expedited. I am not in a better position to say how far the new Magistrates are suitable, but I hope to look into the question during my tour.

18. Though there may be difficulties ahead, I am on the whole by no means pessimistic about the general situation in the United Provinces. It is perhaps rash to give an opinion after a very short experience of the Province, but the Cawnpore settlement has given me some grounds for optimism.

Yours sincerely,
M.G. HALLETT

ENCLOSURE TO NO. 58

CUTTING FROM THE *PIONEER* DATED JUNE 23RD, 1938

United Provinces *Kisans* warned by Governnment

Landlords can take action

"If they default they will not be benefited by the provisions of the proposed Tenancy Law" – this is the latest warning of the United Provinces Government to the tenants on their reluctance to pay rents.

The communiqué, issued by the Government on the subject, adds that it is open to a landlord to take action for recovery of rents or for ejectment of the defaulting tenant.

The Press communiqué says:

"It has been reported to Government that in certain areas tenants are showing disinclination to pay rents for *rabi* 1345 *Fasli*, as they hope that the new Tenancy Act will reduce them and presumably this reduction will have a retrospective effect and the rents for *rabi* 1345 *Fasli* will also be reduced.

"The Government once more desire to make the position clear. The recovery of arrears due for *kharif* 1344 or earlier "kishts" has been stayed under the Stay of Proceedings (Revenue Courts) Act and tenants are entitled to have all payments they now make credited towards the current rent or the arrears, if any, of *rabi* 1344 or *kharif* 1345 *Fasli*. The arrears of rent of *rabi* 1344 and *kharif* 1345 as well as the current rent for *rabi* 1345 are recoverable in the ordinary course of law and if a tenant withholds payments, it is open to a landlord to take action for the recovery of these rents or for the ejectment of the tenant in default of payment according to the provisions of the Agra Tenancy Act and the Oudh Rent Act.

ARREARS AND RENT

"A tenant who now pays in full the arrears of *rabi* 1344 and *kharif* 1345 and the rent for the current instalment of *rabi* 1345 need have no fear that he will be deprived of the benefits of the coming legislation; but a tenant, who fails to pay up and thereby renders himself liable to ejectment and is subsequently ejected, will of course lose its benefits.

"The Government wish to impress upon tenants generally the advisability of paying these demands punctually and fully in their own interests for, if they default and are subsequently ejected, they will not be benefited by the provisions of the proposed Tenancy Law."

59

HALLETT TO BRABOURNE
R/3/1/73

Confidential *July 15th, 1938*
No. U.P.-113

My dear Brabourne,

As I am on tour I have not my papers to hand, but I wrote to you a short time ago about Police medals and about the question of consulting the

Ministers. On thinking over the matter I thought it better to ask the Premier definitely what his opinion was, as Police medals stand on rather a different footing from other honours and titles. I think it is as well that you should see his reply and enclose a copy of his letter of July 13th, 1938, and of my letter to him. I will discuss with him as proposed and shall follow the line indicated in His Excellency Lord Linlithgow's letters on this subject. Clearly the system of granting medals must be continued. I am afraid my recommendation for these medals, both King's Police Medal and Indian Police Medal, will be rather late in consequence, but I trust that will not cause you or your Staff any inconvenience.

Yours sincerely,
M.G. HALLETT

ENCLOSURE 1 TO NO. 59

HALLETT TO PANT

No. U.P.-105 *July 8th, 1938*

I understand that you informed Sir Harry Haig that you did not wish to be consulted or to have anything to do with any recommendations for honours and titles which he might make, as the Provincial Assembly had expressed its desire that the award of such honours and titles should be discontinued. I feel it necessary, however, to make certain whether this decision of yours also applies in the case of medals for the Police force for which members of that force alone are eligible. There are two medals of this type, namely:

(1) The King's Police Medal which is awarded by His Majesty and for which members of all police forces and fire brigades throughout the Empire are eligible. This medal is awarded either for acts of exceptional courage or for conspicuous devotion to duty.

(2) The Indian Police Medal, for which members of a recognised police force or a properly organised fire brigade within the Indian Empire alone are eligible, is awarded by His Excellency the Viceroy and is given (*i*) for conspicuous gallantry, and (*ii*) for valuable services characterised by resource and devotion to duty, including prolonged services of ability and merit.

A number of recommendations for both these medals either for deeds of conspicuous gallantry or for valuable services have been prepared by the Inspector-General of Police. I should be glad to know whether you would like an opportunity of seeing these and of expressing any views about them. You may possibly feel that the case of such medals, which are awarded to members of disciplined forces for exceptional services and for acts of exceptional courage performed in the course of their duties, stands on a different footing from that of other titles and honours; and that any Government, no matter how equalitarian in principle, will find it necessary to give recognition and encouragement of this kind to members of its security forces. As police forms one of the subjects in your own portfolio, I should be especially glad to know your views on the proposed awards if you can see your way to give them; and, if you are willing, I will send the papers to you, for your opinions on the various proposals.

ENCLOSURE 2 TO NO. 59

PANT TO HALLETT

July 13th, 1938

Thanks for your letter of 8th in which you have referred to proposals for awarding the King's Police Medal and the Indian Police Medal to deserving members of the police force in this Province. You are doubtless aware of the policy of the Congress towards the general question of conferment of titles and distinctions. The matter was discussed by our Provincial Assembly and a recommendation that this practice should be discontinued was made by the House. I had occasion to speak to Sir Harry Haig about this subject more than once. I in fact urged that no honours and titles should be conferred in this Province and expressed my inability to have anything to do with any such matters. I also requested him to convey to His Majesty through the proper channel the wishes of the House in this connection.

I quite see the force of your remark that police medals stand on a somewhat different footing from other titles and honours. It would be more in accord with our policy and wishes of the Legislature if such medals were no longer awarded in our Province. I do not know if we are bound to continue this system even if we do not ourselves feel disposed to do so. I am giving thought to this matter and shall be glad to have an opportunity of discussing it with you before any final decisions are reached. It will obviously be somewhat embarrassing to me if these medals are given to officers and men about whose efficiency, character or integrity I do not hold any complimentary opinion or may have my own doubts. It may even tend to undermine discipline and bring about unnecessary friction.

As I understand that you are coming here on or about the 24th I need not say more as I shall then have an opportunity of speaking to you about it.

60

HALLETT TO BRABOURNE
R/3/1/73

Secret
No. U.P.-124

Camp,
July 22nd, 1938

My dear Brabourne,

I enclose, as usual, the official report, dated July 18th, 1938. It is, as usual, rather short and continues to exhibit some of the defects on which I commented a fortnight ago.

2. I think it desirable to start off my report with giving some account of my recent tour and of the impressions which I formed during it. I visited Jhansi and Agra, both very interesting places from the sight-seeing point of view. My visit to each place coincided with heavy rain which was badly needed, in particular for *kharif* cultivation, for although there was some rain early in June, there had been a long break in the monsoon and conditions in these two divisions had not been too pleasant.

3. I had numerous interviews with both officials and non-officials. The non-officials were of course mainly landholders and "loyalists", and if one was guided solely by their views, one would form a very pessimistic view of the situation. They can see no good in any of the activities of the Congress Ministry and many of them reiterate the old request that "Government" should help them, a request which shows that even now they fail to appreciate the new Constitution. I try to reassure by pointing out that under a democratic constitution even a minority can have a good deal of influence on the policy of Government and that if they organise themselves effectively, they may succeed in getting some modification of the Tenancy Bill. I am afraid that I may be guilty of making too frequent references to Bihar, but I find it difficult to refrain from reference to the fact that many of the rights which it is now proposed to confer on tenants in Agra and Oudh have been enjoyed in Bengal and Bihar for many years and also to the fact that in Bihar many of the points in dispute have been settled by compromise. I recognise, however, that comparisons are dangerous and that there are many material differences between the two

provinces and that here in the United Provinces the left wing is probably stronger than elsewhere and has more influence with the Ministry.

4. In forming an opinion of the situation in these two divisions, I have felt it wiser to rely on the opinions of the Commissioners, District Magistrates and Superintendents of Police whom I met and on facts reported by them. I made a particular point of enquiring about (*a*) progress of collections; (*b*) increase of crime; (*c*) effect of speeches of irresponsible agitators and (*d*) cases of interference by Congress workers with the normal activities of Government officers, in particular those of the Police. My enquiries were necessarily somewhat superficial and hurried and the impressions based on them may be incorrect. But as I have on more than one occasion said to His Excellency Lord Linlithgow, I always feel that even hurriedly formed opinions may be of some value to the Governor-General and the Secretary of State in forming some appreciation of the situation.

5. It is I think clear that if the Province were getting out of hand, and if there was a growing spirit of lawlessness and an ever-increasing contempt for law and order, the outward indications of these developments would be difficulties over collection of revenue, and a marked increase in crime, both crime against property and against the person. I refer below to collection of revenues, but I may say here with reference to my tour that none of the District Officers seemed to be very much worried over collections. As regards crime, it must be stated at the outset that dacoity has always been prevalent in these two divisions, mainly because many of these districts are adjacent to Native States. The general opinion which I formed was that dacoity has increased to some extent this year as compared with 1935 and 1936 when it reached a very low level, but officers who were in these districts 10 or 15 years ago tell me that it is far less than it was at that time. I am not apprehensive about the temporary increase and feel that the Police are dealing with dacoity efficiently. Dacoity is however primarily professional crime and it seemed to me that if general lawlessness was increasing, it would be reflected not so much in the dacoity figures as in the figures for burglary, theft, riot, assault, &c. Under these heads there has undoubtedly been some increase but the increase is not yet serious. Various reasons were given; in one district it was said to be due to the fact that the Police were weakened owing to deputations to Cawnpore and other trouble centres – a fact which shows the desirability of increasing our Police reserve; in another it was attributed to the Hardwar Mela and the influx of pilgrims; in some districts the District Magistrates and Superintendents of Police did consider there was growing lawlessness

and that the Police and the Magistracy were experiencing greater difficulty than before over controlling criminals. In one district the local officers considered an increase in the number of murders (17 as against 14, 9 and 6 in the corresponding periods of previous years) as due to this cause, but personally I should regard this increase as fortuitous. In another district an increase of 20 per cent in riots was said to be due to aggressive action by the tenants.

On the whole, my general impression, which I give for what it is worth, is that the new Constitution and the appointment of Congress Ministries might have led to a far more serious increase in crime and general lawlessness.

6. Another point which impressed me was that though in most districts Congress workers are not creating any trouble, yet in some, left wing Congressites are doing a good deal of mischief. There was, while I was there, some trouble over jungle cutting in Lalitpur, an out-of-the-way sub-division of Jhansi district, which I was told was largely due to one agitator; in fact the area seemed to be getting rather out of hand. The Commissioner[32] with my approval recommended vigorous enforcement of the law, if necessary with the aid of more Police, but I have not seen yet what action the Premier has taken; a newspaper report says he has sent a Parliamentary Secretary to effect a compromise! In Aligarh (Agra division), where there are a good number of Muslim landholders, there may be agrarian trouble. In Hamirpur (Jhansi division) the notorious Parmanand is making numerous objectionable speeches. But anti-British speeches do not have much effect in a district which never even has a British officer. However, I will persist in my efforts to induce the Premier to take action against this firebrand. It is always difficult to estimate the effect of objectionable speeches and indeed the effect may not be obvious immediately, but I reminded the Premier the other day that terrorism in Bengal and the terrorist mentality was largely due to the spate of objectionable speeches and literature.

7. From about two districts I had complaints of interference by Congress workers with criminal investigations, but the District Magistrates were in touch with Congress leaders and getting some help from them, so I hope this will not become serious. Government officers on the whole seemed in good heart and one at least told me that the Police and Revenue officers were more cheerful than six months ago. It is very difficult to estimate the position especially for anyone like myself, who is new to the Province. At times I feel that I am unduly optimistic and underestimate the power of the left wing which is undoubtedly strong in this Province, certainly far stronger than in Madras and Bombay and probably stronger than in Bihar.

This opinion is based largely on conversation with Bamford who is staying with me. But though the left wing is strong, and vocal, the right wing is still numerically stronger and my Ministry, though they have of course offended some of their followers, appear to be in a pretty strong and sure position. But all this speculation is rather rash!

8. So much for my tour, which included also a very pleasant visit to Dayalbagh, the religious and industrial settlement near Agra, of which you have no doubt heard. I am going out shortly to Allahabad and Fyzabad, and this tour includes short visits to Gorakhpur, where floods seem to be rather serious, and to Benares.

AGRARIAN SITUATION

9. *Collections.* – I have referred above to collections. In a summary, based on Commissioners' reports up to the middle of June, my Revenue Secretary[33] observes that Land Revenue collections are on the whole not satisfactory. The percentage of collections is only 35 per cent as compared with 43 per cent last year and a rather higher percentage in previous years. Canal dues are rather better. I have examined carefully the most recent reports from Commissioners and these confirm me in the impression that trouble, whether over collections or crime, is confined to those districts where there are irresponsible and virulent agitators. I may quote the Commissioner of Bareilly[34] who writes as follows:

"Shahjahanpur has been more plagued than any other district in the Division with the irresponsible type of village agitators and it is quite clear, as the tahsildars themselves admit, that the local tenants still think they have only got to hold out a little longer to secure further remissions. In this district it will take more than the recent communiqué to disabuse them of this idea and unfortunately their spirit is also affecting the adjacent Bisalpur tahsil in Pilibhit."

The opinion given by the Commissioner of Allahabad[35] is also worth quoting:

"The general position regarding crimes of violence is disquieting. Undoubtedly there is, speaking broadly, diminished fear of the consequences of taking the law into one's own hands. Speakers who impress on villagers that if they only band together they need not fear the Police and are irresistible cannot be acquitted from all responsibility for the deterioration."

From Gorakhpur also the District Magistrate[36] reports that relations between zamindars and tenants are steadily getting worse, but the Commissioner[37] considers that the outlook is more hopeful as a result of the Premier's visit on July 8th. He adds:

"He made it quite clear that tenants must pay their lawful rents and they must be non-violent in their relations with the zamindars. It was arranged that the Conciliation Board which had already been constituted but had not so far done very much good should persevere in their efforts to settle amicably disputes referred by zamindars and tenants.

"But there is one condition which is absolutely necessary if the peace of the division is to be preserved and that is that agitation should cease. There has been more than enough political propaganda already as I have pointed out before."

10. These extracts from the Commissioners' reports are rather depressing, but in other districts either the situation is not so difficult or preventive measures are being effective and there do not appear to have been any serious riots. The Premier appreciating fully the dangers of the situation recently proposed to issue the letter of which I enclose a copy; this is the first draft. On seeing it I said I agreed with the measures proposed, e.g. rectification of grievances, preventive rather than punitive measures, cancellation of gun licence, &c. But I pointed out for his consideration that the first paragraph tended to put the blame mainly on the landholders, which I did not think was entirely correct and that if this leaked out, as it probably would, it might make his position *vis-à-vis* the landholders more difficult. I recognised of course that the letter also told District Officers to help landlords as well as tenants.

COMMITTEES OF THE LEGISLATURE

11. The Select Committee is discussing the Tenancy Bill and appears to be making slow progress, but it is rather difficult to tell from the proceedings exactly how matters stand. Another Committee from which I am receiving daily reports of its meetings is dealing with Local Self-Government, village panchayats, &c. Some of the proposals seem rather radical, but it is not easy to see what form the final report will take. This may of course give rise to the communal question of joint versus separate electorates.

CAWNPORE

12. I have heard no further news of Cawnpore lately but enclose for your record a printed copy of the Government communiqué issued on July 6th.[38] The District Officer[39] is staying with me at present and he seems satisfied with the situation and with the action taken by Government.

RELEASE OF PRISONERS

13. I have not received my Premier's reply to my long note about Chauri Chaura prisoners. There was another case arising out of a civil disobedience riot, in which after a Sub-Inspector had been killed, the Police shot a good many of the rioters. This was in Sir Malcolm Hailey's time. The accused, about 9 or 10 in number, who were convicted were sentenced to transportation for life, and at that time Sir Malcolm considered the sentences far too severe, having regard to the punishment inflicted on the rioters. The late Government reduced the sentences in some cases of prisoners who appealed, to 10 years, but even at that time it was felt that a further reduction might be made. My Minister in charge of Jails suggested releasing all the remaining prisoners forthwith; I suggested that the better course would be a reduction of all the sentences to 8½ years, which means that remissions will be taken into account and releases will not be simultaneous. I enclose an extract from my note on the case and of the Premier's reply. I think this is fairly satisfactory; it was very difficult to resist reduction of sentences.

COMMUNAL SITUATION

14. There is not much to add regarding Hindu-Muslim situation, but a recent riot at Pilibhit, which possibly you noticed in the Press and which is mentioned in the official report, shows how easily such riots may start; in this case it was due to a quarrel over the price of a mango. Incidents such as this show the dangers of the present communal tension.

15. There are some signs, not possibly very marked, that recent events in Palestine had caused greater interest to be taken in that question. But I do not think that Muslims generally take much interest in the question. The Depressed Classes – I had an interview with one of their leaders in Agra – seem to consider that they are rather neglected by the Government; they claim more posts in Government services and consider also that more members of their classes should have secured appointments as Honorary Magistrates.

HONORARY MAGISTRATES

16. As I have already reported, the delay over these appointments continues to cause a congestion of petty criminal cases. The Premier recently suggested appointing temporarily to relieve the situation pleaders or

advocates from adjacent districts on a fee of Rs. 150 a month plus travelling allowance. I do not like this even as a temporary measure; it goes contrary to the whole principle of Honorary Magistrates and may be the thin end of the wedge. I am therefore having the matter discussed in Council. I find it rather difficult to ascertain the quality of the newly appointed Magistrates and during my recent tour heard various accounts of them. A good number of those who have held these posts in the past have been re-appointed and that is satisfactory.

RURAL DEVELOPMENT SCHEME

17. As far as I could make out during my tour, very little is being done in actual practice. Some of the agencies which did useful work in the past, e.g. students of the Christian College at Agra, have been discarded. The Premier and other Ministers have had discussions with Government officers in some districts and are showing no signs of leaving out Government officers, for they recognise that they will be useful.

I am afraid the letter is already unduly long, but I hope you will find it of interest. I may conclude by saying how much I appreciate your very helpful comments on my reports.

Yours sincerely,
M.G. HALLETT

ENCLOSURE 1 TO NO. 60

DRAFT CIRCULAR TO ALL U.P. DISTRICT OFFICERS

Subject – Tension between zamindars and tenants

Sir,

I am directed to address you on the situation arising out of the tension between zamindars and tenants in certain parts of the Province. You are no doubt conscious of the fact that there has been a general awakening among the tenants in recent months and along with this has appeared a keener appreciation of their position and rights. While formerly the tenants were even servile in certain places, they have ceased to be so and are no longer as docile and submissive as in the past. They are learning to claim their legal rights and are not prepared to submit ungrudgingly to unlawful or excessive demands. This attitude of theirs is particularly distasteful to those zamindars who had the benefit of their ignorance and weakness in olden days and who had almost a free and unfettered sway in the backward tracts. It has been reported to Government that in certain places, zamindars have been reluctant to give receipts, that they have made efforts to realise the arrears of rent which have been suspended and that in certain cases payments made for current dues are credited towards suspended arrears. Instances are also believed to have occurred of *sir* tenants being forcibly ejected from their holdings. Zamindars are also reported to have enlisted the services of bad characters in certain areas for bullying and harassing the cultivators. On the other hand, it has also been reported that tenants have in a few cases taken the law in their own hands, for example, by attempting to get hold of fields from which they had been lawfully ejected or which they had mortgaged. Such complaints against tenants are, however, not general and their number is almost negligible.

2. While Government have no reason to believe that the situation in the Province generally has in any way deteriorated, they consider that the greatest vigilance is required on the part of the district authorities. There is a feeling in certain quarters that the tenants' complaints are indifferently treated by the local police. Government wish to emphasize the fact that it is the duty of the District Officers to take prompt action on all such complaints. District Officers will no doubt consider preventive measures as preferable to penal action and as being not only more fruitful but also less harmful. It may be desirable to make use of Section 107 or Section 145 of the Criminal Procedure Code, to cancel or suspend firearms licences and to get such weapons belonging to licensees or exemptees deposited in police stations and malkhanas wherever there is any apprehension of breach of the peace. I am to point out that, if genuine grievances are not redressed speedily, sullen irritation attended by a feeling of helplessness follows which may lead to serious and ugly developments later. The time factor is very important in such cases.

3. In carrying out these instructions, Government confidently expect that the District officers will exercise the utmost tact and restraint in so far as may be compatible with the performance of their important duties. They expect that officers will be absolutely fair and impartial as between zamindars and tenants and, while protecting tenants from high-handed actions, will be ready to give legal assistance to zamindars if they are faced with any difficulty in realising their legitimate dues. In this connection, it is important that cases filed by zamindars should be promptly decided, and other steps provided for by law to assist them in making collection taken, where there is a deliberate refusal on the part of tenants to pay their just dues.

4. I am further to say that Government consider it important that they should be posted with up-to-date information regarding agrarian questions. With this end in view, they desire that speeches delivered at agrarian meetings, whether they are zamindar gatherings or *kisan* conferences, should be reported by the police along the lines laid down in demi-officials Nos. N.325-Police, and 1855-Police, dated December 3rd, 1937, and April 21st, 1938 respectively, and such reports submitted to Government as promptly as possible.

5. Finally, I am to add that sufficient staff should be posted in places where the District Magistrate considers this to be absolutely necessary. If any special request for additional staff is received from any individual District Magistrate, Government will be prepared to consider it.

I have, &c.,

ENCLOSURE 2 TO NO. 60

EXTRACT FROM NOTE BY HALLETT[40]

July 10th, 1938

Question of the release of the Gulaothi Riot Case prisoners

10. Hon'ble Minister suggests that in all these seven cases, the period of imprisonment remaining should be remitted. This will mean that all will be released simultaneously. This will no doubt look like a response to the resolutions recently passed by the Congress Committees, &c., but I would ask Government to consider very carefully whether it is desirable to sanction releases in response to resolutions of political parties. I quite admit that a democratic Government has to consider the views of its party, but Government has also to consider other matters, such as I have suggested earlier in this note, the effect of such releases on law and order generally. If these persons are released, though guilty of taking part in a serious riot in which a Sub-Inspector was killed, might it not be urged that there are many other cases of riot in which the accused should similarly be released?

11. It seems to me that the salient part [?point] in this case is that it was recognised from the beginning that the sentences were too severe; in consequence some were reduced to 10 years and even that reduction was done with the assumption that the case for their release would be considered at an early date.

12. I would suggest that it would be better in this case for Government

to pass an order reducing the sentences on all these prisoners to, say, nine years. This will mean that all will be released in the very near future or probably immediately. It will also mean that they will not all be released simultaneously, and also that those who have behaved best in jail and have earned most remissions will go first. I think it is desirable in the interest of jail discipline that a well-behaved prisoner should get released earlier than one whose jail record is bad.

13. My suggestion has very nearly the same effect as that proposed by Hon'ble Minister. I would not object to reducing their sentences to 8½ years. But I think if we proceed in this way, the action taken will be more justifiable.

ENCLOSURE 3 TO NO. 60

NOTE BY PANT

July 14th, 1938

Question of the release of the Gulaothi Riot Case prisoners

It is not necessary for me to deal with this case at any length. H.M.R. has given cogent reasons in support of his order for the release of those prisoners. His Excellency has covered the entire ground in his minute. There is no doubt that from the outset even a sentence of ten years was regarded as more than the accused deserved, and it is borne in upon me by a perusal of the notes which were recorded when the incident was quite fresh and facts were fully known that these prisoners would be let out of the jail any time after they had served five years and before the expiry of ten. If H.M.R. sees no difficulty I would reduce the sentence in each case to eight and a half years. Their conduct in jail seems to have been uniformly good except in the case of Lakhpat about whom the entry is "fair" and of Mansa about whom it is shown as "indifferent". I do not, however, appreciate the reasons for the disparity in the likely dates of their releases. About some the year "1950" is given, obviously because no application for mercy had been filed and consequently no reduction had been made. But Mansa whose conduct is shown as indifferent is to be released on 1st May 1939. He happens to be the first in the order in which releases will follow. I think it would be fair to grant remissions to all of them on the same scale on which it has been allowed in the case of Mansa.

I do not think this will have any effect on the law and order position.

These prisoners have, I believe, no political convictions and they are not habitual criminals. Still I should like them to be released in batches. Further before they are actually released I would also ask them not to give cause for any embarrassment but to quietly retire to their respective villages without any fuss. I believe they will have no objection.

GOVIND BALLABH PANT

61

HALLETT TO BRABOURNE
R/3/1/73

Secret
No. U.P.-142

Camp,
August 7th, 1938

My dear Brabourne,

I enclose as usual the official fortnightly report dated August 1st.

GENERAL

2. The most disquieting feature of the report is the statement that both Muslims and zamindars are collecting bodies of volunteers. This point had occurred to me also from reading police reports and other sources of information. But the reports are all rather vague and it is not by any means clear whether any practical steps have been taken to collect volunteers and to arm them or whether the proposal is still merely under discussion. Apart from Muslims and zamindars' volunteers, and one Superintendent of Police,[41] whom I met lately from Farrukhabad, told me that the Hindustani Seva Dal, formerly a revolutionary body which was proscribed, had held a training camp at which volunteers did squad drill, &c.[42] The difficulty of appreciating the exact position is that one has to rely on scattered reports. I am therefore asking the Premier to get the C.I.D. to give a considered appreciation of the situation from such information as they have on record, supplemented if necessary by further enquiries from the districts. Clearly if a large number of volunteer bands come into existence, we shall have numerous clashes and may revert to the conditions that prevailed in the middle ages.

3. Another point to be noted in the report is that the Palestine situation is attracting more notice in the Urdu Press. I have no reason to believe

that it is attracting very much notice outside the Press, for Muslims are preoccupied with their own local quarrels and with the League-Congress controversy. I have discussed the communal situation here in Allahabad with the local officers. There is of course a risk of trouble at the Ram Lila festival next month, but it looks to me rather as if the people might have learnt a lesson from the riots of last March and April. The local officers seem to have done very well on that occasion and to have taken effective action to disarm potential rioters; they were in fact quite happy to deal with the situation as soon as Government gave them a free hand.

4. I have again studied Commissioners' fortnightly reports with care; those before me are for the first half of July.

COLLECTIONS

Collections are on the whole progressing satisfactorily; thus in Meerut no difficulty is anticipated over making full collections before the end of September; Jhansi reports that collections in all districts are above the estimate which is satisfactory seeing that there are many places where tenants have paid their rents in part. Gorakhpur, especially Gorakhpur District, does not report a very good percentage, but made good progress during the last fortnight. Benares is also not very good. Fyzabad reports that collections do not compare unfavourably with last year. The net result for the whole Province is that 76 per cent of the current land revenue has been collected as against an average of the three previous years of 80 per cent.

AGRARIAN SITUATION

In the reports dealing with this point there are some reassuring features, though the position in the eastern districts is not too good. However, we seem to be getting through the sowing season without any major disturbances and that is to the good. Ballia district, for example, says that "agrarian situation has eased very much and with the termination of the sowing season the crisis is over." Gorakhpur is not happy; it is a very large and difficult district and suffers from floods and agitation. The Commissioner reports that the District Congress President (Saxena) is very hostile to the administration and in particular to the Collector, Pedley, whom he recently accused of being "in open alliance with the forces of lawlessness". I have a very good opinion of Pedley, but I am afraid the Premier is influenced by his supporters, for he recently expressed the opinion that Pedley was not sufficiently sympathetic to the tenants. This was before I heard of the accusation of an "alliance with the forces of lawlessness", but the report makes clear the reasons for the Premier's opinion. Many districts report a large number of complaints that the tenants have been dispossessed by the landlords; when there are definite complaints, prompt action is taken under Section 145, Cr.P.C., or other appropriate sections and attempts are made, often with some success, to settle the matter on the spot. I feel, however, that Congress in this fight with the landlords are exaggerating their case. Thus the Collector of Cawnpore reports that the local Congress Secretary complained to him that tenants were being forcibly dispossessed of their land; the Collector had himself received no specific complaint and the Congress Secretary does not seem to have produced any. There are no doubt oppressive landlords in some of the more backward tracts, but I cannot believe that the majority of the landlords are as black as they are painted by their opponents. On the other hand, landlords exaggerate their difficulties and the following extract from the report of the Meerut Commissioner[43] gives an example of this:

"I have recently been touring over the division, and here and there I have heard complaints from zamindars that they are not receiving their rents; but, while there is no doubt that collections of rent do not grow easier with the progress of time, I am not at all inclined to believe that their lament is strictly true for some of them are quite ready to say that they have not collected a shell, which is an imaginative statement of their difficulties. The Court of Wards appears to have no difficulty in collecting its rents, and that serves as a gauge."

5. *Legislature.* – While in Lucknow, I discussed private members' resolutions in my Cabinet. One which had secured first place in the ballot recommended that in all complaints of corruption against the Police, the enquiry should be by a committee consisting of the I.G., another police officer and three M.L.As. The Premier was prepared to take a sound line and recognised the objection to a committee with a non-official majority. The difficulty is that the Police in this Province has a somewhat elaborate form of Court Martial for the trial of departmental proceedings, and I hope my Ministers will devise something more satisfactory and will provide for the proceedings to be conducted by the District Magistrate and Superintendent of Police. When this resolution came on for discussion, it was not moved, on the ground that an opportunity would be given to the Assembly to discuss the Anti-Corruption report generally. Other resolutions call for no comment, but I was glad to see that by deliberately spinning

out the discussion on the question of compulsory vaccination, my Government avoided rather a dangerous resolution advocating all the numerous measures designed to help those who had been punished for participation in Civil Disobedience.

6. Detailed proposals regarding debt legislation have been put before Government by the Revenue Secretary, Mr. Mudie. Briefly he is against debt conciliation boards and in favour of an agricultural marketing and financing corporation. I admit that I do not much like the proposal and speaking with very little knowledge of this difficult problem, I may say that I prefer the village *bania* to a Government department or quasi-Government organisation. However my Government have not yet given their views and I hope to discuss the question again when I return to Lucknow. I feel that in all these matters it is better to play for time.

7. The Tenancy Bill is making slow progress in Select Committee and it now appears very unlikely that the report will be ready before the end of August, if then. I presume a good deal of negotiation is going on and I cannot at this stage foretell what the final decision about "sir" lands will be. The Ministry show no anxiety to hasten a decision about the question of an enhancement of revenue.

8. As I have told you by telegram, Mrs. Pandit is going on "leave". I suppose that is constitutional and as I have said, I have no objection to her work being split up between the other Ministers. It will not lead to efficiency, but that cannot be helped. Local self-governing bodies in this Province cannot be more inefficient than they are at present.

Since writing above, I have received your telegram[44] for which many thanks. I am taking necessary action.

9. While in Allahabad, I have had an interview with Sir Tej Bahadur Sapru. He felt very strongly over the Central Provinces affair which he regarded as a denial of democratic Government. He thought Wylie could not possibly have acted otherwise and might even have gone further.[45] We then went on to the question of Federation; he does not think that Jawaharlal Nehru or Subhas Bose will ever agree to it; they are irreconcilable; Gandhi, Patel and Desai and probably the majority of Congress will accept it subject to modification of the provisions regarding indirect election and election in the States. Satyamurti would accept it if the chapter about discrimination were omitted. Speaking generally, he felt the most dangerous tendencies at the present time were the tendency towards dictatorship, which might be either fascist or communist and the attack of the propertied classes. He has of course his own views about the Federal Court, but he thought a

good time would elapse before cases, e.g. in regard to Tenancy Legislation, came before it. He seemed to suggest, though only incidentally, that the Orissa landholders had a stronger case than Bihar.

10. Sapru's opinion on the Central Provinces crisis is of course similar to that of all the old liberals (Chintamani gave me a similar view) and probably has a good deal of support in Congress circles. I have just been reading Gandhi's reply to Khare and his critics and his attack on Wylie, which you and he had anticipated. I feel that if Gandhi still retains his influence with Congress and over Congress Ministers, his article in the *Harijan*[46] will not make the position of a Governor or indeed of members of the services easier; it may have the effect of making Congress Ministers, who as far as my experience goes, are prepared to accept at least in minor matters the advice of the Governor and of the permanent staff, far more obstinate and difficult. Even though there have been few, if any, occasions on which a Governor in the exercise of his individual judgment has had to overrule the Ministers, I feel that the mere fact that cases are referred to him has had a controlling and restraining influence. Gandhi with his usual cunning has emphasised again the "fight"; he contends that Wylie's action has "killed the spirit of the compact between the British Government and the Congress". "If a fight is to be avoided, Governors must recognise the Congress as the one national organisation that is bound one day or other to replace the British Government." A statement such as this may encourage Congress subordinates to interfere more than at present with the Police or District Officers and that I regard as far more dangerous in the long run than disputes between a Governor and his Ministers. Gandhi omits any references to the Muslim League which is by no means a power to be treated with contempt, and it is quite possible that on this occasion we may have a good deal of support. But I have always felt that it is dangerous to under-estimate Gandhi's influence, and though I may be wrong – I hope I am – I feel that his very direct intervention in the Central Provinces crisis is an event of very great importance. I cannot suggest any means of meeting his move, but it is clear that Governors in Congress Provinces must keep closely in touch. I have no doubt that Your Excellency will do all you can to help us.

11. Such District Officers as I have met during my visit to Allahabad have been in good heart. As Your Excellency observed in your reply to my last report, there is a good deal of difference between the views of senior and junior officers, but if junior officers are happy and holding their own it is a satisfactory feature of the situation. I am encouraged by the

Lansdowne incident which I have separately reported;[47] Pant has written to me to say that he took action as suggested by me and hence Saksena did not attend. This is good and I am thanking him for what he has done.

Yours sincerely,
M.G. HALLETT

62

HALLETT TO BRABOURNE
R/3/1/74

Secret *August 23rd, 1938*
No. U.P.-157

My dear Brabourne,

I send as usual the official fortnightly report. It is open to the same criticisms as previous reports. The floods have been very serious in certain districts, but as I gathered from my recent visit to Fyzabad, the local officers are taking all possible steps to deal with the emergency. It may be that some of the measures taken by Congress Government tend to lessen the power of a District Officer and it is certain that many of the suggestions made to them by their followers have this object in view, yet in spite of this, when an emergency arises, either because of a flood or other natural disaster or because of a communal riot, all turn to the District Officer for help, and District Officers, even though they are not as good as in the old days, rise to the occasion and do most valuable work, which is appreciated.

2. I have had a very interesting visit to Allahabad with short trips to Benares and Fyzabad. In the latter district I paid a visit to the sacred city of Ajodhya where the Mahants of one of the largest temples gave me a very loyal and respectful reception. As I rode through the streets of the town, I was much impressed by the respectful salutations of the populace. Another interesting feature of my Fyzabad visit was that two of the leading Congressmen, including the President of the District Congress Committee, came and had interviews with me; it was a refreshing change to hear a different point of view from that put forward by most of my "mulakatis". I feel that tours are most valuable, as they enable one to meet local officers and non-officials and to form a more correct appreciation of the situation than it is possible to form at headquarters, reading Police reports and dealing with voluminous files. In Allahabad I paid an informal visit to the

University; the Police were a bit apprehensive of a hostile demonstration from some students, but all went well and I spent an interesting two hours seeing a University working.

3. As regards the general situation, the last fortnight has been quiet. Heavy rain always damps the ardour of the agitator and prevents the assembly of large crowds! The agrarian and communal situation remains much the same; both are rather disquieting and my paragraph below on Tenancy Legislation gives also my views about the agrarian situation. There have been two or three rather serious cases of riot with murder and in some of these it appears pretty certain that the zamindars were the aggressors. Such cases are bound to occur as long as the Tenancy Bill is on the anvil.

4. In regard to communal matters, I note that the Muslim League Council held a meeting recently in Cawnpore at which leftist tendencies were apparent in some of the resolutions; no doubt these were mainly with a view to secure support of Muslim workers of that town, as well as to discredit Congress. Congress were for example charged with duplicity in dealing with the labour problem, in that though the Congress Committee had professed to support the strikers, the Congress Government had adopted an attitude of neutrality. Another resolution was to the effect that office bearers in the Muslim League should not accept office in any landlord organisation. There have also been two or three cases of communal rioting and in each case the cause of the dispute was a very petty matter.

5. Palestine affairs continue to be discussed in meetings and in Agra the Muslim League Council is said to have boycotted British goods. I still feel doubtful whether this agitation reaches the Muslim masses; the fight with Congress is still far more important and there are some reports before me of the intention to enrol large bodies of volunteers. I am afraid I cannot yet give any more definite information about the question of volunteers, to which I referred in my last letter.

6. In the industrial areas there have been one or two lightning strikes of a minor character, but generally I think the action taken by Government over the Cawnpore strike has had a tranquillising effect. I am paying a short visit to Cawnpore this week and shall no doubt hear more of the employers' views of the situation. A Police report says that in the Mazdoor Sabha elections, the communist group have a majority, but it does not appear to be overwhelming and there are disputes over the election of office bearers.

7. *Tenancy Legislation.* – The Bill is making slow progress owing to numerous discussions by the Government with all the various parties. It is

possible that the Select Committee's report will be ready early in September and it may be possible for the Assembly to start discussion about September 6th, but I do not feel by any means certain.

8. I gather both from my Revenue Secretary[48] and the Nawab of Chhatari that the Taluqdars are being very obstinate in the matter and will not agree to any compromise. They pinned their faith first of all on the possibility of the legislation being disallowed by the Federal Court or some other authority. Now apparently they think that before the Bill becomes law there will be a crisis, either as a result of a European war or of a dispute over Federation or some other reason; they think that if there is a crisis, involving suspension of the Constitution, the Bill will be dropped but as the Nawab has told them, even if the Constitution were suspended, it would be probably necessary for the Governor to enact this or some similar bill and it is far more in their interest to get some form of compromise and get the credit for it. The view taken by persons whom I met on tour, both officials and non-officials, was that it is most desirable to get the question settled one way or the other; it is this uncertainty which is causing the situation to deteriorate. This too is my view; the longer these discussions go on, the greater will become, at least in this Province, the power of the left wing. It is in the interests of that wing to play for time. I doubt whether I can do much in the matter, but if I see any Taluqdars, I will impress on them this point of view.

9. As regards the general situation, the collection of revenue in most districts appears satisfactory, but I am not very happy about the increase in crime and I enclose a copy of a letter which I have just written to my Premier. I have put my views mildly in the first instance, but I do feel that in some districts the position of the subordinate Police is difficult. No doubt in the old days the Sub-Inspector was not above reproach; he probably relied too much on the use of Section 109 or 110 Cr.P.C.; now he is diffident of using these sections and does not know exactly how to adapt himself to the changed circumstances. He realises also that his local M.L.A. can ask questions in the Assembly about his conduct and there is no doubt in my opinion that questions in the Assembly have a most demoralising effect on the administration. I see no direct method of combating this evil but in a note which I have written, regarding Secretariat procedure, in which I have dealt with the general question of the work, I have suggested that Ministers should endeavour to restrain their followers from being too inquisitive, but I doubt whether it will have much effect.

10. I am very grateful to Your Excellency for all the help which you

have given me over the Lansdowne affair. I hope the action we have taken will keep things quiet there for some time.

11. Mrs. Pandit has left and I have passed orders transferring her departments to the other Ministers.[49] I will send a copy of the order. I think the procedure was correct, but it is rather an anomalous position. It is satisfactory however that the joint responsibility of the Cabinet has been emphasised.

12. In dealing with proposals for recruitment to the I.C.S. and I.P., my Premier shows a tendency to cut down the number of European recruits. I will write separately about this.

Yours sincerely,
M.G. HALLETT

ENCLOSURE TO NO. 62

HALLETT TO PANT

No. U.P.-156

Camp,
August 22nd, 1938

My dear Premier,

I have examined the last batch of fortnightly reports received from Commissioners with some care, for there are some points in them which cause me some anxiety and which I consider it right to bring to your notice, although I have no doubt you have yourself noted them. But your work must be so heavy these days that it must be no easy matter for you to deal with it and my object in writing to you is to help you as far as I can.

2. The reports regarding collections are satisfactory, but I am not happy about what I may call the "crime" position. I have endeavoured to get information about this during my tours, and the general impression which I formed is that though the situation has not got out of hand in any district, there is a general increase in crime.

3. My view that the increase in crime needs careful watching is confirmed by the Commissioners' reports. Thus the Commissioner of Meerut[50] reports as follows:

"There is a general and alarming increase in burglary in almost every district. I have been watching the figures with anxiety for some time past, and the problem at its present rate of increase will soon be a serious one. Meerut reports three dacoities during the period; in one of these a villager was shot dead, while in another a cartman was wounded by a bullet."

4. From the Commissioner of Agra's report,[51] I make the following extracts:

"Stubbs[52] reports an agrarian riot resulting in a murder. He observes a definite tendency to increased disputes over land between landlords and tenants, not always leading to violence, and attributes this to apprehensions regarding the new Tenancy Bill. Undoubtedly this Bill is having a very unsettling effect in the rural area in all districts."

"Naqvi reports the continuance of meetings in the rural area of the Aligarh district organised by Thakur Malkhan Singh, M.L.A., at which very intemperately worded speeches are delivered. At one held on July 29th a notorious goonda, who has now enrolled himself as a member of the Congress party, sang a bhajan in which the British were accused of dishonesty and zulm and unhappy references made to incidents during the Mutiny. The bhajan concluded that the first duty of the audience was to turn the British out of India. For this purpose a speaker advocated the enrolment of an army of 35 crores of volunteers, who would be prepared to face death. Thakur Malkhan Singh himself advised tenants to fight their zamindars boldly and face death in the Act. He stated his determination to bury the zamindars in a ditch, and expressed the view that the first duty of the Congress party was to turn the British out of India. Naqvi considers the speeches delivered at this meeting to be actionable, and is reporting them separately."

"In Naqvi's view the agrarian situation in the district is fast deteriorating as a consequence of this propaganda. He writes that 'intemperate speeches and absolutely false propaganda are the order of the day. Innumerable difficulties between the zamindars and tenants crop up as a result'. The position seems to be worst in Atrauli tahsil, where most of the zamindars are Muslims. Here the agitation is taking a communal turn. It seems that Th. Malkhan Singh's faction of the local Congress party has enrolled *goondas* as Congressmen. In Naqvi's view they are intentionally creating communal bitterness. He concludes: 'I cannot speak too strongly of the danger of class warfare in Atrauli tehsil if these present activities are allowed to continue.' I share his apprehensions fully. Th. Malkhan Singh, M.L.A., appears to be wholly irresponsible and to be determined to cause trouble. As Government are no doubt aware, there has been a split in the local Congress party at Aligarh. Th. Malkhan Singh, M.L.A. heads one faction, and Sri Jwala Prasad Jigyasu the other. I do not know which of the rival factions is reckoned to be supporting Government. If political influence can be brought to bear on Thakur Malkhan Singh to restrain him, then it seems to me exceedingly desirable that such action should be taken, failing which it seems to me essential that action of a preventive nature should be taken on the usual lines. As a start I would advise that the full reporting of the speeches delivered at Thakur Malkhan Singh's meetings be ordered."

I formed the opinion when on tour at Agra that Aligarh was a difficult district partly because of the mischievous activities of Thakur Malkhan Singh, partly because agrarian disputes were likely to develop on communal lines.

5. From Bareilly the Commissioner[53] reports that crime has been fortunately light, but adds the significant fact that burglaries are up about 50 per cent in Bijnor, Budaun and Moradabad. I recognise that some Congress workers are giving great help to the authorities, e.g. this report states: "In Pilibhit Th. Bhagwan Singh M.L.A., has given sage advice at various village meetings to help the Police in the prevention and detection of crime, as at present the Congress is being blamed for its increase."

6. From Allahabad I extract the following:

"Burglary his again been very bad in Fatehgarh and Fatehpur. Walley remarks that he has been discussing the problem with the Superintendent of Police,[54] but so far their efforts do not appear to have produced any reduction. The figures were 67 as against 15 in the corresponding period of last year. The position is causing not a little anxiety. On the other hand the Fatehpur Police have rounded up some dacoits, who were wanted for numerous recent dacoities. It remains to be seen however whether they will be convicted."

"Two cases have occurred in Allahabad of the local Congress Mandal holding an inquest in a case of accidental death in the rural areas. A report was sent to the Police station, but the local Mandal disposed of the body without waiting for news to reach the Police. The Superintendent of Police[55] has protested strongly to the Secretary of the District Congress Committee and asked him to prevent such occurrences in future."

7. From Jhansi it is reported that there was a marked rise in burglary in Jhansi district.

8. Gorakhpur reports as follows: "Gorakhpur reports two murders and two dacoities and an increase of burglary, the number of cases being 77 as against 55 in the previous fortnight and 31 last year. There were 8 cases of cattle theft and 8 riots."

"Of the riots one was a serious agrarian riot in village Indarpur of Purandarpur Police Circle. This has been reported separately in the Collector's D.O. No. 1401 to the Chief Secretary, dated August 4th.[56] There seems to be no doubt that the trees were cut by the tenants and the fact that they could do so shows to what a pitch the spirit of lawlessness has reached. According to the Magisterial enquiry zamindars put themselves in the wrong by using fire-arms after all the trees had been cut down and when there was no justification. They will be prosecuted for rioting and proceedings under Section 107 will be taken against both parties."

9. Benares reports: "Both Benares and Mirzapur report an increase in crime generally." "The Collector of Benares[57] reports that he is receiving reports of forcible dispossession of agricultural land although the sowing season is practically over. 35 fresh reports were reported from Benares tahsil and 70 from Chandauli tahsil." "Mirzapur – Further enquiries made by the Collector of Mirzapur[58] show that in a few cases, Congress Mandals and rural development officers are taking upon themselves the responsibility of disposing of judicial cases."

10. Lucknow reports: "Burglaries are on the increase. One gang has been rounded up but the other is active. Rae Bareli – There were 44 burglaries as against 32 last fortnight. Action under Section 110 is expected. Hardoi – Burglaries have gone up from 50 to 105, due to inadequate patrolling in the water-logged areas and defective surveillance where cholera is raging. Kantas and spears have been banned, night patrolling intensified, and necessary action is being taken by the Police."

11. I think you will agree with me that these reports show that the situation must be carefully watched. Some Commissioners in their reports refer only to dacoities and murders and the more serious and spectacular crime, but if we are to appreciate the position correctly, we must know about all forms of crime and an increase in the number of thefts, burglaries and assaults is as much an index of disturbed conditions as are increases in dacoities or murders. I would suggest therefore asking all Commissioners to pay special attention to this point in their reports and if there has been a substantial increase, to give their views as to the reasons for it and as to the measures which may be taken to prevent it. Similarly we should get the views of the I.G.[59] and D.I.G. It is desirable not merely to compare the statistics for the current year with those of last year, and the comparison is more valuable if it is made against the average of the last 3 to 5 years.

12. If crime has increased, many of the causes are obvious. Agrarian agitation, communal disputes, industrial strikes are all bound to create a spirit of unrest and lawlessness which in turn create an increase in crime. What action can be taken to improve the situation is a more difficult problem. As long as the Tenancy proposals are under discussion, agrarian agitation is bound to increase and though I do not wish to unduly hasten the discussions, I feel there is considerable force in the observation of the Commissioner of Agra that the Bill is having an unsettling effect in all

districts. This is a view that has been put before [me] by many persons whom I have met during my tours.

13. It is possible that in some districts the increase in crime is due to the fact that the Police are inadequate or that the strength of the district force has been depleted by the necessity of deputing Police to storm centres such as Cawnpore or Allahabad. The I.G. has, I believe, submitted proposals for increasing the Police reserve and though fortunately at present most districts are fairly quiet (heavy rain always stops disturbances!) we cannot tell when we shall have a fresh outbreak and we should be prepared for it.

14. Then there is the problem of the irresponsible agitator and in this connection I invite your special attention to the report of the Collector of Aligarh. The view that I formed during my tour is that in most districts there is plenty of co-operation between local officials and Congress leaders, but in some districts certainly agitators, such as Thakur Malkhan Singh, are making the task of the Police far more difficult. I think I saw in the Press a complaint made at a Congress meeting that the Police had not changed their methods with the advent of the Congress Ministry and I feel that criticism such as this does not make the position of a Police officer very easy.

15. There is also of course the question of various associations attempting to create bodies of volunteers, a matter which I referred to you a short time ago.

16. I am not in any way unduly apprehensive about the present position, but we must not allow it to get out of hand and I should like to have a discussion with you about it.

Yours sincerely,
M.G. HALLETT

63

HALLETT TO BRABOURNE
R/3/1/74

Secret
No. U.P.-158

August 27th, 1938

My dear Brabourne,

I am afraid my absence on tour has delayed my reply to your letter of 4th August 1938 about the Rural Development grant[60] and I apologise for it.

2. You point out that one of the objects of the scheme, possibly the main object, was to maintain the position of the District Officer as head of the district. I recognise that this was one of our objects at that time, but to put it somewhat crudely it was also an election device to take the wind out of Congress sails. Gandhi had put forward his Rural uplift scheme, which though applauded by some persons in England, was really doing nothing. We wanted to show that our officers could do something better and it was with that object that the money was made over to the District Officer.

3. It is now implied that if this money is taken away from the District Officer, his position as head of the district will be affected. Some senior officers no doubt hold that it is the general policy of Congress Government to do down the District Officer. They base their opinion on these proposals and on other proposals such as those for the separation of judicial and executive functions, for the constitution of anti-corruption committees, &c. No doubt extremists without any practical experience of the difficulty of administration do regard the presence of members of a Secretary of State's service in the post of District Officer as an obstacle in the way of obtaining complete independence and of destroying British Imperialism. But my experience of two Congress Ministries leads me very definitely to the view that the growing realisation of the difficulties of administration tends to make them appreciate the value of the District Officer; I would also add, in particular, of the British District Officer. They realise that he is particularly valuable in times of emergency, whether the emergency is due to natural calamities or communal or agrarian disturbances. On such occasions they are by degrees showing more inclination to leave decisions to him and not to interfere; this was the case here when there were communal riots in Allahabad and when the strike was on in Cawnpore. I feel therefore that the District Officer, provided he is a man of character, and personality and courage – and some of the young civilians in this Province possess these qualifications, though some, I admit, are rather below standard – will hold his own. It may no doubt be that in future he will not be so much the father of his district, concerned with all branches of the administration, but will have to concentrate more on the maintenance of law and order and in this Province with the inter-connected agrarian and tenancy problems and that in regard to other problems will have more of an advisory position. But I see no reason why his prestige should diminish.

4. The present position seems to me to be much the same as that which occurred after the introduction of the last reforms. Previous to that District

Officers had been Chairmen of District Boards and Municipalities; after the new Constitution of 1919 came in, they were deprived of these posts and at that time many officers resented being deprived of work which was definitely interesting and for the benefit of the people; it was thought then as is thought now that this would destroy or reduce the position of the District Officer. No doubt it did to some extent, but I have been a District Officer both before and after this change was made and I must confess that I feel that my position as District Officer without being Chairman of the District Board was as strong as the position I had enjoyed when combining these two functions.

5. For these general reasons I am not against some change in the position of a District Officer in regard to Rural Development Scheme, and in fact I would say that some change was inevitable after Congress Ministries had accepted office. It was however desirable to see that the change was not too drastic and that the District Officer was not left entirely out of the picture.

6. Before however I elaborate this point in greater detail, there is one further point which I would make. Under the old scheme, the total amount placed at the District Officer's disposal as a discretionary grant was not large, possibly he had about Rs. 10,000 in all. The mere fact that he had these sums under his control for expenditure in a district containing thousands of villages, that he was able to help a very few of these villages, did not really contribute very much to his position or prestige. His prestige is far more enhanced by the action which he takes in an emergency. It must be remembered that giving out what are in effect doles may please the small percentage of the population benefited thereby, but will leave the great bulk of the population indifferent and possibly antagonistic.

7. I now refer more directly to the position of Rural Development in this Province. The Ministry was full of enthusiasm for Rural Development and held strong ideas on the subject of how it should be done. His Excellency Sir Harry Haig felt that it was both constitutionally necessary, and also desirable, to let them try out their schemes to the fullest possible extent, with as little interference as possible, in fact to give them their head. There were in fact three schemes in this Province:

(*a*) the original Provincial Rural Development Scheme according to which work was concentrated in six circles, of about 12 villages each, in each district;

(*b*) the Government of India scheme mentioned above, which provided additional finance for scheme (*a*) plus money for expenditure on certain specified purposes in the rural areas; and (*c*) the Ministry's own scheme which was originally intended to be run mainly by non-officials.

8. Of these, (*a*) and (*c*) would be financed by funds provided by the Provincial Government and it was impracticable for Haig or myself or any other Governor to prevent them devising their own organisation and there was a risk that they would try to have an extremely non-official agency. It was also clear that the organisations required under (*a*) and (*c*) above could not continue separately. The old staff must be brought into or swallowed up in the new organisation and the work in the old villages carried on under the new auspices. His Excellency Sir Harry Haig believed that the enthusiasm for rural development of the Ministry, and of a good many members of the Congress party and of the staff selected for the new organisation, was genuine; and that in spite of actions of individuals or even of District Associations here and there, the primary aim of the directors of the scheme was the improvement of village conditions and not the creation of a political organisation in the rural areas. Starting with a strong prejudice in favour of making the movement entirely non-official, those at the head of affairs, and particularly I believe the Hon'ble Minister of Development, were convinced by the logic of facts and the absence of any tangible results from Mr. Paliwal's efforts, that it was essential to make use of the experience of officials and to enlist their sympathy in order to get any persistent driving power into the scheme. They have latterly aimed, I believe, at making much more use of the influence and special facilities possessed by the District Officer for carrying on work of this nature; but have been forced to some extent to camouflage their change of policy in this respect in order to evade the criticisms of their more ignorant and prejudiced followers. In their latest scheme the influence and responsibility of the District Officer is therefore to be more indirect than direct and will vary to some extent with his personality and with local circumstances.

9. It would obviously have been an unworkable and uneconomical arrangement to have kept two organisations, one for the old scheme (*a*) directly controlled by the District Officer, and one for the new scheme under popular control, working simultaneously and in rivalry in each district. It was, therefore, inevitable to amalgamate schemes (*a*) and (*c*); and it seems to me to be equally necessary to amalgamate scheme (*b*). The District Officer in dealing with a matter of this kind cannot work *in vacuo*. He must work through an organisation. The whole aim of the movement is to encourage self-help in the villages and that must be done by encouraging the growth of a non-official organisation. The money allotted by the

Government of India must be spent with the co-operation and for the benefit of the village organisations. It seems to me very difficult to devise a scheme by which this money would still be allotted and controlled by the District Officer, while the funds provided by the Provincial Government would be allotted and controlled by the district organisation, although such an arrangement might increase the District Officer's influence to a small extent. The difficulty would appear to be that the District Officer is a servant of the Provincial Government and therefore subject to direction from that Government. He cannot function entirely independently of the Local Government, as thereby a vicious dyarchical system would be set up, which would not make the position of the District Officer *vis-à-vis* the Ministers at all easy. The position of District Officers *vis-à-vis* Ministers seems to me to be improving and I should be reluctant to hinder this development.

10. I have talked to a good many District Officers on tour. Most of them seem quite satisfied that if, as is being done, an S.D.O. is Secretary of the local executive committee, they will be able to exercise a good deal of control. In fact I agree with Stephenson's view rather than with Dible's. The Ministry were, I think, anxious to bring in the District Officer, but had to do so unobtrusively and I think they are *bona fide* in this matter. The Secretary in the department[61] who has seen it at all the various stages of development also agrees with this view.

11. I recognise that it would be possible for the Government of India to withhold this grant, though I believe there is some amount already transferred to the Local Government and at their disposal. It would be clearly difficult to withdraw any sums already transferred and I would be very reluctant even to suggest withholding further payments. Such action would only create friction with the Ministry and our only chance of success is to work harmoniously with them and to prevent, as far as possible, any serious deterioration. The new scheme has not made very much actual progress and therefore the payment of any further grants might be held up to see if my anticipations regarding its development are correct. The Government of India can still lay down without objection any conditions regarding measures on which this money should be expended and I would suggest that it should be primarily on water-supply and communication; there is less room for leakage in these schemes. The allotment should still be as far as practicable on a contributory basis. This has in fact been proposed by the Local Government in their official letter. Further than that I would not go, though I am afraid the Hon'ble Finance Member may

not like even this departure from the original scheme. Changed conditions however justify a change of policy. I am definitely of opinion that if this is done, it will not result in the money going into party funds.

12. As regards paragraph 4 of your letter, I recognise that the staff employed will be large, but I think that is to a large extent inevitable, in particular in regard to agricultural development but the cost of this will come from Provincial money and if, as I have said, conditions regarding how the Government of India money is to be spent are imposed, it will ensure that that money is spent on something practicable. We cannot stop the Local Government spending their money as they think best and even if we assume that their methods are rather those of Tammany Hall,[62] it may have ultimately the desirable result of strengthening the right wing and preventing a return of the left wing, which would be far more dangerous. Possibly this is rather a cynical view![63]

Yours sincerely,
M.G. HALLETT

64

HALLETT TO BRABOURNE
R/3/1/74

Secret
No: U.P.-167

September 6th, 1938

My dear Brabourne,

I enclose as usual the official report which is somewhat sketchy. But the monsoon is always a quiet time politically and floods and rain prevent agitation. The report is also optimistic and I think, on the whole, some degree of optimism is justifiable.

2. *Floods.* – Interest during recent weeks has centred largely round the floods which have done a lot of damage in the districts bordering on the Ghaghra and Rapti rivers in the Fyzabad and Gorakhpur divisions. You will have noticed that I and the Premier issued a joint appeal for funds; this was his suggestion entirely; the desirability of issuing an appeal had occurred to me, but I thought it better that he should make the first move. This is satisfactory. Another very satisfactory feature of the situation is that the Ministers with whom I discussed the question at a Cabinet meeting lasting three hours before I left Lucknow are very full of appreciation of

the work of District Officers and their subordinates. Ibrahim, the P.W.D. Minister, wrote a long note on the subject, an extract from which I annex to this letter. The Cabinet also decided that all relief work should be under the control of the District Officer. This rather goes to support the view that I put forward in my letter about Rural Development, that the Ministry, having by experience learnt to appreciate the work of District Officers, are not anxious to leave them out of the picture. The Cabinet were also very reasonable in their proposals for relief; I was afraid they might be rather unduly liberal over gratuitous relief, but they fully realised that this was demoralising and did not go as far as I would have gone myself. Thus the floods have had some advantage.

3. In other districts the rainfall has on the whole been satisfactory, though there has been a shortage in some areas. A curious feature of the monsoon has been heavy cloud bursts in some places, e.g. recently I see Allahabad had over 10 inches.

4. *Revenue Collections and Crime.* – The reports of Revenue collections continue satisfactory while crime as usual in the rains has decreased. The Premier discussed with some Police officer the general question of the increase of crime, but I do not know quite what happened at it. The Inspector-General in a report attributed the increase to the fact that owing to the lack of Honorary Magistrates, stipendiary Magistrates could not take up enough cases under Sections 110 and 109, Cr.P.C. I do not myself regard this as the root cause which undoubtedly is that owing to the momentous change in the Constitution, men's minds are unsettled. It does however show the importance which is attached in this Province to the preventive sections which appear to me to be used far more freely than in Bengal and Bihar where, thanks to various rulings of the High Court in the old days, we were somewhat diffident of using them. I am inclined to think that the feeling against the Police is perhaps due to the too free use of these sections, but this is hardly a question which I can take up during the short time remaining to me.

5. *Agrarian Situation.* – Looking through Commissioners' reports, I note the following points bearing on the agrarian situation. From one district of Allahabad it is said that feelings between Congressmen proper and Congress socialists are acute and such agitation as there has been has been rather of the left wing nature. The Commissioner of Meerut[64] notes that owing to the discussions on the Tenancy Bill many attempts to establish possession are being made, both sides being to blame; he is not, however, alarmed at the number of cases instituted. Agra reports that in Aligarh District speeches have been less objectionable than before; the

Commissioner[65] also reports activity in enrolling volunteers – a subject to which I refer below. Bareilly reports that lawless ideas or at any rate speeches appear to be gaining ground and also notes signs of activity in forming and training volunteer corps. He mentions that the President of the Congress Committee in one district has dismissed his Secretary for attempting to intimidate a tahsildar, "a measure of co-operation for which we are very grateful". In Jhansi agrarian agitation is centring on the question of pasture lands for cattle and jungle rights; even when the Revenue officials succeed in effecting settlement, they are usually broken the next day. The Congress leaders seem to give little help to the authorities. In the other divisions floods have attracted more attention than agrarian questions.

6. *Tenancy Bill.* – It is difficult to find out exactly how matters stand in regard to the Tenancy Bill. There have of course been lengthy discussions and various rumours in the papers most of which are usually contradicted next day. I have seen the draft report of the Select Committee as prepared by the Secretary in the Revenue Department[66] under somewhat vague instructions from the Premier. As far as I can see, it goes rather far in the matter of *sir* lands limiting the amount to 50 acres, but whether this will be the final proposal is obscure.

7. *Communal Agitation.* – This continues to be a cause of anxiety. You will have no doubt seen in the Press the reports about the riot over a procession in Allahabad; the most satisfactory feature was the prompt and effective steps taken by the local officers to stop further trouble and restore confidence. There was also another riot in Fyzabad, where the Police had to open fire under the orders of the S.D.O., a Sikh I.C.S. officer.[67] The Muslims have published articles demanding a non-official enquiry and the immediate transfer of all the officers concerned. Pant raised this question at the last Cabinet meeting and both he and his colleagues took a sound line, agreeing that if any enquiry were made it should be made by a senior British I.C.S. Judge. They decided, however, to wait till the detailed report by the Deputy Commissioner (Stephenson) had been received. Their attitude was satisfactory and the incident does not appear to be attracting attention.

8. As I have noted in previous letters, the official report usually puts the blame on the Muslim League and there is no doubt that Muslim Leaguers keep a very watchful eye on all that Government does with a view to proving anti-Muslim bias. For example, when I visited Cawnpore recently a Muslim Leaguer complained that in housing schemes carried out by the Improvement Trust, Muslims did not get a fair deal; their lands were acquired and they did not get any new lands. Statistics given me by the

Collector[68] show that this allegation was ill-founded. In another district, Azamgarh in Gorakhpur Division, the District Officer[69] was inclined to the view that the Hindus were the aggressors and were trying to interfere with cow-sacrifice. In many places the feelings between the communities are accentuated by fights on local bodies, Municipal and District Boards. For all these reasons there is always a chance of row [*sic*], but luckily my local officers have so far seemed quite competent to deal with trouble when it breaks out.

9. *Volunteer Organisations.* – I am still without very much further information about the development of volunteer organisations, but a recent report from my C.I.O. shows that Congress propaganda during the last fortnight has paid special attention to the enlisting of volunteers. Over 50,000 volunteers are claimed to have been enrolled, but inside information indicates that actually only about 11,000 have been enlisted. Cawnpore has offered 5,000, Aligarh 2,000, Benares 1,500, Mirzapur and Naini Tal 700 each. It is further reported that during June about 300 men were trained in camps and 500 more in July. It is proposed to arrange camps in Etah, Muttra and Fyzabad during September.

10. I may also mention that I have recently seen a document which has its humorous as well as its serious side. This document contains the instructions issued to "all Secretaries of the district and city committees and the captains" (I am not quite sure what this means) on the organisation of the Congress Volunteer Corps. A copy of this document has been sent to the Director, Intelligence Bureau.[70] The Corps is to include "Muslims, Christians and women folk in as large a number as possible". The course of instruction covers the following heads and sub-heads:

(*a*) Physical (drill; rifle drill with lathis; exercises).

(*b*) Mental instruction, to be given four hours daily for a total of 160 hours (Congress organisation; geography; Satyagraha; preaching; economic conditions of India; Hindu-Muslim problem; volunteer organisations; health and cleanliness; training camp; first aid work in rural areas).

(*c*) Practical – to be given for three hours daily for a total of 120 hours (spinning; singing; national flag; bugle; control; signalling; office organisation work).

The Officers' course is rather more elaborate, but on the same lines, and includes under the physical head horse-riding and cycling (one sub-head under the former is "knowing at least walking and trotting"). These heads of instruction may appear somewhat cryptic, but it appears pretty clear that if an organisation developed on these lines, the nucleus of an efficient non-violent civil disobedience army will be created. I am inclined to think that the organisation will exist only on paper, but developments clearly need watching both here and elsewhere.[71]

11. In this connection I may refer to another rather interesting matter which has come to my notice. Some time ago the Home Department of the Government of India issued a letter to certain Governments about anti-air raid precautions. It was merely sent to us for information, clearly because there is not much risk of air raids reaching the United Provinces. The Premier sent it to the Education Minister saying that he took a lively interest in this question. The latter wrote a long note trying to prove that the United Provinces was not safe from air raids, apparently on the ground that aeroplanes might land on the hinterland of Orissa or Bengal and attack towns such as Benares or Cawnpore from there. He went on to suggest that we should undertake measures to create an air defence organisation which I understood to be something quite different from merely taking precautions to protect the civil population from the possible danger of air attacks. I returned the file saying that, speaking as a layman, I thought that aircraft could hardly operate as far away from their base as to be able to attack the United Provinces, but further pointing out that constitutionally air defence measures could not be regarded as a Provincial subject. I have heard nothing more about the file.

These are possibly somewhat trivial matters to mention to you, but may be of some interest.

12. *Anti-recruitment Propaganda Bill.* – Reports show that the left-wingers in particular are trying to make capital out of the Anti-recruitment Bill, which has also been attacked at some Muslim meetings, though it is defended by the Muslim League. I do not think this agitation as yet has much support from the right wing and as it appears that, as a result of amendments made in the Assembly, it will not be very easy to take action under the Bill, I doubt whether the agitation will develop to any alarming extent. I am however writing to Craik[72] to ask him to keep me or Haig informed of the progress of agitation in the Punjab.

13. In regard to this Bill, may I venture to make one suggestion? I never heard of the Bill till I read about it in the Press. Surely in all cases in which the Central Government intends to introduce a Bill which has an indirect, if not a direct, bearing on law and order, Governors should be told of their intentions, even though it may not be desirable to tell a Local Government.[73]

14. *Palestine Agitation.* – There are still frequent references to this in the reports, and August 26th is said to have been observed as Palestine day throughout the Province, some objectionable speeches being delivered,

but I am still not apprehensive. C.F. Andrews, writing to the Congress Foreign Secretary, has I see from an intercepted letter advocated the cause of the Jews and Congress may take that line.

15. *Separation of Judicial and Executive.* – Dible who was put on to examine this question has written a very valuable note which I have seen and discussed with him. Whether I shall be able to make any further progress with this matter before I leave I do not know. As His Excellency Lord Linlithgow suggested some time ago, it is far better to play for time. I hope it may be possible for Haig or myself to get the Cabinet to agree to trying the measure experimentally in a few districts. Dible has made it clear that apart from communal, agrarian and labour agitation, conditions are not normal largely owing to the dislocation of work caused by the dismissal of the old Honorary Magistrates and the appointment of a new lot. Till it is known what work will be disposed of by Honorary Magistrates, it is impossible to say what Judicial staff will be required. Dible has also raised other important questions, e.g. the position of the executive Magistrates *vis-à-vis* the Police and the position which will arise in an emergency such as a flood. All these questions will need careful consideration.

16. *Honorary Magistrates.* – I have seen the files regarding the appointment of Honorary Magistrates in some districts, and as far as I can judge, appointments are not being made merely on political considerations. Attempts are being made to secure retired officers, and in many cases senior vakils are selected. I must admit, having rather a prejudice against the old type of Honorary Magistrate, who traded on his loyalty, was insistent on his claims for recognition and was generally not very competent. The new lot may be better or at any rate not worse.

17. *Labour Situation.* – If one believed newspaper reports, Cawnpore is becoming a refuge for all the Communists in India and that complaint was of course made to me by some of the millowners during my short visit to Cawnpore. They complained also of the constant meetings and processions organised by the Reds. In this as in other cases it is extraordinarily difficult to estimate the effect of these meetings or the cumulative effect of the shouting of Red slogans. The Reds appear to have captured the Mazdur Sabha and some of the gentlemen I met in Cawnpore – other than millowners – took the optimistic view that responsibility would beget reasonableness. Let us wait and see. Difficulties may arise in the near future over the question of recognition of the Mazdur Sabha by the millowners.

18. This is possibly the last fortnightly report that I shall send you, but

I spend three or four days in Lucknow before I make over to Haig on the 17th, and I will try and write a short final report.

Yours sincerely,
M.G. HALLETT

ENCLOSURE TO NO. 64

NOTE BY IBRAHIM (EXTRACT)[74]

Floods in the United Provinces

Undated

I saw towns and villages both. Everywhere public expressed their deep gratefulness to the district authorities – Revenue and Police officials – for the timely and valuable assistance rendered by them. Non-official organisations also praised them highly for their excellent rescue and relief work. Government officials had to work amidst many handicaps and under most difficult circumstances and yet they could rescue all. The loss of human life nowhere exceeds five souls, and this too was not due to any lack on the part of officials but to accidents either in coming from or going to some place or the sudden collapse of a house.

Congressmen according to the version of officials rendered considerable help by men and money and fully co-operated with them in rescue and relief work. In Gonda, Gorakhpur and Basti some Muslim Leaguers also took keen interest along with the officials. Khaksars in Bahraich really did good work for which Government authorities there are very grateful to them. The B.&N.W. Railway Authorities also took very keen interest and gave prompt assistance to district authorities by placing at their disposal wagons and buildings for sheltering refugees and providing travelling facilities for officers and distressed people both. Kapurthala and Balrampur Estates specially and others generally were reported to me to have been of great help to the officials. Besides this they rendered direct assistance also to the sufferers. Private charity also was not lacking in providing food and shelter to the distressed. Thousands of people have been fed by those who felt for them. In order to be brief I do not mention here individuals – officials or non-officials – who have done meritorious work. All the officials deserve Government thanks for what they have so selflessly done. There are some like Deputy Commissioners of Bahraich, Gorakhpur, Gonda and Basti,[75] whose names may be specially mentioned, but I think when we receive more detailed reports from districts we will be able to choose to whom special thanks of Government should be conveyed.

I do not know how far my honourable colleagues will agree with me, but I who is more or less an eye witness now suggest that we should in some appropriate form reward both Government officials and such non-officials as have done good work. This reward may take the form of certificates and entries in the service books and annual remarks. If this idea is entertained details may be settled later.

65

HALLETT TO BRABOURNE
R/3/1/74

Secret *September 15th, 1938*
No. U.P.-173

My dear Brabourne,

I am very grateful for your letter of September 11th, 1938,[76] in reply to my last fortnightly report. May I say how very helpful your letters always are and how valuable I find this free interchange of opinion? I am glad you find my "reasoned optimism" encouraging. I feel that at times I am possibly too optimistic, but my own experience of two Congress Ministries leads me to the view that under normal conditions responsibility is begetting reasonableness. I have also found my Ministers here ready to discuss any matters which I wished to discuss, and in some minor cases when I considered a decision deserved reconsideration, I have had no difficulty in securing their agreement with my views. Over the Cawnpore strike they held the balance fairly between the two parties, and as I was told by the Premier the other day, they have gone some way to meet the demands of the landlords in tenancy matters, and have accepted their suggestion regarding realisation of rent. The whole question is now to be discussed by the landlords with the Working Committee, though Pant agreed with me that the Committee would know little of the intricacies of tenancy law in the United Provinces. In law and order matters, they do not follow the lines adopted in the past by a bureaucratic Government, but the agrarian or communal situation though still giving cause for apprehension has not deteriorated as much as might have been expected. Pant has on the whole showed himself ready to back up officers; he appreciates their services and I am fortunate in having very good young officers in the most troublesome districts, – Hancox at Cawnpore, Whittle at Allahabad, Pedley at Gorakhpur, Stephenson at Fyzabad and Naqvi at Aligarh. Of course Pant is always reluctant to take action under the criminal law against public speakers and dislikes Section 124-A, almost as much as he did when in Opposition. But there is no doubt that prosecution under this or any similar section would attract attention to speeches which otherwise would not have much influence. Pant, however, does a good deal behind the scenes to control speeches (Gwynne who has recently come back as Chief Secretary confirms me in this view); he is against any open advocacy of violence and though disliking Section 108 of the Criminal Procedure Code, has encouraged officers to take proceedings under Section 107.

2. Another point which I cannot refrain from making is that grossly inaccurate reports not infrequently appear in the Press, not merely in communal papers but in others. Thus the *Pioneer* recently had headlines, telegrams and articles from which one would infer that the district of Bijnor was going up in blue smoke owing to the quarrels of Harijans and caste Hindus. There had been a certain number of disputes about the use of wells, but most of them had been satisfactorily compromised; there had also been one riot case in which both sides were to blame, but the district officer's report[77] showed that the situation was not getting in the least out of hand.

3. I am very glad to see the opinion which you have given in paragraph 2 of your letter that the best counter move to the organisation of volunteers will be to canalise all their energy into regular channels and to try to link it up with the regular Defence forces. I had formed somewhat the same opinion when dealing with my Government's proposals for military training and with a request which they have made to the Defence Department for help in this matter. Their proposals, which include training in the "Art of war" to be given by young officers who have just left Dehra Dun, could easily be subjected to caustic and sarcastic criticism as being impracticable. But I have written to His Excellency the Commander-in-Chief to treat this kindly, for I feel that if my Ministers establish contact with the Army staff, it can do no harm and may do a lot of good. General Lindsay whom I have kept fully informed of these discussions, I think, shares my views.

4. With the situation in Europe being what it is, it seems inappropriate to write about all these minor affairs. If a crisis develops, the action to be taken by Congress will depend on the High Command; but we are bound

to have numerous "alarums and excursions", to say the least. Though we may at present disregard objectionable speeches, it would be impossible to be so tolerant under those conditions. We should need all the officers we can get hold of, and in my view all I.C.S. and I.P. officers on leave should be immediately recalled. Another matter which we should have to take up here would be an increase of our Police force. The I.G. Police put up proposals some time ago, but unfortunately did not supply adequate detailed information in support of them, and for this reason as well as because the situation in Cawnpore, Lucknow and Allahabad had improved, the case has made little progress. I will draw Haig's attention to it. I am afraid there are some Police Officers who somewhat resent Government's demand for information, and do not realise that in many cases the information is needed to defend the Police from attacks.

5. I have a final Cabinet meeting tomorrow when we may discuss the Anti-Corruption Report and also some questions connected with the Public Service Commission. I shall probably find it desirable to leave most of these points for Haig to deal with. The flooded areas had further heavy rain a week or ten days ago, and I am afraid the distress has been intensified.

Yours sincerely,
M.G. HALLETT

66

DONALDSON TO PUCKLE
R/3/1/74

D.O. No. 1615-G.S.P.

Camp,
September 16th, 1938

My dear Puckle,

Sir Maurice asked me to send you the enclosed copy of an article by our Education Minister, Sampurnanand, which he thought might interest you.

Yours sincerely,
J.C. DONALDSON

ENCLOSURE TO NO. 66

ARTICLE FROM THE *CONGRESS SOCIALIST*, BOMBAY, SEPTEMBER 3RD, 1938

Problems of a Congress Minister by Sampurnanand, Minister for Education, United Provinces

The first problem of a Congress Minister has to face is himself – his psychological make-up. The man who has gone through the hectic days of 1921, the dark days and years following the suspension of non-co-operation, the Civil Disobedience struggles of 1930-2, with experiences of underground work on a scale till then thought impossible, has got these experiences woven into the very fibre of his being.

We do not talk of Swaraj in a purely intellectual sense. We have seen, where we have not experienced, suffering – the mental and physical torture of our comrades through the years. We have been rebels.

Now we have to adjust ourselves to new surroundings. We have to work within the four walls of the Government of India Act, against which we revolt with every fibre of our being. It is not easy.

We feel like kicking over the traces. Believe me, not one of the Ministers I know does not, immersed in his files, pine for the old days. We live in an atmosphere of unreality. There are many of us who would like to get out of it. But there we are.

The machine. – Our next problem are our subordinates – the instruments through which we must function. They have, as a whole, adjusted themselves to the new environment admirably. In the vast majority of cases we have no complaint against them. The lower grade of Indian official, more than the Englishman, finds it difficult, however, to reconcile himself to democracy. He looks upon it as unreal – a passing phase, a bad dream.

There is, as a result, a silent, mental non-co-operation on their part. It constitutes a serious brake on our work. It is a splendid machine – meant to be fool-proof. But it was not, and is not, a machine devised for Independence, for revolutionary times and changes. Red tape certainly is one of our problems.

To my knowledge, there is no historical parallel to the circumstances in which we accepted office. A people struggling for national Independence, meaning to continue to fight for it, stop half-way to accept administrative responsibility! This is a contradiction in our position which also creates difficulties.

Constructive work, properly so called, can be thought of in terms of decades, if not generations. But here – we may have to leave our places at any moment. So we have to devise yearly and six-monthly programmes and projects. And this with a bureaucratic machine which is static, not dynamic.

In the United Provinces we have five Universities of which three are under the Government of India. This year we decided to give 2 of them some help. Pandit Govind Ballabh Pant, the Premier and Finance Minister, and I decided the matter in conversation in exactly two minutes. But we have not been able to give effect to our decision for three or four months! Red tape will have its way.

Had there been a complete capture of power, it would all have been very different.

Hopes deferred. – Another problem is that created by the hopes and expectations roused in the minds of our masses. One has only to see and meet people to realise the difference. There is visible hope, confidence that was not there a year ago. It is *their* Government. In the United Provinces when the man in the street talks of the *sircar* he thinks of the Congress Committees.

Hence the great amount of work done by these Committees. Complaints of tenants against zamindars, of the public against officials, of wives against husbands have all to be dealt with.

And every day, sheafs of such complaints are forwarded by Congress Committees to us. We suffer from an *embarras de richesse* in the way of advice. If you don't take any notice of them, people get angry. You can't afford that – these are democratic times.

The amount of psychological energy available today needs to be seen to be believed. The problem is how to harness it, how to satisfy the expectations roused.

It all shows what could be done under a real national government if only all the brains and energy could be harnessed.

The Link. – An allied problem is the Congress worker. He has been our colleague in the fight. Today, he is *par excellence* the man on whose information we can rely. He is also the exponent of our policy. He has to bear the pressure from both sides.

The Congress Working Committee has in its infinite wisdom thought fit to decide that we Ministers may not serve on Congress Executives. This has to an extent cut us off. We can only feel the pulse of the organisation through the Congress worker.

He feels we are where we are because of him and he cannot understand why we do not always abide by his advice. He thinks he has a lien on your time.

Your Congress worker has formed a certain picture of what a Congress Minister should be like. Sometimes, we fail to live up to his picture. Then he discovers we have feet of clay.

A Thorn. – The problem created by communal leaders is, for us in the United Provinces at least, a thorny one. There is unprecedented and cold-blooded misrepresentation by the Muslim League of all we do. Much good work has in consequence to be stopped.

The United Provinces Cabinet had made up its mind to restore the fullest civil liberty. It has tried to stick to that resolve but I confess we have had to go back on it a little. The Province has become a happy hunting-ground for people from neighbouring Provinces.

The Muslim League knows that in the United Provinces there can never be a Muslim League Government which will have to face problems. So today they are amongst the most radical of politicians! No measure of reform is good enough for them. But when in private we ask whether they will support a radical measure, some of them frankly say they will absent themselves from the Assembly on that occasion!

There are others also who have abused the civil liberty extended, but the most guilty are the communal leaders.

Everything we do is, according to them, with the one aim of destroying Muslim culture and establishing a Hindu raj in the Province!

We may not put down even the preparations for communal riots because immediately there would be the cry of "Repression".

There are other problems – that, for instance, of finance. With a grant of Rs. 2,000, I am expected to solve the problem of unemployment! What I am doing with it is to provide employment to two clerks and two peons.

All this may help others to assess things correctly when preparing balance-sheets for Congress Ministers. But they should also remember that on them no less than on us lies the responsibility for the experiment.

NOTES

1. Not included in R/3/1/73.
2. Mr L.P. Hancox acted as District Magistrate, Cawnpore between 13 May and 16 September 1938 while Mr L. Owen was on leave.
3. In his letter of 7 May 1938 to Governors, Lord Linlithgow expressed the view that there had been a substantial modification in the attitude of Congress

to Federation at any rate on the part of the right wing. Instead of outright rejection, there had been a move in the direction of acceptance subject to bargaining. Linlithgow asked Governors for a confidential appreciation of the atmosphere and position on Federation in their provinces.

4. In a lengthy answer to a question in the Indian Legislative Assembly on 10 March 1938, Sir James Grigg stated that the early achievement of Federation represented the considered policy of both the British Government and the Government of India. See *The Legislative Assembly Debates*, 1938, Vol. 2, p. 1666.
5. This is a reference to a speech made by Lord Zetland at the annual Bombay Dinner in London on 27 May 1938. Zetland said there was not the least likelihood of the British Government or Parliament being willing to consider, before even Federation had come into operation, any alteration in its structure.
6. Mr Mubashir Husain Kidwai.
7. Mr Srikrishna Sinha was the Premier of Bihar at this date.
8. Sir Sikander Hyat Khan and Mr A.K. Fazl-ul Haq were the Premiers, respectively, of the Punjab and Bengal at this date
9. Lord Linlithgow minuted: 'P.S.V. – Whether one agrees or not, Hallett makes some interesting points. My own view is that he fails to give Gandhi his full value, and fails to realise that – unless Congress can get an arrangement with the Muslim League favourable to Congress – it is very probable that Congress will take Federation with a few inexpensive trimmings within the Act; the Service p[oin]t is of importance. S./S. must know Hallett's views.'
10. Mr R.M. Saner.
11. See No. 33, note 2.
12. Lieutenant-Colonel A.E. Clarke.
13. Not printed.
14. Lord Linlithgow minuted: 'P.S.V. – It would be foolish to promote a 1st rate row over this incident. I think Hallett should make a strong *personal* appeal to Pant to point out to the Parliamentary Secty. that speeches of that kind are better left unspoken. Report fully to S./S.'

    Correspondence on the Lansdowne incident continued through the summer of 1938. Eventually the G.O.C.-in-C., Eastern Command agreed to terminate the expulsion order on Mr Rup Chand Varma and recommended a refund of the fine imposed on him. On 20 September 1938 the U.P. Government expressed its gratitude for this action. R/3/1/74.
15. The text of the U.P. Government's Resolution on the Cawnpore Labour Inquiry Report is printed in Basudev Chatterji (Ed.), *Towards Freedom: Documents on the Movement for Independence in India, 1938.* Part II (New Delhi: Oxford University Press, 1999), pp. 1692-1701.
16. In paragraph 2 of his letter of 3 June 1938, Lord Linlithgow said he felt the best prospect of a solution of the dispute lay in Pandit Pant getting the two parties together round a table and giving out a fairly definite hint of pressure. R/3/1/73.

17. The last paragraph of the Resolution was entitled 'Hopes for future'.
18. Lord Linlithgow minuted: 'The point of not allowing those who have *not* taken the oath of secrecy to see secret papers must be preserved at all costs.'
19. Cf. *U.P.P., 1936-7*, No. 85, paragraph 8.
20. Mr W. Christie.
21. This inspection was probably carried out by Mr P.W. Marsh.
22. John Gunther, *Inside Europe* (London: Hamish Hamilton, 1936.)
23. Lord Linlithgow minuted: 'Very nice of him to find time.'
24. R/3/1/73.
25. No. 51.
26. The full text of the Mazdur Sabha's conditions for accepting a settlement, dated 2 July 1938, is printed in Chatterji, *Towards Freedom*, Part II, pp. 1705-6.
27. Sir John Ewart.
28. Mr C.W. Grant.
29. Mr J.E. Pedley.
30. See Enclosure 2 to No. 6.
31. See *U.P.P., 1936-7*, Appendix 17.
32. Mr F.W.W. Baynes.
33. Mr R.F. Mudie.
34. Mr P. Mason, Commissioner, Rohilkhand Division.
35. Mr T.B.W. Bishop.
36. Mr J.E. Pedley.
37. Mr C.W. Grant.
38. Not included in R/3/1/73.
39. Mr L.P. Hancox.
40. Only this extract is printed in R/3/1/73.
41. Mr E.S. Thomson.
42. Lord Brabourne minuted: 'We are taking this up.'
43. Mr M.H.B. Nethersole.
44. In his telegram 1036-G of 6 August 1938 Lord Brabourne suggested that they follow the same procedure with Mrs Pandit's leave as was proposed in 1936 when the Raja of Bobbili (then Chief Minister of Madras) wished to take leave. This was to the effect that if the Chief Minister intended to be out of India for a considerable period, he should resign his office and be re-appointed on his return. However if Pandit Pant would not agree to this procedure, Brabourne would take no further action. R/3/1/73.
45. In the Central Provinces there had been differences between Dr N.B. Khare (the Premier) and some of his Congress colleagues in the Ministry dating from soon after the time when Congress had taken office. On 20 July 1938 Khare resigned because of a lack of harmony in the Ministry. In taking this action he had not consulted either the Congress Working Committee or the Congress Parliamentary Committee. Three of the Ministers refused to submit

their resignations without consulting Congress and on 21 July the Governor (Sir Francis Wylie) dismissed them. Subsequently Wylie asked Khare to form a new Ministry. However this new Ministry lasted for only a few days before Khare was forced to resign again. A Congress Ministry led by Pandit R.S. Shukla took office on 29 July. On 2 October the Congress Working Committee disqualified Khare from Congress membership for two years.

46. Writing in the *Harijan* of 6 August 1938 Mahatma Gandhi said that 'if Dr. Khare was impatient of his recalcitrant colleagues he should have rushed, not to the Governor, but to the Working Committee and tendered his resignation'. Moreover in acting as he did, Sir Francis Wylie had 'betrayed a haste which I can only call indecent.' Gandhi continued: 'Of course, the Governor's action conformed to the letter of the law, but it killed the spirit of the tacit compact between the British Government and the Congress.' This was a 'gentlemen's agreement in which both are expected to play the game.'
47. In his letter U.P.-140 of 6 August 1938 Sir Maurice Hallett told Lord Brabourne that Pandit Pant probably used his influence to keep Mr Saksena and other leaders away from a Tilak Day meeting at Lansdowne. As a result of this, and perhaps because of the heavy rain, nothing objectionable occurred. R/3/1/73.
48. Mr R.F. Mudie.
49. See 'Principal Holders of Office', at start of volume, note 1.
50. Mr M.H.B. Nethersole.
51. It would appear from the *U.P. History of Services, 1939* that Mr W.C. Dible continued with his duties as Commissioner, Agra Division while working on the question of the separation of the judicial and executive functions of district officers.
52. Mr J.L.C. Stubbs was Magistrate and Collector, Muttra.
53. Mr P. Mason, Commissioner, Rohilkhand Division.
54. Mr G.S. Kher, S.P., Fatehpur.
55. Mr E.F.G. Chapman.
56. Mr J.E. Pedley was Collector of Gorakhpur.
57. Mr R.V. Vernède.
58. Mr H.E. Barlow.
59. Mr B.G.P. Thomas acted as Inspector-General of Police, U.P. between 5 August and 26 September 1938 while Mr Horton was on leave.
60. In his letter of 4 August 1938 Lord Brabourne said that he felt difficulty over the U.P. Government's proposal to merge the old and the new schemes of rural development. One of the important objects of the old scheme was that the Government of India's contribution should be used to enable the district officer to maintain his position. In the U.P. scheme, on paper, the district officer was out of it altogether. Brabourne had spoken to Mr Stephenson and Mr Dible. Stephenson was unperturbed and felt that any district officer worth his salt should be able to control the policy of the Rural Development

Association. Dible, however, considered the whole scheme was part of a considered policy to push the district officer on one side. In paragraph 4 of the letter, Brabourne feared the U.P. scheme would create an army of functionaries and there would not be much money over for things like drainage and water supplies. R/3/1/73.

61. Mr P.M. Kharegat.
62. Tammany Hall was the name given to the United States Democratic Party political machine which played a major role in New York City politics from the 1790s to the 1960s. In 1932 the machine suffered a severe setback when the Mayor of New York was forced from office because of corruption. Tammany never fully recovered after this.
63. In a letter of 21 September 1938 to Lord Zetland on the U.P. Government's rural development proposals, Lord Brabourne said that Sir Maurice Hallett's letter did not reassure the Finance Member of the Government of India, Sir James Grigg. Brabourne had shown the letter also to Sir Henry Craik, Governor of the Punjab. Craik 'points out that one obvious weakness of the United Provinces' scheme is that it creates an army of functionaries, without particular technical qualifications, the filling of whose appointments will in consequence give enormous scope for political jobbery, and says that a scheme very much on the lines of the United Provinces' scheme has been tried in the Punjab and has been found to be a failure.' Craik recommended that the Government of India made certain conditions in connection with their grant and some of these were actually made. MSS.EUR.F 125/6.
64. Mr M.H.B. Nethersole.
65. See note 51 above.
66. Mr R.F. Mudie.
67. Mr M.S. Randhawa.
68. Mr L.P. Hancox.
69. Mr R.T. Shivdasani.
70. Sir John Ewart.
71. Lord Brabourne minuted: 'Yes.'
72. Sir Henry Craik was Governor of the Punjab at this date.
73. Lord Brabourne minuted: 'This *seems* a reasonable complaint. What is the usual practice?'
74. Only this extract is printed in R/3/1/74.
75. These Deputy Commissioners were as follows: Mr B. Prasad (Bahraich); Mr J.E. Pedley (Gorakhpur); Mr A.S. Husain (Gonda); and Mr S. Singh (Basti).
76. R/3/1/74.
77. Rao Bahadur Hukum Singh was Deputy Commissioner, Bijnor.

CHAPTER 4

Documents for 26 September – 31 December 1938

67

HAIG TO BRABOURNE
R/3/1/74

Secret
No. U.P.-175

September 26th, 1938

My dear Brabourne,

I returned on the evening of September 16th and took over charge at once from Hallett, who had very kindly arranged to stay till the evening of the 17th so that we might discuss the various current problems of the Province. I had some very useful talks with him before he left. Since then I have been busy picking up the threads again.

2. In many respects, conditions seem little changed since I went on leave four months ago; but of course events do not stand still. The most crucial problem facing the Province at the moment appears to me to be that of the relations between landlords and tenants. Before I went on leave, the Ministry had introduced their tenancy Bill, providing for a number of important concessions to tenants. They had not, and still have not, produced in legislative form their proposals for dealing with the arrears of rent the collection of which was stayed or, most important of all from the point of view of the landlords, the pitch of land revenue assessment which they had been intending to fix at a rate which seemed to me unreasonably high. The tenancy Bill was to be referred to a select committee, and the Ministers' programme was that the select committee should report with reasonable promptitude and that consideration of the Bill by the Legislature should begin early in August. These anticipations have not been fulfilled, the select committee are still considering the Bill, and have not really reached

firm conclusions. I discussed the situation first with the Premier and Dr. Katju. They professed a desire to reach a reasonable settlement with landlords and declared that they had shown great patience and readiness to consider the landlords' point of view. But they complained that the landlords did not seem to have been in a mood to make any firm settlement, that it was very difficult to get a definite answer out of them on any particular point, and that the landlords' representatives were inclined to say that they could not answer for the attitude of the main body of landlords.[1] I subsequently had conversations with some of the leading landlords, including Chhatari who is the most important figure in Agra, and Jahangirabad who is the President of the Oudh Taluqdars. They both admitted to me that there was some justice in the complaints of the Ministers. It had been arranged that the landlords should send a deputation to Delhi to interview the Working Committee regarding the provisions of this Bill, and they evidently hoped that the Working Committee might be more sympathetic to them than the Ministers were. I urged them strongly to try and reach a definite compromise at once. I pointed out to them that while no doubt the landlords have the power through the Upper Chamber of delaying the whole of this tenancy legislation for a year, it must be anticipated that if they took any such action it would lead to dangerous agitation throughout the villages, and at the end of that time the landlords might find that their own position had been fundamentally weakened, if not destroyed. I urged them to remember that their future depended on re-establishing relations of trust with their tenants, and that this was impossible if it could be represented that they were obstructing all proposals for improvement of the tenants' conditions. On the other hand, if a reasonable measure of reform could be carried now with the consent of the landlords, there was some prospect of conditions in the villages gradually settling down. I found that on points like this Chhatari needed no convincing and even Jahangirabad agreed substantially, though he said that some of the more backward Taluqdars were still anxious to fight for what they regarded as their rights. But he gave me to understand that he had every anticipation that wiser courses would prevail and that when the landlords' representatives went to Delhi they would go there with a real intention of negotiating a settlement and not procrastinating further. I have subsequently heard that the landlords' representatives were quite pleased with their reception at Delhi, and hope that some settlement may be possible, which would doubtless include a decision about the pitch of land revenue and the treatment of the stayed arrears of rent.

3. The attitude of the Ministry in regard to these problems is interesting.

I found Pant and Katju on the whole more conciliatory than I had expected. I surmise that at the back of their minds they realise that if a big fight takes place on these issues, the only party that would really gain in strength, and gain formidably, is the party of the extremists and the Kisan Sabha. I think they probably feel that it is to their interest as well as to the interest of the landlords that a settlement should be reached. At the same time they are in a difficult position, for the Provincial Congress Committee appears on the whole to be dominated by the more extreme views and is strongly opposed to any concessions in the Bill, and even appears to think that the Bill does not go far enough. In these circumstances I doubt if Pant was in fact displeased at the matter being taken up by the Working Committee, and though the position has been carefully maintained that the responsibility for decisions will be that of the Ministers, he may find that the support of the Working Committee will enable him to go a little further in the face of his own extremists than would otherwise have been possible. I expect definite negotiations between the landlords and the Ministers to take place now after a few days. The Revenue Minister, Mr. Kidwai, is I think decidedly opposed to any concessions to the landlords, and I believe there is a good deal of difference of opinion within the Ministry on these questions of agrarian policy.

4. One point that the landlords stressed to me was the continuous agitation that has been carried on in the villages against them. This is being done I think not so much by official Congressmen but by the irresponsible extremist elements. It seems to me this is bound to continue at any rate until the tenancy Bill is passed. The villagers I am told are beginning to get somewhat restive, in that over a year after the Congress Ministry had taken office none of their promises have been carried out. I am quite clear that from every point of view it is most desirable now that the terms of this Bill should be settled and should go through without further delay.

5. There has been a disturbing incident at Cawnpore in connection with the discipline of the Police. As the result of a resolution passed at a meeting of the Cawnpore branch of the United Provinces Police non-Gazetted Officers Association on the 4th September, a circular was sent to Sub-Inspectors by the Secretary of the Association saying that it was intended to observe a fast and say prayers on the 8th September for all members of the Association who were in distress. On the 8th September most of the Muslim Police in the Police lines, who number about 100, and a few Hindus observed the fast; also a few Police in the city. The Secretary of the Association was at once removed from the District and it was hoped that

there would be no further developments. But on the 16th September some unsigned notices were found posted up in the Police lines in which the Police were asked to hold further prayers and observe a fast on the 17th September because of "the oppression which is being perpetrated on us". The immediate cause for this manifestation appears to be the fact that a number of men of the Cawnpore Police have been for some time under suspension on a charge of committing various excesses in a certain village.

6. Prompt action is being taken to deal departmentally with those who appear to have been the ringleaders in this movement. The Premier is very indignant and seems to want to hold an inquisition into the conduct of every single constable. This would I think be unwise, particularly as the Police authorities are satisfied that the situation is perfectly in hand and that no more trouble is to be anticipated. They have in fact been handling the matter sensibly, and I hope the Premier will agree not to disturb the situation unnecessarily.

7. The whole affair however gives rise to some uneasiness, and I am anxious to ascertain whether there were any predisposing causes of a general nature, or whether this affair was merely the result of particular local circumstances and conditions. I have addressed a note to the Premier referring to my numerous discussions with him regarding the treatment of the Police and their behaviour, and suggesting that as soon as Mr. Horton, the permanent I.G., Police, returns from leave at the end of the month, the Premier and I should have a really frank discussion with him and try to ascertain whether there is anything essentially unsound in the present position; and if so, what are the causes and possible remedies. I think I have in previous letters frequently referred to this problem of the relations between the Government and the Police. There have been times when I have felt as very unsatisfactory the attitude of suspicion and distrust which the Premier showed towards the Police. After Horton returned from leave at the beginning of last cold weather there was a marked improvement in the attitude of the Premier; but towards the end of the cold weather there were signs that this improvement was not being maintained, and I see that in paragraph 4 of my letter No. U.P.-78, dated May 13th, 1938, written to Lord Linlithgow a few days before I went on leave, I referred to the fact that appreciation of Police work seemed to be rather markedly lacking particularly in Cawnpore. From conversations which I have had with some senior Police officers since my return it looks as if matters at the very least have not improved. What I propose to take up in particular with the Premier, though I know he will be extremely difficult over it, is the question of action against corruption. It is sometimes said that at any time a policeman

may find himself accused of corruption, and thereupon the Premier's anti-corruption officer and his organisation is brought into action; and though ultimately these officers cannot be punished except as a result of a proper departmental enquiry, they are kept under suspension and put to great anxiety often in cases in which there is really not very much substance. It has also been alleged that these complaints are directed much more frequently against the Muslim than the Hindu members of the force. I do not say that these allegations are correct – indeed I have no doubt the Premier will have a vigorous reply to them – but I think it is time I took up the whole question of this anti-corruption organisation. The Premier himself has always attached the greatest importance to it, and being prepared to believe everything he hears to the discredit of the Police, genuinely thinks that the action is fully justified. I shall try to persuade him that he will get better results by trusting his officers than by appearing to work behind their backs. I shall at the same time try to get down to the causes of the recent marked increase in crime, on which Hallett has commented in some of his letters. The natural supposition would be that this indicates some relaxation either of Police authority or of Police interest. I think the Premier himself is probably somewhat disturbed about this, though he is inclined to deny the facts, having struck out from the draft of the Chief Secretary's fortnightly D.O. for the first half of September a statement that crime presented several serious features, particularly a very large increase in burglary, and that in one district it seemed that there was an increasing tendency for such crimes to be committed by persons who had not hitherto been engaged in crime. I think the Premier probably considers that the Police are deliberately relaxing their efforts because they are opposed to his Government. This I am sure is a complete misreading of the situation. But if men are uneasy and depressed, they naturally will not do their best work and will tend to take the line of least resistance in dealing with crime. I do not say that on examination the considerations I have stated above will necessarily be found to be accurate. I am merely letting you know how my mind is moving at present, and in what direction I propose to try and satisfy myself about conditions in the Police.[2] I do not wish to give an alarmist picture or to suggest that conditions have suddenly deteriorated. To the extent that there is anything wrong it is the result of a slow process and many factors.

8. The elections for the newly constituted Mazdoor Sabha of Cawnpore have resulted in a complete victory for the Communists. This however has not in Government circles given rise to as much disappointment as might have been expected. The fact is that it has been realised for a long

time that the so-called moderate leaders had no control over the men, and that while they talked in a most reasonable way to the Government, they made speeches of a very difficult [?different] purport to the workmen in order to try and maintain a precarious influence. Now at any rate the Government will be dealing with men who actually have the support of the majority of the workers, and as it is believed that they do not at present wish for trouble, the Government are not unduly perturbed.

9. From what I hear I get a general impression that the position of the Ministry has probably weakened during the last few months. The left wing seem to control the Provincial Congress Committee and have been asserting themselves a good deal. I am told that Pant's own position in the Ministry is probably not as strong as it was. Kidwai, a somewhat baffling figure, presenting outwardly a mask of impassivity, commands a great deal more influence than one would suppose from talking to him. He has always been on the side of the left wing, and it is said that he no longer gives quite the same support to the Premier's policy that he used to. Sampurnanand also belongs to the left wing. I have no doubt that Pant can still control his own Ministry and the Party, but he is perhaps meeting with increasing difficulty. On the other hand, the Party will not at present split, and, for instance, if Pant pursues a moderate line in regard to the tenancy legislation I imagine that the malcontents, however, much they may dislike it, will have to acquiesce.

10. Communal feeling does not seem to have improved at all. Indeed, it appears to be particularly bitter, and there is a great deal of ill-feeling in many districts in connection with the approaching Dussehra.

11. I had some conversation with Pant and Katju about the international situation. They naturally did not wish to say anything about the attitude of the Congress in the event of war, as this was a matter which was to be discussed by the Working Committee at Delhi. But it seemed to me clear that their own sympathies were entirely in favour of taking a firm line against Hitler, and that they would not desire to do anything to embarrass the British Government in the event of war, feeling that their own interests are clearly involved.[3] A rather interesting discussion has been proceeding on a file recently regarding air raid precautions. Sampurnanand is not at all satisfied that the United Provinces should be classed as non-vulnerable and seems particularly anxious about Benares where he himself lives. He put up some suggestion that the Province should develop an air force of its own, besides taking certain air raid precautions. I merely mention this as an indication that Congressmen probably realise that in their own interests they should co-operate in the event of war. Actually, however

they are not likely to do so unless they can feel that they are taken into confidence, and are really playing an active and not merely a passive part. No doubt the Working Committee will shortly formulate their views and demands.

Yours sincerely,
H.G. HAIG

68

HAIG TO BRABOURNE
Telegram
MSS.EUR.F 115/10

Important *September 29th, 1938*
No. 178-G

Your telegram 1284-S, September 28th. I returned to Lucknow yesterday morning in order to get in touch with Ministers. Premier also returned yesterday from Delhi and in the evening we had long and friendly talk just before receipt of your telegram.

2. I started by saying I wished to consult him regarding measures that would be necessary immediately on declaration of war. I told him about the draft ordinance and explained that certain extensive powers would be conferred by it on local Governments. I said, however, that it did not seem to me that immediate action to be taken by local Governments would be of any great importance. I mentioned to him various matters, such as Foreigners' Act, registration of aliens, recalling of officers from leave, return of certain officers to military duty, possible strengthening of police force, etc. He did not seem to anticipate any particular difficulty in regard to action which might be regarded as almost routine in the event of war. He showed a little uneasiness about the powers that would be conferred on local Governments, saying that this might place him in a position of having to decide on important matters of policy, a decision which he would not seek to avoid but which might raise vital issues. He then explained to me that the Working Committee had really come to no definite conclusions but had left it to Premiers to comply with the normal necessities of the situation and to refer for instructions if any vital matters arose. He seemed to think that no difficulty need be raised about complying with requests of the Central Government to carry out measures, such as internment of enemy subjects, censorship, etc., which they considered essential. But if the local Governments were asked to take an initiative he seemed to think this might

require reference to the Working Committee. In practice I do not anticipate that he would raise any difficulty about the kind of measures which I understand it would be necessary to take immediately.

3. He then went on to explain more generally the attitude of the Congress. He said that Gandhi held strongly the thorough-going pacifist view that resistance by force to aggression was always wrong, and that there was a fair amount of sympathy for this view in consequence of the non-violent policy which had been preached for so long. I understood, however, that this sympathy was perhaps more intellectual than practical, and he himself though feeling the appeal of Gandhi's views did not seem to hesitate about the necessity for war and its justification if Hitler pursues his present line. But while it seemed that the sympathies of India and its interests ought both to lead Indians to support a war, he said there was a profound difference between entering on a war because Great Britain told them they must and entering on it by a voluntary act, as in the case of Dominions. He said it was a psychological difference of the greatest importance.

4. He did not suggest that Congress would want to make definite conditions. He did not go beyond the position that it ought to be consulted and given the opportunity of supporting the war by a voluntary act. He remarked that in England the leader of the opposition was taken into confidence and consulted. He said that if war was once declared the situation would develop very rapidly and that therefore it was important that the position of the Congress should be cleared up as quickly as possible.

5. I cannot say whether he represents the views of the Working Committee, who may well be determined to make important conditions, but Pant's own attitude suggested that he personally might be satisfied if you were to send for one or more representatives of the Congress, take them into confidence and ask them whether Congress would support the war. I myself have felt for some time that in view of the obvious coincidence of interests between India and Britain, if a war breaks out, it is most desirable to try and enlist the genuine support of the Congress. I presume that if you contemplated anything of the kind you would also at the same time send for the leaders of the Muslim League.

6. I also discussed with him the various conditions that might be anticipated if (*a*) Germany alone were concerned, or (*b*) Italy came in, or (*c*) Japan came in. In the first case India would be little concerned directly. In the second case India would be much more closely interested in connection with Mediterranean and Egypt. In the third case he felt that India would be very directly concerned and that it might be necessary for India to make a really big effort. I thought this view was interesting, besides being essentially sound.

7. I had also seen earlier in the day Sampurnanand my Education Minister. He has a left wing history, though I should not regard him now as representative of left wing opinion. He has no kind of pacifist leanings. He takes for granted the justice and necessity of war and would obviously like India to play its part, provided it can feel that it is its own war. He is particularly interested in the development of an auxiliary air force. His ultimate aim is the development of a national army. But in present circumstances he regards it as a very definite grievance that recruitment for the army from the U.P. has been so greatly diminished. He thinks it is a slur on the province and is sapping the martial spirit which used to exist.

69

HAIG TO BRABOURNE
R/3/1/74

Secret
No. U.P.-176

Naini Tal,
October 10th, 1938

My dear Brabourne,

This is my usual fortnightly report.

I had, after making contacts with Ministers and Secretaries in Lucknow, come up to Naini Tal on the 24th September intending to remain there until the 10th October. On the 27th September, in view of the threatening international situation, I felt it necessary to return to Lucknow and get in touch with the Premier and ascertain his probable attitude towards measures that would be required immediately on the outbreak of war. I sent you a full account of the Premier's attitude which on the whole seemed to me very satisfactory. I have had no conversation with him since about developments following on the Munich agreement, but I should judge that the general advanced Indian opinion in the Province had been clearly in favour of supporting Czechoslovakia and making a firm stand on the issues of principle raised by Hitler's terms, and that consequently there has been much criticism of what appeared to be a surrender of principle in the face of threats. War is to people in India a thing so remote that they are disposed to judge the issues of war and peace with little appreciation of what a war would actually involve. The preservation of peace therefore, which has seemed to be the point of overwhelming significance to British opinion, has here been regarded as secondary to the fundamental issues of policy and principle, as they appear to critics at this distance. When it became apparent that war had been avoided, I returned to Naini Tal again on the 2nd October. The Premier also took the opportunity of the Dussehra holidays to come up to Naini Tal, and I have had some important discussions with him about the state of the Police, which I have reported to you in a separate letter. I leave Naini Tal today for a short tour to Bareilly and Dehra Dun, arriving in Lucknow on the 17th October, which is the day fixed for the meeting of the Legislative Assembly.

2. I have little new information to give you about the tenancy legislation. Pant, when I questioned him, corroborated the information given in the Press that the Working Committee were prepared to arbitrate if the landlords so desired. Pant seemed to think that this was a reasonable proposal and that the landlords were likely to adopt it. He said that something of the sort had been done in Bihar, and he thought that it would be to the advantage of the landlords to have the Working Committee on their side. I felt myself however considerable doubt whether the landlords would care to put themselves in such a position of subservience to Congress authority, and as I have heard nothing more of this proposal, I am inclined to think that it will come to nothing. Pant agreed with me that the matter of vital importance to the landlords is the pitch of land revenue, a matter which has not yet really been decided and has not been embodied in any legislative proposal. He appreciates the point that this issue must be decided as part of any general settlement. He himself is rather going back to the view which he held originally that it would be wiser to leave the principles of land revenue settlement much as they are at present, and take the increased contribution from the landlords not by raising their land revenue but by imposing a special graduated income-tax on agricultural incomes. I myself am rather disposed to think this would be a wiser course. Pant expressed to me the rather surprising opinion that he had little doubt about getting the tenancy bill through the Upper House even against the opposition of the landlords. Whether that is so or not, I remain of opinion that a settlement between the two parties would be the most satisfactory solution. I am entirely in agreement with what you say in paragraph 1 of your letter of 2nd October, and I had mentioned to the landlords whom I saw immediately on my return from England that it was no use their hoping for better things as a result of war. Indeed, my own view has always been that if war came the Congress would be likely to secure more power and not less. I shall be in a better position to judge probable developments about the tenancy legislation after I have returned to Lucknow.

3. One point of very considerable interest is the rebuke which the Congress Working Committee delivered to the Provincial Congress

Committee over their attitude to the Tenancy Bill. I enclose a copy of the Working Committee's resolution. It emphasises very strongly the fact which I have mentioned in my letter of September 26th, that the Working Committee have adopted a much more moderate attitude towards this tenancy legislation than the Provincial Congress Committee. The attitude of the latter indeed is, I think, definitely an embarrassment to Pant.

4. The Dussehra seems to have gone off peacefully everywhere, which is beyond expectation and is a very satisfactory result. But I do not think it indicates any diminution of the ill-feeling between the two communities. That ill-feeling and the political rivalry between the Congress and the Muslim League is, I should judge, operating definitely as a restraining influence on Muslims in regard to Palestine. If they were less deeply involved in their own immediate political struggle against the Congress they might be likely to succumb to an extremist agitation about Palestine. Certainly the long delay in reaching a settlement and the increasing bitterness of the struggle have increased the dangers of Indian Muslims seriously taking up the cause of the Palestine Arabs. One of our most prominent and unreliable Muslim Leaguers in this Province, Chaudhri Khaliq-uz-zaman, has gone off to the Palestine Conference at Cairo, and I hope he will not return with any mischievous ideas or policy.

5. The result of the bye-election in a Muslim constituency in the Budaun district, which had raised a good deal of feeling, has recently been announced. The Muslim League defeated the Congress candidate by a substantial majority. I am told that the Madhe Sahaba controversy in Lucknow is being pushed to the front once more, possibly with the idea of embarrassing the Congress Ministry, and either working up Sunni feeling against them or bringing pressure to bear on them to go beyond the decision they have already taken, and antagonise the Shias and endanger the peace of Lucknow. I have heard nothing more save rumours about the general position of the Ministry, which I referred to in paragraph 9 of my letter of September 26th. I quite agree with you of course that any serious weakening of the Ministerial position would be a disaster. But that it has weakened to some extent seems to be a general impression.

6. I have recently been seeing a number of my Heads of Departments – Education, Irrigation, Buildings and Roads, Forests.[4] On the whole they seem to be getting on reasonably well with their Ministers, though of course in some minor matters both of policy and of administration they do not like some of the actions of the Ministers. Generally speaking, however, the Heads of Departments seem to be adopting a very sensible attitude, and handling the Ministers well. Sampurnanand, the Education Minister,

is undoubtedly a man of considerable ability, and having himself been in his earlier days a teacher, knows a good deal from the practical point of view. I should judge that he is approaching the subject of educational reform on very realistic lines. In the Irrigation Department a committee has been sitting for months charged with the duty primarily of investigating the very difficult problem of canal rates, and also authorised to report on various matters of principle concerned with the administration and organisation of the Engineering services. The Chief Engineer, Irrigation,[5] thinks that no one is in a hurry for the committee to report about canal rates. Meantime, they rove over the whole question of administration and organisation, but so far without doing much harm. I gather that after much discussion the committee have been converted from their original ideas of the desirability of amalgamating the Irrigation and Buildings and Roads branches, and that the members show themselves susceptible to reason and argument when the whole official case is frankly and clearly placed before them. I understand also that they are disposed to favour entrusting District Board public works to the agency of the Buildings and Roads Department, which from the point of view of efficiency would certainly be a most desirable reform, though popular feeling has hitherto been against it. Meantime, another committee charged with the task of recasting the whole system of local self-government has been sitting industriously and is turning out opinions of great length and of a very controversial and, in many cases, theoretical character. I should imagine that there would be endless discussion before any policy on these matters is settled.

Yours sincerely,
H.G. HAIG

ENCLOSURE TO NO. 69

RESOLUTION OF THE CONGRESS WORKING COMMITTEE PASSED AT DELHI ON SEPTEMBER 30TH, 1938

"Resolved that in view of the fact that doubt has been raised regarding the function of the parliamentary sub-committee, the working committee desires to make it clear that in accordance with the resolution appointing it, the parliamentary sub-committee is required to be in close and constant touch with the working of the Congress party in all legislatures in the Provinces: to advise them in all their activities and take necessary action in any case of emergency. The parliamentary sub-committee is entitled to do so *sue moto* and not only on reference being made by the parliamentary parties or the Provincial Congress Committees.

"This committee regrets that the agrarian sub-committee of the United Provinces Provincial Congress Committee should have questioned the authority of the parliamentary sub-committee and passed a resolution to that effect. The United Provinces resolution is particularly objectionable as there is absolutely no justification for the assumptions whereon it is based."

70

HAIG TO BRABOURNE
R/3/1/74

Secret *October 10th, 1938*
No. U.P.-177

My dear Brabourne,

In the course of my fortnightly D.O. No. 175, dated September 26th, 1938, I referred to my uneasiness about conditions in the Police and my intention to have a full discussion with the Premier and the Inspector-General of Police about them. I think it is convenient that I should deal with the result of these discussions in a self-contained letter and not merely include them in my fortnightly report.

2. When I first put to the Premier my proposal to have these discussions, he showed some reluctance, and was inclined to take the line that he was handling the Police to the best of his ability and judgment, and that there was nothing at present which required me to interest myself specially in the problem. After I had reminded him however of my special responsibilities in connection with the Police and my desire to make any contribution that I could at an early stage while it might still be of value, and not wait until anything had gone seriously wrong, he changed his attitude and agreed to the proposed discussion. I arranged that he and I should see Horton, the Inspector-General of Police, on the 5th October and question him frankly about his view of the general conditions, and that on the 6th October the Premier and I should meet by ourselves to discuss the views expressed by the Inspector-General of Police and the Premier's own estimate of the general state of affairs.

3. The Inspector-General of Police said that he was satisfied that so far as the incidents at Cawnpore were concerned they were entirely local in character and that no notices of a similar kind had been distributed

anywhere else in the Province. He was also satisfied that the situation was completely under control at Cawnpore and that no further indiscipline was to be anticipated there. The cause of the trouble was to be found primarily in the action of certain individuals who were being dealt with departmentally. At the same time he felt that the incident was, in his own words, "a straw in the wind" and was an indication that the trying conditions to which the Police had been subjected during the last year had not been without their effect. This view certainly receives corroboration from an incident at Jhansi of a somewhat similar character which happened a few days ago, but was not known to us at the time of these discussions. There also the men in the reserve lines refused to take their food in the common messes. In Jhansi I understand the refusal was a general one. It seems to have been provoked by bullying behaviour by the Reserve Inspector. The officiating Superintendent of Police,[6] a comparatively young officer, does not seem to have dealt with the situation with sufficient vigour, and it was not until the Deputy Inspector-General of Police[7] on hearing of the incident went to Jhansi that the trouble was stopped. Doubtless behaviour at Jhansi was influenced by what had been done at Cawnpore. It is important to realise that both at Cawnpore and at Jhansi the indiscipline did not proceed beyond refusal to partake of food in the common messes, which was a spectacular form of protest. There was no kind of refusal to perform their ordinary duties. There is always the danger that an incident of this kind may lead to imitation elsewhere on the occurrence of any serious local grievance.

4. The Inspector-General of Police while not seriously disturbed at present about the attitude of the men in general said that it was clear that there might be possibilities of their wavering if they came to look elsewhere than to their own officers for the protection of their interests and for rewards and punishments. The particular matters he mentioned as tending to the development of such ideas were:

(*a*) The large volume of complaints and representations sent direct to Government, and particularly any action taken by Government over the heads of local officers on those complaints.

(*b*) The activities of the Anti-Corruption Officer who is working directly under Government.

(*c*) The effect of transfers of officers being ordered from headquarters over the heads of or contrary to the advice of local officers.

(*d*) The number of questions which are asked in the Legislative Assembly about promotions and the cases of individual officers.

5. The main remedy which the Inspector-General of Police suggested

was that Government should put more confidence in its own Police officers and not appear to be working over their heads. He suggested that greater trust should be reposed in the Inspector-General of Police and Superintendents of Police to take steps to remove corruption and introduce better methods of work. Complaints against the Police should be made not to the Government but to the local authorities. It was important that the Anti-Corruption Officer should not be looked upon, as he is at present, as an outside and indeed inquisitorial authority.

6. I talked over all these matters in a frank and friendly manner with the Premier on the 6th October, and on the whole I was favourably impressed by an attitude on his part much more reasonable than he had displayed in previous conversations with me. In the first place, he told me that the Congress authorities themselves are genuinely impressed with the undesirability of individual Congressmen or local Congress Committees attempting to interfere with the administration, and that he was himself fully alive to the disadvantages and dangers of these tendencies. He told me that a resolution had been passed by the Congress Working Committee recently at Delhi which it had been intended to place before the All-India Congress Committee, but unfortunately time had not permitted. He assured me however that the Working Committee attached real importance to this resolution. According to the newspapers, the terms of the resolution were as follows:

"It has come to the notice of the Congress that certain committees interfere with the ordinary administration of the country's affairs by seeking to influence officers and other members of the services. The Congress advises Congressmen not to interfere with the due course of administration. This however does not mean that they are not to render assistance to the members of the services if they are requested thereto by the latter."

7. On the subject of reposing more confidence in Police Officers, the Premier spoke as if he was very genuinely anxious to win the confidence and support of the Police, and he said that he was quite conscious that unless he had this he could not possibly succeed in his general task. He had not yet begun to despair. But it was clear that in many respects he was still dissatisfied about the attitude of the Police in general. He said he was well aware that in the case of Superintendents of Police who were sincerely anxious to carry out the policy of Government, nothing could be more effective than to trust them, and that in fact wherever there was a Superintendent of Police of this type no kind of difficulty was experienced and Police work went on without interference by Government and to the satisfaction of the public. But he held that there were a number of

Superintendents of Police who did not sincerely accept the present position and were inclined to oppose and obstruct the policy of Government. This was what made it necessary for Government to interfere to an extent which they themselves would prefer not to. At the same time he said that he was satisfied that the Inspector-General of Police was genuinely anxious to co-operate with him. He felt, however, that this was not the case with a considerable number of officers working under him, and he thought that the general attitude of Police Officers towards the administration was much less satisfactory than the attitude of Indian Civil Service officers.

8. With reference to the particular suggestions of the Inspector-General of Police he said that the volume of complaints coming to Government was very much less than it had been in the earlier days. This I think is correct, for the dangers and disadvantages of this practice were clearly realised at an early date, and it is a point which I have repeatedly impressed upon him. At the same time the Police are undoubtedly subject to much abuse and criticism, and it would be surprising if this did not produce some feeling of depression or irritation. The Premier realises this and claims to have given the Police some encouragement. But I think he could have done a good deal more, and this is a point which I shall continue to suggest to him.

9. I had a long discussion with him about the functions of the Anti-Corruption Officer and found him more reasonable than I had expected. He pointed out that when in the case of an officer of some position information came to the notice of Government in any way which raised serious doubts about his honesty, it seemed necessary not to ignore that information but to try and find out whether there were really substantial grounds for making a formal enquiry. This could only be ascertained by a preliminary confidential investigation, and this was the work that was entrusted to the Anti-Corruption Officer. If he reported that there was no substance in the allegations, or that there was not sufficient evidence, then no further action was taken. If on the other hand he reported that there was evidence, then Government considered whether formal proceedings should be taken against the officer concerned. The Premier said that when the Anti-Corruption Officer was directed to make a confidential investigation, he always informed the head of the department and got into touch with him. I raised the question whether the head of the department was consulted before it was decided that the Anti-Corruption Officer should enquire. The Premier admitted that this was not the case. I said I thought that this was a very important point and that heads of departments would naturally feel that they were not being treated with confidence by Government if it

was decided, without any reference to them, to make even a preliminary enquiry into the conduct of one of their officers. I think my argument made some impression upon the Premier, and he has promised to consider this matter and let me know his views later. I think myself that it would greatly strengthen the position of the Inspector-General of Police, and indeed is essential, that he should be taken into consultation before it is decided to hold any kind of enquiry through the Anti-Corruption Officer.

10. With regard to transfers the Premier took the line that comparatively few had been ordered, and only for very good cause. I propose to go into this further, and ascertain details, for I can well believe that undue interference of the Minister in transfers of officers of the rank of Sub-Inspectors for instance might have a very unsettling effect.

11. In the course of conversation I drew pointed attention to the danger that if political influence were brought to bear on the Police it was almost certain in this Province, where politics are so largely directed on communal lines, that the influences would be of a communal character, and this might have the most serious effects on the discipline and conduct of the Police. I think there are already signs that the Muslim League is working in this direction. Though the Premier did not say much about this directly, I am convinced that he fully appreciates the point and does not under-estimate the danger.

12. In general it seems to me that the question is one of gradually developing more confidence by the Premier in the Police administration. Interference by Government which is apt to cause uneasiness in the ranks of the Police, or failure to give them sufficient public encouragement, can all be traced to distrust of the conduct and attitude of the Police. Undoubtedly there are in some instances grounds for this feeling, but in many cases I think the Premier suffers from an exaggerated and unreasonable suspicion. This can only be cured gradually. It is I think a hopeful sign that he has definitely confidence in the Inspector-General of Police, and my own view is that his attitude is distinctly less difficult and suspicious than it was a year ago. At the same time I think he is beginning now to realise more clearly the dangers of any weakening in the discipline of the Police and the fact that some of the action that Government has taken in the past must tend to cause uncertainty and uneasiness. I do not think there is any short cut out of our difficulties. We must, with a clear realisation of the tendencies and the dangers, go steadily on trying to create a better feeling and impressing on the Premier, what he himself is already beginning to appreciate, the importance of securing confidence and contentment in the force. During my cold weather tours I shall make it a

point of talking to Superintendents of Police and ascertaining their general views about conditions. I shall encourage the Inspector-General of Police to impress on officers that when there are reasonable rounds for suspecting corruption or misconduct, Superintendents of Police do no good to anyone by trying to shield the culprits or obstruct disciplinary action, but that they must genuinely co-operate in attempting to remedy such defects. I believe in fact that the attitude of Superintendents of Police is normally sensible and satisfactory, but if there were so [?no] exceptions to the proper attitude, the occasions for the Premier's suspicions would be much diminished, and then we should be well on our way to the establishment of sounder conditions.

Yours sincerely,
H.G. HAIG

71

HAIG TO BRABOURNE
R/3/1/74

Secret *October 18th, 1938*
No. U.P.-180

My dear Brabourne,

Many thanks for your letter of October 13th[8] about relations between my Ministers and the police. I agree with you about the great advantage of the Premier making some public pronouncement about the police. Last cold weather I pressed this consideration on his notice a good deal, and he did eventually deliver a speech to a police parade at Cawnpore after some prolonged labour trouble there. Though I believe this did some good, the result did not quite come up to expectations, for his addresses, when once he gets started, tend to become homilies on the duties of the police and exhortations to reform rather than pats on the back for good work. He is in fact very cautious about acknowledging good work. It was only after considerable delay that he could be induced to acknowledge the admirable work done by the police both in Allahabad and Benares during the serious communal disturbances there last cold weather.

2. Recently at the end of August he was moved to action by a considerable rise in crime statistics and also, I understand, by pressure from Hallett on the same point. He called in all the Deputy Inspectors-General of Police and a couple of representative Superintendents of Police from each Range,

and he and Dr. Katju talked to them at length in the presence of the Inspector-General. I understand that the manner of this talk was very good, but the matter was by no means so agreeable. Among other things he developed a thesis that honest police work would always be successful in dealing with crime, because the honest police officer would have assistance from the public, and public opinion would be on his side. From this premise he drew the conclusion that if crime increased in a police circle or a larger area it must be because the officer in charge was not honest. The dangers of this line of argument are obvious. The police officers present at the meeting found him ready to listen to what they had to say, and quite pleasant to deal with; but the impression left on their minds as to the attitude of the head of their department was not a very reassuring one. They felt that he genuinely desired to put down both crime and corruption, but that his ideas as to how to do so were too theoretical. As I have often written before, he is apt to let his theories and principles carry him too far.

Yours sincerely,
HARRY HAIG

72

HAIG TO BRABOURNE
R/3/1/74

Secret and Personal
No. U.P.-181

Camp,
October 19th, 1938

My dear Brabourne,

I am writing in answer to your letter of October 10th, 1938,[9] regarding the proposal of my Government to amalgamate the old and new schemes of rural development. I have read the previous correspondence, and I am very definitely in agreement with Hallett's general conclusions on this matter. Hallett's letter gave a clear picture of the position as it stands at present. I think, however, for a full understanding of the case, it is important to distinguish clearly between two markedly different phases. When the Congress Ministry came into power, one of the most important parts of their programme was a rural development scheme. They had no very clear ideas on the subject except that the scheme must be different from the one which we had been working in the Province since 1935, that it must give quick results, and that it must be essentially non-official as contrasted with our scheme which derived its impetus from official sources. In pursuance of these ideas, and in spite of my warnings, Mr. Paliwal, a member of the Central Legislative Assembly, who was entirely devoid of any administrative experience and was by character and temperament unsuitable, was put in charge of the movement, and it was frankly decided to recruit as workers in the movement mainly Congressmen on the ostensible ground that among no other classes would be found the necessary "missionary zeal". Mr. Paliwal drew up on paper various grandiose schemes, recruited in a manner which aroused a great deal of public criticism 700 organizers, kept official influence at a distance, and hoped presumably for some results. The practical results, however, were negligible, and from all quarters came reports that the organisers were more interested in politics than in rural development, and that the rural development scheme looked like being utilised primarily for Congress propaganda in villages. These reports led to much criticism and put the Ministry on the defensive. At the same time I took every opportunity of emphasising that the organisers were Government servants and must behave in accordance with the code of conduct of Government servants.

2. After some six months of this it was generally realised that the Congress Ministry were getting out of their scheme of rural development very little in the way of practical results and much public discredit. At the same time my own impression was that certainly the Premier and probably most of the other Ministers were really anxious to improve conditions in the villages by means of the rural development scheme and that they were certainly not prepared to spend large sums of money merely on party propaganda. About this time Mr. Paliwal resigned, and there was a fairly long period of reconsideration, out of which has recently emerged the second phase.

3. The second phase represents the scheme which has now been brought into force and is dealt with in our official letter of 7th June 1938. In place of Mr. Paliwal, M.L.A., an officer of the Indian Forest Service[10] has been appointed as Rural Development Officer, and there is no doubt at all that he is making every effort to foster the movement on sound and non-political lines. I enclose, as it may be of interest in this connection, a circular[11] from him which has just reached me giving instructions for the organisation of a rural development week throughout the Province. The staff recruited by Mr. Paliwal has been scrutinised, some of the worst members of it have been removed, and the others have been made to understand that what is expected of them is rural development work and not politics. They are all to undergo special practical training and those who are found to be unfit will be removed. A Deputy Collector on the District Officer's staff is

Secretary of each district association, and the whole work is done in the closest co-operation with the departmental officers in the district. The result is that in effect the Ministry have gone back to the main principles of the scheme which we introduced in the Province in 1935; but they have extended both its scope and the number of villages to which it applies, and are spending a great deal more money. During the period of reconsideration Dr. Katju, the Minister-in-charge, said to me that they had realised they could not get satisfactory results without the co-operation of officials, and that it was essential in the new scheme to secure such co-operation. Though the district officer has no direct connection with the organisation, except that he is charged with a general supervision, and is authorised to draw attention to any features which are undesirable or could be improved, he is in fact, through the Deputy Collector Secretary, able to keep in close touch with what is being done and to influence it.

4. It would be impossible to expect a Congress Ministry to go further than this in the direction of invoking official co-operation in view of the opinions with which they came into office only a year ago. Indeed yesterday's papers record some interesting and heated discussions within the Provincial Congress Committee in which the left wing have been fiercely attacking the Ministry's scheme as having officialised the rural development work. The Ministry, however, have defended their policy, and as far as I know have every intention of pursuing it. I enclose cuttings[12] from the *Statesman* and the *Pioneer* which give a general idea of the trend of these discussions and make it clear how bitterly disappointed the left wing are that the movement has now become one of genuine work for the improvement of the villages and no longer a political ramp for the benefit of the Congress party.

5. Bearing in mind the conditions I have explained above, it seems to me exceedingly important that we should take advantage of the policy of the Congress Ministry as it now stands and give them every encouragement in working out their scheme on existing lines, and that we should not play into the hands of the left wing by doing anything which may be regarded as unfriendly to the Ministry's policy or which suggests that there is some essential antagonism between the "official" and the "Congress" policy. It follows that I am strongly in favour of the Government of India money being made available for expenditure in association with the Provincial scheme.

6. With regard to the two conditions suggested in paragraph 2 of your letter, condition (*a*) follows the lines of conditions that the Government of India made originally when our scheme of 1935 was introduced. It goes

somewhat further, in that I understand about 1½ lakhs annually of Government of India money was being spent on staff. In view however of the very largely increased provision now being made by the Provincial Government, a direction that none of the Government of India grant should be spent on staff would not, I believe, cause embarrassment. I do not think therefore in practice there would be any difficulty about accepting condition (*a*).

7. Condition (*b*), I fear, is not likely to be palatable to the Ministry. The form would be displeasing because it would emphasise the fact that the Government of India reposed their confidence only in the district officers to whom the Ministry are not, for the reasons explained above, entrusting direct functions in connection with the scheme. I quite appreciate the desire of the Government of India to satisfy themselves that their money is in fact being spent usefully, and not on schemes of an unsuitable character, or schemes put forward to gratify influential members of a particular political party. I would suggest however that this object could be sufficiently assured without requiring the sanction of the district officer to the expenditure incurred. At present the Government of India grant, apart from the sum of Rs. 1½ lakhs which, as I have explained above, is being spent on staff, is divided into two parts. In the first place, Rs. 5,000 a year is being placed at the disposal of each district officer for expenditure at his discretion on approved objects. In the second place, a sum, which I understand amounts to 2¼ lakhs a year, is being distributed to districts for expenditure on certain specified purposes, namely, improvement of communications, water-supply and seed. I would suggest that the whole of the Government of India grant should now be amalgamated and treated on one basis alone, and that it should be laid down that it can be spent by the District Association only on certain specified objects. These I would suggest should be:

(*a*) Improvement of communications;

(*b*) Water-supply;

(*c*) Seed;

(*d*) Provision of bulls;

(*e*) Projects of sanitary improvement in villages, e.g. filling up insanitary hollows, paving of lanes, &c.

If expenditure from the Government of India grant is definitely restricted to these objects, all of which are of great practical importance, I do not think it would be necessary for the district officer to sanction the particular items of expenditure, and the Government of India might feel satisfied that their money was being devoted to definite practical objects. The risk of funds of this nature being applied in accordance with political sympathies seems to be not serious. Any tendency of this kind would very soon attract the attention of the district officers who would, I think, be able to correct it. I might add that present tendencies suggest that the district associations may before long be recast so as to make them a more genuine reflection of the opinion of the villages concerned, and this would be all to the good.

8. The third condition mentioned in your letter that the district officer should be *ex-officio* chairman of the district association would, for the reasons I have explained above, be in my judgment impossible for the Ministry to accept, and I am glad to note that you are yourself not disposed to favour it.

Yours sincerely,
HARRY HAIG

73

HAIG TO LINLITHGOW
R/3/1/74

Secret
No. U.P.-185

October 23rd, 1938

My dear Lord Linlithgow,

I am actually writing this fortnightly report the day before you arrive, so Your Excellency has been given little respite on your return from leave. I hope you have come back feeling very much refreshed from your holiday as I did.

2. I left Naini Tal on October 10th, which is the date of my last report to Brabourne, and spent a week on tour in Bareilly and Dehra Dun. At Bareilly I saw all six District Magistrates and Superintendents of Police of the division, and had from them on the whole a satisfactory picture of conditions. In particular the reports I received about the police were generally reassuring. In more than one district I was told that the police are certainly in better heart than they were at this time last year. At the same time there is evidently a good deal of uneasiness in connection with the activities of the Anti-Corruption department. If these could be modified to some extent, a point which I shall be taking up further with the Premier in due course, I think it might have a considerable effect on police confidence. Though the actual number of cases investigated by the Anti-Corruption department is not very large, a single case sometimes tends to

undermine confidence rather widely. One of the chief embarrassments in connection with this matter is the report which was made last May by the committee set up by Government under the chairmanship of Kunwar Sir Maharaj Singh, late Home Member of my Government. Some of the recommendations of this committee seem to me mischievous and dangerous, and if adopted, likely to undermine the confidence of the services generally. In particular I dislike the proposal for district committees, consisting of officials and non-officials, charged with a general supervision of the problem of corruption in each district, and the proposal to establish on a still firmer basis an Anti-Corruption department. There is already a general feeling that the Anti-Corruption department might easily develop into a kind of OGPU.[13] The report was debated last week in the Assembly. Before Hallett left, the Cabinet had started consideration of the report and had accepted a number of harmless recommendations at the beginning. But Hallett had secured the postponement of consideration of the more vital recommendations until the publication of the report of the Bihar Anti-Corruption committee, which he hoped might make more reasonable and less dangerous recommendations. I had been a little apprehensive that with discussion obviously necessary before long in the Assembly the Ministry might press for further consideration of the report and the adoption of definite conclusions in advance of the debate. However they did not suggest this and we had no further Cabinet discussion, and the debate in the Assembly petered out in generalities. I hope this will give us some appreciable respite.

3. The reports I received in the Rohilkhand division of relations between Hindus and Muslims were very discouraging. In most districts it seemed to be felt that not only were relations bad, but that they were deteriorating and communal trouble might be anticipated at any moment. I believe these conditions, which are general throughout the Province, are causing considerable anxiety to the Ministers, though the Premier does not go out of his way to disclose his anxieties to me. This state of affairs is, as I have more than once mentioned before, the inevitable consequence of the present political grouping in the Province, whereby the main opposition to the Government consists of Muslims and almost the whole body of Muslims are in the opposition. Finding themselves unable to effect much by parliamentary methods, they are inevitably tempted to create unrest and disturbance outside the legislature, and there is no doubt that the Muslim League have set themselves quite deliberately to this policy. There are, I believe, a great number of inflammatory speeches and writings on the Muslim side, and of course the Hindus do not refrain from counter-attacks.

Moreover, as I have also mentioned before, it is probably the case that the Hindus are elated by their position of political power and are by no means tolerant or conciliatory. From quarrels over festivals and processions and recriminations about appointments and treatment of individuals the trouble has been spreading to schools, and the Education Minister told me a few days ago that he was seriously disturbed at the extent to which boys of certain schools were being led on to ridiculous communal activities. In Pilibhit, for instance, the Muslim boys claimed to interrupt the school work in order to say their prayers, provoking immediately counterclaims by the Hindus, even though congregational prayers form no part of the religion of the latter. He told me that actually at one stage the Muslim boys collected on the hockey ground to say their prayers at one goal while the Hindu boys collected at the other goal and put up a counter-religious demonstration. The trouble was stopped at Pilibhit by the doubtful and temporary expedient of changing the school hours, making them run from 7 to 12 so that the hours when the Muslim boys claimed to say their prayers were after school time had finished. But this is clearly no final solution, particularly as with the approach of the cold weather it would be impossible to bring the boys to school at 7 a.m. It will probably be necessary for Government to take a firmer and more definite line. There is also of course the much more serious danger that these communal feelings may spread to the police. That would be disastrous. I am glad to think that at present there are no serious indications of this, but it is a matter which has to be watched most carefully.

4. The Premier is very indignant at the general Muslim League agitation and the nature of the speeches and writings, and I believe that he has often considered taking a more vigorous line in the way of prosecution. He is deterred, however, by the fear of provoking still more violent attacks from the Muslim League and by his own general policy of extreme toleration towards undesirable speeches and writings. If he once started prosecuting Muslims on any considerable scale, he could hardly refuse to prosecute many of the more extreme Congress supporters who make constant attacks on the police or on the British connection.

5. The Muslim Press agitated itself considerably about some firing which took place about two months ago at Tanda in the Fyzabad district in connection with some communal outbreak, as a result of which one or two Muslims were killed. A Judge of the Chief Court of Oudh has now been appointed to make an enquiry and the enquiry has just started. I believe the incident has been given quite exaggerated importance, but this enquiry had to be conceded in view of the extreme nature of the agitation.

6. Another problem that is causing the Government some anxiety is the perennial trouble between the Sunnis and Shias of Lucknow over the Madhe Sahaba question. This has been revived recently at the instance of an influential Maulvi of Deoband, Maulvi Husain Ahmad Madni, who has taken up the position that the Sunnis should be allowed on one occasion to assert the right which has been pronounced to be theirs, namely, to recite Madhe Sahaba publicly. I gather that he would be satisfied if this right were exercised on one occasion only and that if after that the Sunnis agitated for a repetition he would have no sympathy with them. In the meantime the local Sunni agitators have raised the question prominently and threatened that unless they receive satisfaction shortly they intend to start civil disobedience. The view of the Ministers seems to be that they should meet the demand of Maulvi Husain Ahmad, and I myself am disposed to think that this is right. They have some hopes that they might get the Shias to acquiesce in this. Negotiations are proceeding at the moment and the whole situation is uncertain and somewhat dangerous. The Premier spoke to me rather strongly on the subject yesterday, and said that it was not fair to have our officers subjected week after week and month after month to this constant strain, never knowing when an outbreak over this question might occur. He is definitely in favour of taking some action which would settle it once for all. The difficulty is that the question is of such a nature that if people wish to make trouble it can never be settled. But I hope that if it is decided to allow the Sunnis to recite the Madhe Sahaba on one occasion the agitation will at any rate die down for some considerable period.

7. The most crucial question facing the Province and the Ministry at the moment is the future of the Tenancy Bill. I gave some account of more recent developments in paragraph 2 of my letter of September 26th, 1938 and in paragraph 2 of my letter of October 10th, 1938 to Brabourne. After the meeting of the landlords with the Working Committee at Delhi, there was a curious lull and no one seemed quite to know what was happening. I have since heard that Vallabhbhai Patel wrote to the Nawab of Chhatari immediately after the Delhi meeting asking him whether the landlords were prepared to discuss the case further with the Working Committee and abide by their decision. Chhatari was away in Southern India and did not get this letter till about ten days later. When he got it he arranged for a meeting of the Agra Province Zamindars at Allahabad, which resolved to authorise a small committee of themselves, known as the negotiating committee, to decide whether they would accept this proposal. Armed with this authorisation Chhatari and the other leading landlords of Agra

sent a communication to the Working Committee accepting their proposal. They did this deliberately without waiting for the views of the Oudh Taluqdars, as they felt it was necessary to give a lead. Meantime, and partly I imagine owing to the delay in action after the meeting of the Working Committee, the more intransigent party of the Oudh Taluqdars had got busy with meetings and statements, reasserting their old demands and advocating a militant policy; and actually while the Agra Zamindars at Allahabad were deciding to agree to arbitration, the Oudh Taluqdars at Unao were nailing their colours to the mast. The Oudh Taluqdars have been particularly provoked by a strong speech which the Premier had made on October 13th at Agra, a copy of which I enclose. I presume that when he made it, he was under the impression that the landlords did not mean to consider the proposal of the Working Committee. He evidently spoke under a feeling of considerable irritation and, as always happens, speeches of this nature provoke counter-speeches of equal violence and heat.

8. The present position is that while, as I have said, the Agra Zamindars have agreed to the proposal of the Working Committee, the Oudh Taluqdars are to meet on the 27th October in order to reach their decision. In order to give them time for consideration the Assembly which met on the 17th October was adjourned after a few days and is now not to meet again until November 10th. The Premier told me yesterday that if the Oudh Taluqdars agree to the proposal of the Working Committee he believes that the whole matter will have been settled before the 10th November, and that on that date it would be possible to proceed with an agreed Bill. Even, however, if the landlords accept the arbitration of the Working Committee, it is certain that the Muslim League will oppose it. But I do not think that their opposition could be very effective if the landlords did not join in.

9. Kunwar Sir Jagdish Prasad was over in Lucknow for a few days at the time when the Agra Zamindars were taking their crucial decision, and he, as one of themselves, gave them what in my opinion was very good advice. I had a long talk with him and found myself completely in agreement with his views. I had indeed already expressed the same views to several of the more prominent landlords immediately on my return from leave. I have since seen several of the landlords (who come to see me at their own request), and I am making it quite clear to them that in my opinion their interests definitely demand that they should reach a settlement now. On this point I have not the slightest doubt. To fight this measure further would greatly embitter the situation, would lead I am afraid to dangerous agitation in the villages, would greatly increase the power of the left wing,

and would in the end achieve nothing for the landlords. They would in fact be in every way far worse off than if they accepted a settlement now. The form of the settlement is of course galling to their pride, and constitutionally no doubt it is open to criticism. But from the practical point of view I can see no alternative. The landlords have not sufficient solidarity to authorise some of their members to negotiate with full power on their behalf, and it has been clear from the proceedings of the last few months that direct negotiations between the landlords and the Ministry lead to no effective conclusions. If the matter is to be settled without delay, which is most desirable, it can only be settled by a definite pronouncement by some authority. Actually it is generally believed that the landlords will get better terms from the Working Committee than the provincial Ministry would be in a position to offer. The Ministry is subject to very severe pressure from the left wing, which demands that there shall be no concessions and on the contrary seeks to stiffen up the provisions against the landlords. I do not think the Ministry are likely to be in a position to give away anything more. On the other hand the Working Committee are believed to have some sympathy with the landlord point of view, and to be very definitely right wing, and they are in a position to oppose the left wing and to enforce their decision upon it. I think that if arbitration is accepted, this will be a very decided triumph for the right wing of the Congress and a great discouragement to the left wing who are opposing the idea strongly.

10. As for the prospects of the Oudh Taluqdars agreeing to arbitration, I think that most of the older and influential Taluqdars are now of opinion that they should agree. The opposition is being led by some of the younger men, with the support and, I think to some considerable extent, under the inspiration of the *Pioneer* which again takes its views to a large extent from Sir Jwala Prasad Srivastava. He himself is not a landlord, and I can well understand that he believes it is worth while attacking and weakening the Congress Ministry without looking too closely to the consequences for the landlords. But I am sure that from the point of view of the landlords and in fact from the point of view of the Province as a whole it is a profoundly mistaken view. The only alternative to a Ministry controlled by Pant is a Ministry controlled by the left wing, and no one can suppose that that would be a change for the better. I hope myself that counsels of moderation will prevail, and that on the 27th the Oudh Taluqdars will agree to the proposal. There will be some support for a middle course, namely, that the Taluqdars should not agree to arbitration but wait and see what the result of the arbitration is, and if it is reasonable, accept it; if it is unreasonable, fight it. But I think there is no doubt that the Congress

Working Committee would not agree to arbitrate at all unless the whole body of landlords agreed to accept their decision. Such a course therefore would mean ruining the whole scheme, and I shall certainly impress that view plainly on any Taluqdars who may suggest it to me.

11. It is not yet clear whether the landlords will try to get as a condition of their agreement any kind of assurance in regard to the vital question of the amount of taxation or extra land revenue that the Government will wish to take from them by a separate legislative measure. They are fully alive to the position and realise that in fact their interests might be much more seriously endangered by the provisions of a measure of this kind than they are likely to be by the Tenancy Bill even if it were to go through unchanged. I am not without hope that if an agreement is reached on the Tenancy Bill, more friendly relations generally will be established between the landlords and the right wing of the Congress, and I am definitely of opinion that this, taking the long view, would be desirable for the future orderly development of the Province. Indeed, it seems to be the best hope of preventing a left wing government after a time coming into power.

12. There is reason to believe that the Ministry may want to consider again, in connection with the Budget, proposals for a cut in pay. This is associated with rumours that the Government of India themselves may be considering something of the kind. I should be grateful if you could let me know whether there is any kind of foundation for this belief.

13. I have had talks with all my Ministers except one, during the last week, and have found them all most friendly and reasonable on the various points we discussed. Mrs. Pandit is due back about the middle of November.

Yours sincerely,
H.G. HAIG

ENCLOSURE TO NO. 73

SPEECH BY PANT AS REPORTED IN THE *NATIONAL HERALD* DATED 14TH OCTOBER, 1938

The international situation, the communal problem and the tenancy policy of the United Provinces Government were explained by Hon'ble Pandit Govind Ballabh Pant, Premier, at a huge public meeting here (Agra) yesterday. A record number of addresses, 25 in number, were presented to the Premier. While those by the Municipal and District Boards were read out the rest were taken as read.

The Premier said that they were fighting against great odds. Their country was engaged in a great fight against a mighty Imperialist Power and they had various reactionary forces within their own country to contend with.

But they were confident of their ultimate success when they would show to the world the way of real peace to this distressed and tormented humanity.

The Great Powers of Europe, added the Premier, were guided solely by the law of the jungle and no moral principles had any hold on them. "They are steeped in violence. One who can go ahead with aggression succeeds, but our country is following a new path of struggle and our weapon is also a new one – that of non-violence."

"Through this weapon we have already achieved wonderful success. The power that the Congress wields today is tremendous and it is no exaggeration to say that no Government can function in this country without the support of the Congress."

COMMUNAL PROBLEM

Proceeding he emphasised the need of Hindu-Muslim unity and appealed to the audience to foster harmonious relations between the communities. He added:

"A community has always the full right to put forward its claims and grievances before the Government, but when there is a deliberate and mischievous plan of dividing the country and creating dissensions with a view to making ordered progress [?in] society impossible the Government must put its foot down on such activities."

The Premier warned mischief-mongers that the Government would give no quarter to those who disturbed the peace of the country and attempted to widen the gulf between the communities. Religion should not be mixed up with politics.

The Premier declared: "Those who invoke the dead to fan communal frenzy are doing the greatest disservice to the country and their own community." He informed the audience that whenever any grievances had been brought to the notice of the Government, it had looked into the merits of the case. It was in keeping with this policy that a judicial enquiry with a Judge of the Chief Court had been instituted into Tanda firing. If in spite of all this some people blamed the Government, it was not only unfair but criminal.

TENANCY POLICY

Dealing with the rent and revenue policy of the Government the Premier referred to the various ameliorative and relief measures in the form of Stay Orders, &c.

He said: "The peasant is the source of livelihood of all people. On him thrives the community. If he is suck[ed] dry whence will you get your nourishment. While he is helpless and poor the exploiters are in prosperity living in luxury in palaces. It is an irony of fate that the toiler is starving and the exploiter is thriving."

Pandit Pant referred to a threat by a Zamindar who said that the Pant Government was extirpating the Zamindar class and that he would make Pandit G.B. Pant his first objective of attack. The Premier added: "But they should realise that the peasant is a power today and no one can do him any harm who stands by the masses."

The Premier welcomed the landlords' threats of satyagraha, and added that such empty threats would not deter the Government from their course of action. He warned the Zamindars that if they did not come to the straight path of justice they would be hastening their own ruin, and that of their future generation. There was only one course open to them, which was that they should accept the Government's measures with good grace.

He pointed out that the argument that Muslims would be adversely affected by the Tenancy legislation was a pure myth. "It is admitted on all hands that the Muslim masses are poorer than Hindus and the policy of the Government is to introduce measures which will benefit the poor. *Ipso facto* our measures will benefit the vast masses of 'Muslim community'."

The Premier concluded: "It does not lie in the mouth of landlords to question the fairness and equity of this legislation. Do not they realise that when they were in power they introduced debt legislation which was highly prejudicial to the interest of other classes. They reduced their huge liabilities to almost nothing and their creditors are left to their own fate."

74

HAIG TO LINLITHGOW
R/3/1/74

Private and Personal
No. U.P.-189

Camp,
October 30th, 1938

My dear Lord Linlithgow,

One of the personal embarrassments that has arisen from having a Congress Ministry in power concerns the case of Rai Bahadur Ram Babu Saksena, who was for a number of years our Director of Publicity. He is a Deputy

Collector who, owing to his qualifications and initiative, was specially selected by Lord Hailey for this post some years ago while he was still comparatively junior in service. Lord Hailey made a great deal of use of him and thought well of him, and I have seen a recent letter which he has given him in which he indicates his opinion that we have certain obligations towards Mr. Saksena. I found him a very enthusiastic Director of Publicity, and there is no doubt that in the conditions which prevailed before the present constitution came into force he did carry out for the Government, in accordance with its policy at the time, a great deal of propaganda which was valuable and effective. From the nature of things the propaganda was largely of an anti-Congress tone, as the Congress were then engaged in an open struggle against the Government. Mr. Saksena's activities were very well known to the present Congress Ministry, and he is naturally anything but a *persona grata* to them. They kept him on in the post for a few months after they took office; but though he adjusted himself to the new conditions and was genuinely prepared to support their policy, they naturally could not reconcile themselves to keeping him in this position. Nor could I regard it as reasonable to press them to do so, quite apart from the fact that I had no power. He was replaced therefore nearly a year ago by a new Director specially recruited for the post, and he has since been on leave. There was talk at one time of providing him with a post of Deputy Secretary in the Secretariat, but it has now become clear that the Ministry are not prepared to do this. Therefore Mr. Saksena's only prospects in the Province are to revert to the ordinary line as Deputy Collector. This means a considerable fall for him both in pay and position, and he is naturally very anxious to avoid it. I think also from my own point of view it is not desirable that a man who identified himself rather unusually with the policy of the previous Government should too obviously suffer for it. I therefore have considerable sympathy with Mr. Saksena's desire to get some employment outside the Province.

2. Mr. Saksena has just received an offer of appointment as Chief Justice in the Kotah State on, I believe, Rs. 1,000 a month, and this he is accepting. He feels, however, that this post does not offer any prospects, and he would be very glad if in the course of the next year or so he could get a fresh start under more promising auspices. He mentioned to me the possibility of some post in the Government of India Secretariat, or an appointment of Trade Commissioner, or some more important post in an Indian State. Mr. Saksena does not under-estimate his abilities and is always inclined to look high. At the same time he is undoubtedly a man of capacity, very industrious, a loyal worker, with considerable experience of affairs,

who has been to England more than once (indeed, he was attending the Round Table Conference in some secretarial capacity), and I think he might prove very suitable for one of the posts to which he aspires. I should personally be grateful if Your Excellency could see your way to doing something for Mr. Saksena, and I think this would also be the view of Lord Hailey.[14]

Yours sincerely,
HARRY HAIG

75

HAIG TO LINLITHGOW
R/3/1/74

Secret
No. U.P.-191

Camp,
November 8th, 1938

My dear Lord Linlithgow,

I am sending my usual fortnightly report, and enclose the official report. I was very glad to get Your Excellency's secret letter of November 1st, 1938, and to know that the general impression you receive on return is encouraging. I wrote last on October 23rd from Lucknow. On October 29th I started on a short tour, spending three days in Agra, three days in Jhansi and two days in Etawah, a fairly typical district not of the first importance in the Allahabad division. I reached Lucknow again on the night of the 6th November. The tour has been useful and has made me realise to what a considerable extent conditions differ in different parts of the Province. As I said in my last letter, I got on the whole a satisfactory picture of conditions in the Bareilly division. I found the Agra division, or at any rate the Commissioner,[15] a good deal more gloomy. One has to make allowance for the fact that the hot weather in Agra has been peculiarly trying, and that on top of other difficulties they are faced with the possibility of scarcity conditions in some of the districts unless the winter rains are good. But, as always, the question whether the administration is hopeful or the reverse, tranquil or worried, depends usually on whether it is subjected to the activities of a very small number of troublesome Congress workers. In the Agra division the Aligarh district suffers from one exceedingly bad and unscrupulous man. The Agra district too has its troubles arising from one or two difficult persons, and also to some extent Muttra. But the other two districts of Etah and Mainpuri, where there are no Congressmen who are out to make trouble, seem to be carrying on under quite normal conditions. In the Jhansi division it is much the same. There the majority of the districts have settled down to reasonably tranquil conditions; but the Lalitpur sub-division still remains an acute storm centre, though the storm is less violent than it was two or three months ago. The trouble there has been deliberately stirred up by certain Congress workers utilising the genuine and serious grievances of a simple, ignorant, and very poor population. The Premier has interested himself in the problem of Lalitpur a good deal, and though the local officers feel that the action of the Government has been weak and that the cultivators have been allowed to go too far in asserting their claims by show of force, the Premier has succeeded in having the principal firebrand removed from the Lalitpur sub-division and his departure has produced at any rate a welcome lull in agitation. There are a number of difficult controversies in Lalitpur, arising out of the relations between landlords and tenants, and the Commissioner[16] is going to Lucknow in the course of the next fortnight to talk them over with the Premier and try to reach conclusions, in which I shall interest myself.

2. In Agra I was met with a general view, not only from officials, that the left wing influence in the Congress is growing, and that eventually it is sure to overpower the right wing. In Jhansi there are certain troublesome left wing people, but on the whole the impression seemed to be that the right wing were in control, if they only chose to assert themselves, and in some districts left wing influence was negligible. At Etawah I found on the whole a peaceful and friendly atmosphere. I came into touch myself with some of the leading Congressmen whom I found exceedingly friendly and very anxious to do what they can to improve conditions in the district. It is doubtless due to this that the district is reported to be quiet, there is no interference with the administration and the police are carrying on their work without difficulty.

3. With regard to the police, it was again in the Agra division that gloomy views were expressed and that in some districts there was a feeling of uneasiness in the police and doubt whether they could depend on their own officers to protect their interests. As usual, these ideas can nearly always be traced to particular incidents, almost invariably connected with the activities of the Anti-Corruption officer. The incidents are few, but they produce a widespread impression. I propose to discuss these matters now that I am back in Lucknow with the Premier as soon as I get an opportunity. Where, as in many districts, there have been no cases in which any policeman could regard himself as having been unjustly treated and

the Anti-Corruption department has not been called in, my impression is that things are settling down not unsatisfactorily.

4. I have observed on my tours some rather interesting differences in the attitude of people towards rural development in different districts. I wrote recently to Brabourne, just before Your Excellency returned, my general impressions of our rural development movement. It might interest you to have a little detail based on recent personal experience. When I was in Bareilly, I had arranged to visit a rural development village. I found on arrival a great concourse of officials who had organised something in the nature of a minor exhibition of the various rural development activities in the district, the village itself and its own affairs being rather pushed into the background. What struck me at once was that the non-official chairman of the district rural development association was not there. I enquired whether he had been informed that I was coming and was told that this had been done; but evidently he had not been in any way pressed to present himself. I considered it to be quite wrong that he should not have been present, and said so. But I believe he is a town man and probably takes little practical interest in the work. At Agra, which is the home town of Mr. Paliwal who was in charge of the whole rural development organisation when it was being used for politics and not for rural development, there is an atmosphere of considerable distrust on the part of the officials, and the work has clearly been allowed to relapse to a great extent. I did what I could to encourage officials to take it up again in earnest, now that the Government really want them to take a hand. When I visited a Government experimental farm near Agra, I found the Chairman of the District Rural Development Association present, and he had taken a good deal of trouble to bring in workers from a number of neighbouring villages to meet me. He seemed keen and practical and anxious to get the support of the officials. In Etawah I found the atmosphere most friendly. I had arranged to see a class where a number of organisers are undergoing an intensive three-months' training, this being part of a scheme to put all the organisers in the Province through this practical course. The chairman of the rural development association who is also the President of the District Congress Committee, was most oncoming. He takes a real interest in rural development and begged me to come out next morning to see one of his rural development villages. There had been some correspondence about my going out to this village, but it had seemed that I could not find time for it. He told me that the villagers would be most disappointed and I consequently arranged to pay a visit the next morning. I found that encouraging work was being done at this village and that the villagers

appeared to be greatly interested. It is true that the village was strongly Congress, but the reception to me was most cordial.

5. On the whole communal relations in the areas I have been visiting are much less strained than they are in the Rohilkhand division. Even in the Agra division the situation does not seem to be acute, though there are always possibilities of trouble in Aligarh; while in the Jhansi division and in Etawah the problem does not seem to be regarded at the moment as one of any very serious difficulty. A sensible Muslim League leader whom I saw in Etawah said that undoubtedly there was a general impression that the Hindus were ruling the country, and that this tended to make the Hindus somewhat intolerant and the Muslims somewhat resentful. But he gave me to understand that the local Leaders on both sides took considerable pains to restrain feelings and were very anxious to prevent any outbreak of disorder.

6. Before I left Lucknow there were some very interesting developments about the Tenancy Bill. As I mentioned in my last letter, the Oudh Taluqdars had decided to meet on the 27th October to reach their conclusions on the question of submitting the matter to the arbitration of the Parliamentary Sub-Committee of Congress. On the evening of the 26th I happened to be giving a rather large party at which several of the Taluqdars were present. I heard at the party that on that day there had been a preliminary meeting of the most important Taluqdars and it had been decided that they would definitely reject the idea of arbitration. Some of them were clearly uneasy about this decision, and I was asked whether I would send for the Raja of Jahangirabad the next morning before the decisive meeting of the Taluqdars took place. I said I should be very glad to see the Raja at any time, but that if he wanted to see me he had better send word. He did in fact send word and I saw him the next morning at 9-30. The meeting was to have taken place at 10, but he postponed it till 11, and we had a very interesting talk for an hour. He told me that opinion against arbitration was decisive. At the same time he himself and many others did not feel at all happy at the prospect of having to fight out these issues to the end. I went over the old arguments with him in favour of reaching a settlement and he agreed once more that they were perfectly sound. In the course of the conversation he told me that some of the Taluqdars were still hoping for intervention by the British Government. I had told him before on more than one occasion that I considered nothing was to be hoped for in this direction, but on this occasion I felt it desirable to speak to him very plainly. I told him quite definitely that in my opinion there was no possibility of the Governor, the Governor-General or the Secretary of State intervening in connection with

this Tenancy Bill to save the Taluqdars from making sacrifices which after all were not very unreasonable. I felt it was desirable to talk quite plainly, because many of these are men who are so anxious to believe that some miracle may save them that they snatch at any chance word of politeness that may be used by anyone in authority and construct on it a complete edifice of illusion. I then said that while I quite recognised that in view of the temper of the Taluqdars it was not possible to pursue the question of arbitration, it seemed to me of the utmost importance that they should in their resolution express themselves as anxious to negotiate further with the Ministry. I found the Raja quite in agreement with this view, and he showed me various drafts which they had under consideration. I suggested that they should make their draft as non-contentious as possible and that they should express their readiness to negotiate with the Ministry with a view to an immediate and final settlement of these issues. I stressed the two words "immediate" and "final", because I knew that the Ministry considered that the landlords had been putting off a decision again and again in an unreasonable way and that they always shied off reaching any firm conclusion. Jahangirabad accepted this, and these words were actually included in their resolution, a copy of which I enclose. Jahangirabad also asked me whether I thought it was advisable for them to say anything about including in the negotiations the question of the enhanced land revenue or agricultural income-tax, in one of which ways the Government propose to get further money from the landlords. I said I thought it was most desirable to include a reference to this, and that it was indeed essential that their discussions should lead to a settlement on these points. I urged them, however, not to widen too much the scope of the discussion but to confine it, if possible, to a few specific issues.

7. On the 28th October after the resolution had been published, I thought it desirable to see the Premier and he arranged to come in the evening. I had a remarkably frank and friendly talk with him on this occasion. I was not sure whether he would be anxious to disclose to me his views frankly on account of the political considerations and tactics involved; but he said he was very glad to put me in possession of his mind. He made it clear that in the light of the Taluqdars' resolution he saw no possibility of the Parliamentary Sub-Committee being prepared to take any action. He said that they were not anxious to participate and that they would only come in if they were satisfied that both parties trusted them and were prepared to accept their decision which would be given in a strictly judicial spirit. I then said that I still hoped strongly that the Ministry would meet the landlords and make a final effort to reach an agreement before the matter

came on again in the Assembly on the 10th November. I said that I had done what I could to impress on the landlords the importance of their reaching an agreement on this measure, and he said he was well aware of this. He himself was clearly ready to reach agreed conclusions if it were possible; but he said he was afraid that the landlords had no one who could really speak for them or would have the courage to reach definite conclusions. I said I quite appreciated the difficulty and that I was not myself sanguine that further conversations would result in a settlement. But the importance of a settlement seemed to me so great that I felt no chance should be omitted, and I urged him to agree to enter into final negotiations provided there were no question of further postponing the date for consideration of the Tenancy Bill, namely, November 10th. He then said that he had been discussing the matter with the other Ministers and that they had practically reached the conclusion that they would have nothing further to do with the landlords and would go straight ahead with their proposals; but in deference to what I said he was prepared to make another attempt. We left the matter at this, and it was my intention the next day before I started on tour to see Jahangirabad and Chhatari and urge them strongly to take the opportunity of final negotiations with the Ministry. After dinner, however, that same evening the Premier rang up and asked whether he could see me again. He came round and told me that on return he found that Jahangirabad and Chhatari had already approached the Revenue Minister and asked for an opportunity of further negotiations with the Ministers, and had suggested the possibility of referring to the Parliamentary Sub-Committee any matters that might remain unsettled. In the circumstances the Premier suggested that it might be better if I did not see Jahangirabad and Chhatari and if they were left to themselves. I accepted this view and did not see them.

8. On the whole I think it has been not a disadvantage that I was away from Lucknow for the last week, as this was a situation which it was better should work itself out. It did not seem to be working itself out very favourably, and on the 2nd November I sent a note to my Secretary, who had been in Lucknow all the time, and asked him to show it to Jahangirabad and Chhatari. I enclose a copy of the note. They expressed themselves grateful for the note and entirely in agreement with it; but they seemed to be doubtful whether it would in fact be possible to bring the landlords to the point of authorising anyone to take decisions for them. The Taluqdars are, I fear, much disunited. Indeed, a cynic might say that they are never united except when they are wrong.

9. Discussions between the Ministers and the landlords started on the

evening of the 7th. I asked the Premier this morning what progress was being made. He said that the discussions were friendly and he seemed to think that agreement was not impossible. He was apparently making clear how far he could go and what points he could not consider. I was glad to find that on the question of enhanced taxation real progress seemed to have been made. The landlords had definitely expressed a view that the present principles and limits of land revenue assessment should be left virtually unchanged and were prepared on that understanding to accept an agricultural income-tax. This is a plan which the Premier himself prefers, though the Government proposals prepared last cold weather had proceeded on the basis of assessing the more wealthy landlords to a higher rate of land revenue. It has been generally realised that one serious objection to such a scheme is that the capital value of land would differ in accordance with the prosperity of the owner, and that the land of the wealthy landowner which would be subject to a high rate of land revenue would have a smaller market value than the land of the smaller landowner. This is obviously an unreasonable and inconvenient position. The Premier seemed to think that on this point and even on the question of the general rate of agricultural income-tax an agreement was likely to be reached.

10. I received on the 25th October a deputation from the Oudh Bar Association who wished to protest against the proposal that the Chief Court should be deprived of its original jurisdiction. They had already laid their views before the Premier and the Judicial Minister, but I thought it not unreasonable that I should receive their deputation in view of the fact that the matter concerned the jurisdiction of a High Court. I did not wish to appear to be uninterested in such a matter. The arguments which they advanced seemed to me to be deserving of careful consideration. I said that they would no doubt recognise that the constitutional responsibility for policy in this matter lies with my Ministers, but that I would discuss the matter fully with the Ministers in the light of this representation. I am not sure whether the Government intend to go on at once with their proposals. They had reached their conclusions, I think a little hastily, and actually before they had asked the Chief Court for their views. This omission has now been remedied, and the views of the Chief Court are awaited.

11. Another matter affecting a High Court has come up recently. There was a sensational incident in Cawnpore. The daughter of a well-known Hindu Vakil eloped with the son of a prominent Muslim merchant, and apparently the girl embraced Islam and was duly married to the boy. A charge of abduction was brought against the boy. After some weeks the

girl was discovered and pending the trial of the criminal case, her father made a claim to custody of the girl under the civil law. The High Court were moved to intervene and transferred the civil proceedings to themselves. Meanwhile, the girl and her father disappeared and have not yet been found. The whole matter has given rise to acute communal feeling both in Cawnpore and also in Allahabad, and allegations were made against the impartiality of one of the Muslim Judges of the High Court. An application was made to the Provincial Government to transfer the case to another High Court under the amended form of Section 527 of the Criminal Procedure Code. The grounds advanced were that there was danger of a breach of peace owing to acute communal feeling, and that on the same ground they could not expect a fair hearing in the Province. The Minister for Justice, Dr. Katju, who is perhaps naturally inclined to accept the Hindu version has taken a perfectly proper line. He asked the High Court for their comments and enquired from the District Magistrates of Cawnpore and Allahabad[17] whether they anticipated any difficulty in maintaining order if the case continued as at present. Armed with the replies of these various authorities which were on the lines to be expected he has rejected the application for transfer. I had discussed the matter with him at an early stage and made it clear that I wished to see the case before any orders were passed. But when it came up to me the opinions expressed and the conclusions reached were in my judgment entirely correct. The case has drawn attention to the peculiar form which the law has now assumed. Had we wished to transfer the case, we should have had to obtain the approval of another Provincial Government to its being sent to their High Court. If it were being transferred on communal grounds another Province might be very reluctant to take it over. I cannot feel that the provision as it stands at present is very satisfactory or practical. I recognise the objections to this power being exercised by the Federal Government, but I should have thought it was preferable to place it in the hands of the Governor-General. On the other hand, if it is felt that this power is in effect one which should practically never be used, then the present provision is well enough adapted to policy.

12. While I was at Agra I received a letter from the Maharaj Rana of Dholpur asking me to come over and see him if I could possibly manage a visit. As he is an old friend, I went over to tea one afternoon. I found him as firmly opposed to Federation as ever and exceedingly pessimistic about conditions in general, including the affairs of British India. I tried to convince him that so far as this Province is concerned prospects were not nearly so gloomy as he seemed to think. He gave me to understand that he

expected there would be strong opposition among the States to Federation, but I expect the wish is father to the thought.

13. With reference to paragraph 7 of your letter of 1st November,[18] I asked Pant this morning whether there was any likelihood of his going to Delhi for the Marketing Conference. He told me he could not get away, but that he hoped to be going later possibly in connection with some conference of Finance Ministers. I should very much like Your Excellency to meet him. I think you would find him an interesting and rather attractive personality. I am sure these conferences at the Centre are of value in many ways.[19]

Yours sincerely,
HARRY HAIG

ENCLOSURE 1 TO NO. 75

CUTTING FROM THE *HINDUSTAN TIMES*,
DATED OCTOBER 29TH, 1938

The following resolution was passed at a meeting of the Taluqdars held at Lucknow on October 27th, 1938, under the Presidentship of the Raja of Jehangirabad:

"This meeting of the landlords of Oudh is of the opinion that it is desirable that the entire land question, including matters relating to land revenue and other matters affecting land, should not be dealt with piecemeal but at one and the same time and this meeting would welcome an agreement on the entire question so that the landlords and Taluqdars may have a complete picture of the future before them.

"This conference, however, feels that a permanent and satisfactory solution of such diverse and important problems, upon the proper solution of which the peace and prosperity of the Provinces depends, can only be achieved by goodwill and mutual agreement. The imposition of any decision arrived at without the concurrence of those vitally affected by it is not likely to establish that healthy atmosphere which is essential for a peaceful solution of the problem.

"In case the Congress Parliamentary Sub-Committee is willing to settle all outstanding agrarian problems by negotiation and mutual agreement, the landlords of Oudh would be glad to meet them with a view to an immediate and final settlement of the points at issue and will leave no avenue unexplored for the purpose."

ENCLOSURE 2 TO NO. 75

HAIG TO DONALDSON
Note

November 2nd, 1938

The position as I see it is as follows. The problem is to reach a final and authoritative conclusion before the Assembly meets on November 10th. This can be done either by a decision taken by an outside authority, or by agreement between the Ministry and the landlords.

2. The first alternative really means arbitration. The Taluqdars have rejected this; but still suggest in the end "representing" their case to the Parliamentary Sub-Committee. The question is what would happen after such representation? Would the conclusions of the Parliamentary Sub-Committee be accepted automatically by the Taluqdars or not?

3. The position of the Parliamentary Sub-Committee, as I understand it after my conversation with the Hon'ble Premier, is that they are only prepared to intervene in the role of arbitrators and not as mediators. If both sides trust them sufficiently to be prepared to accept their decision, they will give a decision. If not, they will have nothing to do with the matter.

4. If that is the correct appreciation of the position of the Parliamentary Sub-Committee (and from their point of view it is perfectly reasonable) then I see no possibility of a solution by means of the Parliamentary Sub-Committee. The Taluqdars would only go so far at the most as to say that they would consider the conclusions of the Parliamentary Sub-Committee, and I do not think this could satisfy the Sub-Committee. I therefore assume that no solution can be found on these lines.

5. The alternative is agreement between Government and the landlords. As a result of my conversation with the Hon'ble Premier I believe that the Ministry would be prepared to meet the landlords of Agra and Oudh together in a final effort to reach a decision. This agrees with what you report in your note.[20] I am myself strongly in favour of this, though I realise that the chances of an agreement being reached are not good; but even so an attempt should be made.

6. What I had intended to say to the Raja of Jahangirabad and to the Nawab of Chhatari had I seen them was:

(*a*) That in my judgment it was a matter of crucial importance for the landlords to reach a settlement on this Bill and also on the land revenue question.

(*b*) That time is short and they must be prepared to take definite decisions.

(*c*) That the only practical way in which the matter can now be handled is for the landlords to select a very small number of their body, not exceeding at the outside three representatives of Agra and three representatives of Oudh (and less if possible); that they should give them full authority to conclude a settlement and that they must have the courage to reach decisions.

7. The Hon'ble Premier is doubtful whether the landlords will be in a position to reach conclusions, and that is really the crux of the matter.

8. I think the landlords inevitably will get less out of the Ministry than they would have got from the Parliamentary Sub-Committee. That cannot be helped, but the fact should be recognised. The Ministry are clearly not in a position to give away much on the Tenancy Bill, but they might reach a reasonable solution on the land revenue issue, and the landlords should reach their conclusions immediately about this and try and get the consent of the Ministry to proposals on lines which would be agreeable to them.

9. My advice would be that they should confine negotiations strictly to the minimum of points, which would probably include only the outstanding issues on the Tenancy Bill, which were to have been referred to arbitration, and the question of the demand that is to be made on the landlords either in the shape of a higher rate of land revenue, or the imposition of agricultural income-tax and the amount of that demand, i.e. the rates to be settled. If the discussion is widened beyond certain quite specific points, no conclusions will be reached, and it may be taken as certain that the Ministry will not hold their hand beyond the 10th November, but will have to proceed then with the Tenancy Bill.

76

HAIG TO LINLITHGOW
R/3/1/74

Private and Personal *November 9th, 1938*
No. U.P.-192

My dear Lord Linlithgow,

I hear that my Ministers propose to take up formally and at once the question of abolishing the posts of Commissioners. I do not yet know how far their recommendations would go, whether, for instance, they would merely revive the proposal which was sent up by the Provincial Government in the time of Lord Hailey for reducing the number of Commissionerships from ten to five, or whether they would propose on principle to abolish Commissioners altogether. I understand that they are likely to argue the case on broad grounds of administrative principle, favouring a system of centralisation and expanding the Secretariat, and abandoning the old principle of trying to co-ordinate policy locally on which our present system rests.

2. As I shall clearly have to give my own views on these proposals when they come up, I should be very grateful if my knowledge of the discussions on the subject could be brought up to date. I am well enough acquainted with the general trend of arguments up to the time I left the Home Department in 1934, but since then I think some reduction has been made in Commissioners in the Central Provinces, and I see that one out of the two Commissioners in Assam has just been abolished, and it is stated in the Press that the abolition of the second will come under consideration.[21]

Yours sincerely,
H.G. HAIG

77

HAIG TO LINLITHGOW
R/3/1/74

Secret *November 16th, 1938*
No. U.P.-196

My dear Lord Linlithgow,

I am greatly obliged for Your Excellency's secret letter, dated November 12th, 1938, regarding the possibility of a cut in the pay of the services.[22] I quite appreciate the position and am grateful to you for putting me in possession of what can be said at this somewhat indefinite stage. Your letter reached me very opportunely, for yesterday evening we discussed in Cabinet two important proposals regarding the pay of the services. I should in any case have been reporting them for Your Excellency's information, but they also raise certain important questions of policy regarding which I should like your advice.

2. The first is a complete scheme for reduced scales of pay for new entrants to our Provincial Services, class I and II, and other comparable posts. New reduced scales of pay for future entrants were introduced from

July 4th, 1931, and the scales of pay of the Provincial Services were at that time reduced by amounts generally ranging between 25 and 33 per cent of the rates of pay then in force. The scales now proposed, which are to be made applicable to persons entering Government service on or after July 1st, 1938 (a preliminary warning having already been issued that those appointed after that date will be put on the new scales of pay) involve further substantial reductions. Broadly speaking, the Provincial Services, class II, will be on a time-scale from Rs. 200 to Rs. 500, which in the case of the Provincial Civil Service, executive and judicial, will rise to Rs. 600, and in the case of the Police to Rs. 550. Class I services will be roughly on the scale of Rs. 500 to Rs. 750, selection posts from Rs. 900 to Rs. 1,100, and the highest pay fixed for the head of a department is Rs. 1,200. These rates are of course on our present ideas distinctly low, but the Ministers regard them as sufficiently liberal. Their general view really is that too high a standard of living has been set for the services in the past, and that the scales now proposed, though low in comparison with recent ideas, are quite adequate for a country whose general standards of living and resources are as low as they are in this Province. The general scales, I understand, are pretty close to those already accepted in Madras and proposed in other Congress Provinces, and as this is clearly a matter that the Ministers can decide for themselves, I have, after the usual expressions of caution, not opposed the introduction of these scales which were approved at the Cabinet meeting last night.

3. There is one point, however, which I have reserved for further consideration. When reduced scales of pay were introduced in 1931, they were not made applicable when an officer was promoted to a higher post borne on the same cadre to which he belonged and which was deemed to be reserved for him. The Ministers while agreeing that the new scales of pay in general should only apply to new entrants are not prepared to agree that this particular rule should be continued. Their proposal is that when an officer is promoted to a selection post which might be regarded as belonging to the cadre of his own service, he should only draw the new reduced scales of pay in such a post. It is said that this follows the rules made by the Madras Government nearly a year ago. The arguments brought forward by the Ministers are that it is important to do what can reasonably be done about expediting the realisation of the economies arising from the new scales of pay, and that the disparity between the new and the old scales is so considerable that on administrative grounds it is desirable to reduce it as rapidly as possible. They also argued that up to about the year 1919 the scales of pay were very much lower than they became afterwards,

and that therefore officers who entered the services about that time had nothing like the expectation of promotion that they have since secured. They went further and said that their own policy, if they could have a free hand would have been definitely to cut down the scales of pay for the existing officers, but they realised obviously that that would provoke opposition from me, and they were therefore content to leave the regular time-scales for those already in service untouched.

4. The exact effect of these proposals on the various services will have to be examined by me in some detail before I can appreciate precisely what is involved. But the question will arise whether, if I think that it will affect a number of existing officers seriously, I should press my opposition to the point of refusing to agree to the proposals of my Ministers, or whether I should be prepared to acquiesce. In this connection it seems to me a point of considerable importance that this principle has already been accepted and introduced in Madras, and I should be grateful if Your Excellency could let me have any information that may be in your possession about this, as well as your advice as to my general attitude. My own feeling at present is that it would perhaps not be wise to refuse to accept the advice of my Ministers on this point.[23]

5. The second question is that of the reduction of special pays and compensatory allowances. This is a matter that has been under consideration for a very long time, and it involves an immense amount of detailed scrutiny. Proposals have now been prepared by the Chief Secretary and Finance Secretary,[24] and with certain modifications approved by the Premier as Finance Minister. These special pays and compensatory allowances had already been scrutinised in 1932 and 1936 and reductions made. The present proposals would give an annual saving in special pay of approximately 1,05,000 out of a total of 7,75,000, and in compensatory allowances of 1,26,000 out of a total of 12,17,000. These results are not in themselves very startling, but of course will affect a large number of individual officers.

6. The Premier explained at the Cabinet meeting that he himself was on principle definitely opposed to giving special pay at all. He felt that, with the present system of remuneration whereby all the members of a service were guaranteed reasonable rates of pay on the time-scale, they ought to take the rough with the smooth, and as they do not get reduced pay when they happen to be filling comparatively easy posts, so they should not get increased pay when they happen to be filling more exacting ones. But though this is his general outlook, he is prepared to a large extent to accept

things as they are and merely to adjust the system, instead of proposing its complete abolition.

7. The Premier further stressed the point that, when they came into office, one of the principal items of their programme was to reduce the cost of the administration which, according to them, was unduly high. Though they were able to make proposals for reduced cost in the future by the new scales of pay now contemplated, very little impression had been made on the actual cost of the administration, and they were particularly anxious to be able to show their followers that they were doing something in this direction even though it might not be very substantial. From this point of view they did attach very special importance to carrying through these reductions in special pay, but they were quite prepared to handle the question in a moderate way. He further developed the argument that reductions of this kind might do something to mitigate the intensity of the feeling regarding the unreasonably high scales of pay of the all-India services. He said that this was going to be in the future a very serious problem. I said that these reductions in special pay would not go far to reduce the gap between the all-India Services and the Provincial Services, and indeed as special pay was being cut down for all services, it was not likely to have any appreciable effect in this direction. On the contrary, as they were intending to introduce still lower rates of pay for the Provincial Services, the disparity would become more marked. He admitted this, but said that the mere fact that something was being done to reduce the remuneration of the all-India Services would have a definite psychological value. Later in the discussion it evidently occurred to him that this line of argument might suggest to my mind, as in fact it had, that they had no intention of trying to reduce the pay of existing members of the service. He therefore said he hoped that I should not assume that they had no such intention. They might in fact wish to propose, quite apart from the schemes at present under consideration, a reduction in the rates of pay of existing Government servants. Finally, he said that it was exceedingly difficult to justify the retention of these additions to pay for the higher paid services when inferior and menial servants were employed on most insufficient rates of pay. He said that they felt very strongly about this, and that there was no doubt the rates of pay of inferior servants ought to be increased substantially in order to give them a living wage.

8. The proposals for reducing special pay for the all-India Services will have to go to the Secretary of State, and the proposals for the Provincial Services bring in my individual judgment. I understand from Thorne's

official letter No. 36-2-G.-II/37, dated September 14th, 1938, and the letter from the Auditor-General to the Secretary to the Government of Central Provinces and Berar, Finance Department, dated July 22nd, 1938, which was enclosed, that an order for the abolition or reduction of special rates of pay of members of the Provincial Subordinate Services appointed before April 1st, 1937, will also be a matter for my individual judgment. I have made these points clear to my Ministers and said that I would have to take some time to consider the position and to look into these very numerous and detailed proposals. I shall endeavour to follow the general principles reproduced in Thorne's letter of 14th September 1938. But broadly speaking I shall be faced with the problem whether I am to accept the general position of the Ministry, that considerable reductions should be made in special pay and compensatory allowances up to the limit of what might be considered reasonable, or whether I should adopt a rigid attitude and refuse to agree to any proposals for which there was not a perfectly convincing case. My own inclination very strongly is to adopt the former line, in which case I should probably agree to nearly all the proposals put forward. They have not, so far as I can judge, been framed in an unreasonable spirit, granted the fundamental position that there should be substantial reduction in the cost of the special pays, and that the whole principle of special pay should be viewed a good deal more strictly than it has been in the past. I think, in view of the correspondence that has passed between us, that Your Excellency will be in agreement with this general outlook. This attitude would have been strengthened if it were possible to assume that I could stand fast on the question of the substantive pay of existing members of the services. This however is a point on which, in the light of Your Excellency's letter of November 12th, 1938, I cannot feel very confident. It is I think beyond question that if the Government of India make a cut in the pay of their own services it would be impossible for the Governor to resist similar proposals made by his Ministers. It may no doubt be the case that the financial necessity of the Government of India might be represented as more urgent than that of the Provincial Government. But apart from the fact that we could always make out a strong case for the necessity of securing additional funds by means of retrenchment (e.g. proposals to raise the pay of the lower paid servants) there is the broad, general consideration that if the Government of India under official control adopts the policy of making a cut in the pay of its own servants, it is not politically reasonable to prevent a provincial Ministry doing the same thing, when this is in fact one of the important points of their policy and one which they have been severely criticised for not bringing into effect. I am sure that Your Excellency will agree that the decision of your Government on a cut in pay will not be a decision merely for the Government of India, but will in effect be a decision for the Provincial Governments as well.

9. So far as this Province is concerned, I should be very sorry to see that decision taken. I think myself we should stand firm on our present position of maintaining the existing scales of pay for those now in service. On the other hand I think the comparatively small concessions contained in these proposals about special pay might reasonably be made, and would help to lessen the pressure to which the Ministry are undoubtedly subjected in the direction of reducing the pay of the services. I would therefore propose, subject to Your Excellency's advice, to go into these questions of special pay with the general idea of accepting all those which do not seem to me to be manifestly unreasonable. I think this attitude might be adopted whatever may be the outcome of the proposals regarding a cut in pay. I have to reach decisions on this question of special pay without unreasonable delay, and I do not think I could let them hang over until the question of a cut in pay is likely to be settled. If there is to be no cut in pay, the reduction of special pay, as I have said, will ease the position. If there is to be a cut in pay, the small additional burden represented by the cut in special pay will not be of very great significance compared to the general cut in pay, and will not add appreciably to the discontent that would be caused by the cut in pay.[25]

Yours sincerely,
HARRY HAIG

78

HAIG TO LINLITHGOW
R/3/1/74

Secret
No. U.P.-198

November 22nd, 1938

My dear Lord Linlithgow,

I enclose as usual the official fortnightly report. These reports tend to be rather meagre and while I readily accept the suggestion made in paragraph 10 of your letter of 15th November, that I should comment on the information they contain, wherever comment is of value, I fear in many cases there is not much that deserves comment. The fact is that from the beginning Pant has shown a definite inclination both to omit the statement of inconvenient facts and to cut out from the draft any comments which are not in accordance with the impression he wishes to create on the public. In any case the Province has during the fortnight under report been quiet, and the administration has been proceeding with little incident. The future however may not be so tranquil, and I deal with certain important aspects below.

2. The official report is quite right in saying that the topic of absorbing interest at the moment is the future of the Tenancy Bill. In my letter of 8th November I brought my account of the negotiations up to the evening of the 7th, and I reported an attitude on the part of the Premier which seemed both friendly and reasonably hopeful. Nevertheless, when the discussions on the Bill were due to start in the Assembly on the 10th November no settlement had been reached. I was still hoping that conversations would continue, and that possibly before matters had proceeded far in the Assembly, a settlement would be made. The zamindars held a meeting at Bara Banki on the 13th November, which had been arranged before, and it passed the usual strong resolutions; but I did not think any particular significance attached to these. On the 16th November, however, the Premier made a speech in the Assembly which appears to have been both uncompromising and threatening. I enclose the version of the speech given by the *Pioneer.* The speech was actually delivered in Hindustani, and the *National Herald*, which is the Congress paper in Lucknow, gives a milder version. But I fancy the *Pioneer* account is nearer the truth, and indeed Jehangirabad assured me that the speech was much stronger even than appeared in the *Pioneer* report.[26] In particular the Premier threatened that deficiencies in the Bill would be removed, meaning that left wing amendments would be introduced and carried. I confess I was surprised and disappointed at this development. On the 17th November I happened to have important conversations with some of the landlords. My first visitor was Nawab Sir Muhammad Yusuf. He had been taking a prominent part in the meeting at Bara Banki and I had always looked upon him as definitely opposed to any compromise. I was consequently surprised when he assured me that there was every expectation that the landlords would in fact ask for the intervention of the Parliamentary Sub-Committee, and that he was convinced that this was a wise course. He said that the speeches and resolutions were merely a demonstration, but that the main body of the landlords realised the importance of reaching a settlement and not carrying on a struggle, the result of which would be likely to be their virtual destruction. He looked forward to the time when the Congress right wing

will need the help of the landlords and will be prepared for ask for it. But in the meantime it was essential that the landlords should, as far as possible, keep their existence as a separate body and their organisation intact and vigorous.

3. My next visitor was the Raja of Jehangirabad. I have never seen him so moved. He had been deeply affected by the Premier's speech in the Assembly the day before. He declared that apart from the attacks on the landlords and the threats to make the Bill worse, the Premier had reproached the Taluqdars for their past attitude of loyalty to the British, and had made it clear that they were being punished for having sided with the British. He said that the Premier had now thrown off the mask, and revealed his real feelings. He might speak in a moderate way to me, but his true desire was to destroy the landlord class. I argued with him that the course of action hitherto followed by the Premier as well as the whole trend of his conversations with me did not support this view. He said, however, that the Premier's attitude in the conversations before November 10th had created on the minds of the landlords the impression that he did not really want a compromise, and he said that actually on that morning the Premier had admitted to the Nawab of Chhatari that this was correct. At the end of our interview the Raja told me that the landlords had been considering the question of approaching the Parliamentary Sub-Committee, but that in view of this new attitude of the Premier he felt that such a course might be not only humiliating but useless. He asked my advice. I said that this was an important matter which I should like time to consider, and I suggested that Chhatari and Jehangirabad should come to me in the evening if they wished to discuss the matter further.

4. In the evening Chhatari and Jehangirabad did come to me and explained the position. Chhatari was much less perturbed about the attitude of the Premier than was Jehangirabad, who was still much upset. Chhatari had on the 16th been in communication with Bhulabhai Desai and had asked whether, if the landlords passed a satisfactory resolution, the Parliamentary Sub-Committee would be likely to agree to intervene. Desai appears to have said that the matter was out of his hands and that it depended on the attitude of the Parliamentary Sub-Committee. On the morning of the 17th Chhatari had rung up Patel at Wardha and had put the same question to him. Patel had given a non-committal answer, saying that he would have to consult his colleagues. But he finally said that it was necessary to know what was the attitude of the Premier to these ideas. There at the moment the matter rested.

5. Chhatari while agreeing that the Premier was in a very un-

accommodating mood, so far as concerned direct negotiations between the landlords and the Ministry, and that in fact in the conversations preceding the 10th November he had not been prepared to make any concession, said he was convinced that the Premier was still favourable to the idea of intervention by the Parliamentary Sub-Committee and would welcome it. The position presumably on this reading of it is that the Premier feels that in view of left wing influence in the Province he can make no further concessions to the landlords. He does not really wish for a fight, and would be glad to have a settlement reached through the intervention of the Parliamentary Sub-Committee who would be in a position to defy the left wing in the Province. We discussed the situation at some length. Both Chhatari and Jehangirabad were clearly of opinion that it was of great importance to reach some settlement. It also seemed clear that if the Bill went on the chances of a settlement at any later stage would be exceedingly remote. In these circumstances they both said that there appeared to them to be no alternative to approaching the Parliamentary Sub-Committee. Such a course was exceedingly distasteful to Jehangirabad, but in the larger interests of the landlords he was prepared reluctantly to swallow his pride. He told me that though the Taluqdars would not be unanimous on such a course, he was confident that there was a considerable majority which would support it. I said in the end that the course they proposed seemed to be the only one now open. They were obviously relieved to get this endorsement of their proposal and they said they would go off at once to see the Premier and ask him whether he would support the idea of a reference to the Parliamentary Sub-Committee. If he agreed, they thought it should be possible to get the matter settled.

6. I understand that when they approached the Premier he seemed to think that it might be very difficult at this stage to bring the Parliamentary Sub-Committee in. The situation had changed owing to the pronouncement of Subhas Chandra Bose,[27] the statement issued by Vallabhbhai Patel,[28] and particularly the return of Jawaharlal Nehru[29] who would have to be consulted and was likely to be opposed to any concessions to the landlords. Pant appears to have agreed to communicate with the Parliamentary Sub-Committee and express his willingness to accept their intervention. But he was evidently not sanguine that anything would come of this, and there has been no further information. I may mention that in the draft of the official fortnightly letter Pant struck out a slightly hopeful reference to this matter in the Chief Secretary's draft and substituted in his own hand, the following:–"There has been considerable delay and one does not know if any such arrangement will be reached."

7. My own reconstruction of the matter is that before the 10th November, Pant had come to the conclusion that he could not afford to antagonise the left wing by making any concessions to the landlords. I think it is possibly true, as several of them have assured me, that the landlords were very anxious to reach a settlement and would have been content with comparatively little. I think the impending return of Jawaharlal Nehru was undoubtedly a factor in the situation. Pant's speech in the Assembly on the 16th November closed the door on negotiations with the Ministry and he has since been considering with some anxiety what are the possibilities of being able to get the Bill through the Upper House. He has always expressed a belief that he might be able to do it, and I am not sure that the landlords are at all confident that they could throw it out. In any case events seem to be leading steadily up to a trial of strength. The only chance of avoiding this now lies with the Parliamentary Sub-Committee. I have little doubt that Pant would welcome this solution just as the majority of the landlords would; but I fear the opportunity has passed and they have reached this position too late. The landlords are still passing bellicose resolutions and had a big meeting last Sunday at Sitapur. In these gatherings the more moderate men like Jehangirabad do not seem to be able to hold their own, but from what he tells me he has undoubtedly a majority on the actual body of Taluqdars. There is no doubt that in the last few months the landlords have strengthened their organisation greatly and extended it to include a considerable number of the petty landlords, who in the aggregate have a good deal of influence. If it comes to a fight, I think their opposition will not be negligible, and as I have said we may be in for seriously disturbed conditions.

8. I am afraid from what you say in paragraph 1 of your letter of the 15th November, that I have created an impression about conditions in the Agra division which I had not intended. I did not myself get any idea that conditions had deteriorated since Hallett's visit in July, or that they were in general particularly disturbing. Indeed, I had meant to suggest that where the administration was encountering difficulties it was usually traceable not so much to general conditions as to the influence of one or two men, and I had myself drawn from this rather reassuring conclusions. Certainly there is no trouble anywhere in the Agra division comparable to the conditions that exist in the Lalitpur sub-division, where though things have improved considerably since last July the administration is faced with a really difficult problem, which requires careful handling. I mentioned in my letter that the Commissioner[30] was coming to Lucknow to discuss Lalitpur affairs with the Premier. On the whole the discussion has been

satisfactory. The Premier has agreed to action being taken under Section 107 and Section 108, Criminal Procedure Code, if necessary, against any speaker who is really stirring up dangerous feeling, and armed with this authority the Commissioner thinks that the temperature is not likely to rise again formidably. But there are a great many difficult points of controversy still unsettled, and it looks as if it may not be possible to get them determined until certain settlement operations which are just starting have been concluded. It is evident, however, that the Premier is fully alive to the situation, and is prepared to take a stronger line than he had agreed to a few months ago.

9. In all these matters one sees the ceaseless pull between the right and the left wing. In your letter of the 15th November Your Excellency said that Pant's difficulties are probably not negligible in dealing with the left wing. I would myself put the case more strongly. I think he is subject to constant and serious embarrassment from his left wing and that he will find this particularly in dealing with the Tenancy Bill in the Assembly. Indeed, if Jawaharlal Nehru throws his weight against him, he may have to make large concessions to the left wing in this matter. I am afraid I get the general impression that the left wing is gaining in strength.

10. I have taken up with the Premier recently a number of features in the administration which seem to me rather disquieting.

(*a*) Recent reports have been mentioning a large number of objectionable speeches. I called the attention of the Premier to these, and in particular asked him to discuss with me certain speeches which had been made by one Batliwala who at one time gave the Madras Government a lot of trouble. I had a general talk recently with the Premier regarding these speeches. His general line was that he himself was watching them also, that in many cases he had called for detailed reports, and that these did not fully bear out the impression given by the summaries in the police reports, but that he realised that if objectionable speeches were having any effect it will be necessary to take some action. Batliwala appears to have been induced to leave Cawnpore where he had been making some particularly bad speeches; but if he returns I hope the Premier can be screwed up to do something about him. Another exceedingly bad speaker is the Bihar Kisan Sabha leader, Swami Sahajanand, who has been making a tour in this Province and outdoing our local orators. He too, however, has now left us. On this subject of speeches it may interest you to see the copy of a letter that has just been issued to all District Magistrates, informing them that speeches delivered at communal meetings and at agrarian meetings should be reported by the police unless they consider reporting to be unnecessary in any particular case. This completely shifts the previous emphasis, and will result in much more extensive reporting of the speeches that are delivered.

(*b*) I had a somewhat disquieting report from our C.I.D. about the renewed activities of revolutionaries. I have asked the Premier to discuss this with me, but we have not yet had time to get down to it.

(*c*) What seems to me the most disquieting feature at the moment is the movement to organise and train large bodies of militant volunteers. I think the simplest thing will be to enclose a copy of a note, dated November 18th, which I have addressed to the Premier. The matter I find had been mentioned in its earlier stages by Hallett in his letters of August 7th and September 6th, but he had not at that time received the detailed C.I.D. reports. It seems to me desirable at this stage definitely to challenge the principle of the movement and endeavour to get my Ministers to realise how dangerous it is. So far as the Congress volunteers are concerned, this is an example of left wing activities which Pant would, I feel, have great difficulty in controlling or opposing. But the very obvious communal danger, if these Congress and Muslim volunteers are to go on drilling and organising, may bring him to take some action. There is something to be said for trying to divert these militant ideas into a system of military training in schools which the Ministry have been anxious for some time to introduce and about which both Hallett and I have been in correspondence with the Commander-in-Chief. But of course there is the danger that the military training in schools will simply be used to strengthen and reinforce the movement outside. If these volunteer forces are allowed to develop unchecked, I fear they may become a formidable menace.

(*d*) So far as the Police are concerned, I have little fresh to say except that I am taking up the whole question of the functions and procedure connected with the Anti-Corruption officer and if I can get the Premier to agree to some considerable modification of these which I have in mind, I feel that one of the main sources of uneasiness in the Police will be removed.

11. One of the nominated members of the Legislative Council, an Indian Christian, died recently, and I am beginning to consider filling the vacancy. At a recent interview the Premier mentioned the matter to me and said he hoped I should make a nomination before the 1st December when a joint session of the two Houses will be held to deal with certain financial bills. I let the topic drop and he did not press me. But a few days later he sent me word by the Chief Secretary that he was greatly interested in this nomination and hoped that he would have an opportunity of discussing the matter with me. From what the Chief Secretary told me, it was clear

that he wants to have a safe vote for the Congress with a view to improving his chances of being able to carry the Tenancy Bill in the Upper House. I have of course no intention of making my nomination on any such consideration. I shall discuss the matter with him when I have cleared my own ideas as to the men who might possibly be nominated, but I shall be careful not to compromise in any way my own position. As a further illustration of the anxiety of the Government about votes in the Upper House, I may mention that not long ago a member whom I had nominated to represent the scheduled castes came to see me and said he was being pressed by the Government Whips to vote for the Government and that they told him that as he had been nominated by the Government he was bound to support them. I told him that of course this was wholly incorrect, that he had been nominated by me and not by the Government, that he had no obligation to Government, and that he was free to give his vote in accordance with his own judgment and conscience.

12. On another point of some constitutional interest I was rather amused to find that in connection with an amendment of the Income-tax Bill in the Central Assembly, Vallabhbhai Patel had sent a telegram to the Premier asking him to telegraph to the Government of India in particular terms on behalf of the Provincial Government supporting the Congress point of view. A telegram on the lines suggested was duly despatched; but no doubt it was fully realised in the Finance Department that this support from the Provincial Governments to this particular amendment is neither spontaneous nor considered.

13. I have written to Your Excellency at some length about the proposals in connection with the scales of pay for new entrants to the services and the reduction of rates of special pay which the Ministry have just put up. All through these discussions, though the matter is hardly raised on the surface, one feels the underlying hostility to the rates of pay fixed for the all-India services. I have often speculated on what Pant's real attitude to the European members of the services is. He recognises fully the value of the work they do. He is glad enough to use good Europeans in the difficult and important districts which he knows they are likely to be able to handle best. But behind all this possibly lies a strong desire to be rid of us, and a readiness to face the consequential loss of efficiency. While he appreciates the work of our best European officers, I think he feels that the average European though he has certain qualities which perhaps the average Indian does not possess, is on the other hand lacking in others which he regards as equally or more important, which the Indian has. Recently while looking through a file about recruitment for the Indian Police, which was discussed

at some length in Hallett's time, I found the following passage in a note recorded by the Premier on the 22nd August 1938: "There is an insistent and urgent demand among all sections of Indian thought today that Indian agency should be substituted as rapidly as possible for European agency in the cases of the I.C.S. and the I.P., and as I observed before this question is likely to form a major issue of Indian politics in the near future." I should judge that that represents a deep conviction of his, and that he is right in thinking that before long the issue may be forced to the front.

14. Colonel Muirhead and Mr. Keeling[31] were staying with me last week, and I think they were able to pick up a fairly good idea of our conditions in the short time available. Muirhead had long talks with Pant and with the Speaker, Purshottam Das Tandon, and was greatly interested. He also spent a long day in Cawnpore and saw something of district life in Fyzabad.[32]

Yours sincerely,
HARRY HAIG

ENCLOSURE 1 TO NO. 78

CUTTING FROM THE *PIONEER*,
DATED NOVEMBER 17TH, 1938

Debate in the United Provinces Legislative Assembly on November 16th, 1938

United Provinces Tenancy Bill

PREMIER'S SPEECH

Pandit Govind Ballabh Pant, the Premier, who spoke next, was the fourth member of the Cabinet to take part in the discussion on the general consideration of the Bill.

He said that the Bill was an important piece of legislation and deserved dispassionate consideration by all members. Several members had put forth criticisms merely to cloud the issues. Some had talked of Imperialism, others on local Self-Government and Independence. Several members had imputed political motives to the Government for bringing out the Bill. The only motive of the Government said the Premier, was to give relief to about five crores of agriculturists of these provinces to help them live like human beings. No one could question that motive. The question that could arise was whether this legislation was the correct way of achieving that objective. If not, then they had to consider how best to improve the Bill to achieve that object.

The Premier recalled an interesting talk which the Finance Minister[33] of this Government's predecessors had with an operator over the telephone. The Finance Minister had put in a trunk call and when he could not get it in time he telephoned the trunk and told the man on duty that he was a non-co-operator. The operator on duty replied: "Sir, I am neither a non-co-operator nor a co-operator. I am a simple operator." (Laughter.) The Premier said this Government was also an operator. The Government were just finding ways and means of improving the lot of the poor agriculturists.

Proceeding the Premier said that both the Socialists and the Opposition members had suggested radical changes in the Bill. Most of the suggestions had no bearing at all on the Bill. What was needed was a certain amount of sacrifice by the zamindars. They had built many public institutions, such as universities and hospitals. They had made big sacrifices. They had with these sacrifices established friendship with people thousands of miles away. (Congress members, "hear, hear".)

Having made those sacrifices surely the zamindars could make a little sacrifice for their countrymen, the agriculturists, who had served them so long. (Congress applause.) "It is not fair that 98 per cent of the agriculturists should remain illiterate while 2 per cent of us should be able to get very high education. Why can't your spirit of sacrifice rise to the occasion?" asked the Premier. He deplored that during the seventeen or eighteen years of their rule in these provinces the zamindars had not given to the agriculturists such paltry rights as to fill the posts of patwaris and constables.

Sir Muhammad Yusuf. "They had not been precluded from getting that training."

The Premier: "I welcome interruptions, but I do not value all interruptions."

Turning to the argument of Nawab of Chhatari that a grant of relief of Rs. 2 per annum to the agriculturists would not help them, the Premier said that when a small salt tax of Rs. 1-4-0 was imposed there was a countrywide agitation against it. The reason was that the agriculturists were so poor that they were not able to bear any taxation. Therefore any relief that could be given to them would go a long way to ease their economic position. "You cannot call yourselves friends of the agriculturists without doing anything for their relief" said the Premier.

Turning to the negotiations that the zamindars had been carrying on among themselves and with the Government to come to a settlement, the Premier said that the Government had not relaxed their efforts to find ways and means of helping the agriculturists despite the speeches made by the zamindars at Unao and Rae Bareli.

"We were not afraid," continued the Premier, "we continued our efforts; if no settlement or a decision was reached by you it was no fault of the Government. You do not want to reach a decision. To come to a decision one must have strength which you people have not got. (Congress "hear, hear".) But we have the strength to come to a decision. This you will see in the proceedings of the next few days. (Congress applause.) This Bill has some deficiencies which will be removed. (Prolonged Congress applause.) This Bill will emerge from the House like pure gold which has been tested by fire. (Congress applause.) I am not stating it as a challenge because we are a Government and we have certain duties towards you also. We are also responsible for you. But for the sake of the country's good we have to bring into operation our principles." (Congress applause.)

Proceeding the Premier said that it was curious that the zamindars should accuse the Government of being dishonest in their efforts to do good to the agriculturists. The zamindar members contended that whatever was being done by the Government for the agriculturists was the result of pressure of the zamindars. If trying to be just to the zamindars was dishonesty then, said the Premier, the Government would show them how to be honest and would see to what extent the zamindar members were prepared to agree to their really honest efforts to ameliorate the lot of the agriculturists. (Prolonged Congress applause.)

Some members of the Opposition had argued that the sub-tenants had been given no concessions. The Premier asked if it was not a fact that when this question came up for consideration certain members of the Opposition had wanted the existing position to continue.

He told Mr. Ishaq Khan that there was no need to quote his (the Premier's) views expressed some years ago. He moved with the times unlike the zamindars and naturally changed his views. His whole complaint was that the zamindars did not move with the times.

As regards the Muslim personal law, the Premier said that as a non-Muslim he did not know whether to speak on this matter, but as he had some difficulties, he asked whether or not the Muslim Taluqdars of the British Indian Association were following the Muslim personal law. To the arguments from the zamindar members on this subject his reply therefore was "Physician, heal thyself".

He asked the Muslim League members whether the Muslim personal law was being followed by the Governments of Sir Sikandar Hyat Khan in the Punjab and Mr. Fazlul Haq in Bengal.

The Premier then hurriedly replied to the arguments advanced by the Opposition members against the provisions of the Tenancy Bill.

He assured Mr. Walford that he would be amazed to see after two years what the United Provinces Government had done for the agriculturists, in comparison to what the other provincial Governments had done.

ENCLOSURE 2 TO NO. 78

GWYNNE TO ALL U.P. DISTRICT MAGISTRATES

Confidential

Police Department, Government,
United Provinces, Lucknow,
November 12th, 1938

I am desired to invite your attention to the correspondence resting with Mr. Panna Lal's endorsement forwarding copy of his demi-official letter No. 4390/VIII-1238 of 15th March 1938 on the subject of reporting of speeches. I am to make it clear that speeches delivered at communal meetings, i.e. meetings organised by communal organisations or addressed by communal leaders, and speeches delivered at agrarian meetings should be reported by the police, unless you consider such reporting to be unnecessary in any particular case. You may, whenever you so desire, depute a magistrate to attend any such meeting. I am to request that these instructions should be carefully noted and carried out.

Yours sincerely,
C.W. GWYNNE

ENCLOSURE 3 TO NO. 78

NOTE BY HAIG SENT TO PANT

November 18th, 1938

My attention has been directed recently by various reports to the organisation and training of large numbers of volunteers in the Province which is at present going on. On making enquiries about this I find that the matter was taken up by Sir Maurice Hallett last August in a note which he addressed to the Hon'ble Premier. At the end of his note he reached the conclusion, which is that which I had already formed for myself before seeing the papers, namely that it was very desirable that the C.I.D. should collect the reports received, give their appreciation of the situation as based on these reports, and in particular say whether these volunteer bodies have been formed and are functioning, or whether they exist merely on paper. I have now seen the reports prepared by the C.I.D. to comply with this note of Sir Maurice Hallett's. There is a report dated 8th September and another dated 12th October.

2. I find the information contained in these reports decidedly disquieting. It seems that apart from certain smaller organisations which may require careful attention, particularly the volunteers of the Youth League which appears to be connected definitely with revolutionary and terrorist ideas, there are two large bodies of volunteers which are now apparently being trained actively. These two bodies are (1) the Congress Volunteer Corps or Army, and (2) The National Guard organised by the Muslim League. With regard to the Congress Volunteer Corps it is said: "However peaceful and legitimate may be the objects of this organisation the reported teachings of certain persons at meetings of volunteers or held for the purpose of encouraging the enlistment of volunteers are likely to have a harmful effect, and a vast body of youths imbued with militant ideas are not likely to remain peaceful for long. Some of the teachings referred to above are that volunteers though now armed with lathis will later be provided with rifles, that the volunteer corps would shortly replace the police who would be disbanded and that they should be prepared to fight." As regards the National Guard it is said: "The formation of the National Guard by the Muslim League to function opposite the Congress Peace Brigades in certain districts is likely to be a matter of serious importance in time to come. The statements by four Frontier Muslims at Meerut that the National Guard would not remain non-violent if the necessity arose, the drilling of volunteers, who are required to keep a lathi and a knife, at Ghazipur, and the fact that it has been organised in opposition to the Congress Peace Brigades makes it clear that the 'Guard' is out for trouble if necessary. In addition to the National Guard there are Muslim League volunteer organisations in certain districts of which members are trained in drill, dressed in uniform and armed with lathis and spears. These and the National Guard will, no doubt, eventually join hands."

3. These passages are taken from the report of 8th September. The supplementary report of 12th October mentions that the number of volunteers in the United Provinces has reached considerable proportions and that the information is that these figures are steadily increasing. Mr. Thomas wrote as follows: "The figures of particular note are those of

the Congress Volunteer Army and the Muslim League Volunteer Corps (including National Guards). These two organisations representing the two most important political parties of the time would appear to be vying with each other in regard to the strength of their volunteer organisation. Apart from the dangerous potentialities attending the existence of such large bodies of semi-trained men, there is no gainsaying the fact that they are likely to be lacking in discipline and efficient leadership at moments when such qualities may be most necessary. They are systematically being taught on most militant and aggressive lines and a still greater danger lies in the functioning side by side of two such rival bodies at times of communal or political unrest." Mr. Thomas also states: "In most districts the volunteers of the various organisations are usually armed with lathis and wear a distinctive uniform and, in the case of the Congress volunteers and Muslim League and National Guard volunteers, carry a flag. In all cases training on military lines is advocated and in the majority of districts is actually put into practice. Training camps are gradually increasing and in the case of the Jaunpur Youth League training camp it is specially noted that a most undesirable type of youth is being attracted and that the camp is more or less a revolutionary training centre."

4. The whole scheme for the enlistment and organisation on military lines of volunteers seems to me full of potentialities of danger. It is difficult to understand for what purpose these volunteers are being organised save ultimately with the idea that their military training and force will be used for purposes of violence or intimidation. They do not seem to me to be consistent with the ordinary ideas of peaceful democratic organisation. The idea seems to me far more akin to that of the Fascist or Nazi bodies which have in fact imposed their will on their respective countries through organisations of this type.

5. Apart from this general objection of principle, there is the most obvious danger, as brought out in the C.I.D. reports, of these rival bodies of Hindus and Muslims coming into conflict. The whole development seems to me menacing and sinister, and I should like to invite the very serious attention of the Hon'ble Premier to it. I should value a discussion with him on the subject. The attitude of the Government is clearly a matter of the greatest importance. I gather that hitherto Hon'ble Ministers have been inclined, and perhaps not unnaturally, to extend some support and encouragement to the Congress volunteers; but I feel it is necessary for us to take full account of the situation and try to look ahead and see where such a movement may be likely to lead us.

79

HAIG TO LINLITHGOW
R/3/1/74

Secret
No. U.P.-199

November 23rd, 1938

My dear Lord Linlithgow,

I think it may interest you to hear at once of a conversation which I had yesterday afternoon with Mrs. Pandit shortly after my fortnightly report No. U.P.-198 of November 22nd was written. This was my first interview with Mrs. Pandit since her return. I always find her very frank, and she is essentially a moderate-minded person. She is thus a valuable link, as through her brother[34] she is in the closest touch with extremist opinion and policy. She said to me yesterday that the public expected her to be "red" and she often finds it very difficult to live up to this expectation.

2. I was discussing with her the general situation in the Province as she found it on her return, and she seemed decidedly apprehensive. She said that the position of the Ministry was, in her judgment, definitely weaker than it had been, and that while a year ago there had been plenty of casual and unorganised criticism of the Ministers, now it seemed to her that the criticism had become organised and insistent. She said that Pant was being continually attacked for his moderation. It was said that he has done nothing which a Liberal would not have done, that he is too friendly with the Governor and too much under his influence, and that he is becoming a second Chhatari.[35] These criticisms are of course very far from being justified; but it is significant if, as she assures me, they are being made now as part of a regular policy. This affords strong corroboration of the view I expressed in my letter of November 22nd, that the left wing was gaining in strength. It seems clear that it is becoming more and more aggressive and is now launching a definite attack on the right wing of the Ministry. The Ministry is in any case divided, for Kidwai and Sampurnanand are plainly in sympathy with the left wing. Mrs. Pandit is obviously a supporter of Pant, and she is perturbed. She says that the Ministry is being attacked very strongly for not going much further in the direction of making concessions to the tenants, and that it is being suggested that the Congress are taking a more advanced line in States like Rajkot than they are in this Province where they form the Government. She told me she thought we should have a very troublesome cold weather, and she

evidently looks with some apprehension on the Congress meeting in February. It is possible that her views may have been coloured at this moment by the visit of Subhas Chandra Bose, who obviously has been anything but helpful to the more moderate Ministers; but I have no doubt that, broadly speaking, she is right and that we must expect the left wing to become more and more aggressive and, I fear, powerful. You will understand that this will make Pant's position very difficult.

3. I should be grateful if Your Excellency would treat this information as strictly personal. I am sending a copy of this letter to the Secretary of State.

Yours sincerely,
H.G. HAIG

80

HAIG TO LINLITHGOW
R/3/1/74

Secret
No. U.P.-205

December 4th, 1938

My dear Lord Linlithgow,

I send herewith for your information a copy of a note recorded on the 21st November by my Premier regarding the formation of District Advisory Committees, which has just reached me With regard to the merits, or rather demerits, of this particular proposal, and the line that should be taken with reference to it, I will address Your Excellency when I have been able to consider it carefully and in detail, and when I have received the note which the Chief Secretary is preparing on the subject. But I feel sure you would like to be aware at once of this proposal.

2. I am myself considerably impressed by a growing feeling that an attack on a broad front is being made on the whole machinery of the present administration, and I think we ought to frame our policy with reference to that view. I mentioned in a recent letter the probability, already foreshadowed by my Premier, of an attack on European recruitment for the services. An attack on their pay may be developed at any moment, and I have with me now the proposals of my Ministers for the abolition of all posts of Commissioners, a matter on which I shall in due course address Your Excellency officially. Now comes this proposal for the constitution of District Advisory Committees. We have already under consideration a

scheme for the separation of judicial and executive functions, which will soon be coming up for final consideration. I think it is necessary that all these matters should be viewed in relation to their cumulative effect in shaking and weakening the administrative structure. Side by side with this we have the activities, which I recently mentioned to Your Excellency, for the formation of an extensive Congress Army (as they themselves call it) of volunteers.[36]

Yours sincerely,
H.G. HAIG

ENCLOSURE TO NO. 80

MINUTE BY GWYNNE

December 2nd, 1938

Hon'ble Ministers:

The attached note on the subject of the formation of District Advisory Committees, which has been prepared by the Hon'ble Premier, is circulated to Hon'ble Ministers under Hon'ble Premier's orders. I am preparing a further note on the subject and will circulate it to Hon'ble Ministers as soon as it is ready.

C.W. GWYNNE
Chief Secretary

ATTACHMENT

NOTE BY PANT

November 21st, 1938

The question of the establishment of District Councils to assist District Officers in the administration of the district has been engaging my attention for a considerable period. We have appointed a number of committees in districts from time to time to deal with specific questions. Some of these are, I believe, still in existence. The Anti-corruption Committee presided over by Sir Maharaj Singh have recommended that committees composed of officials and non-officials should be formed in every district to deal with matters pertaining to corruption. Their recommendation is embodied in paragraph 22 on page 8 of their papers. I am of opinion that a permanent committee should be formed to assist the District Officers in all those matters for which independent permanent committees have been considered necessary as well as for other purposes which I will indicate later. It will no longer be necessary to appoint any *ad hoc* committees for temporary purposes once such a Council has been established.

The subject is not new. It was raised before the Decentralization Commission in 1908. One of the main objects of the inquiry of the Commission was to devise means for bringing the district administration into closer touch with the people. This course was supported by leading independent public men of the day in our Province. Of the 84 non-official witnesses who gave evidence before the Commission 71 were in favour of this proposal. It was also approved by the non-official Europeans who were examined by the Commission. However, nothing came out of this inquiry, although in our Province the leading public men including Madan Mohan Malaviya, Sir Sundar Lal, Raja Sir Rampal Singh, Nawab Sir Muhammad Muzammi Ullah Khan and the Revd. Greaves were among its supporters.

In 1912 Mr. Gokhale moved a resolution in the Governor-General's Legislative Council to the effect "that steps should now be taken to bring the district administration into closer touch with the people by creating, as far as possible, in every district in the provinces a District Council composed of not more than nine members, partly elected and partly nominated whose functions should be merely advisory to begin with, and whom the Collector should ordinarily be bound to consult in all important matters." As usual Mr. Gokhale made a very elaborate and reasoned speech in support of his motion. In the course of his speech he urged that a body so formed, sitting round a table with the Collector and meeting once a month, would be able to dispose of a lot of business on the spot, which at present involves endless delays and indirectly to get rid of a lot of poison which now gathers in a district from day to day and which tends to vitiate the air in a manner truly regrettable. He also replied to the criticism that such committees should tend to impair efficiency of administration [?by arguing that] the association of a Council with the District Officer would greatly increase it. District administration, he said, is the real ground of contact between the bulk of the people and the Government and that no expansion of the legislatures, unless supplemented by the creation of advisory councils, would fully meet the requirements. In 1922, Pt. Gokaran Nath Misra moved a similar resolution in the United Provinces Council recommending to the Government to appoint advisory committees in all the districts consisting of non-officials including the members of the Council to advise the Collector on important matters relating to the administration of the district. The Government accepted the scheme in principle and undertook to try it in a few selected districts. Nothing was, however, done and the question continued to agitate the public mind. In November 1936 the United Provinces Legislative Council adopted another resolution asking Government to establish such Councils in districts. Soon after our assuming office a resolution, of which notice had been given by Professor Krishna Chandra, was tabled in August 1937, recommending to Government that advisory committees should be formed in each district to advise and help the District Magistrate in the discharge of his functions. The resolution was, however, not reached. There is little doubt that if it had been discussed it would have received support from all sections of the House and Government would have accepted it.

Far-reaching constitutional changes have taken place since the Decentralization Commission examined this question. We have now the system of Provincial Autonomy and ministerial responsibility covers the entire field of administration. The bureaucratic system has been replaced in the provinces by popular and democratic Government. It would be a legitimate question whether the need for such Councils subsists even after the introduction of the system of responsible Government. I personally feel it has become still greater. The field and the structure of administration must be regarded as one integral and whole unit. A change merely at the top unaccompanied by any readjustment at the base is bound to be incomplete, unsuitable and unsatisfactory, even from the purely administrative point of view. The various parts of the machine should work in unison, so that there may be no clogging of the wheels, no deadlocks and no jerks. The maximum efficiency cannot be ensured unless there is a stable equilibrium. The system of democratic Government ultimately rests on the sanction of the people and it cannot effectively function except with their willing co-operation. Such co-operation cannot yield fruitful results if it is confined to the top. It may even become a source of em barrassment and weakness to the administration as a whole if a friendly attitude towards the Government is not accompanied by mutual active trust at the bottom. With the stirrings of new life, new forces with a different outlook must also come into existence and as the people become more and more conscious of their [?new position] vigilance should increase and along with it the criticism of public acts of public servants should become more and more vocal and widespread and so will be the demand for the removal of grievances. The public attitude will be determined to a very large extent by the trust enjoyed by the administration in any particular locality. To some extent it must also depend on their knowledge of the limitations and handicaps under which Government have as a rule to function. Even to maintain peace and control crime public co-operation is absolutely essential. The Police do not receive adequate support at the hands of the public. The executive agency of the Government is looked upon with suspicion in some places and there is a lack of the appreciation of the difficulties of the officials and of the *bona fides* of the public workers. Besides, with the change in the system of Government the function of the district authorities is no longer merely formal or concerned with the maintenance of public peace and the prevention and control of crime, but it must be formative and constructive as well. There is a natural anxiety to raise the economic, moral and material level of the community with the result that nation-building activities claim constant attention and the District Officer has to see not only that the people in his district live peacefully and are not maltreated and robbed but he must also devise measures calculated to make them happy and prosperous. His task is stupendous. Several of our districts are [as] big, if not bigger, than some of the foreign and Indian States. In the exigencies of public service District Officers are frequently transferred and specially in the hot weather junior officers have to be placed in charge of districts, sometimes with little knowledge of the locality and little experience of the conditions in which they have to work. I consider it essential in the interest of the administration that the District Magistrate should be assisted by a Council which should be more or less a miniature of the Government at the top. The contact between the Government and the members of the legislature and especially those belonging to the party in power may give cause for misgivings if there are no legitimate avenues of approach and association between the District Officers and the members of the legislature. Similarly, the confidence of the people may be shaken, howsoever well-meaning and capable a Government be, if there is constant friction between the leaders and the officers in the districts. It is necessary to ensure a smooth working of the machine in order to avoid waste and to achieve the best return for the public money.

When this proposal was discussed in the past it was suggested that the members should be partly elected and partly nominated. To this certain objections were raised. It was argued that such a procedure would call for the preparation of an electoral roll, the prescription of an electoral procedure with the processes of nomination, scrutiny, election and all the attendant inconvenience and expense. I appreciate the force of these objections and I am opposed to fresh elections also on other grounds, as I do not want a body in the districts that would not be in harmony with the legislature which is ultimately responsible and which for the time being mirrors public opinion. I also agree that the committee should be fairly small, and that its function should be advisory and not binding on the District Magistrate. A great deal can be achieved by mutual consultation. I believe that the appointment of such committees will have a very wholesome effect. Misapprehensions will be allayed, if not removed altogether, and the District Officers will receive intelligent support and ready co-operation to a much larger degree than at present. The responsibility for the administration will as heretofore rest on the shoulders of the District Magistrate, but his burdens will be lightened. I believe that a great deal of distrust is due to lack of knowledge and when opportunities for a frank talk are available the mist will disappear. I also know that the members of the legislature, especially belonging to the party on whom the responsibility of administration is cast for the time being, are bound to act in a responsible manner. I am not without hope that in many cases an agreement will be reached and even where it is not, the tension will be relieved by mutual discussion. The proceedings of the committee should be confidential. The statutory and general responsibilities of the District Magistrate will not be diminished in any way by the coming into existence of these committees. Matters need not necessarily be decided by votes, but the District Magistrate will take account of the sense of the committee and it will be to his advantage if he has some means of measuring the public barometer.

The committees may consist of the District Magistrate, the Superintendent of Police, the local M.L.As. and M.L.Cs., the President of the District Bar Association and two or three men nominated by Government. The same member of the legislature will not be on the committee of more than one district. When he represents a constituency which extends to more than one district he will make his choice of the particular district committee on which he would like to serve. The committees will be given power to co-opt members for special purposes. I mention some of the matters on which the committee will advise the District Magistrate:

I – Selection of honorary magistrates.

II – Temperance and prohibition movement.

III – Measures for furthering the rights and amenities of scheduled castes.

IV – Anti-corruption measures to be dealt with in the manner recommended by the Maharaj Singh Committee.

V – False reports, unjustifiable attacks and interference with public servants.

VI – Extension of the operation of Acts to new areas.

VII – Legislative proposals.

VIII – Matters pertaining to religious endowments.

IX – Organization of relief measures on the occasion of famine, floods, fires, earthquakes, cholera and other natural calamities and epidemics.

X – Social measures, such as the control of gambling, traffic in women and prevention of child marriages.

XI – Local publicity to remove misunderstandings and to contradict false or malicious propaganda.

XII – Reclamation of criminal tribes.

XIII – Need for the imposition of punitive police and the enrolment of special police officers.

XIV – Recommendations about remissions and suspensions of land revenue.

XV – Cancellation and restoration of the exclusion from the Arms Act of such arms as swords, spears, &c.

XVI – Special measures required for the maintenance of public peace and tranquillity, and for the control of crime.

XVII – Agrarian and labour troubles.

XVIIII – Regulation and control of fairs, festivals and religious processions.

XIX – Constructive planning.

The list above is not exhaustive. Still I am not particularly keen that all these items should be taken up by these committees forthwith. The first 12 seem to me to be completely harmless and unobjectionable. We may make a start with these and then extend the scope later. All district committees need not necessarily exercise identical functions. There will be nothing to prevent the District Magistrate from referring to the committee any other matter not covered by the categories indicated above. The members of the committee may refer any question of general interest to the District Magistrate and if he considers it advisable he may include it in his agenda. Meetings of the committee may be held whenever necessary, ordinarily once a month. The committee will not have anything to do with matters pertaining to the appointment, preferment, &c. of public servants or with the grievances of any particular single individual. I feel that the District Magistrate will find the committees a source of strength and that his co-operation with them will make for better, more efficient and more popular administration in districts. With goodwill on both sides, with a sense of responsibility and a desire to promote the welfare of the public the occasions for any disagreement should be very rare.

Chief Secretary will please prepare a note for the Council of Ministers on this subject and in the meantime circulate this.

G.B. PANT

81

HAIG TO LINLITHGOW
R/3/1/74

Secret *December 6th, 1938*
No. U.P.-206

My dear Lord Linlithgow,

I enclose the official fortnightly report. It does not contain much of special interest. The passage dealing with the Cawnpore labour trouble was amended by the Premier so as to make it more colourless. I shall later in this letter deal with the Cawnpore situation at some length. As I remarked in my last fortnightly report of November 22nd, the Province is at present quiet, but it is very necessary to consider with attention possible developments.

2. In my last report I brought the Tenancy Bill situation up to the point that the Taluqdars were reluctantly prepared to accept arbitration by the Parliamentary Sub-Committee, but that it was doubtful whether the latter would agree. After a short time it became apparent that the Parliamentary Sub-Committee were not prepared to intervene. The Taluqdars held a meeting while this point was still unsettled, but decided, quite rightly in my opinion, not to divide themselves and make a public declaration of the willingness of the majority to accept arbitration while it was still not certain whether the Parliamentary Sub-Committee would agree. This particular solution may now, I think, be regarded as dead.

3. Soon afterwards my own apprehensions about the course of the discussions on the Tenancy Bill were greatly relieved by conversations I had with the Revenue Minister, Kidwai, and with the Premier. Kidwai is generally regarded as something of a left winger and is believed to have been hostile to any concessions to the landlords. When talking to him I made the point that if the Bill was seriously amended in the direction of satisfying the left wing, it would make it so much the less likely that it would get through the Upper House. He surprised me by saying that it was not in fact the intention of the Ministry to allow the Bill to be substantially amended in the left wing direction, that they contemplated

passing it as it stands, and that in fact they would probably be prepared to make provision for sale of holdings as an alternative to the ejectment procedure, which he thought would go far to remove the difficulties felt by the landlords over the ejectment provisions. I said that if that was the position, it seemed to me advisable that they should give some hint to the landlords that this was what they had in mind. At present, as far as I could judge, the landlords were intending to fight the Bill by all possible means and this would prolong the controversy and raise the temperature. The next day I spoke to the Premier and he corroborated the views expressed by the Revenue Minister, though he seemed more cautious in saying that certain amendments would probably be passed which would naturally be in favour of the tenants. But he also said that the intention of the Ministers was to pass the Bill substantially in its present form. He also spoke as if he was anxious to make some concessions to the landlords on the ejectment issue. I made the same point to him about not letting the controversy go too far. I may add that about the same time the Premier thought it necessary to issue a press note to try and tone down the speech which he had made in the Assembly on the 16th November, which I referred to in my last letter. I enclose a copy of this communiqué.

4. Since then the consideration of the Bill in the Assembly has started on a restrained note, and I think, if the Ministers stick to the intentions they have declared to me, that they will without much difficulty, though doubtless after a somewhat prolonged discussion, get the Bill through the Lower House, and that they will also be able to get it through the Upper House. I have, however, just heard a somewhat disturbing piece of information. The late Revenue Secretary,[37] who has recently returned from leave, has been retained temporarily at headquarters to do some special work in the Revenue Department, and he told me that he has been asked by the Ministers to work out proposals for reducing the rent-roll of the Province by 6½ crores from the pre-slump 1931 rent-roll. The 1931 rent-roll amounted to 18¼ crores; at present, after the remissions given for the slump, it stands at 15 crores; and the proposed reduction would bring it down to 11¾ crores. There is some reason to think that this proposal is the result of an undertaking that the Premier gave to his party last July. It has been pointed out to the Ministers in the Secretariat noting that the reductions they propose could not be effected under the principles for the fixation of rent laid down in the Tenancy Bill as it stands at present, and that if they wish to have a legal basis for such action, they would have to make some amendment in this clause. It has also been pointed out that these proposals would involve a large loss of revenue and would roughly reduce land

revenue from 6 crores to 4½ crores. I confess I am at a loss to understand what the intentions of the Ministers are. The Premier had given me clearly to understand that he did not contemplate, as a result of this legislation, any considerable reduction in present rents. I have no doubt he has also conveyed that impression to the landlords. If he now tries to reduce rents by over 3 crores (a proposal in my opinion quite unjustifiable on merits) he will provoke the strongest opposition which is likely to lead to this particular provision in the Bill being rejected in the Upper House. I can only hope that he is merely trying to pacify the left wing by having the proposal examined then showing them on the basis of the Secretariat noting that it involves a loss of revenue which cannot be faced. The point of course is one with which he has long been perfectly familiar.

5. I mentioned in my last letter that I was taking up the question of volunteer organisations with the Premier. My conversation with him was far from satisfactory. He could give me no reasonable explanation why it should be necessary to have uniformed volunteers trained on military lines to carry out the policy of the Congress, while for a convinced democrat he seemed to me to regard somewhat lightly the danger that a force of this kind would be developed so as to impose the will of the party on the rest of the people. He said that while of course he differed from any such ideas, opinion in the Congress might change; it was at the moment in favour of non-violence; but if the majority changed their views other methods would prevail. I said that surely it was the duty of those who were in a position of power but did not believe in such developments, to do all they could to prevent them. He admitted this somewhat tepidly. I was left with the general impression that while it was impossible to expect the Congress to stop the volunteer movement, they might be induced to look a little more closely to its methods and check the militant spirit which is being shown. With regard to the Muslim and other volunteers he was quite prepared to agree that the spirit was one of violence and he was alive to the objections. But he asked how it was possible to stop these developments. He said that orders had already been issued authorising District Magistrates to prohibit processions in which swords and spears were carried; but he did not see how it was possible to go any further. At the same time he did seem quite prepared to consider any means for discouraging the spread of activities of this kind. We finally decided that we would both consider the matter further, and see whether we could think of any methods of diminishing the risks of the development of this body of volunteers on dangerous lines. On the whole I got the impression that he feels that little or nothing can be done to check the Congress volunteers.

6. I spent three days in Cawnpore, from the 27th to the 30th November. Just before I went, there was talk of the unemployed wanting to bring a deputation to me, and organise a demonstration. I got the Premier to communicate with Mr. Bal Krishna Sharma, who is the most influential Congressman in Cawnpore, and this was stopped. I enclose a copy of a statement put out by Mr. Sharma which shows a very reasonable spirit. There was no demonstration and no kind of unpleasantness. While at Cawnpore I had a number of important conversations with officials, employers and Congress workers, and, just before I left, with three representatives of the unemployed. From these conversations I drew the conclusion that conditions in Cawnpore were much less satisfactory than I had supposed. I had hoped that after the settlement of the general strike less summer, labour was on the whole settling down, and though I knew that the communists had captured the Mazdur Sabha, the official attitude towards this was that the communists at any rate were in control of the Mazdur Sabha which their predecessors had not been, that they were not anxious to cause trouble at the moment, and therefore their capture of the organisation need not create any alarm. I found, however, that the communists were in fact very active, that there was a good deal of preaching of revolution, that provocative meetings were being held at the mill gates and undesirable and insulting slogans were shouted, and that generally labour was being kept by this artificial agitation in a state of unrest. The employers were very critical of the Government, and said that it would require little action on their part to put down this communist agitation. They declared that the great majority of the labourers were only anxious to be allowed to go on with their work, but that it was a characteristic of Cawnpore labour that a few determined men could lead the mass in a direction in which they did not want to go. They complained particularly that this communist movement was being definitely encouraged by the attitude of the Ministry, and maintained that if it were not for this attitude the communists would lose support rapidly. I discussed the general situation with Mr. Bal Krishna Sharma, the leading Congressman in Cawnpore, who has ever since the Congress Ministry took office pursued a tortuous and unreliable course, and has undoubtedly been encouraging the communists. He spoke to me in a most moderate way and said that the last thing he wished to do was to injure the industrial interests of Cawnpore, that he merely wished to get reasonable trade unions established, and so on. It is difficult to discover what is really going on beneath the surface in Cawnpore. But what disturbs me is the attitude taken by the Premier which I shall describe later. The action which it seemed important to take was:

(*a*) to deal with some of the violent speakers,

(*b*) to stop the provocative meetings at the mill gates.

General orders had very recently been issued by the Ministry to the effect that District Magistrates might take action under Section 107 or even Section 108 of the Criminal Procedure Code to check speeches advocating violence. These orders had not yet reached the District Magistrate,[38] but I told him about them, and said that it seemed to me that under those orders he would be able to do what was necessary about the speakers. At the end of my visit a sudden strike broke out in one of the smaller mills. Simultaneously there was a fracas at the gate of one of the most important mills as a result of a communist demonstration. Thereupon the District Magistrate issued an order under Section 144, prohibiting these mill gate meetings and the shouting of slogans. In this way one of the remedies required had already been applied, and it only remained to see that the Premier would back up the District Magistrate.

7. I saw the Premier soon after my return from Cawnpore and told him of the general state of feeling I had found there. He took a very unsatisfactory line about the attitude of the Government to the communists, and I could really get nothing out of him. With regard to the immediate action taken, he said that he would not interfere with the order of the District Magistrate under Section 144, though he himself would have preferred to see it expressed differently. As to the prosecution of speakers, he was not prepared to let the District Magistrate have a free hand, but promised to discuss the whole matter shortly with the District Magistrate with a view to reaching a decision. I hope these measures will lead to an improvement in the immediate situation. I may mention that the strike has already come to an end; but the Premier's general attitude about this matter left on my mind a disquieting impression, as if he were really hardly a free agent or was afraid of opposing the extremists in Cawnpore.

8. I mentioned above the circular to District Magistrates about using Sections 107 and 108 of the Criminal Procedure Code, and I enclose a copy.[39] This is an encouraging step, and I hope may enable District Magistrates to control more effectively the revolutionary speeches that have been made rather freely, particularly in the east of the Provinces. It suggests that the Premier is anxious not to let this go too far. At the same time the result of some careful scrutiny of brief descriptions of speeches contained in the Police Abstracts goes to show that they very often give a misleading impression and exaggerate the nature of the speech. The police have again been exhorted to scrutinise carefully the accounts which they give of speeches in the Police Abstract. Another encouraging step that has

been taken recently by the Government is a circular on discipline in schools, a copy of which I enclose.[40]

9. I attended today the annual police parade, and I enclose a copy[41] of the speech I made. The parade was one of the best I have seen, the men were very smart and moved excellently. I had asked Pant whether he would attend this parade and he considered the matter for some time. In order to facilitate his attendance, I arranged to distribute the ordinary Indian honours such as Khan Bahadur and Rai Bahadur, at an investiture, and to confine the distribution on the parade to the Police Medals which the Premier has himself recognised as an appropriate form of reward. However, in the end he decided not to come. I think he was probably reluctant to play a secondary part on such an occasion. I notice that recently Brabourne in Calcutta allowed the Home Minister[42] to address a parade while he himself distributed the medals. Such a procedure, however, would not at this stage of development be suitable in this Province. The attitude of the Ministry to the police has been in many respects so unsatisfactory that I feel it might have shaken the confidence of the police if the Governor had appeared to be divesting himself of the functions they were accustomed to see him perform. Moreover, I could not be sure what the Premier would say. With the best intentions he cannot avoid lecturing the police on these occasions, and they do not greatly appreciate this. He made a speech to a police parade recently at Sitapur which was on the whole more satisfactory than many of his utterances on this subject. I asked him whether I could refer in my speech to his unavoidable absence and express his appreciation of the work of the police, but he clearly did not like this idea and said that he was going to address a parade at Moradabad shortly when he would be able to say what he wanted. So I left the matter alone.

10. You will have gathered from what I have said above, particularly in connection with volunteers and the Cawnpore labour situation, that I am not very happy about the present attitude of Pant. I feel that he is finding the left wing too strong for him, and that he may progressively subordinate his views to theirs. At the same time, he will continue to put forward proposals, such as I have mentioned separately, for the abolition of Commissioners and the constitution of district advisory committees, which appeal to him as being in the direct line of succession from demands of the early days of Congress, and at the same time are sure to be welcome to the left wing as weakening the machinery of the administration.

11. The growing strength of the left wing in this Province does not to my mind represent any calculated policy of the Congress.[43] Indeed, one would suppose that it cannot be agreeable to the Working Committee. I

regard it as a spontaneous expression of certain forces of discontent (and perhaps ambition) which are steadily gaining strength, and I fear these forces are not going to submit willingly to control. The danger is that the Ministry may not have the resolution, or perhaps the strength, to be able to face them and that the whole situation may steadily deteriorate. It is probable that Jawaharlal Nehru's return has already proved an encouragement to the left wing.

12. We have just concluded the first joint session between two Houses which has been held anywhere in India under the new Constitution, or indeed at all. The procedure worked quite smoothly, and I think the legislators felt a certain satisfaction in the idea that they were making history. The result of the joint session was of course never in doubt. The two Bills under consideration provided for increases in Court fees and Judicial stamps, bringing in between them considerable new revenues. The Upper House jumped at the opportunity of being able to pose as protectors of the poor and champions of the popular cause of avoiding taxation. But the Government had their followers well under control, and the figures of the divisions gave them a majority of about 80.

Yours sincerely,
H.G. HAIG

ENCLOSURE 1 TO NO. 81

CUTTING FROM THE *PIONEER*,
DATED NOVEMBER 24TH, 1938

The following Press note has been issued by the Director of Public Information, United Provinces:

"The speech of the Premier in the Assembly on November 16th has been misrepresented in its reference to the Zamindars' generosity in the past.

"What the Premier meant to convey, and in fact actually said, was that, while they had contributed to many public institutions, such as universities and hospitals, their generosity really has had the effect of immediately benefiting the middle classes and city or town dwellers and incidentally, also, people thousands of miles away, and did not benefit the tenants and dwellers in the countryside who were in greater need of such services."

ENCLOSURE 2 TO NO. 81

CUTTING FROM THE *NATIONAL HERALD*,
DATED NOVEMBER 27TH, 1938

Cawnpore,
November 26th, 1938

Mr. Bal Kishen [Krishna] Sharma, President of the City Congress Committee of Cawnpore, has issued the following statement to the Press with regard to the Governor's visit and the proposed Bekar Sabha's demonstration in Cawnpore:

"I learn that the Bekar Sabha of Cawnpore is organising a demonstration of factory workers of the city. It so happens that the day of the demonstration coincides with the day of the Governor's arrival. So far as I know, the demonstration is neither directed against the Government nor against the Governor. The demonstrations do not mean any personal affront to the Governor. It is only with a view to drawing the attention of the Cawnpore public as also of the Local Government to the acute problem of unemployment in Cawnpore, that the demonstration in question has been staged. The unemployed workers wish to evoke the sympathy of the Cawnpore public to the plight they are subjected to.

"I, therefore, hope that the demonstrators will do nothing by way of shouting slogans or by demonstrating in front of any particular spot which may be interpreted to involve any expression of protest against the Governor's personality."

82

HAIG TO LINLITHGOW
R/3/1/74

Secret
No. U.P.-208

December 19th, 1938

My dear Lord Linlithgow,

Paragraphs 2 and 3 of Your Excellency's secret letter, dated 5th December 1938,[44] deal with considerations which have been very much in my own mind ever since I returned from leave, and I am glad that you have brought them out specifically. I have thought that the best way of dealing with them is to put down my ideas in the form of a memorandum, which I enclose. I am sending a copy of this letter and the memorandum to the Secretary of State.

Yours sincerely,
H.G. HAIG

ENCLOSURE TO NO. 82

MEMORANDUM BY HAIG

Secret *December 19th, 1938*

Appreciation of existing position

Since I returned from leave in September, I have been receiving information from various sources that the left-wing in this Province is gathering strength, that its activities are now a definite embarrassment to what is in the main a right-wing Government, and that the Government is increasingly disposed to give in to left-wing pressure. I think it is fair to say that this is the common impression in the Province. From my own dealings with the Ministry in the last few months I draw a similar conclusion. It seems to me that there are indications that the Premier is finding it difficult to stand up to left-wing pressure.

(*a*) His attitude about communism and particularly the activities of the communists in Cawnpore is unsatisfactory, and indicates an unwillingness or fear to take action against a comparatively small body of men, who do not belong to the Congress and are doing a good deal of mischief.

(*b*) His attitude towards the movement for the formation of militant Congress volunteers is equally unsatisfactory, though I recognise that it would in any case be very difficult for him to oppose a movement which has secured the support of the Congress organisation.

(*c*) I am receiving from the Ministry a series of proposals which would have the effect of weakening the administration seriously.

(*i*) They have formally proposed the abolition of the posts of all Commissioners.

(*ii*) They are formally considering the appointment of advisory committees for district officers, ostensibly with powers limited to advice, but with the clear intention that the advice should be followed. There is an obvious intention that the members of the Congress Party in the districts should obtain a controlling influence over the district administration.

(*iii*) Far-reaching proposals for the reorganisation of local bodies are contained in the report of a committee which has been sitting for many months past presided over by one of the Parliamentary Secretaries. The most important proposals of this committee are for the establishment of village Panchayats to cover every village in the Province. It is proposed to give the village Panchayats very extensive and unsuitable powers, including apparently control over chaukidars and the enlistment of "civic guards". It is proposed also to establish Judicial Panchayats with dangerously wide powers. The Ministry have not yet considered their attitude to these proposals, but the fact that they have been made under the auspices of a Parliamentary Secretary is of some importance.

(*d*) There are also various items of general policy which suggest the same conclusion, in particular the attitude about rents. Though the Premier has given both myself and the landlords to understand that he does not contemplate any reduction of rents below the rate to which they were reduced in the remissions given on account of the 1931 slump, and has recently reiterated this intention to me, there seems to be no doubt that some months ago he made a promise to the Party that he would reduce rents by 6½ crores, and if possible 7 crores, below the pre-slump level. This would involve a reduction of rents by some 3½ crores from the present level and would involve grave complications of various kinds. The Premier seems at present uncertain what to do about this problem. It is likely to be a crucial test of how far he will submit to left-wing pressure. In some respects however the Ministry show signs of pursuing a reasonable course. It is perhaps the case that at certain points they give way to pressure, and when there is no special pressure they maintain their own line.

2. There is a good deal of talk of growing dissatisfaction among the propertied classes and moderate men of all kinds at the disturbed conditions, the increase in crime, the loss of respect for authority, which have to some appreciable extent been the results of nearly 18 months of Congress administration. The policy of the Congress Ministry has given rise to:

(*a*) a fairly general sense of uneasiness among moderate persons;

(*b*) some loss of business by shopkeepers;

(*c*) industrial unrest and consequent loss to capitalists as well as workers;

(*d*) agrarian unrest and threatened loss of income and certain rights by landlords.

It has not escaped notice that while the Government are vigorous in their attack on corruption in the Services, Congress workers are to an increasing extent following those courses which are denounced in the case of the Services, and that the Congress authorities seem singularly reluctant to check these malpractices among their own supporters.

3. In spite of all that is being done or attempted for the villagers they are only doubtfully grateful. They have been led by the general election campaign and the constant Congress agitation in the villages since then to expect much, and are getting into a habit of thinking that Government must do for them everything they desire. They seem to be paying more attention to what has not been done than to what has been done. As an illustration of this feeling, I observed in a rural development village which I visited recently, where some substantial improvement seems to have been effected and the village looked reasonably prosperous, that the villagers concentrated on lamenting their poverty, and presented a long series of complaints with a view to reduction of rent, increase of irrigation and so on, none of which appeared to have much substance. This spirit is encouraged by the left-wing agitators who are always leading the villagers to expect far more than any Government can give them.

4. The Muslims are strongly opposed to the Government and the Muslim League movement shows sings of great vitality. It has captured practically the whole body of Muslims in the Province and is working under aggressive leadership.[45] Communal relations are naturally bad throughout the Province, and the antagonism between Muslims and Hindus and the consequent fear of disturbances is one of the main anxieties of the Ministry.

5. As against this discontent, which is either sectional, as in the case of the Muslims, the landlords and the industrialists, or vague, as in the case of men of moderate views, we have to place the immense prestige that Congress have won in the Province since the general election, and particularly since they took office, the authority they possess and exploit fully by virtue of being the Government, the nationalist sentiment which extends probably to a much larger proportion of the population than one might suppose, and is greatly reinforced by Hindu feeling and ideas of Hindu raj, the great personal popularity of Pandit Govind Ballabh Pant whose name is known throughout the Province. These are very important assets and far outweigh the factors of discontent mentioned previously. There is in my opinion at the present time no sign at all of the possibility of any Government being formed in this Province other than a Congress Government.

6. The administrative machinery is still intact. Tendencies towards the formation of a parallel administration which were observable in the first few months after the Ministry took office have gradually died down. They were not in my view part of an official policy, but were a spontaneous

expression of the ideas of Congressmen in the first flush of enthusiasm when they came into power. But there are now signs, as I mentioned in paragraph 1, of a deliberate policy of weakening the administrative machinery by changes in the organisation. Though the machinery is still intact, the authority of the administrative services is not what it was. There is a general feeling that if a Government officer does anything displeasing to members of the public, it is always possible to appeal either direct or through the intervention of some local Congress authority to the Premier with a hope that some result will come of it. This feeling again is possibly less strong than it was; but while we are settling down now to conditions of equilibrium, it is a somewhat different equilibrium to that which existed before the Congress Ministry came into office and it means a certain loss of authority.

7. The Courts maintain their authority, aided by vigorous action taken by the High Court to deal with numerous cases of Congressmen trying to interfere with the course of justice. The Ministers themselves have not shown any great scruple in their attitude to cases in which they had any political interest, but I think this tendency can be, and is being, kept within bounds, and is much less marked than it was.

8. The police have probably suffered more than any other part of the machine in loss of authority for the reasons generally explained in paragraph 6, which affect the police in particular; and they have also lost confidence to some extent owing to the anti-corruption activities launched by the Ministry, and a feeling that those who had antagonised the Congress in the old days were likely to be victimised. I think this process has probably been arrested, and I am even hoping that there may be some improvement, for the Premier has certainly shown a realisation of the fact that he must have an efficient police force if order is to be kept in the Province. The discipline of the police is in my opinion still intact and they could be relied upon to act vigorously, if given a lead.

9. Apart from administrative difficulties, the services, and particularly perhaps the provincial and subordinate services, are generally somewhat resentful of their treatment by the Congress Government. Privileges and allowances are cut down wherever they can be, and there is recognition of the fact that the Ministry would like to go much further on this path. There is some inevitable apprehension that they are not safe against attacks on fundamental things, like their pay. There is a feeling that members of the services are not really trusted, that political considerations and personalities have too much sway, that transfers in the case of the non-protected services are made too lightly on personal grounds of favour or the reverse. Some

of course identify themselves with the Congress, but on the whole the members of the very important provincial executive service, for instance, have maintained a spirit of independence and indeed an attitude of criticism towards the Government beyond what could have been expected. The reason is partly that they do not like the new system which has affected their authority and made things in many ways more difficult for them, and partly, without doubt, the fact that a great many of them are connected with landlord families and have landlord sympathies.

10. This is generally the situation as it appears to me at present. When I went on leave in May, I thought that we were on the up-grade. We had overcome many initial difficulties, the Ministers seemed to be showing an increasing sense of responsibility and were getting more and more occupied with practical administrative considerations. I hoped that we were gradually settling down, and undoubtedly we should have, if the right-wing could have had their own way. When I returned from leave, the left-wing seemed to me definitely stronger than it had been, and I now have a feeling that the process of improvement has been arrested, and that we may begin to slip down. There is nothing really to show for this as yet administratively. It is rather a question of the minds of the Ministers and their general policy. It is possible that I am attaching too much importance to certain tendencies, but what I have said certainly represents the view that generally prevails. There is always the possibility that the Working Committee may bring pressure to bear on the Ministry from the other side. So far they do not seem to have done much in this direction; but if left-wing influence became too pronounced in the United Provinces it is not impossible that the Working Committee might come into action. That is indeed, I think, the best hope for the future.[46]

POSSIBLE DEVELOPMENTS IF LEFT-WING GATHERS STRENGTH

11. If, however, we are to assume that the left-wing will continue to gather strength, I should not anticipate an open breach between the right- and left-wings. I think the Working Committee would undoubtedly assert itself to stop this. Ruling out therefore an open breach, there would remain two possible developments:

(*a*) Pant would remain in office with perhaps some left-wing accession to his Ministry.

(*b*) Pant would be displaced without any open breach and a Ministry, left-wing or predominantly so, would be gradually installed.

Of these two alternatives I consider (*a*) more probable. Pant would be likely to cling to office and to subordinate his views to the extent necessary to the left-wing. In spite of the heavy burden of work, I believe he enjoys the power and position immensely, and I think he would make every effort not to surrender it. The choice between the two alternatives would hardly lie with me, but I consider that (*a*) would be decidedly the easier position to deal with, for Pant's own natural moderation would act as some kind of brake, though not a very reliable one, on policy.[47]

12. The effects that might be anticipated from a growing left-wing policy are:

(*a*) Increasing agrarian difficulties, tenants getting out of hand, landlords in self-defence organising themselves better and forced to fight for their existence. Conditions of disorder would gradually develop.

(*b*) Growth of revolutionary and communist feeling, directed both against the general political and social order and against the British connection and the British people. It is impossible to tell at what point this feeling, which would be steadily worked up, might become really formidable.

13. We have got to realise that with a situation of this kind at some point conditions of disorder would arise that could not be tolerated. A crucial question is, whether we should wait for this stage or anticipate it. On the whole my view is that we should wait as long as is at all possible without running the risk of complete collapse.

(*a*) There is really no going back on the constitutional experiment. Even if it breaks down for a time, it will have to be renewed before long. Therefore unless we are to have the same administration back again and go over the same ground once more, we must allow a left-wing administration to discredit itself as much as possible and prove unmistakably its dangers and disadvantages.[48] This would afford the only chance of a more moderate administration being formed after a break-down.

(*b*) If we took action too soon, sympathy would be aroused for the popular Government. At the time of the ministerial crisis in February last it was very noticeable how most even of those who were strongly opposed to the policy of the Congress Ministry did not want it to fall altogether and the system to break-down.

14. It is perhaps probable that if the Ministry felt the situation getting out of hand, they would themselves force some issue and resign. We should have to be careful at that stage to avoid being put in the wrong on a weak case.

GENERAL POLICY

15. From the above I would draw the following conclusions about policy:

(*a*) We must retain intact the framework of the administration. There should be no hesitation in rejecting proposals, such as the abolition of Commissioners, &c. which are going to weaken this seriously.

(*b*) We must retain the confidence of the services and keep them in reasonably good heart. For this purpose we must not agree to anything that injures them fundamentally, such as reduction of pay, or makes them feel that they cannot depend on the reasonable support of the Governor. These are the two key positions which we must defend. Without them, we cannot retrieve the situation if a break comes; with them, we should be able to.

(*c*) We must on the other hand, if the Government comes under the domination of left-wing influences, put up with policies which are dangerous to the peace of the Province, until the point of breaking clearly arises. It would be necessary continually to point out the dangers, to draw the attention of Ministers constantly to the effect of what they are doing or leaving undone; but we should not in my opinion, force (or risk) a break down on a disputable apprehension of disorder. This means of course taking certain risks, but I think we should take those risks with our eyes open and relying on (*a*) and (*b*). If, however, the confidence of the services were being seriously affected by development under (*c*), then this would be a good cause for acting without further delay.

16. If things are allowed to come to a point at which the dangers become clearly apparent to the public, there is always the possibility that public opinion may assert itself and bring about a more moderate policy. Constitutionally it seems right to pursue this line and trust to the normal balances of a democratic constitution as far as possible. Further, in the special conditions of India and the nationalist complications of the situation, I feel that this is from the practical point of view the wise course.[49] I should like to emphasis the point that I am in this memorandum assuming a deterioration in the situation, which may in fact never occur. I do not wish it to be understood that I am at present expecting these developments, but we have to consider possible eventualities. Further, I recognise that what I have suggested above can only indicate a general outlook on these problems and cannot be taken as a settled guide to conduct in particular circumstances; but it is desirable to be clear about our general outlook, and particularly about the points on which we must stand firm.

H.G. HAIG

83

HAIG TO LINLITHGOW
R/3/1/74

Secret *December 23rd, 1938*
No. U.P.-210

My dear Lord Linlithgow,

I am writing this under rather severe pressure on my time, as there is always a great deal to do before the Christmas holidays begin. Moreover for the month of January I shall be based on Allahabad and seeing less than I otherwise should of my Ministers, so I have made a point in the last few days of having a long talk with each of them.

2. With reference to the very interesting questions raised in Your Excellency's letter of 5th December, about possible developments in this Province, I have sent you a full appreciation of the position as I see it, and I will not attempt to repeat what I have said there. In one important respect I think there are signs at present that the right-wing are holding their own, and that is in connection with the Tenancy Bill. The discussions on the Bill are pursuing a normal course, the large number of amendments are being disposed of steadily, there is no attempt at obstruction on the part of the Opposition, and no unreasonable heat has been introduced into the debates; above all there seem to be no inconvenient attacks on the Ministers from their own side. Very little change is being made in the Bill. The Revenue Minister told me yesterday that in regard to the ejectment procedure, which is probably the point which most closely affects the interests of the landlords in view of its bearing on their ability to realise their rents, the Ministry is contemplating including two additional alternative procedures which would to my mind greatly improve the prospect of rents being paid punctually. The anticipation of the Ministers is that the Bill will get through the Lower House by the beginning of February, and that with comparatively small changes they will also be able to get it through the Upper House. If these anticipations are realised, the Bill should be finally passed, I suppose, by about April; and if passed in the form now contemplated, I should regard it as a satisfactory solution of the problem. It will however be far from satisfactory to the left-wing, and it is not certain how the villages will receive it. But on the whole it must have a tranquillising effect, and it will I think help the right-wing to keep left-wing agitation in the villages under control, which I am sure is

their very strong desire. Mrs. Pandit told me two days ago that there was no enthusiasm for the Bill in any Congress circles and she thought that agitation would continue in the villages after it was passed. But though there may be no enthusiasm for it, I am convinced that it will be on the whole a valuable measure, and will greatly improve the position of the tenants. At the same time the landlords may perhaps count themselves lucky to escape with nothing more drastic.

3. I mentioned in paragraph 4 of my letter of December 6th that the question had been raised of making a very drastic reduction in rents. I have had some talk since then both with the Premier and the Revenue Minister on this point, and though they are somewhat vague, I get the impression that neither of them in fact contemplates any large general reduction in rents and that they are manoeuvring to hold off proposals that are doubtless being pressed upon them by the left-wing. It is evident that they have no intention of making any modification in the Tenancy Bill which would justify reductions of rent on a large scale.

4. The Taluqdars have recently held their election for the Presidentship of the British Indian Association, which has been vacated by the Raja of Jehangirabad at the end of his term. The two candidates were the Raja Bahadur of Tiloi and the Raja of Salempur. The former is a man of limited intelligence and no strength of character. He has been conspicuous in the past for little except the size of his debts, and belongs to the class of unsatisfactory and useless landlords. The Raja of Salempur, though also considerably in debt, is a man of different calibre, with an intelligent outlook and a fairly long history of political activities. He was Minister of Education in my minority ministry The election was very closely contested and Tiloi was successful by 147 votes to 145. It is generally believed that Tiloi owed his election to the strong support he received from the Congress. Today he came to see me and seemed very anxious for my advice and guidance, which surprised me, as I thought from what I had heard that he had put himself completely into the hands of the Congress. I asked him on what issues the election had been fought, and he said that it was primarily the issue of reaching a settlement with the Congress or putting up a vigorous opposition to them, but that this had been complicated by the raising of the Hindu-Muslim issue, a new and unfortunate development, for the Taluqdars have hitherto been very free from communal feeling among themselves. In the result all the Muslims voted for Salempur, who also had the support of an appreciable bloc of Hindus who wished to follow a policy of strong resistance to the Congress. Tiloi's supporters included however quite a number of reasonably-minded Taluqdars. In view of his

undoubted association with Congress during the election, I was somewhat amused to find that he was inclined to criticize the Tenancy Bill and to hope that I might save the Taluqdars from it. I made it clear to him, as I had already on many occasions to his predecessor, that I saw no prospect of feeling justified in interfering with the Bill as it stands at present, and he did not press the point, but departed reiterating his hope for my support and guidance.

5. A question of great importance to the general administration of the Province, and particularly to villages, is likely to be raised before long as a result of the report of a committee which has been sitting for many months about local self-government. Their proposals are in many respects startling and unpractical, and they will, I feel, meet with a great deal of opposition. But Mrs. Pandit told me that the present idea of the Ministry is to leave for the moment the proposals regarding the reorganisation of the municipalities and district boards, and to concentrate on the formation of village panchayats and the grant of powers to them. This will be done by a Village Panchayat Act which is already being drafted in accordance with the general lines of the committee's proposals. But the policy has not yet been considered by the Government. I do not know how far the Government will really be prepared to go when they are confronted with practical criticisms on these proposals. I hope perhaps it may be possible to keep them within reasonable bounds, but the decision is likely to depend very much on the struggle between the left- and right-wings, and it is not unlikely that the Ministry will be prepared to go a good deal further than they really think wise in order to do something to meet left-wing influence. The Legislature will be very fully occupied with the Tenancy Bill and the budget up to the end of March, but it is not impossible that this Village Panchayat Bill may be introduced in April. The Ministers seem to have made up their minds to sit continuously from the 3rd January up to the middle or end of April. This will involve a very heavy strain upon them.

6. In my last letter I wrote at some length on the Cawnpore situation. I was over there for one night recently in order to attend the jubilee dinner of the Upper India Chamber of Commerce, and I had a further talk with the District Magistrate.[50] He is pleased with the effects of his order under Section 144. It has had the result of practically stopping undesirable speeches and demonstrations organised by the communists. At the moment therefore he is not pressing for any action in the direction of prosecution in respect of the speeches of any individuals. His anticipations for the future, however, are not hopeful, and he thinks it more than likely that next hot weather will see a renewal of the strike. I felt it necessary in my

speech at the jubilee dinner to refer to the relations between capital and labour and also the communist menace. In regard to the latter I had to speak with considerable caution, as it was no use my denouncing communist activities at a time when my Government were really not prepared to do anything effective about them. Consequently what I said was perhaps a good deal less than my audience would have liked. On the whole, however, I think it was worth saying. I enclose a copy of my speech.[51] I am coming more and more to the view that the real trouble in Cawnpore is that Pandit Bal Krishna Sharma, whom I mentioned in my last letter and who is an exceedingly ambitious opportunist, has a very strong position in Cawnpore which the Ministry dare not challenge. I think that accounts for many of their vacillations in matters affecting Cawnpore. In a recent conversation which I had with Dr. Katju, who is the Minister for Industries, he hinted to me pretty plainly that that was the root of their difficulties.

7. The police situation is I think more hopeful. I have heard from various sources that my speech on the occasion of the police parade in Lucknow was greatly appreciated by the inspectors and sub-inspectors, particularly because it gave the police praise, to which they had been for some time unaccustomed. This is of course only a transitory influence. What is much more important is that the Premier recently visited the Police Training School at Moradabad, and the Inspector-General of Police who accompanied him was more than pleased with his attitude and with the impression he made on a considerable number of police officers with whom he came in contact there. The Premier himself was very well impressed by the work that is being done at the Training School and by the standard of the cadets, and I hope that this visit will have done a good deal to promote an understanding on both sides which is the only foundation for better relations. I have had no further talk with the Premier on the anti-corruption issue, as I wished him to ponder over the general suggestions I have made in my note. But I was particularly glad to find from the Inspector-General of Police that the Premier in his address to the police at Moradabad appeared to have gone a long way towards adopting the general attitude which I had commended in my note. He stressed in particular the fact that members of the police force must be under the control of their own officers in all disciplinary matters. He urged the necessity of the police force as a whole setting itself loyally to carrying out the policy of the Ministry, and I hope that he will really take my advice and depend on the police themselves to proceed against corruption rather than rely upon an outside organization.

8. The Anti-Corruption Report, however, still remains an embarrassment.

In my opinion it contains certain ill-considered and dangerous proposals. Sir Maharaj Singh, its author, feels obviously that his credit is involved in the carrying out of these recommendations and is continually pressing the Government as to what action they are taking on the report. I do not think that they themselves regard it with as much admiration as its author does; but it is a popular cry and it is difficult to continue to do nothing. The Ministers therefore have asked that we should resume consideration of the report in Cabinet at the point at which it was left when Hallett took it up shortly before I returned from leave.

9. You may have seen in the papers various accounts of the Lucknow University convocation which I attended. The convocation address was being given by Pant, and I felt it was important in the interest of our general relations before the public that I should make a point of presiding on this occasion at the convocation. The Vice-Chancellor[52] had assured me that he anticipated no kind of trouble or unpleasantness from the students and told me there was no question of Congress flags. I had asked the Premier several times for an advance copy of his convocation address, but I finally received it only on the evening of the day before it was to be delivered. I think it was quite true that it had only just been finished. In everything he does, he has to work against time. When I saw the address, I was sorry to find that he had instructed so much politics into it, though the general tone was reasonable. There were two passages in particular which I felt were embarrassing to me. The first was a very strongly worded denunciation of the German behaviour towards the Jews which I thought might, in view of the circumstances of the case and of my presiding, provoke a protest from the German Consul-General. The second was an outspoken condemnation of the attitude of the Prime Minister in regard to Czechoslovakia. At the end of the address also he spoke of an independent India in a way which was not very suitable to the occasion. I got my Secretary to ring him up that evening and say that I felt difficulties over these passages. He said he was sorry about it, that he would certainly have modified them if he had any idea that I should object to them, but that the address had gone for printing and that it was too late to make any changes. I decided that the best course would be for me to make some remarks of a general character in the way of comment after his address.

10. Half an hour or so before the convocation was due to start some of the students proceeded to hoist a Congress flag on one of the domes at the far side of the quadrangle in which the convocation was being held and therefore facing me as I sat on the dais. It appears that as soon as this was noticed, the Vice-Chancellor sent up some chaprasis with orders to pull

the flag down. But this move was observed and loud cries of protest were raised. The Vice-Chancellor fearing that there might be something of a tumult just at the beginning of the convocation decided to leave things alone. Actually when our procession marched in there were still some cries of *Inqilab zindabad* going on, but these died down as soon as we had taken our seats. At Lucknow a practice prevails different to that followed at Allahabad and Agra. At the latter universities the names of all the students who are to receive particular degrees are read out and they stand up in their places and the degree is then conferred. At Lucknow the practice is that the students as their names are read out file up in front of the Chancellor, bow and pass on. Two or three of the students rather ostentatiously did not bow when they came before me, but on the whole their general attitude was perfectly respectful and polite, and by the time it came to my giving away the medals the atmosphere which at the beginning had been a little tense seemed to me to have become decidedly friendly. Pant's convocation address was then delivered and was received without any particular enthusiasm. Forty-five minutes of reading tries the patience of most audiences. When he had finished I got up and spoke briefly without notes, which in contrast to Pant's reading was, I think, effective. I enclose a record of what I said.[53] My remarks were received very well by the students and at the same time, as I heard afterwards, pleased the old-fashioned people of whom a large number were present. I was applauded at least as loudly as the Premier, and on the whole I felt that the proceedings which might have been rather difficult went off well.

11. About ten days ago I went on a short tour which included two days going round the newer tube-well areas where the wells were only finished about a year ago. I was anxious to see how they were doing in a year which was obviously going to test somewhat severely the amount of the sub-soil water-supply. We had always realised that the worst conditions would be a failure of the monsoon, which would in itself deplete the sub-soil water, followed as it must be by an intensive demand for irrigation in the *rabi*. These are precisely the conditions prevailing in the western districts, and the wells that I visited, mainly in the Budaun district, had been working practically without intermission for over twenty hours a day for the last 2½ months. I was assured, however, that this had not apparently affected the water level, though of course it had dropped in consequence of the lack of rain in the monsoon. The wells were giving their full supply of water, and I found on an average that 300 acres of *rabi* were being irrigated by each well. That means that in this district alone the tube-wells are doing over 100,000 acres of irrigation in a year in which without the

tube-wells there would have been the greatest difficulty over the *rabi* crop. I understand that in other areas the results are much the same, and financially this year the tube-wells are likely to show an appreciable profit. There is no doubt to my mind that the scheme has very fully justified itself.

12. While I am on the subject of rural conditions, I may mention that my Minister for Communications has worked out a very comprehensive scheme for improving the communications of the Province. If the scheme can be put through, many rural areas will be opened up with great advantage to themselves. The scheme involves raising a loan of about 1½ crores on the basis of the proceeds from our own motor vehicles tax, and it contains fairly comprehensive proposals for providing the income which will be necessary for the upkeep of the additional length of roads. Some of the roads would be metalled, others would provide only for wheel tracks and others would be unmetalled. The Minister himself is prepared to go a long way in the direction of special taxation to aid this scheme. I do not think the Ministry as a whole would support the taxation of carts which he proposes. But at least the scheme is a good one, and approached in a practical spirit, and I mention it as an interesting and encouraging example of the practical side of the activities of the Ministry.

13. There was considerable discussion recently in the Assembly about a case in which the Ministry had decided to release a man who had been convicted of murder. I have not really seen the papers recently, but I have some recollection of the case. The District Magistrate and the Commissioner made a representation to Government that a certain man who had been convicted of murder in a communal affray in Saharanpur was believed by local opinion to be guiltless and to have been wrongly implicated. The case came up under the old constitution, and I took the line that we could not allow ourselves to be influenced by local gossip as against the findings of the Courts, and we refused to interfere. The case was again taken up under the present constitution and the Minister of Justice went into the details with considerable care. He convinced himself that in fact a certain point in the case had been overlooked by the Courts and that had this point been brought before the Courts they would have been bound to acquit this man. The matter came up in the time of Hallett and I understand he pointed out all the implications of the case and the matter was considered by all the Ministers. They decided to support the Minister of Justice and orders were issued for the release of this man. The action taken was attacked, as it was bound to be attacked, on communal grounds by the Muslims. I think myself it is only in the very rarest cases

that a Government ought to take the responsibility of actually releasing a convicted murderer, which amounts to declaring their own belief that he was wrongly convicted. But in this case at any rate the matter was gone into most carefully and was dealt with strictly on the merits as they appeared to the Ministers.

14. My Minister for Education, Sampurnanand, who lives at Benares, told me while we were discussing Federation recently that an attack was about to be launched on the Benares State because they were not prepared to concede a constitution. I had heard nothing of this, and I am not sure how far he was talking with inner knowledge and how far he was basing himself on a paragraph in the papers which I have since seen. But I am rather afraid that as he is himself a resident of Benares, he was talking with some inner knowledge and that a definite attack on the State administration may be in contemplation. If this is so, I fear the State will not be well placed, for the agitation will no doubt be directed from Benares city and I doubt if the administration is of a kind which would be able to handle such an agitation successfully. I mentioned the matter to the Premier who told me he had heard nothing about it, but he was going to Benares and he promised to look into it. I feel sure he would not desire to encourage anything of the sort.

15. Affairs are going on quietly in the Province as indicated by the official fortnightly report which I enclose. Our main anxiety at the moment is to have satisfactory winter rains which would do an immense amount of good in the west of the Province. In my recent tour I visited Shahjahanpur, an area where dacoity has been particularly bad. This is naturally a somewhat turbulent district and I think the police administration has for a time been rather ineffective. Special measures however are now being taken to deal with the dacoity problem, and with a new and vigorous District Magistrate just appointed[54] I hope that conditions will before long be restored to normal. There is no particular political problem there. It is rather a matter of administration.

16. I was most interested in what you wrote in paragraph 6 of your letter about the volunteer movement and the proposals that are being put forward for military training in schools. It is difficult to know what is the best line to take in regard to the latter. I fear it would not be at all easy to combat it directly. There is I think a great deal to be said for Hallett's view of trying to guide it. The volunteers are, or may be, a more formidable proposition.

17. I was amused by what you tell me about reporting in the House of Lords some time ago.[55] We certainly have difficulties with our present

system of reporting and the use of two languages and three scripts. Did you know that the debates now blare forth on to the public highway through a loud speaker?

With all good wishes for the New Year.

Yours sincerely,
H.G. HAIG

84

HAIG TO LINLITHGOW
Telegram
R/3/1/74

Most Secret *December 28th, 1938*
No. 187-G

Your Excellency's most secret letter of December 22nd regarding constitutional position in the event of war.[56] I will attempt in the first place some estimate of probable attitude of my Government towards war measures, based on their general outlook and conversations I had with Pant in September.

(*a*) I think they would be prepared to carry out general policy of Centre in matters of routine character.

(*b*) Difficulty might arise as soon as they were asked to take action on their own which was in conflict with their normal policy for instance in regard to interception or detention of individuals.

(*c*) If full legal powers were possessed by Centre and responsibility for all action directed to prosecution of war were clearly on Congress I think Ministers would find their position less difficult. This does not necessarily mean that there would not be a break. That would depend on All-India Congress policy. If Congress wanted a break in the event of war there would be one. If they did not want a break it is probable that a system under which the Centre issue instructions in all matters of this kind would give less occasion for trouble than a system which required a definite degree of voluntary co-operation from Provincial Governments.

2. I agree that powers now suggested for Centre would be necessary for the effective conduct of war. I also (agree) that their existence would smooth the path of Provincial Government if it did not wish to refuse to co-operate. But it is one thing to appreciate the advantage of powers if they were in existence; it is quite another thing to hold that powers which unfortunately are not in existence should be taken at once. My view is that it will certainly

be necessary to take powers if war breaks out. The purport of the question appears to be whether they should be taken now or at outbreak of war.

3. It is difficult to speak with assurance about probable political reactions of proposing these amendments now. But it is clear that opportunity for criticism and misrepresentation would be very wide and I think it would be a grave mistake to underestimate the probability that a controversy seriously disturbing present political conditions would develop. How far such controversy would be carried would depend presumably on general policy of Congress Working Committee. But more extreme elements in Congress would I should judge do all they could to exploit the situation. My own Ministers are very jealous of any appearance of invasion of their powers by central authority and it seems to me likely that there would be protests by Provincial Governments against legislation proposed. There would also be much talk about Imperialistic wars and it would be assumed that we should be engaged in a war unjustifiable from the point of view of India. We should have to meet criticism based on hypotheses and prejudice would be created. Situation would give rise to sufficient embarrassment and political difficulties, to put it at its lowest, as to make it in my opinion very desirable to avoid these results if any other reasonable alternative is open.

4. So far as I can judge I should (consider) that it would meet practical requirements if powers were taken immediately on outbreak of war. When we were on brink of war in September it appeared to me that it was likely to be some time before India would be seriously affected and fully involved in consequences of war. If that is so then the arguments for making amendments now instead of on outbreak of war seem to resolve themselves into certain practical difficulties of preparing Rules which, while I do not underestimate them, should not in my opinion be decisive in a matter like this. Admittedly the taking of these powers on outbreak of war might be a contributory cause or quiet [*sic*] pretext for Congress to refuse their co-operation. But if that is their mood a break would in any case be inevitable. If Congress were in a co-operating mood and war one to which (it) could hardly regard itself indifferent, I think powers of this kind might be accepted without much difficulty when emergency was actually upon country. It is my definite belief that powers would be far more strongly resented if they were taken now than if they were taken on outbreak of war.

NOTES

1. Lord Brabourne minuted: 'I suspect that the landlords are putting off a settlement in the hope that War may bring an end to the Congress Govt.!'
2. Lord Brabourne minuted: 'A state of affairs which may well become serious if not checked.'
3. Lord Brabourne minuted: 'Good.'
4. These heads of departments were respectively Mr R.S. Weir (Education), Mr Wajahat Hussain (Irrigation and Buildings and Roads) and Mr E.A. Smythies (Chief Conservator, Forests).
5. Mr M.R. Richardson.
6. Mr W.A.C. Pearce.
7. Mr K.M. O'Riordon was the Deputy-Inspector of Police whose responsibilities included supervision of Jhansi Division.
8. R/3/1/74.
9. In his letter of 10 October 1938 Lord Brabourne asked Sir Harry Haig whether he agreed with the views on the U.P.'s rural development proposal expressed by Sir Maurice Hallett in No. 63. In addition Brabourne asked for Haig's views on two suggestions which had been made: (*a*) that no part of the Government of India's grant should be spent on the salaries of paid officials; (*b*) that all expenditure from Government of India grants to the District Association should be sanctioned by the District Officer. As indicated in paragraph 8 of Haig's present letter, Brabourne mentioned that a third suggestion had been made but he did not wish to pursue it. R/3/1/74.
10. Mr M.D. Chaturvedi.
11. Not included in R/3/1/74.
12. Not printed.
13. OGPU was the early security and political police of the Soviet Union.
14. Lord Linlithgow minuted: 'P.S.V. – I should be happy to help Mr. Saksena if that is possible.'
15. Mr W.C. Dible.
16. Mr H.S. Ross, Commissioner of Jhansi, had returned from leave on 18 October 1938.
17. The District Magistrates of Cawnpore and Allahabad at this date were respectively Mr L. Owen and Mr G.W.M. Whittle.
18. In paragraph 7 of his letter of 1 November 1938, Lord Linlithgow said he hoped he might have the chance of seeing Pandit Pant if he was coming to Delhi. R/3/1/74.
19. Lord Linlithgow minuted on 10 November 1938: 'P.S.V. – Paras. 1, 2 and 3 make rather disturbing reading. The question is whether I ought to represent to the Governor the need for active pressure by him upon his Chief Minister and Colleagues towards moving them to giving better support to their Executives in the divisions mentioned. It is really little use for the G[overno]r to write that these most disquieting signs are due to the machinations of a

few rascals. The point is that the D.Os. and the Police have their tails down, and that bad conditions prevail. I do *not* like this letter.'

20. Mr Donaldson's note is not included in R/3/1/74.
21. Lord Linlithgow replied on 30 November 1938 and enclosed a note by Mr E. Conran-Smith, Joint Secretary of the Reforms Department of the Government of India. The note concluded with the following statements: 'There has therefore been no change in the attitude of the Government of India and the Secretary of State since 1934 in regard to proposals for the abolition of Commissionerships. Such proposals would not be considered favourably if they were dictated by purely political objects or a desire to attack the Services. . . . [T]he Government of India continue to regard with suspicion any general move for abolition of Commissioners as such in pursuance of the general policy of the Congress of weakening the district administration and isolating the Governor from his District Officers. . . . The need for Commissioners would be especially urgent if the Governor were at any time compelled to assume control under Section 93 of the Government of India Act.' R/3/1/74.
22. In his letter of 12 November 1938, Lord Linlithgow said that there were no concrete proposals before the Government of India at that time for cuts in the pay of its services. The Viceroy was unable to say whether a deterioration in the financial situation would make it necessary to consider so drastic a step. R/3/1/74.
23. Sir Harry Haig wrote again to Lord Linlithgow on 19 November 1938 with respect to paragraph 4 of the present letter. Haig said he had had examined the proposal that existing rates of pay should not be continued in the case of officers promoted to higher posts borne on the cadre of the service. It appeared that in some cases an officer would be entitled to less pay on promotion than he would receive on the time-scale of his previous post. The officer would therefore remain on the time-scale and receive nothing on account of promotion. Haig now felt that there might be a very strong case for refusing to accept the advice of his Ministers on this point. R/3/1/74.
24. Mr W. Christie.
25. Lord Linlithgow replied to this letter on 7 December 1938. Linlithgow was asking the Governor's Secretary in Madras to supply Sir Harry Haig's Secretary with information on the Madras experience. Linlithgow would await Haig's further recommendations following his study of the Madras material. The Viceroy noted that Haig was inclined to accept the general position of the Ministry that considerable reductions in special pay and compensatory allowances should be made up to the limit of what might be considered reasonable. Linlithgow saw no reason to advise Haig in a contrary sense. Ibid.
26. Lord Linlithgow minuted: 'Does not the G[overnor] get an official Report? It seems to me extraordinary that the Governor of a province should not be able to know precisely what his P.M. said in the provincial legislature.'

27. The *Leader* (Allahabad) of 10 November 1938 carried a report from Cawnpore dated 8 November. According to this Mr Subhas Chandra Bose had sent a telegram to the Cawnpore Congress President which read: 'The parliamentary sub-committee has decided not to interfere with the pending tenancy legislation. The matter therefore rests with the Assembly. I hope the public and the Kisans will be satisifed.'
28. In a lengthy statement issued in Bombay on 12 November 1938, Sardar Patel said that the Congress parliamentary sub-committee, in agreeing to arbitration in respect of the U.P. Tenancy Bill, had done so on the basis that its arbitration had to be accepted as final. The Oudh Taluqdars had rejected this but had asked the Congress sub-committee to negotiate a settlement. The sub-committee felt no useful purpose would be served by taking up this request.

    Patel acknowledged that the Nawab of Chhatari was still pursuing the arbitration proposal but Patel added: 'now it is too late to mend matters'.
29. Pandit Nehru had been away from India from the beginning of June 1938 in order to visit Europe.
30. Mr H.S. Ross.
31. Lieutenant-Colonel A.J. Muirhead was Parliamentary Under-Secretary of State for India and Mr E.H. Keeling was his Parliamentary Private Secretary.
32. Lord Linlithgow recorded two minutes on this letter as follows: (1) 24.11.38. 'P.S.V. – This is a disturbing letter and I feel bound to send a copy of it to S./S. It is of interest to note the curious fact that para. 8 shows something like resentment at the suggestion that the Agra Division is deteriorating, while the rest of the letter is full of gloomy prognostications. I note, too, the complete lack of touch between the Governor and the P.M. over the Tenancy Bill issue. I have the impression that this estrangement is increasing. Then again, there is the very significant passage analysing the P.M.'s probable feelings towards the British – a new note for Haig to sound. I think the time is approaching for another talk with Haig, perhaps in Feb[ruar]y. Much as I wish to avoid bringing matters to a head in that way. But a visit up here need not involve censure, or the appearance of it.' [For Linlithgow's earlier discussions with Sir Harry Haig, see *U.P.P., 1936-37*, Appendices 11 and 12.]

    (2) 1.12.38. 'P.S.V. – *Later.* I am content to comment on his p[oin]ts (*a*) the impression from this letter that the Governor is not as much in the confidence of his P.M. as is desirable; (*b*) the subject of the pencil marginal note on p. 2' [Presumably a reference to Linlithgow's minute in note 26 above.]
33. Sir J.P. Srivastava.
34. Pandit Nehru.
35. The Nawab of Chhatari had been Governor of the U.P. in 1928 and 1933 and Premier April-July 1937.

36. Lord Linlithgow minuted: 'P.S.V. – Inform other G[overnor]s and ask them to keep an eye open for early signs of any such movement in their own charges.'
37. Mr A.A. Waugh.
38. Mr L. Owen.
39. Not included in R/3/1/74.
40. Not printed.
41. Not printed.
42. Khwaja Sir Nazimuddin was Home Minister in Bengal at this date.
43. Lord Linlithgow minuted 'P.S.V. – I am coming to feel that the trouble is in part due to the Premier's mental make up. He is the one P.M. and his Govt. the only Govt. in a *big* province which does not stand up to challenge. We may be sure that Pant misses it somewhere, or he would not have failed to make good for the inner circle of Congress.'
44. In paragraphs 2 and 3 of his letter of 5 December 1938 to Sir Harry Haig, Lord Linlithgow said he was greatly interested in Haig's account of his talk with Mrs Pandit given in No. 79. Linlithgow shared the concern felt at the increase in the influence of the left-wing on the U.P. government. The Viceroy said he had not been entirely satisfied in the past with Pandit Pant. However he readily agreed that:

    'the alternatives to him are not easy to find, and that within reason therefore we must be prepared to put up with certain things which we do not much like. I do not dispute that the answer to many of our difficulties might well be that the type of situation which shows signs of beginning to emerge is in effect implicit in the Act; that the risk of the Left-Wing preponderance becoming dominant is inherent in the system of government which has been established, and that we must not take it unduly tragically if that result comes about.'

    It may be that Haig would feel that there was nothing to be done but watch the situation and only move should the swing to the left-wing become too pronounced. On the other hand Linlithgow wondered 'what policy it would be wise for us to adopt should pressure of a Left-Wing character on a Right-Wing Prime Minister lead or oblige that Prime Minister to support courses the adoption of which on a long view in our judgment cannot but be detrimental to the future of constitutional government….' Linlithgow looked forward to Haig's comments. R/3/1/74.
45. Lord Linlithgow minuted: 'Has it any *organisations* in the villages?'
46. Lord Linlthgow minuted: 'A broken reed when Mr. G[andhi] leaves the world.'
47. Lord Linlithgow minuted: 'The only ultimate refuge is in a split in C[ongress], with the right joining moderate opinion in defence of the rights of property. For that Pant may yet prove to be the right man.'

48. Lord Linlithgow minuted: 'But for *this* purpose Pant is better in opposition, surely.'
49. Lord Linlithgow minuted: 'I quite agree. Another way of saying the same thing is that no one yet knows whether Indians as a whole are, or are not, capable of developing those natural protective or resistive qualities by which an experienced electorate sees through the wiles of the more blatant and damaging forms of vote catching, and – on the whole – tends to reȧct away from those extreme courses which, if pursued, must lead to anarchy, or a revolution from one side or t'other.
'Plainly, our job, now that the decision to try out representative Government has been taken, is to so play the hand as to encourage by every means the growth of those normal and healthy responses, while seeing to it that the administrative machine and the respect for law and order don't quite disappear in the process.'
50. Mr L. Owen.
51. Not printed.
52. Sheikh Muhammad Habibullah.
53. This record is not included in R/3/1/74.
54. Mr W.W. Finlay had been appointed District Magistrate of Shahjahanpur on 2 December 1938.
55. In paragraph 11 of his letter of 5 December 1938, Lord Linlithgow recalled that when he had entered the House of Lords thirty years previously, members were given ten days to check the galley proof of the report of their speeches. This allowed for a considerable embellishment of what had actually been said. R/3/1/74.
56. In his circular letter of 22 December 1938 to Governors, Lord Linlithgow explained that his Government had been anxious for some time past about the constitutional position of India in relation to the conduct of a war. While a proclamation of a state of emergency under the Government of India Act transferred concurrent legislative powers to the Centre in respect of Provincial subjects, it did not transfer corresponding executive authority. It had therefore been suggested that an amendment to the Government of India Act should be made and the Viceroy enclosed a considerable amount of correspondence elaborating the idea. Linlithgow sought Governors' views and in particular an assessment of probable political effects in their Provinces. R/3/1/74.

Appendices

APPENDIX 1

LINLITHGOW TO HAIG
MSS.EUR.F 115/12

Secret and Personal

The Viceroy's House, New Delhi,
February 1st, 1938

My dear Haig,

You will remember that on the 24th December[1] I wrote to you on the subject of the circular letter[2] issued over Mr. Gwynne's signature to District Magistrates regarding their relations with the Congress and I there expressed my apprehensions regarding the possible effect of such a circular on the minds of Government servants so long as they regard those instructions as binding on them. A cutting from the *Hindustan Times* of the 22nd December has since come to my notice reproducing a circular alleged to have been issued by the Superintendent of Police, Meerut,[3] to all police subordinates of that district in amplification of the U.P. Government's circular. If such a circular was really issued by the Superintendent of Police I can only feel that the fears which I expressed earlier have soon been warranted, and I should be very glad of any information which you can give me as regards the circumstances of its issue and its effect on the minds of the subordinates addressed. *Prima facie* I can hardly conceive a circular more likely to have a depressing effect upon the local police. Its general tone is such as to place all police officers in the dock and to inform them that their only hope lies in submitting themselves to the methods adopted by the local Congress Committee "to convert them from their evil ways". The circular as a whole appears to give an official status to the Congress party organisation in the district and to place the local police under its disciplinary supervision.

2. Apart from that aspect of the circular, the publicity given to these orders appears to be open to serious objection. It is a fundamental principle that instructions to the police should issue only in the form of departmental orders which are unpublished official records and should not be treated as official communiqués or be given to the press. The most that would have been permissible in such a case would have been to publish a brief statement to the effect that the principles laid down by the Provincial Government for the guidance of its officials in respect of their relations with the public had been communicated to all concerned in the form of detailed official instructions. But to allow the actual instructions to be published – especially instructions in such terms – seems to me to be most detrimental to the discipline and morale of the police.

3. No doubt this circular of the Superintendent of Police is as little to your liking as it is to mine and I hope that you have in the meanwhile been able to do something, as suggested in my previous letter, to remove any misapprehensions among officials to which the previous Government circular may have given rise. It would seem, however, most necessary to correct the ideas of the Superintendent of Police, Meerut, on this subject, since I can hardly imagine that an officer capable of issuing such a circular is fit to command the police force of a district so long as he remains in his present frame of mind.

Yours sincerely,
LINLITHGOW

APPENDIX 2

COMMUNIQUÉ BY DONALDSON
MSS.EUR.F 115/22B

Lucknow,
February 15th, 1938

The Council of Ministers of the United Provinces raised not long since with His Excellency the Governor the question of the release of the fifteen prisoners classed as political who are still serving sentences imposed by Courts in the United Provinces for offences which are, with one exception, directly connected with methods of violence. The question of the release of the so-called political prisoners in the United Provinces has a history dating from the assumption of office by the present Ministers. At a very early stage general orders were issued for the release of political prisoners who had not been engaged in acts of violence but whose offences were for the most part connected with the law of sedition. Very shortly afterwards the Ministers raised the question of the release of prisoners convicted in connection with offences of violence, whose crimes had some political background. Those for whose release they pressed in particular were the prisoners who had been convicted in the Kakori case, which dealt with an elaborate conspiracy extending over a considerable period in the course of which a number of dacoities and murders were committed. After considerable discussion and anxious consideration the Governor agreed at the end of August to release of a batch of ten prisoners including six convicted in the Kakori case. The release of the Kakori prisoners was made the occasion of widespread demonstrations of a revolutionary character which made a great impression on the public mind. For a time the policy of gradual release of prisoners guilty of acts of violence was suspended owing to the unexpected and disturbing nature of these demonstrations and the public reaction to them. Subsequently about the end of October when the Ministry again took up strongly the question of further releases, His Excellency agreed to the release of five more prisoners. The policy of gradual release was again suspended owing to the activities of the Kakori prisoners, which came to light in October and November, in touring round the province, making speeches of a revolutionary character and in certain cases inciting to violence. The activities of these men proved very disturbing to the United Provinces Government, which found it necessary at the end of December to issue a most serious warning that they could no longer refrain from prosecution in the case of speeches inciting to violence, and that they held themselves free to institute proceedings without any further warning against any individual who offended in this manner. The more active of the Kakori prisoners had been at this time arrested in Delhi for breach of an order and were convicted and sentenced to certain terms of imprisonment. Partly as a result of this and partly as a result of the warning issued by the Government the stream of dangerous speeches was checked and the atmosphere in the province became more tranquil.

Early in January the Ministry again took up the question of releasing the remaining political prisoners. After close and frequent discussions, in the course of which the Ministers explained their hopes that the release of the remaining prisoners would not lead to any renewal of violent activities or the propagation of ideas of violence, the Governor expressed his willingness to consider further the question of release of individuals on an examination of their records and connections.

The Ministers however found themselves unable to accept this course and formally advised the Governor to agree to the immediate release of the fifteen prisoners. Of these six have been actively engaged in the terrorist movement, four of them being regarded as important members of the terrorist party, and one of these as a prominent organiser. The remaining prisoners include one communist and the others have been convicted for the most part of robbery or dacoity.

These were the circumstances in which the advice of the Ministers for a general and immediate release was tendered to His Excellency. The Governor has taken steps to draw the attention of his Ministers to the serious nature of the issues involved, to the importance of maintaining the sanctions of law, to the dangers of giving further encouragement to the revolutionary movement, and to the responsibility of Government to the law-abiding public for the security of life and of property in the province. His Ministers were however unable to modify their advice to him and he accordingly reserved the matter for consideration and referred it to the Governor-General. The Governor-General thereupon issued instructions to him under Section 126 (5) of the Government of India Act, and in the light of those instructions His Excellency the Governor has found himself unable to accept the advice of his Ministers who have in consequence tendered their resignation. His Excellency has informed them that he notes that they have tendered their resignation, but that before accepting it he must consider the alternative arrangements to be made to enable the King's Government to be carried on.

[J.C. DONALDSON]
Secretary to His Excellency the
Governor, United Provinces

APPENDIX 3

STATEMENT BY PANT[4]
MSS.EUR.F 115/22B

February 18th, 1938

A communiqué stating the Governor's case as regards the release of political prisoners and explaining his views in the matter appeared in the newspapers yesterday in the name of Mr. J.C. Donaldson, Secretary to the Governor, United Provinces. I have on a close examination found that it is somewhat incomplete, if not inaccurate.

However, one significant fact, which is of paramount importance, distinctly emerges out of the statement namely that although the Governor was not satisfied about the wisdom of the course decided upon by the Ministers he did not think that his special responsibility for any grave menace to peace or tranquillity in the province was involved in the matter of release of these prisoners. The Governor-General too seems to have shared this view as neither the Governor has taken action under Section 54, Clause 1, nor the Governor-General, in accordance with Section 54, Clause 2, of the Government of India Act. The Governor-General's instructions under Section 126, Clause 5, are apparently based on extra-provincial considerations and in these circumstances the explanation for the Governor-General's interference should be found elsewhere beyond our own province. The narrative given in the Governor's communiqué being restricted to events that happened inside the province itself is thus hardly relevant.

Still I should like to advert to certain facts that the Governor's Secretary has mentioned in his historical retrospect. At least three points are conclusively established by his narration of facts: (1) that the Ministers throughout showed remarkable patience, (2) that they acted with great restraint having repeatedly suppressed their own better judgment out of regard for Governor's wishes, and (3) that they throughout took a realistic view of the situation and fully took facts into account in regulating their course of action from time to time.

As the communiqué states, soon after assumption of office by them, the Ministers pressed for the release of political prisoners of this class, there was "considerable discussion and anxious consideration" for more than a month and ultimately 10 prisoners were discharged in August. As to the rest, the Ministers stayed their hands out of deference for the Governor's views.

The communiqué proceeds to say that the Ministry again "took up strongly the question of further release", but as the Governor expressed his difficulty in releasing more than five prisoners, the Ministers again yielded and agreed to wait further for the release of the remaining prisoners. These five were released in October and there have been, according to the communiqué, "close and frequent discussions" since.

During this interval the Ministers thoroughly examined and noted the individual cases of at least seven prisoners and they definitely suggested their release early in January. One of them actually spitted blood about that time and his release was also recommended on medical grounds for prolonged treatment in a decent sanatorium by no less a person that the superintendent of his jail in the second week of January. Nevertheless not a single prisoner had been released since October.

A lot of the valuable time of the Governor and of the Ministers was taken by these interminable and inconclusive discussions. No release had been allowed in the course of the last three and a half months. Thus a stalemate had been reached for all practical purposes. At the same time the question of release of political prisoners had become progressively still more important and, owing to their resort to hunger-strike in certain provinces, even grave.

We had to take active measures to dissuade the prisoners in our province from adopting such embarrassing methods and they respected our advice. Public criticism of our omission or inability to release them was gathering fresh momentum every day. In some cases it was actually getting bitter. The atmosphere for serious constructive work on which we wanted to concentrate was visibly disturbed and the tension was increasing.

It was equally obvious that the release of a few individuals would not meet the situation. On the contrary, every person who was let out took it as a point of honour to work for the release of those left in jail. The speeches and the energies of the Kakori prisoners, to which reference has been made in the communiqué, had been directed to this end and it was not inconceivable that had all prisoners been released in the beginning, the released prisoners would not have had the occasion for their agitation.

I should also like to point out that of the speeches referred to by Mr. Donaldson the worst were made not by the released Kakori prisoners but by one who was discharged by the Punjab Government after he had fully served out his term of 21 years' imprisonment. If I am not mistaken, only two Kakori prisoners delivered speeches which were considered actionable. As the communiqué points out, we were fully satisfied that the release of these 15 prisoners would not "lead to any renewal of violent activity or propagation of ideas of violence" and we had taken good care to assure ourselves in this respect. That these prisoners had been convicted of offences involving violence was of course well known and, as the communiqué points out, we had already released prisoners who had been charged with robbery, dacoity, etc. So no new principle was involved.

It is necessary to precisely define here the proposition for which the Ministers had sought the Governor's assent. There was, in fact, no serious objection to the examination of individual cases but the real question was as to who should do so – the Ministers or the Governor. The principle being accepted, the working and execution of it was no more than a matter of detail to be left to the Ministers concerned.

We were oppressed with the nauseating futility of interminable discussions and it was no longer possible to put off the final decision. We tendered our advice and requested the Governor to confide in our judgment as responsible Ministers in charge of law and order as regards these 15 cases and asked him not to stand in the way of our determining the time and pace of these releases.

The Congress session was approaching fast. The release of political prisoners had always held a prominent place in the Congress programme. The session would naturally like to take stock of the achievements and omissions of the Congress Ministers. The danger of hunger-strike was not yet past and, whatever view one might take of such practices in abstract theory, their practical reactions could not be ignored by a popular Ministry, especially when it had sought the suffrage of the people on a definite programme which included the release of prisoners as one of its items.

So we had no doubt as to the minimum requirements of the situation. We, therefore, wanted to ensure a position in which we could definitely declare at Haripura that there was no danger of any resistance to the release of these prisoners from any quarter and that the decision solely rested with us. It was exceedingly repugnant to our sense of self-respect to take shelter under the plea that we were powerless to effect such releases.

Four of these prisoners were of no more than 17 or 18 years of age at the time of their conviction, eight I believe, were between the ages of 18 and 35, several had already served long terms of imprisonment and four I think, were due to be released between three and nine months.

The issue was really very narrow, namely whether the Governor should reject the advice of the Council of Ministers if he did not find himself in agreement with them as regards the release of one or two or a few more individuals out of 15. It would be a mockery even of the provincial autonomy provided in this grotesque scheme of the Government of India Act if the Governor were allowed to override his Council in these matters of detail regarding individual cases.

However I have no desire to discuss the constitutional aspect as I am concerned for the moment only with the Governor's communiqué.

The communiqué has laid some stress on the demonstrations that accompanied the release of the Kakori prisoners in August. Six more prisoners were, however, released thereafter in October one of whom was a prominent member of the Kakori group. By that time the excitement associated with these demonstrations had worked itself out and we were all agreed that further releases need not be postponed on that account.

It is worth remembering that the releases of these six prisoners were not marked by any such scenes. They were not accorded any reception and they quietly made their way to their respective residences from jail. It was evident that the levity which marked the release of the Kakori prisoners in the first flush had completely vanished by the time of these releases in October. In fact, meanwhile, there had been a distinct change in the public feeling. Mahatma Gandhi had strongly condemned such action. It had also been disapproved by Pandit Jawaharlal Nehru. The mistake had been candidly confessed by those who had taken part in these demonstrations.

The political tranquillity of the province was not seriously disturbed at any time, whether by demonstrations or by speeches. And the ripple had completely subsided by the time these 15 cases were taken up for consideration.

The Ministers, though naturally reluctant to use the coercive apparatus of State, had made it perfectly clear that whenever necessity arose they would do so. In fact, they did not hesitate to take such steps when occasion demanded, as at Cawnpore. And, as the communiqué states, they had always issued stern warnings to stop objectionable speeches. They abhorred the idea of shirking their responsibility or taking shelter behind the Governor's special powers.

APPENDIX 4

RESOLUTION OF ALL-INDIA CONGRESS COMMITTEE
MSS.EUR.F 115/8

Haripura,
February 21st, 1938

In accordance with the direction of the Faizpur Congress, the All-India Congress Committee decided in March 1937, the issue of acceptance of office in the provinces and permitted Congressmen to form ministries provided certain assurances were given by or on behalf of the British Government. These assurances not being forthcoming, the leaders of the Congress parties in the provincial assemblies declined at first to form ministries. Thereafter there was considerable argument for some months regarding these assurances and various declarations were made by the Secretary of State for India, the Viceroy and the Governors of the provinces. In these declarations it was definitely stated, among other things, that there would be no interference with the day to day administration of the provincial affairs by the responsible Ministers.

Experience of office by the Congress Ministers in the provinces had shown that at least in two provinces, the United Provinces and Bihar, there has in fact been interference in the day to day administration of provincial affairs as shown hereafter. The Governors, when they invited the Congress members to form ministries, knew that the Congress election manifesto had mentioned the release of political prisoners as one of the major items of Congress policy. In pursuance thereof the Ministers began the release of political prisoners and they soon experienced delay, which was sometimes vexatious, before the Governors would endorse the orders for release. The way releases have been repeatedly delayed is an evidence of the exemplary patience of the Ministers. In the opinion of the Congress release of prisoners is a matter coming essentially within the purview of the day to day administration which does not admit of protracted discussions with the Governors.

The function of the Governor is to guide and advise the Ministers and not to interfere with the free exercise of their judgment in the discharge of their day to day duty. It was only when the time came for the Working Committee to give the annual account to the Congress delegates and to the masses of the people backing them, that the Committee had to instruct the Ministers, who were themselves sure of their grounds, to order the release of political prisoners in their charge and to resign if their orders were countermanded. The Congress approves of and endorses the action taken by the Ministers of the United Provinces and Bihar and congratulates them on it.

In the opinion of the Congress, the interference of the Governor-General with a deliberate action of the respective Prime Ministers is not merely a violation of the assurance above referred to, but it is also a misapplication of section 126(5) of the Government of India Act. There was no question of a grave menace to peace and tranquillity involved. The Prime Ministers had, besides, in both the cases satisfied themselves from assurances from the prisoners themselves and otherwise of their change of mentality and acceptance of the Congress policy of non-violence. Indeed, it is the Governor-General's interference which has undoubtedly created a situation that may easily, in spite of the Congress effort to the contrary, become such a grave menace.

The Congress has, during the short period that Congressmen have held office, given sufficient evidence of their sacrifice, administrative capacity and constructive ability in the matter of enacting legislation for the amelioration of economic and social evils. The Congress gladly admits that a measure of co-operation was extended by the Governors to the

Ministers. It has been a sincere effort on the part of the Congress to extract what is possible from the Act for public good and to strengthen the people in pursuit of their goal of complete independence and the ending of the imperialistic exploitation of the masses of India.

The Congress does not desire to precipitate a crisis which may involve non-violent non-co-operation and direct action consistent with the Congress policy of truth and non-violence. The Congress is, therefore, at present reluctant to instruct the Ministers in other provinces to send in their resignations by way of protest against the Governor-General's action and invites His Excellency the Governor-General to reconsider his decision so that the Governors may act constitutionally and accept the advice of their Ministers in the matter of release of the political prisoners.

The Congress regards the formation of irresponsible ministers [ministries] as a way of disguising the naked rule of the sword. The formation of such ministries is calculated to rouse extreme bitterness, internal quarrels, and further deepen the resentment against the British Government. When the Congress approved of the acceptance of office, with great reluctance and considerable hesitation, it had no misgiving about its own estimate of the real nature of the Government of India Act. The latest action of the Governor-General justifies that estimate, and not only exposes the utter inadequacy of the Act to bring real liberty to the people but also shows the intention of the British Government to use and interpret it not for the expansion of liberty but for its restriction. Whatever, therefore, may be the ultimate result of the present crisis, the people of India should realize that there can be no true freedom for the country so long as this Act is not ended and a new constitution, framed by a constituent assembly elected on the basis of adult franchise, takes its place. The aim of all Congressmen, whether in office or out of office, in the legislatures or out of legislatures, can only be to reach that goal even though it may mean, as it often must mean, the sacrifice of many a present advantage, however beneficial and worthy it might be for the time being.

On behalf of the United Provinces Governor it has been stated that the demonstrations organized to welcome the Kakori prisoners and the speeches delivered by some of them had interfered with the policy of gradual release of the political prisoners. The Congress has always discouraged unseemly demonstrations and other objectionable activities. The demonstrations and speeches referred to by the United Provinces Governor were strongly disapproved by Mahatma Gandhi. Pandit Jawahar Lal Nehru, president of the Congress, had similarly taken immediate notice of the indiscipline which was thus betrayed. Nor were they ignored by the

Ministers. As a result of these corrective steps public opinion rapidly changed and even the persons concerned came to realize their mistake. And when six prisoners, one of whom was a prominent member of the Kakori group, were released subsequently, about two months after the release of the Kakori prisoners, no demonstrations were held in their honour nor any reception accorded to them.

Nearly four more months have since elapsed and any delay in releasing the remaining 15 prisoners only on account of demonstrations or speeches connected with the prisoners released in August is utterly unjustified. The responsibility for the maintenance of law and order is that of the Ministers and they are entitled to perform their functions in such manner as they deem proper. It is their business to weigh all the relevant factors in the light of the prevailing circumstances but their decision once taken ought to be accepted and enforced. Any interference with them in the exercise of their powers in the normal day to day administration is bound to undermine and weaken their position. The Congress Ministers have more than once declared their determination to take adequate action in the matter of violent crime and the risk run in releasing prisoners, specially when they have abjured the path of violence, is altogether imaginary. The Congress has given during the past months ample evidence of its desire to take a severe notice of indiscipline and breach of the code of non-violence that the Congress has laid down itself. Nevertheless the Congress invites the attention of Congressmen to the fact that indiscipline in speech and action calculated to promote or breed violence retards the progress of the country towards its cherished goal.

In the pursuit of its programme of release of the political prisoners, the Congress had not hesitated to sacrifice office and the opportunity of passing ameliorative measures. But the Congress wishes to make it clear that it strongly disapproves of hunger-strikes for release. Hunger-strikes embarrass the Congress in the pursuit of its policy of securing release of the political prisoners. The Congress, therefore, urges those who are still continuing hunger-strike in the Punjab to give up their strike and assures them that Congressmen will continue their efforts to secure the release of detenus and political prisoners by all legitimate and peaceful means.

In view of the situation that has arisen in the country, the Congress authorises the Working Committee to take such action as it may consider necessary and to take the direction of the All-India Congress Committee in dealing with the crisis whenever the necessity arises for it.

APPENDIX 5

STATEMENT BY LINLITHGOW
Cmd. 5674

February 22nd, 1938

The history of the difficulties which have arisen in the United Provinces and Bihar in connection with the release of prisoners described as political prisoners is well known. In both Provinces discussions regarding the release of prisoners in this class have, for some time past, been proceeding between Ministers and Governors; and Governors throughout made it clear that they were ready and willing to examine individual cases and would not stand in the way of release, unless where circumstances were clearly such as to involve responsibilities laid upon them by the Act. The principle of individual examination was well established over many months in Provinces where Congress is in power. It was equally established in other Provinces, and Mr. Gandhi himself has proceeded on this basis in his recent discussions with the Government of Bengal. It was thus no new thing.

2. Discussions regarding release after examination of individual cases were still proceeding, when on 14th February a demand was tendered by the Premiers of Bihar and the United Provinces for immediate general release of all prisoners classed as "political" in those two Provinces. In the case of Bihar that demand, received by the Governor at 1 p.m., called for action by the Chief Secretary in this case by 4 p.m. the same day. In the case of the United Provinces the time limit set for compliance was, also, brief to a degree. In the case of Bihar the Premier[5] made it clear that as a matter of principle he could not agree to individual examination. In the case of the United Provinces, after much discussion Ministers made it clear that a policy of gradual and individual release would not satisfy them.

3. The prisoners in question are almost without exception persons convicted of violence or of preparation for specific acts of violence, by normal criminal courts. The nature of their offences has been indicated sufficiently in the statements issued by the Governors. Their record is such that individual examination was called for, not merely for the reason I have given, but in the interest of public safety, and that examination was equally essential in the interest of maintenance of sanctions of law, and of authority and position of courts.

4. In these circumstances, having regard to the responsibilities which,

under the Constitution, are placed upon the Governor-General, the Governors of both Provinces, after consulting their Ministers, referred for my instructions the advice which their Ministers had tendered. Having regard to the circumstances described above; to the essential necessity of considering the reaction on adjoining Provinces of the release of these prisoners; and to the fact that acceptance of the principle that terrorist convicts should be indiscriminately released without regard to individual considerations would be highly dangerous, and in view of the history of terrorism in the past could not fail to give impetus to fresh terrorist organisation in Bengal, careful consideration left me with no choice but to conclude that issues involved were such that it was incumbent on me to issue an instruction to those Governors under provisions of Section 126 (5) of the Act. That section empowers the Governor-General to issue orders to Governors of Provinces as to the manner in which the executive authority thereof is to be exercised for the purpose of preventing any grave menace to the peace and tranquillity of India or of any part thereof. To acquiesce in the immediate and indiscriminate release of prisoners with records of violent crime would have been to strike a blow at the root of law and order in India; dangerously to threaten peace and good government; and to run a grave risk to peace and tranquillity; all the more so since this categorical demand took no account of possible reactions of certain releases on the position elsewhere, or of the reiterated readiness of Governors to examine individual cases.

5. The Governors, on receipt of my instructions, informed their Ministers that they could not accept their advice on this matter. The Ministers therefore tendered their resignation.

6. The Governors concerned, and I, so far as I am concerned, have done our utmost over the last seven months to work in harmonious co-operation with the Congress Ministries of both these Provinces and all possible help has been lent them. There has been no foundation over that period for any suggestion that it is the policy, or desire, of the Governor-General or of the Governors to impede or interfere with legitimate activities of these Ministries, or to take any step the necessity for which was not imposed upon them by the terms of the Act. That is equally true today.

7. I have made it clear that in issuing the instructions I did, I had no hesitation in feeling that a grave menace to the basis of law and order, and so to the peace and tranquillity of India, would have been involved in acceptance by the Governors of demands of such an order presented to them in such a manner.

8. As regards the particular issue of the release of prisoners, so far as

the Governors are concerned there is no going back on the policy of readiness to examine individual cases, and the Governors remain ready to agree to release, after examination, where no undue risk in their own Province, or in other Provinces, is involved. There is no impropriety, whatever may be suggested to the contrary, in their requiring such individual examination, or in their declining without it to accept the advice of their Ministers. Ministers are responsible for law and order. But they are so responsible under the Act subject to the responsibility of Governors to ensure the peace and tranquillity of their own Province; and the Governors are bound to have in mind the corresponding responsibility that falls on the Governor-General for the peace and tranquillity of India or any part thereof. Neither a Governor nor the Governor-General will wish to see his responsibility attracted, but, as I made clear in my message of last June, where that responsibility is in fact attracted, neither the Governor nor the Governor-General can shrink from discharging it.

9. Finally, and this I wish particularly to emphasise, there is no foundation for the suggestion that the action I have taken is dictated by a desire to undermine the position of Congress Ministries. The record of the last seven months should have made it abundantly clear that the Governors and I myself are only too anxious to lend all assistance that we properly can within the framework of the Act to any Ministry in power in a Province. Neither the Governors nor the Governor-General have any desire to interfere, or any intention of interfering with the legitimate policy of a Congress or any other Government. The action taken was designed to safeguard the peace and tranquillity of India and, incidentally, to uphold the sanctions of law and orderly functioning of the constitutional machine. That action leaves it open to Ministers, in consultation with the Governors, to pursue a policy of release of prisoners, and they need anticipate no difficulty now, any more than in the past, in securing the friendly and ready co-operation of the Governors in individual examination. I am glad to think that in no quarter is there manifest any disposition to extend the area of difficulty beyond the limits of the position which I have described, and it is my sincere and earnest hope that it may shortly be possible to return to normality and that in the two Provinces most concerned Ministers in discussion with the Governors may find themselves able to resume their interrupted labours.

APPENDIX 6

PRESS STATEMENT BY GANDHI[6]
MSS.EUR.F 115/8

February 24th, 1938

I have read the Governor-General's statement with the respect and attention it deserves. I had hoped that it would give some satisfaction as was given, at least to me and, if I may say so, to a large number of Congressmen, when he made a pronouncement upon the Congress demand for certain assurances as a condition precedent to acceptance of ministerial responsibility by Congress members of the provincial legislatures. It reads like a special pleading unworthy of a personage possessing unheard of powers.

No one has questioned the propriety of examining the cases of prisoners to be discharged but what I have questioned and the Congress most emphatically questions is the propriety of such examination by the provincial Governors in provinces said to be enjoying complete provincial autonomy. The duty and right of examination belong solely to the responsible Ministers as I understand the Government of India Act and the convention in responsibly governed Colonies.

The Governors' duty and right are to advise their Ministers on questions of broad policy and warn them of the danger in their exercise of certain powers but having done so, to leave their Ministers free to exercise their unfettered judgment. If such were not the case responsibility would become a perfectly meaningless term and the Ministers responsible to their electors would have as their share nothing but odium and disgrace if their responsibility had to be shared with the Governors in the daily administration of affairs by law entrusted to them.

It is hardly graceful for His Excellency to quote against the poor Ministers their non-exercise of their undoubted powers to prevent the Governors from examining individual cases. The Congress Resolution describes their forbearance as exemplary patience. I would venture to add that probably it was also the inexperience of the Ministers who were totally new to their task.

I am afraid, therefore, that unless this crucial question is decided in favour of the Ministers it will be difficult for them to shoulder the grave responsibility that the Congress has permitted them to take over.

I am glad His Excellency has drawn public attention to the method I adopted in Bengal. He might have noted also the difference between Bengal on the one hand and the United Provinces and Bihar on the other. In Bengal I was dealing with a Government which was not bound by the Congress manifesto in any shape or form. The Ministers there, rightly or wrongly, would not listen to wholesale discharge of convicted prisoners. I was treading upon very delicate ground in pursuance of my promise to the prisoners. My motive was purely humanitarian and the only weapon that I had at my disposal was an appeal to the humanity of the Bengal Ministers and I am glad to be able to testify that I was not speaking to hearts of stone.

The situation in the United Provinces and Bihar is totally different. The Ministers there are bound by the manifesto which gave them victory at the polls. They had not only examined the cases of all prisoners whose release they were seeking but, being fully aware of their responsibility for the due preservation of peace in their provinces, they had personally secured assurances from the prisoners in question that the latter no longer believed in the cult of violence.

One thing in His Excellency's statement gives me the hope that the impending crisis might be prevented. He has still left the door open for negotiations between the Governors and the Ministers.

I recognise that the notices were sudden, because in the nature of things they had to be so. All parties have now had ample time for considering the situation. In my opinion the crisis can be avoided if the Governors are left free to give an assurance that their examination of the cases was not intended to be a usurpation of the powers of the Ministers and that since the latter had armed themselves with assurances from the prisoners they were free to release them on their own responsibility and I hope that the Working Committee will leave the Ministers free, if they are summoned by the Governors, to judge for themselves whether they are satisfied by the assurances they may receive.

One thing I must say in connexion with the exercise by His Excellency of his powers under Section 126(5) in the light of his argument justifying the use of sub-section 5 of Section 126. I have read the whole of it. It is entitled "Control of Federation over the Provinces in certain cases". Unless the sub-sections have no connexion with one another and are to be read independently of one another my reading is that in the present case the exercise of powers under sub-section 5 of Section 126 is a manifest misapplication. But here I am treading on dangerous ground. Let lawyers decide the point. My purpose in making this long statement is to assist in the peaceful solution of the crisis that has suddenly appeared.

APPENDIX 7

PANT TO HAIG
MSS.EUR.F 115/8

Lucknow,
February 24th, 1938

Dear Sir Harry Haig,

I have carefully studied Mahatma Gandhi's statement since I saw you this morning. According to my reading of it, he has laid down three principles regarding the release of prisoners, namely: (*i*) that cases should be individually examined, (*ii*) that the right and duty of such examination belongs solely to Ministers and (*iii*) that before releasing prisoners Ministers should assure themselves fully that the prisoners no longer believe in the cult of violence. He has laid great stress on the Ministers making themselves solely responsible for the examination of individual cases. I find that he has in fact gone to the length of criticising the Ministers in his own way for sharing this task with Governors in the past. He attributes this to their unfamiliarity with their constitutional position. For your convenience I will quote a few sentences from his statement:

"No one has questioned the propriety of examining the cases of prisoners to be discharged. But what I have questioned, and the Congress most emphatically questions, is the propriety of such examination by provincial Governors in provinces said to be enjoying complete provincial autonomy. That duty and right of examination belongs solely to responsible Ministers as I understand the Government of India Act and the convention in responsibly governed Colonies....

"It is hardly graceful for His Excellency to quote against poor Ministers their non-exercise of their undoubted powers to prevent Governors from examining individual cases. The Congress resolution describes their forbearance as exemplary patience. I would venture to add that probably it was also the inexperience of Ministers who were totally new to their task. I am afraid, therefore, that unless this crucial question is decided in favour of Ministers it will be difficult for them to shoulder the grave responsibility that the Congress has permitted them to take over....

"In my opinion the crisis can be avoided if the Governors are left free to give the assurance that their examination of cases was not intended to be a usurpation of the powers of Ministers and that since they had armed themselves with assurances from the prisoners that they were free to release them on their own responsibility."

It is necessary to bear these points in mind in arriving at a solution. The Ministers' duty of examining individual cases and securing dependable assurances from prisoners with due regard to the responsibility they owe for the peace and tranquillity of the province before releasing any person has to be accepted and, in order that they be held answerable by the public for the due discharge of their duty in this regard, it has to be made clear that the responsibility for individual releases is theirs.

I will be meeting you tomorrow. In the meantime I thought that it would be helpful if I made this attempt to clarify the position in the light of Mahatmaji's authoritative statement.

Yours sincerely,
G.B. PANT

APPENDIX 8

STATEMENT BY HAIG AND PANT
MSS.EUR.F 115/22B

February 25th, 1938

We have had a full discussion between ourselves about the present situation and recent developments. We have arrived at agreed conclusions, and the Hon'ble Ministers are accordingly resuming their normal duties.

The cases of certain prisoners classified as political have been individually examined, and the Governor will be soon issuing orders, on the advice tendered to him by his Ministers, to remit, under section 401 of the Code of Criminal Procedure, the unexpired portion of the sentence in each case and to order their release. The cases of the remaining prisoners are being individually examined by the Minister concerned and appropriate orders will be similarly passed thereon within a short time.

We have had also a long discussion on the mutual relations between the Governor and the Ministers. We discussed the recent statement of H.E. the Viceroy along with the views of Mahatma Gandhi on it and also the resolution passed at Haripura about the resignations of Ministers and the previous statement made by H.E. the Viceroy last summer. There is no reason to fear any usurpation of or interference with the legitimate functions of the responsible Ministers. We are both desirous of maintaining healthy conventions and with goodwill on both sides we hope that we will succeed.

APPENDIX 9

HAIG TO PANT
MSS.EUR.F 115/22B

Immediate *February 26th, 1938*

Dear Pandit Govind Ballabh Pant,

I have just seen a file in which H.M.J. has directed, without any kind of detailed examination, the release of a large number of the political prisoners. This is completely out of accord with the agreement we reached when I discussed the matter with you on the morning of the 24th. It might, in my opinion, create a very serious situation if Dr. Katju, who I see is leaving for Allahabad tonight, were to make any statement with regard to these prisoners before I have had an opportunity of discussing the matter with you and him.[7]

Yours sincerely,
[H.G. HAIG]

APPENDIX 10

LINLITHGOW TO HAIG
R/3/1/73

Private and Personal

The Viceroy's House, New Delhi,
February 27th, 1938

My dear Haig,

I realise that you have inevitably been working under circumstances of very considerable difficulty, and I realise a little, too, the nature of the strain which has weighed upon you during the last few days in connection with the resolution of the crisis which has arisen. You will not, therefore, think any critical comment which I may make upon the terms of the communiqué finally agreed between you and Pant is due to lack of appreciation of the position. But I confess that while what is done is done, I feel considerable uneasiness that it should not have been possible to secure the drafting amendments which, on my instructions, were put to your Secretary.[8] As regards the reference to conventions, I readily agree that the modification which you persuaded Pant to accept takes the sting out of the sentence in question, though I would still have been happier had there been no reference whatever to conventions in the statement, since the term, suitable as it may be in connection with our own flexible and unwritten constitution, is one open to very considerable misrepresentation, at any rate at this stage when we are dealing with a written constitution such as that provided under the Act. I would have much preferred, too, that we should have been able to avoid the use of Gandhi's phrase "usurpation of or interference with the legitimate functions of responsible Ministers".

2. Finally, I cannot but regret the absence of the amendment which I suggested in the last sentence of the first paragraph,[9] the absence of which seems likely to cause us some embarrassment in the light of press comment of today. I readily recognise that on a strict and cautious reading of the draft as it stands, it is arguable that nothing positively incorrect is said in it. What I am afraid of is that the statement does on this point appear to me (and had from the time when I first saw it) to give a misleading impression, and that advantage may be taken of the position by Congress to suggest that there has been a climb down on the part of the Governor or the Governor-General: and an abandonment of the position that Ministerial responsibility for law and order is subject to the special responsibility of the Governor, an impression which we should both be most anxious to avoid. The position is of course as set out in the penultimate paragraph of my statement, and if there is a debate in the House of Lords, I will suggest to the Secretary of State that he should take the opportunity to reiterate what I have said there, while I will also endeavour to find some opportunity of doing so myself.

3. The extent to which any failure to make my intentions, or the importance which I attached to the amendments I suggested entirely clear, was due to the failure of the human machinery working by telephone in circumstances of considerable pressure, is difficult to assess; and as I have made clear, I think, I fully recognise the great strain under which you are working, and the difficulty which must inevitably be experienced by anyone other than the person actually conducting the negotiations, in assessing the actual atmosphere at the time, and the extent to which it would be wise or unwise to press a particular point. But my own impression has been very strongly that Congress were so concerned to resume office that they would not have broken on drafting amendments such as I had suggested, and I feel that, if we could have secured them, our own position would have been more satisfactory than at the moment I think that it is.

Yours sincerely,
LINLITHGOW

APPENDIX 11

HALLETT TO BRABOURNE (EXTRACT)[10]
L/P&J/5/266: FF. 219-20

Secret *September 24th, 1938*

I have been back in Bihar for such a short time that it is not very easy to give my fortnightly appreciation.

2. Before talking of Bihar, I must refer briefly to my last days in the United Provinces. We had a Cabinet meeting the day before I left at which we decided one or two minor matters. The two main items on the agenda were, first, the report of anti-corruption committee, and secondly, the Public Service Commission. The latter question we could not take up and I have had to leave it for Haig. In regard to the former we dealt with some of the non-contentious recommendations which do little more than reassert or amplify slightly the Government Servants Conduct Rules e.g. it was decided to prohibit *dalis*[11] entirely. Katju observed in his somewhat cynical manner that when the report was discussed in the Council, there were two points of view; some members thought the bribe-giver should go free, others that the bribe-taker should be let off; the result he observed would be that all were to be let off! The Cabinet seemed to wish to have the report considered by the Assembly and did not seem very anxious to take up contentious questions. I suggested that they might do well to await the report of the Bihar Committee which, as far as I know, has gone into the question with more care and in greater detail.

3. As regards the Tenancy Bill I understood both from Pant and the Nawab of Chhatari that Government have made some concessions to the landholders in regard to the provisions for the realisation of rent; as regards *sir* lands, persons paying Rs. 250/- or less as land revenue will not be affected by the proposals and they form a pretty large percentage of the landholders. I gathered that the landholders' object in discussing the question with the Higher Command was to stop the provincial Government making more concessions to the Left Wing, which is in my view quite a real danger. Pant optimistically believes that the Bill will get through the lower house in six weeks but I feel very doubtful.

Pant and Katju both called on me on the day of my departure to say goodbye and were very friendly.

APPENDIX 12

PRESS COMMUNIQUÉ ISSUED BY U.P. GOVERNMENT
L/P&J/7/2587: FF. 40-1

November 10th, 1938

QUESTION OF THE RECITATION OF THE MADHE SAHABA

The Government of the United Provinces in a statement to the Press says:

There is some unrest at present in the public of Lucknow on the question of Madhe Sahaba, and there are some parties who are attempting to launch civil disobedience movement. The right of Sunnis to recite Madhe Sahaba had been in dispute for the last 35 years. The present Government in their resolution clearly recognized this right. So far as the exercise of this right is concerned the Sunnis are free to recite Madhe Sahaba in their houses and mosques, and on the occasion of Milad-i-Sharif without any interference, but the convening of special meetings exclusively for reciting Madhe Sahaba or to take out processions are matters which create a danger of disturbance of peace.

GENERAL CONTROL

Government is, therefore, obliged to exercise that right of general control which it has to prevent breaches of public order. For some time past Government have been intending to allow Sunnis to have public recitation of Madhe Sahaba in the manner mentioned above, provided there is peaceful atmosphere in the town of Lucknow, but Government regret that some time on account of threats of civil disobedience and some time for other reasons, no such peaceful conditions could establish themselves.

At present Government is having talks with Shias on the one hand and on the other with Sunnis (Majalas-i-Ahrar, Maulvi Abdul Shakoor's party and others) to bring about an amicable settlement of this question. In view of this it is not proper for Government to announce any decision of their own. Government appeal to all to create a peaceful atmosphere in the city. Either the talks will lead to some fruitful result, or Government will in the near future make an announcement of their decision.

APPENDIX 13

HAIG TO HALLETT
MSS.EUR.F 115/11

Secret *November 29th, 1938*
No. U.P.-203

[My dear Hallett,]

Many thanks for your secret letter No. 2113-G.B., dated November 25, 1938.[12] The position about our Tenancy Bill is, I now think, decidedly more hopeful than it seemed to me when I wrote my last fortnightly report. I think there is a fair chance that we may get it through without provoking a serious conflict. Nevertheless, about the general situation as it has developed in the Province, I continue to feel decidedly uneasy. It will of course be a matter of the greatest importance if we can avoid a serious agrarian clash, and at the moment I am inclined to think that we have less dangerous agitation going on in the villages perhaps than you have, judging from your report of the 24th November to the Viceroy, which I read with very great interest. As you know, the only two areas at present where there is danger of serious trouble of this kind are Gorakhpur and Lalitpur. About the former I have heard nothing lately, and I regard this consequently as good news; and as for Lalitpur, tension is greatly relaxed. But it is the general swing to the left that disturbs me, and about the fact of it I do not think there can be much doubt. It is true that Pant is so friendly, so reasonable, and puts his case with such skill that after talking to him I cannot help feeling reassured; but I fear the facts are against him, and I get in the aggregate a great deal of information which is in conflict with his professedly optimistic outlook.

2. I see that you look upon these left wing activities as a preparation for a campaign against federation. I had not thought of them myself in this connection, and had indeed been assuming lately that Congress would probably swallow federation under protest. I have been looking on our left wing activities rather as a spontaneous expression of certain forces of discontent (and perhaps ambition) which are steadily gaining strength, and whatever may be the decision of the Congress about federation, I fear these forces are not going to submit willingly to control. The danger is that the Ministry may not have the resolution, or perhaps the strength, to be able to face them and that the whole situation may steadily deteriorate.

3. I will have a copy of my C.I.D. report about revolutionary activities sent to you.[13] It is a report by the provincial C.I.D. covering the six months ending September 1938. The Youth League in its various manifestations seems to be particularly active.

4. I had a talk with Pant recently about volunteers and could get nothing very satisfactory out of him. Indeed, he expressed with regard to the Congress volunteers ideas so unconvincing that I felt he knew he was not in a position to do anything about it and was simply fencing with me.

5. I am writing from Cawnpore where the atmosphere is not happy. Revolutionary speeches and incitement of labour go on unchecked. Owen thinks that the settlement of last summer is nothing more than a truce, and that we are bound before long to have another crisis, and that things will not settle down until the matter has really been fought out. I am disappointed, for I had thought the atmosphere in Cawnpore was improved. It is I think in certain respects, but I fear the agitators will see that things never settle down.

6. I saw recently a copy of the report of your Retrenchment Committee, which has a close bearing on certain proposals which my Ministers have put up and about which I have addressed the Governor-General. I think it may interest you to see my two letters to him, and I enclose copies.[14] I made a reference to the possibility of a cut in pay owing to the somewhat cryptic reply which I received from him to an inquiry I made on the subject. Please keep this entirely to yourself and do not refer to it in any correspondence with the Viceroy, as his letter to me was marked secret, and I am sure he wants even the possibility of such a thing kept very strictly confidential at the moment. I think myself that particularly in view of the disquieting developments which I am now beginning to anticipate, it would be a very grave mistake to upset our services by agreeing to any cut in pay.

7. On the subject of special pay, I imagine the proposals of your Retrenchment Committee are much on the same scale as those which my Government have put up. I should be glad to know whether you are being pressed to take action; and if so, what you contemplate doing. I am glad to see that your Committee have not sought to follow the system apparently adopted in Madras which seems to me, as I said in my second letter to the Viceroy, to be exceedingly difficult to justify.

Yours sincerely,
[H.G. HAIG]

NOTES

1. See *U.P.P., 1936-7*, Appendix 16.
2. See *U.P.P., 1936-7*, Appendix 9.
3. Mr G.G. Field. In his circular, as reported in the *Hindustan Times*, Mr Field 'pointed out to all ranks that it is their duty to co-operate with the leaders of Congress in this district and to afford them all support that they legally can in their campaign to better the lot of the villagers.' Station officers must receive complaints from Congress officials 'in a spirit of friendliness. Any rudeness or other ungentlemanly conduct towards them would be taken serious notice of.' Finally the Superintendent of Police drew attention to the determination of the present Government to stamp out oppression and corruption among Government officials. If police officers did not take notice they had only themselves to blame if sterner measures had to be adopted in the end.
4. The text of Pandit Pant's statement reproduced here is taken from the file copy of a cutting from the *Pioneer* of 20 February 1938.
5. Mr Srikrishna Sinha.
6. Two earlier statements by Mahatma Gandhi on the constitutional crisis were made on 16 and 18 February 1938. These are printed in Basudev Chatterji (ed.), *Towards Freedom: Documents on the Movement for Independence in India 1938*, Part II (New Delhi: Oxford University Press, 1999), pp. 1168-9, 1173-4.
7. There is no reply to this letter on the file.
8. In telegram 312-G of 25 February 1938, the Viceroy gave Lord Zetland details of the changes he had asked Sir Harry Haig to make to the draft of the Statement by the Governor and Pandit Pant (Appendix 8). The changes requested were: '(*a*) in discussion re-draft sentence which refers to "appropriate orders" being issued by Governor: (*b*) substitute for "usurpation of the legitimate functions of responsible Ministers" the words "misunderstanding between us"; and (*c*) in particular avoid reference to conventions in last sentence which, as originally drafted, ran "to establish healthy conventions".' L/P&J/8/649: f. 107.

   A full account of the telephone discussions on 25 February 1938 between Mr Laithwaite and Mr Donaldson is given in a minute of Donaldson's dated 28 February on MSS.EUR.F 115/22B.
9. The reference would appear to be to the last sentence of the second paragraph in the statement as issued.
10. Only this extract is on the file.
11. The word intended here may be '*dalali*'. See Glossary.
12. In his letter of 25 November 1938, Sir Maurice Hallett said he had read No. 78 with great interest. He agreed that the whole danger was of surrender to the left wing but in Bihar they were possibly a little better off as their most contentious tenancy legislation had been passed.

Hallett was concerned to have further details of the renewed activities of revolutionaries in the U.P. [See No. 78, paragraph 10 (*b*).] He noted that in Bihar they had similar volunteer camps among Kisans, particularly in the troublesome district of Gaya, but as yet they were not very effective. He agreed that the most dangerous aspect of the volunteer movement was its bearing on the proposals of the U.P. and Bihar Ministries to start some form of military training. MSS.EUR.F 115/11.

13. The C.I.D. report is not on the file.
14. The copies are not on the file. The letters were presumably No 77 and the letter of 19 November 1938 summarised in No. 77, note 23.

Index

Certain terms, such as Hindus, Muslims and United Provinces, occur in almost every document and have therefore not been indexed. For the same reason there are no index entries for Lord Linlithgow as Viceroy nor for Sir Harry Haig as Governor of the United Provinces. Lord Brabourne is not indexed for the time that he was Acting Viceroy and Sir Maurice Hallett is not indexed for the time that he was Acting Governor of the U.P. Footnotes are indexed under the document to which they are attached. References to documents in the Appendices are preceded by the letter 'A'.

The index entries refer to document numbers